ALL ABOUT THE Girl

ALL ABOUT THE Girl

CULTURE, POWER, AND IDENTITY

EDITED BY

ANITA HARRIS

WITH A FOREWORD BY **MICHELLE FINE**

ROUTLEDGE
NEW YORK AND LONDON

Published in 2004 by
Routledge
270 Madison Avenue
New York, NY 10016
www.routledge-ny.com

Published in Great Britain by
Routledge
2 Park Square
Milton Park, Abingdon
Oxon, OX14 4RN
www.routledge.co.uk

Routledge is an imprint of the Taylor & Francis Group.
Printed in the United States of America on acid-free paper.

10 9 8 7 6 5 4 3 2 1

Library of Congress Cataloging-in-Publication Data

All about the girl : power, culture, and identity / edited by Anita Harris.
    p. cm.
Includes bibliographical references and index.
ISBN 0-415-94699-9—ISBN 0-415-94700-6 (pbk.)
1. Teenage girls. 2. Young women. 3. Women—Identity. 4. Feminist theory.
    I. Harris, Anita, 1968-
HQ798.A56 2004
305.242'2—dc22

2004006781

Contents

Acknowledgments   ix

Foreword   xi
  MICHELLE FINE

Introduction   xvii
  ANITA HARRIS

PART 1   Constructing Girlhoods in the
Twenty-First Century

1   Notes on Postfeminism and Popular Culture:
Bridget Jones and the New Gender Regime   3
  ANGELA McROBBIE

2   Women, Girls, and the Unfinished Work of
Connection: A Critical Review of American
Girls' Studies   15
  JANIE VICTORIA WARD AND BETH COOPER BENJAMIN

3   Good Girls, Bad Girls: Anglocentrism and Diversity
in the Constitution of Contemporary Girlhood   29
  CHRISTINE GRIFFIN

4   From Badness to Meanness: Popular Constructions
of Contemporary Girlhood   45
  MEDA CHESNEY-LIND AND KATHERINE IRWIN

PART 2   Feminism for Girls

5   Feminism and Femininity: Or How We
Learned to Stop Worrying and Love the Thong   59
  JENNIFER BAUMGARDNER AND AMY RICHARDS

6   Girl Power Politics: Pop-Culture Barriers
        and Organizational Resistance   69
        JESSICA K. TAFT

7   Mythic Figures and Lived Identities: Locating the
        "Girl" in Feminist Discourse   79
        JENNIFER EISENHAUER

8   "I Don't See Feminists as You See Feminists":
        Young Women Negotiating Feminism in
        Contemporary Britain   91
        MADELEINE JOWETT

PART 3 Sexuality

9   Pretty in Pink: Young Women Presenting Mature
        Sexual Identities   103
        KATE GLEESON AND HANNAH FRITH

10   Talking Sexuality Through an Insider's Lens:
        The Samoan Experience   115
        ANNE-MARIE TUPUOLA

11   Shifting Desires: Discourses of Accountability in
        Abstinence-only Education in the United States   127
        APRIL BURNS AND MARÍA ELENA TORRE

PART 4 Popular and Virtual Cultures

12   Where My Girls At? Black Girls and the
        Construction of the Sexual   141
        DEBBIE WEEKES

13   Spicy Strategies: Pop Feminist and Other
        Empowerments in Girl Culture   155
        BETTINA FRITZSCHE

14   Jamming Girl Culture: Young Women and
        Consumer Citizenship   163
        ANITA HARRIS

15   Girls' Web Sites: A Virtual "Room of One's Own"?   173
        JACQUELINE REID-WALSH AND CLAUDIA MITCHELL

PART 5 Schooling

16   Pleasures Within Reason: Teaching Feminism
        and Education   185
        NANCY LESKO AND ANTOINETTE QUARSHIE

17 Girls, Schooling, and the Discourse of Self-Change:
    Negotiating Meanings of the High School Prom   195
    AMY L. BEST

18 Gender and Sexuality: Continuities and Change for
    Girls in School   205
    MARY JANE KEHILY

PART 6   Research With and By Young Women

19 Colluding in "Compulsory Heterosexuality"? Doing
    Research with Young Women at School   219
    KATHRYN MORRIS-ROBERTS

20 Speaking Back: Voices of Young Urban Womyn
    of Color Using Participatory Action Research to
    Challenge and Complicate Representations of
    Young Women   231
    CAITLIN CAHILL, ERICA ARENAS, JENNIFER
    CONTRERAS, JIANG NA, INDRA RIOS-MOORE, AND
    TIFFANY THREATTS

21 Beneath the Surface of Voice and Silence: Researching
    the Home Front   243
    ADREANNE ORMOND

22 Possible Selves and Pasteles: How a Group of Mothers
    and Daughters Took a London Conference by Storm   255
    LORI LOBENSTINE, YASMIN PEREIRA, JENNY WHITLEY,
    JESSICA ROBLES, YARALIZ SOTO, JEANETTE SERGEANT,
    DAISY JIMENEZ, EMILY JIMENEZ, JESSENIA ORTIZ, AND
    SASHA CIRINO

Contributor Biographies   265
Index   271

Acknowledgments

The idea for this book developed out of the Monash University Centre for Women's Studies and Gender Research conference *A New Girl Order?* held at King's College, London, in 2001. I would like to thank my co-convenors, Maryanne Dever and Ceridwen Spark, as well as Kirsten McLean for her assistance, and the staff at King's College and the Menzies Centre for Australian Studies. All the participants and presenters made the conference very lively and engaging. Thanks are also due to Michelle Fine for her support, not least in the form of the Foreword for the book. I am grateful to Mari Shullaw at Routledge London for helping the project move forward, and to Ilene Kalish at Routledge New York for her ongoing support and for suggesting such a snappy and thought-provoking title! The anonymous reviewers offered very helpful suggestions and all of the contributors have worked hard to make my task as editor easier. I am thankful also for the support of my colleagues in the School of Political and Social Inquiry at Monash University, and the financial assistance provided by a Faculty of Arts Project Completion grant. Much appreciation to the Benedykt Café for the lattes, and friends and family, especially Michael Ure, for their love and for listening.

Foreword

Michelle Fine

All About the Girl

A thank-you note

In the spirit of the post-Foucaultian confessional, I must admit that I love women's bathrooms. The neoliberal global economy renders women's bathrooms a shared fate with juries, libraries, and highways—all remainder public spaces. Spaces where we confront the "between," where we can still meet ourselves and each other. Women's public bathrooms open spaces not already hyper-commidified, Gap-ed, privatized, and colonized. Nestled inside this space for labia only swells a profoundly gendered world in which we can produce, consume, critique, engage, witness, eavesdrop, separate, and join. The long arm of the global market is barely visible, held off at the door by a collective of women who usually just need to pee. And yet there are always leaks....

> Need condoms?
> Tampax?
> Diapers?
> Cards?
> Mouthwash?
> Horoscope?

Wanna Weigh Yourself?

Rare are the spaces in which girls and women gather as girls and women. It's hard to find spots where self-consciously gendered (not necessarily feminist or postfeminist but gendered) politics can pollinate among strangers, unencumbered by the suffocating grasp of commodification—although it's always in the air freshener.

In this heterotopia of girls'/women's privacy and intimacy, *we* can be seen, heard, watched, and smelled, and still act *as if* no one is watching. Crouching in liminality between full exposure and existential solitary, we are at once with and alone. We can "do" the politics of intimate daily life among a group of relative strangers, joined by a thin reed of biology. Like Web sites, zines, chain letters, soap operas, protests, and rallies, all (a)part, for a moment, we create a world. I smile, ironically, as I invent this segregated space with radical possibility, although really I long for the physical, ratty, mildew-couched, poster-filled "My best friend is a man, but would you want your sister to marry one?" women's centers that decorated my late teens and young adulthood. In today's new gender regime, you must qualify with a badge of (dis)honor to enter a space explicitly for girls and women: battered, teen and pregnant, or anorexic.

So I felt as if I were coming home to a virtual, transnational women's center when reading *All About the Girl*. The volume hosts a textual pajama party for girls, and girl wannabes, across the globe. Immersed in a semifictional community of *us*, theory, methods, ethics, lipstick, rape, consumerism, and politics get an airing. The essays cast a wide net, historically and internationally, to catch, and constitute, an *us*.

In bathrooms, *we* brush our teeth, stare at our butts, check out our swollen wombs, help baby boys urinate, teach children not to stare or laugh, kiss a lover, write on walls. We are fully embodied; at once raw and performing. And if we're really lucky, we can enjoy years and generations of scribbling on the bathroom stalls. We can read decade-old conversations among girls and women about loving Tommy, hating bitches, sucking cock, caressing Connie's breasts, heartbreaks and heart throbs. In the textual commode, you may consume (read) and produce (write). Or you can just listen, as mothers and children negotiate, "Are you done yet?" Friends giggle about boys, girls, bodies, clothes, and performances. Older women lower themselves onto the seat. Just the generation who believes they have to put paper down or squat is the one least physically capable of doing either. You may wander past a woman with her life in a paper bag in the corner, not begging, willing to accept. Sleeping, a smile, her eyes betray a life. You'll act as if you don't smell.

There is no neutral space in the women's bathroom. The net is wide, and you can't opt out.

With praise and delight, *All About the Girl* delivers the best of women's bathrooms. Conversations, sounds, smells, memories, bodies, histories and futures, production and consumption, scars and pleasures, etched in stories of girls and feminisms past and future, near and far. This book weaves an *us* with differences marked and theorized: lipstick scorned and adorned; cleavage buried and blossoming; a black eye, don't ask but nod knowingly. In this volume we delight in the radical possibilities of (re)theorizing girl, reframing the waves feminism, troubling the Anglocentric and white laminations of postfeminist theory, combing through the knotted hairs (what Angela McRobbie calls the "double entanglements") of global capital and the production of gender, "race," and age, and exploding what constitutes method, evidence, consciousness, and activism.

With the clever analytic eyes of editor Anita Harris and the collective of authors, *All About the Girl* advances, as it establishes, a critical space for girls' studies. With great insight about how history, political economy, and the media shape representations and embodiments of gender, race, ethnicity, class, sexuality, and age, the chapters also reveal the ways in which "waves" of feminism alter the ideological fashions designed for girls. As a collective, the chapters theorize gender and girls in global relation to capital and consumption, and in localized relation to place and politics. Deeply rooted in the United States, Canada, Great Britain, Australia, Samoa, and New Zealand, the chapters both interrogate local shapings of gender and connect the global ribs that sculpt bodies through gender, race, ethnicity, class, age, and geography. Perhaps most stunning, these chapters articulate a critical theory of feminist method, troubling what constitutes evidence, epistemology, and activist research. The chapters elevate gossip, zines, girls' magazines, teen quizzes, comics, television, popular culture, proms, Web sites, stereotype stickers, and the nail-polished trivia of everyday life as empirical archives of social reproduction and struggle. This volume marks a cross-disciplinary turning point by establishing the field, insisting on globally analytic and locally deep work, and radically reimagining feminist methods for girls' studies.

So, if this were a bathroom wall, I would scribble on about three of my favorite, thick, messy struggles in the book.

irony: The title of the book forecasts the ironies that season the volume: *All About the Girl.* While *All* signifies a blasphemic slip/slap toward totalizing knowledge, *the Girl* performs unapologetically as singular and multiple, representational and idiosyncratic, blond, Samoan, pink, queer, goth, performing slut, enacting academic success, coherent and fractured, assured and ambivalent, resisting and reproducing. The category "girl" is at once presented and it vibrates throughout the volume, in good critical intellectual tradition.

struggle: Between chapters, important, contentious struggles surface about the "waves"— their wisdom and hegemommy — between girls and women. More precisely, a vibrant and provocative set of tensions emerges about the relation of second- and third-wave feminisms, the metaphor of waves, the familial roots of the word *generation,* and the sense of loss between women and girls. While these debates are much needed, much appreciated, and profoundly unresolved, the arguments echo but also resist the wisdom of Lillian Hellman's book title *Pentimento.*

As I read across the manuscript, I conjured a thick, wet canvas upon which our many feminisms have been painted. I relived the luscious spaces

I've enjoyed between girls and women. And yet, in the never coincidental slip of the fingers, I typed *vicious* as I thought *luscious*. Fingers speak.

The volume elicits reflexive, unsettling vibrations, tinged with nostalgia, resistance and wonder at the declaration that we are decidedly "post" feminist. While the dangling hairs of prior feminisms can be found ambivalently in the "third wave" there is a theoretical demarcation at the post feminism that troubled me. I found myself more comfortable with the language of *a new gender regime* than a demarcation of *post,* yearning for more generous border guards of "herstory," willing to snorkel for material passing through the leaky and porous membranes separating the waves.

The relation between the waves is critical to analyze for *partial continuities*, not simply distinctions. We must wonder—on the canvas, in the waves, in the bodies, and through the collective body of girls and women, in the "post"—where live the outrage, analysis, knowledge, critique shouted and stuffed back into our bodies; protested and commidified? What carries forward over time? What is displaced, obliterated, destabilized, and what survives transgressively? Perhaps we need to excavate those bathroom walls, diaries burned, tears on pillows, scratchings on the walls of mental institutions to learn what girls/women knew then and have drowned since, for each generation to discover anew. Maybe we need to invent traditions of passing down oral histories, secrets, whispers, and screams of girls/women—before, within, and across homes, communities, cultures, and nation-states.

freedom in pink—girls at the global cash register: Across chapters a(nother) critical conversation percolates over the political economy of girls as citizens, consumers, producers, and simply as exploited bodies. These chapters theorize the neoliberal discursive shifts, from constraint to "choice," from liberation to (neo)liberal.

Reading the manuscript, I flashed to a conversation I had recently with a friend who described her visit to a "baby farm" in Texas. A fortysomething, Jewish, lesbian-hoping-to-be-mother, an artist, eager to adopt, she flew to Texas, to a well-known and frequented ranch where pregnant teens who want to relinquish their babies go to be well fed, educated, and nurtured through the pregnancy. Prospective adoptive parents pay $25,000 for the *opportunity to be interviewed,* submit portfolios of what they will deliver if they are granted the right to adopt. They listen to panels of postbirth mothers reflecting on how they selected the "perfect" family for their child, hearing, most typically:

> I was looking for a family with young parents, like in their early twenties, with a stay-at-home mom, good Christians, a dog, and the family I chose for my baby gave me a car after Tommy was adopted.

You can imagine how well my friend fared.

Subverting class domination for a magical moment, wealthy adoptive parents sit pretty and morph into commodities, while poor and working-class (white) birth mothers don a glass slipper as agents of "choice." In drag as powerful decision makers, for a split second the cumulative constraints on their lives masquerade as freedom and autonomy. Such well-crafted moments of "both/and/between," hazy and vivid ambivalence, domination and resistance, seduction and loss, vivify this book and force us to retheorize "choice" within conditions of enormous constraint glamorized with neoliberal commodification.

All About the Girl overflows with the polyglossia of women's bathrooms. Exposing the scars of global politics as they cut through the fabric of girls' daily lives, we also witness the (dis)comforting joys and transgressions girls today engage in language and bodies. This collection of essays helps us to analyze the juicy and dangerous, hilarious and disturbing intersections of the global political economy, social movements of resistance, and thong underwear; helps us conceptualize the youth patois, embroidered with the words of subversion and offense: "re-vulva-lution," "bitch," or "fed-up honey."

All About the Girl stands as a textual museum of girls' lives, representations, and politics; indeed, a transnational conversation "between." And, better than bathroom walls, this conversation you can take to bed.

Introduction

Anita Harris

Good girls, bad girls, schoolgirls, Ophelias, third wavers, no wavers, B girls, riot grrrls, cybergURLs, queen bees, tweenies, Girlies: young women suddenly seem to be everywhere. They are the new heroes of popular culture, the dominant faces on college campuses and the spokespeople of public education campaigns. They are wooed by advertisers and recruitment companies alike. Feminism has furnished young women with choices about sexuality, chances for education and employment, and new ways of asserting autonomy and rights. These changes in possibilities and expectations for young women are reflected everywhere, from the sassy icons of the culture industries to the proliferation of government-funded girl power programs. At the same time, rising rates of arrest, incarceration, un- and under-employment among young women are a troubling counterpoint to images of over-achieving, consumer-oriented girlpower. While some privileged young women are indeed reaping the benefits of new opportunities, those without economic or social capital are slipping through the ever-widening holes in what remains of our social safety nets. Education, employment, health and safety are precarious experiences for many girls who bear the full impact of economic rationalism, new security concerns and the dismantling of welfare. Young women appear to have it all, and yet many constitute those hardest hit by the effects of the new global political economy on jobs, resources and community. How do they survive and flourish in a world of greater choices and opportunities, but fewer structures of support?

Contemporary analytical frameworks for interpreting girls' lives are complicated by the intersections of constraint, autonomy and selective freedoms that they embody. Western girls' studies today must begin the encounter with young women who are standing at the corner of feminism and neoliberalism.[1] This book embarks on this project by bringing together work by scholars, researchers and activists from a wide range of disciplines and international backgrounds to explore issues concerning young women as we move into the new century. It includes research about, with and by young women in North America, the U.K., Europe and the Pacific, and reflects on the ways that class, culture, ethnicity and sexuality are shaped by and shape experiences of girlhood in these contexts. Among the questions it addresses are: How are young women positioned and how do they position themselves in the changing postindustrial and postmodern Western world? How has girlhood itself taken on new meanings as we enter the twenty-first century? Who speaks for young women and girls? What is the future of feminist inquiry into the lives of young women? In this regard, girls' studies must move forward into an unknown and somewhat unexpected landscape, and at the same time must draw on its long tradition in feminist interdisciplinary work.

Girls' studies have a strong transnational and cross-disciplinary history, even if the nomenclature itself is more recent. The field was borne out of the commonplace disregard for issues of gender within youth studies and age within women's studies. The circumstances and experiences of young women had been systematically overlooked in research and policy until the feminist interventions of the late 1970s and early 1980s. These interventions occurred in a number of different countries, out of many different disciplines, but coalesced into a loose thematic focus that can be characterized as "girls' studies." The nature of this earlier work yielded an important legacy. In the U.S. context, the work of Michelle Fine was among the first to account for the discursive possibilities as well as safe spaces in the lives of young women that make self-expression and autonomy imaginable. Her famous essay on "the missing discourse of desire" and her research on the importance of understanding intersectionality in young women's identities ushered in a new area of critical investigation. Also in the U.S., the groundbreaking work of feminist psychologists introduced the idea that conventions of adolescent development theory missed valuable information about young women's experiences. The Harvard research on Women's Psychology and Girls' Development, which includes the work of Carol Gilligan, Lyn Mikel Brown and Jill MacLean Taylor among others, researched the now popular idea that girls lose their resistant and authentic voices when they engage with cultural requirements to shape their identities in line with dominant femininities.[2] Prior to this, in the U.K. girls' studies first emerged out of the Marxist analyses of cultural life that developed at the Centre for Contemporary Cultural Studies in the late 1970s. Christine Griffin's *Typical Girls?* and Angela McRobbie's *Feminism and Youth Culture* were important works that linked young women's

---

[1] See Aapola, Gonick and Harris, forthcoming 2004.
[2] This framework has been popularized more recently by the bestseller *Reviving Ophelia*, and currently informs many programs and policies for girls.

choices and material circumstances with popular images and expectations of young femininity.

Although there was a considerable Atlantic divide in terms of disciplinary traditions and conceptual frameworks regarding feminist work about girls, a shared body of knowledge and a political research agenda were developed across these differences which became the basis of the broad field of girls' studies. For example, the construction of girls' identities at the intersection of class, race, and gender has remained an important conceptual frame for more recent work, such as Heidi Safia Mirza's *Young, Female and Black*, and *Growing Up Girl* by Valerie Walkerdine, Helen Lucey, and June Melody. Cultural studies approaches, which were first popularized by this earlier work on the construction of young femininity such as Leslie Roman and Linda Christian-Smith's edited book *Becoming Feminine*, have also been central to shaping contemporary girls' studies. There has been a recent explosion of texts in this field, including Susan Hopkins' *Girl Heroes* and Catherine Driscoll's *Girls*. Edited U.S. collections as diverse as *Urban Girls; Delinquents and Debutantes; Girl Power*, and *A Girl's Guide to Taking Over the World* offer interdisciplinary perspectives on diverse groups of girls, often centering their own voices. Internationally, the discipline of education has also been integral to the development of the girls' studies agenda. The examination of schools as sites where femininities are constructed through hegemonic discourses of nation, gender, sexuality and culture, and resisted by girls themselves, is a key plank of feminist education studies. This body of work includes Australian and New Zealand/ Aotearoa texts such as Jane Kenway and Sue Willis's edited book *Hearts and Minds*; Pam Gilbert and Sandra Taylor's *Fashioning the Feminine*; Lesley Johnson's *The Modern Girl*, and Alison Jones' *"At School I've Got A Chance."* More recent work in this tradition includes *The Company She Keeps* by Valerie Hey; Mary Jane Kehily's *Sexuality, Gender and Schooling*; and North American books like Amira Proweller's *Constructing Female Identities* and Marnina Gonick's *Between Femininities*.

These key texts establish the terrain of feminist work about and with young women through the twentieth century and into the twenty-first.[3] This tradition has established some fundamental issues for girls' studies: the relationship between popular cultures, material conditions and gendered identities; the role of social institutions such as school and the media in shaping femininities, and the places and voices young women utilize to express themselves. However, girls' studies is now at a turning point, and this book marks the beginning of a new focus on the meanings of girlhood and opportunities for young women in the context of three major changes for the field. First, whereas a "first wave" of girls' studies aimed to expose

---

[3] This overview is, of course, partial. Most notably, there has also been considerable work on the relationship between young women and feminism, and a whole body of literature about third wave feminism itself. This is interrogated closely in Part 2 of this book.

and rectify the oppression experienced by young women, today it tackles the legacy of its own interventions. Researchers, commentators, and activists now grapple with pervasive assumptions about young women's newfound freedoms, in part enabled by feminism, in the context of an increasingly inequitable distribution of resources among girls. That is, there exists a sharpening bifurcation between young female "haves" and "have nots," but far greater access to discourses of power on the part of all. Second, while early girls' studies sought to highlight the experiences of young women as young women, more recent work has questioned the capacity of this "cohort" approach to adequately attend to the complex and multifarious nature of girls' identities. That is, the differences between young women need as much attention as the features that are shared. Finally, contemporary researchers are learning the lessons generated by a now long history of working with young women. Some of the young women who were studied by the "first wave" of girls' studies theorists are now researchers themselves. Concerns about "over-researching," the value of research to girls themselves, and the ends to which research is put have come to the fore. Increasingly, young women are conducting their own projects or making informed decisions about participating—or not—in the research of others.

Earlier feminist work about young women keenly anticipated a time when girls would enjoy greater freedoms and opportunities, and yet now that we are in such a moment, these experiences are not straightforward, nor equally available. The category of "girl" itself has proved to be slippery and problematic. It has been shaped by norms about race, class and ability that have prioritized the white, middle class and non-disabled, and pathologized and/or criminalized the majority outside this category of privilege. As critical psychologist Sarah Carney writes, "Although all girls are surveilled, not all girls' bodies are of concern all of the time."[4] The question of who a girl is, that is, how she comes into our purview as a girl, has become part of the work of girls' studies itself. Even the issue of how old a "girl" is—previously a fairly simplistic categorization of females between the ages of approximately 12 and 20—has been complicated by both the "tweenies" phenomenon and the "Girlie" movement, which together "girlify" 7 year olds in midriff tops and 40 year olds with Hello Kitty barrettes. Further, the assumption that the job of (older) feminists is to help young women speak out and take action has also been problematized in the light of the misuses to which girls' voices have been put. These issues have generated a refinement and revitalization of girls' studies: a project which is at the heart of this book. The complex questions about creating a relevant and vital agenda for girls' studies form the backdrop against which different dimensions of girls' power, cultures, and identities in the twenty-first century are explored.

---

[4] Carney 2000: 123.

The book is divided into six parts. The themes of each have emerged out of the contemporary research agendas that currently characterize girls' studies, although they are not exhaustive. Feminism, sexuality, popular culture and school are central issues in young women's lives across the Western world. The book opens with a set of chapters that tackle contemporary constructions of girls and girlhood in the new millennium. It then pursues those key issues of feminist agendas, sexual autonomy, the culture industries and education to understand how different young women across the Western world enact political, cultural and personal expressions, and perform the new kinds of identity work that is now required of them. It closes with a section that discusses emergent methodologies for research with young women that account for the changing times within which they live.

Part 1 attends to the shift in representations of girls and girlhood within media, policy and the academy into the 2000s. As Angela McRobbie points out in her opening chapter, popular constructions of young women currently take place within a "cultural space of postfeminism." She argues that sexual politics are displaced in the larger project of the production of young women as the ideal self-inventors in an individualized risk society. In contrast to this, Meda Chesney-Lind and Katherine Irwin examine the development of a counterpoint to the girl as ideal citizen. They map the shift in representations of "bad girls" from the image of young women as dangerous criminals in the 1990s to the backstabbing bullies of the 2000s. Both of these chapters suggest that the public debates that focus on middle class white girls in the new millennium serve to empty out class and race politics from discussions of youth futures. Janie Victoria Ward and Beth Cooper Benjamin then map the development of girls' studies in the U.S., and argue that the agenda of early work in this field has been depoliticized in the process of mainstreaming. They call on researchers and practitioners to re-engage in multidimensional, interdisciplinary and intergenerational approaches to young women to address the larger systems of oppression and opportunity that shape their lives. Christine Griffin also takes up these themes in her chapter, demonstrating how and why some girls have been "invisibilized" in youth research, and documenting the impact of ethnocentrism on girls' studies in her analysis of the girlpower debate.

Part 2 covers the sometimes rocky terrain of the relationship between girls and feminism. It focuses on the meanings of girlhood, rather than the role of young women, in contemporary feminism. The chapter by Jennifer Baumgardner and Amy Richards marks out this ground by declaring a rupture between the waves specifically around images of the girl. They argue that a third wave of feminism can be characterized by its desire to embrace "girlness"; writing that "the ascent of the 'girl' as a strong and distinct identity is probably one of the best examples of what differentiates Third Wave feminists from Second Wave feminists." Jessica Taft pursues this idea in examining the notion of girlpower. She argues that girlpower operates as a shifting set of strategies that can be used to both depoliticize young feminism and operationalize new kinds of resistance to dominant ideals of femininity. Jennifer Eisenhauer builds on this debate about where girlness fits into feminism by examining conventional feminist representations of the girl as a state of *becoming*. She argues provocatively that the girl has traditionally been an object for feminism rather than a subject in her own right. The chapter by Madeleine Jowett rounds up this section by investigating how some young women, positioning themselves as entitled agents rather than undeveloped pre-feminists, are interpreting and shaping feminism for new times.

Part 3 addresses changing meanings of sexuality and sexual maturity for young women. It is widely accepted that the sexual revolution and the second wave of feminism have created new possibilities for sexual expression for this generation of girls. Kate Gleeson and Hannah Frith point up some of the complexities at work in adopting a subject position as a sexually desirable and desiring girl. They suggest that young women's expressions of sexual autonomy—as indicated by something as seemingly innocuous as their clothing choices—demonstrate the careful work they must do to enjoy new found freedoms and yet not appear too sexual. Anne-Marie Tupuola considers some of these issues in a cross cultural context, suggesting that assumptions embedded in adolescent development theory—for example, of sexual freedoms in the liberal West versus sexual oppressions in the traditional Pacific—do not hold up when examining young women's sexual and cultural identities as increasingly heterogenous, transient, and globalized. April Burns and María Elena Torre then play out some of these arguments in a policy context, asking what happens when conventional discourses of adolescent sexuality are operationalized to shape young women's pathways towards academic and professional success. They document the agendas and effects of abstinence-based sex education in the U.S., and explore how academic success and chastity are linked together for young women.

Part 4 examines new intersections between young women and popular cultures. It offers a complex reading of girls as both consumers and producers of cultures of music, fashion, style, and play. Debbie Weekes opens the section with an analysis of young African-Caribbean women's ambiguous relationship to ragga and rap music. She discusses the ways young women can use this music to celebrate Black female sexuality and politicize Blackness. However, this requires a constant and simultaneous effort to subvert sexist portrayals of women. She argues that age may be a significant factor in the strategies girls generate to criticize and resist "slack" lyrics. In the following chapter Bettina Fritzsche pursues this notion of active consumption in her analysis of young Spice Girls fans. She suggests that this girl group operates not so much as role models who are either "good" or "bad" for the cultivation of feminist outlooks in young women, but instead represent a "toolbox." Girls can legitimize their own identity

choices, which are often unconventional, by drawing sometimes very tenuous but strategically important connections with the Spice Girls' image
and philosophy. Anita Harris then analyzes the constitution of young
women as consumer citizens through the girl culture industry. I suggest
that this is being met by a "culture jamming" counter-move by some
young women who find ways to re-introduce production and creativity
into experiences of citizenship, and create new places for community and
activism. In the last chapter of this section, Jacqueline Reid-Walsh and
Claudia Mitchell discuss young women's creation of websites as a kind of
"virtual bedroom culture." They argue that webpages are both a private
and public space for young women to play, produce, and consume. Their
work suggests that an examination of virtual space is increasingly important in a contradictory historical moment; that is, young women have
never been more entitled to take their place in the public sphere, and yet
spend more and more leisure time in the home.

Part 5 explores one of the key institutions in young women's lives, that
of the school. The chapters here look at school as a site for the production
of new kinds of femininities. Mary Jane Kehily indicates how conventional
constructions of gender and sexuality in classrooms exist in tension with
new images and experiences of young women as free agents shaping their
identities without the constraints of traditional feminine mores. Through
her question, "What is new and what has remained the same in the everyday social worlds of girls in school?" she demonstrates the complex work
of negotiating new and old sex-gender hierarchies. Amy L. Best takes up
this theme of negotiating old and new gendered and sexual identities in
her chapter on the meanings of high school proms. She argues that the
prom is an opportunity for young women to create identities as something
other than school students, and to try out ways of presenting adult and
sexual selves. The school's complicity in the production of the prom as a
transformative experience also indicates how educational institutions
operate to shape new subjectivities for young women based on notions of
personal effort and work on the self. Nancy Lesko and Antoinette
Quarshie examine this idea from another angle by reflecting on their
teaching practice and the stories women tell about their girlhoods in an
educational context. They suggest that such "biomythographies" can open
up spaces for connecting, deconstructing, and questioning universalizing
notions of womanhood and girlhood.

Part 6 deals with new approaches to research about girlhood, including
frameworks for shaping projects with or by young women. It opens up
some of the complexities of research from the perspective of both "insid-
ers" and "outsiders." Feminist methodology has long taught the value of
research that engages individuals as active participants, and this lesson is
coming to bear on girls' studies. Kathryn Morris-Roberts opens the section with a brave account of the difficulties she faced in negotiating collu-
sion/intervention in homophobia as a researcher in high schools. She

illustrates the complexity of researcher responsibility by inviting readers into her process of critical reflexivity. In the following chapter, Caitlin Cahill, Erica Arenas, Jennifer Contreras, Jiang Na, Indra Rios-Moore, and Tiffany Threatts discuss their experience of participatory action research. They demonstrate that such research also contains hierarchies, negotiations and vulnerabilities, and offer their reflections on the process by which their team created the Fed Up Honeys project, by and about young urban women of color.

Adreanne Ormond then offers an important intervention into the debate about "insider" research, illustrating how a shared experience of place and culture with research participants can sometimes prevent researchers from seeing differences. She argues that we need to be attentive to and respectful of the political ways that youth can actively construct researchers as outsiders, in order to preserve their right to keep knowledge to themselves and to control public representations of their circumstances and opinions. The book concludes with a celebratory chapter by Lori Lobenstine, Yasmin Pereira, Jenny Whitley, Jessica Robles, Yaraliz Soto, Jeanette Sergeant, Daisy Jiminez, Emily Jiminez, Jessenia Ortiz, and Sasha Cirino about the "possible selves" project they developed and their experience of engaging with an international academic community to share their findings. They argue that research shaped and owned by young women is valuable both for its own intrinsic objectives and its capacity to re-position young women as agenda setters for policy and project managers for research on their own terms.

This book is titled, somewhat playfully, *All About the Girl.* It tells us many things about the contemporary situation of young women in different circumstances, but it deliberately does not aim to tell us *all* about *the* girl. A desire to know and analyze young women has often concealed another agenda: the regulation and surveillance of their behavior. Against this, the work contained in this book suggests that there is no universal, one-dimensional girl about whom we can know everything. The category of "girl" is constantly being constructed and deconstructed, and young women themselves are an incredibly diverse and dynamic population. Further, the material in this book suggests that the future of feminist inquiry into the lives of young women does not lie in seeking to know all. Rather, it is in creating opportunities for alliances, finding places and resources for young women to develop their own research, articulating issues and debates that need to be heard, and respecting their rights to keep some stories to themselves.

References

Aapola, Sinikka, Marnina Gonick, and Anita Harris (forthcoming 2004). *Young Femininity: Girlhood, Power and Social Change.* London: Palgrave.
Carlip, Hilary (1995). *Girlpower: Young Women Speak Out,* Warner Books, New York.

Carney, Sarah K. (2000). "Body Work on Ice: the Ironies of Femininity and Sport," Lois Weis and Michelle Fine (Eds.), *Construction Sites: Excavating Race, Class and Gender Among Urban Youth*. New York: Teachers College Press.

Driscoll, Catherine (2002). *Girls: Feminine Adolescence in Popular Culture and Cultural Theory*, Columbia University Press, New York.

Fine, Michelle (1988). "Sexuality, Schooling and Adolescent Females: The Missing Discourse of Desire", *Harvard Educational Review*, 58, (1), February, pp. 29-53.

Gilbert, Pam and Sandra Taylor (1991). *Fashioning the Feminine*. Sydney: Allen and Unwin.

Gilligan, Carol, Nona P. Lyons, and Trudy J. Hanmer (1990). *Making Connections: The Relational Worlds of Adolescent Girls at the Emma Willard School*. Cambridge: Cambridge University Press.

Gonick, Marnina (2003). *Between Femininities*, State University of New York Press, Albany.

Greene, Karen and Tristan Taormino (Eds.) (1997). *A Girl's Guide to Taking Over the World: Writings From the Girl Zine Revolution*, St Martin's Press, New York.

Griffin, Chris (1985). *Typical Girls*, Routledge and Kegan Paul, London.

Hey, Valerie (1997). *The Company She Keeps: An Ethnography of Girls' Friendship* Open University Press, Buckingham.

Hopkins, Susan (2002). Girl Heroes: *The New Force in Popular Culture*, Pluto Press, Annandale.

Inness, Sherrie (Ed.) (1998). *Delinquents and Debutantes: Twentieth-Century American Girls' Cultures*, New York University Press, New York.

Johnson, Lesley (1993). *The Modern Girl: Girlhood and Growing Up*, Allen and Unwin, Sydney.

Jones, Alison (1991). *"At School I've Got A Chance" Culture/Privilege: Pacific Islands and Pakeha Girls at School,* Dunmore Press, Palmerston North.

Kehily, Mary Jane (2002). *Sexuality, Gender and Schooling*. London: Routledge/Falmer.

Kenway, Jane and Sue Willis (eds.) (1990). *Hearts and Minds: Self-Esteem and the Schooling of Girls*, Falmer, London.

Leadbeater, Bonnie J. Ross and Niobe Way (eds.) (1996). *Urban Girls: Resisting Stereotypes, Creating Identities*. New York: New York University Press.

McRobbie, Angela (1976). *Feminism and Youth Culture*. London: Macmillan.

Mirza, Heidi Safia (1992). *Young, Female and Black*. London: Routledge.

Pipher, Mary (1994). *Reviving Ophelia: Saving the Selves of Adolescent Girls*. New York: Grosset/ Putnam.

Proweller, Amira (1998). *Constructing Female Identities: Meaning Making in an Upper Middle Class Youth Culture*. Albany: State University of New York Press.

Roman, Leslie and Linda Christian-Smith (eds) (1988). *Becoming Feminine*. London: Falmer.

Taylor, Jill MacLean, Carol Gilligan, and Amy M. Sullivan (1995). *Between Voice and Silence: Women and Girls, Race and Relationship*. Cambridge: Harvard University Press.

Walkerdine, Valerie, Helen Lucey, and June Melody (2001). *Growing Up Girl: Psychosocial Explorations of Gender and Class*. London: Palgrave.

PART 1

Constructing Girlhoods in the Twenty-First Century

Notes on Postfeminism and Popular Culture: Bridget Jones and the New Gender Regime*

ANGELA McROBBIE

This chapter is based on work in progress, its tone is deliberately open-ended, and it quite consciously takes liberties with academic procedures by skimming the surface of popular cultural texts and commenting on observable social behaviors. It first proposes that through a complex array of machinations, elements of contemporary popular culture are perniciously effective in regard to the undoing of feminism; it then proposes that this is compounded by some dynamics in social theory which appear to be most engaged with, and hence relevant to, aspects of gender and social change; and finally it suggests that by means of the tropes of freedom and choice which are now inextricably connected with the category of young women, feminism is aged and made to seem redundant. Feminism is thus cast into the shadows, where at best it can expect to have some afterlife, and where at worst it might be regarded ambivalently by those young women who must in more public venues stake a distance from it, for the sake of social and sexual recognition. Let me start with the film *Bridget Jones's Diary* (released 2001); my claim is that it marks the emergence of a new cultural norm, which can be understood in terms of postfeminism.[1] Without attempting a full definition of this overused term, I propose instead a complexification of the backlash thesis which has

*This essay was first delivered as a lecture at Yale University in October 2002. I thank Vron Ware and Paul Gilroy for inviting me.

had currency within forms of journalism associated with popular feminism (Faludi 1997).

My argument is that postfeminism actively draws on and invokes feminism as that which can be taken into account in order to suggest that equality is achieved, in order to install a whole repertoire of meanings which emphasize that it is no longer needed, a spent force. This is particularly prominent first in *The* (U.K.) *Independent* newspaper column "Bridget Jones's Diary" then in the book and film. Postfeminism is, for me at this stage, an enabling concept for the examination of a number of intersecting but also conflicting currents. These include shifts of direction in the feminist academy, as well as generational and political repudiations of feminism from a variety of directions. The notional consent, frequently invoked across political culture—that gender equality was a not unreasonable claim, now happily achieved—permits a wide range of responses, many of which indicate relief and closure; that there is no longer any need for sexual politics, which in turn gives license for such a politics to be undone. Broadly, I am arguing that for feminism to be taken into account, it has to be understood as having already passed away. This is a movement detectable across popular culture, a site where "power ... is remade at various junctures within everyday life, [constituting] our tenuous sense of common sense" (Butler et al. 2000: 14).

Some fleeting comments in Judith Butler's short book on Antigone suggest to me that postfeminism and the new gender regime can be explored through what I would describe as a double entanglement, that is, the coexistence of neoconservative values in relation to gender, sexuality, and family life (for example, George Bush supporting the campaign to encourage chastity among young people) with processes of liberalization in regard to choice and diversity in domestic, sexual, and kinship relations (for example, full recognition that gay couples are now able to adopt, foster, or have their own children by whatever means), and alongside this the coexistence of feminism as at some level transformed into a form of Gramscian common sense, while also fiercely repudiated—indeed, almost hated (Butler 2000; McRobbie 2003). The "taken into accountness" permits all the more thorough dismantling of feminist politics.

It may be helpful to suggest some sense of periodization with 1990 (or thereabouts) as a turning point, marking the moment of definitive self-critique in feminist theory. At this time the representational claims of second-wave feminism come to be fully interrogated by postcolonialist feminists like Spivak, Trinh, and Mohanty, among others, and by feminist theorists like Butler and Haraway who inaugurate the radical denaturalizing of the postfeminist body (Spivak 1988; Trinh 1989; Mohanty 1995; Butler 1990; Haraway 1991). Under the prevailing influence of Foucault, there is a shift away from feminist interest in centralized power blocs (e.g., the state, patriarchy, law) to more dispersed sites, events, and instances of power conceptualized as flows and specific convergences and consolidations of talk, discourse, attentions. The body and also the subject come to represent a focal point for feminist interest, nowhere more so than in the work of Butler. The fact that the concept of subjectivity and the means by which cultural forms and interpellations (or dominant social processes) call women into being, produce them as subjects while ostensibly merely describing them as such, inevitably means that it is a problematically she, rather than an unproblematically we, which is indicative of a turn to what we might describe as the emerging politics of postfeminist inquiry (Butler 1990, 1993).

In feminist cultural studies the early 1990s also marks a moment of feminist reflexivity. In her article "Pedagogies of the Feminine", Brunsdon queried the hitherto assumed use value to feminist media scholarship of the binary opposition between femininity and feminism—or, as she put it, the extent to which the housewife or ordinary woman was conceived of as the assumed subject of attention for feminism (Brunsdon 1997, first printed 1991). Looking back, we can see how heavily utilized this dualism was, and also how particular it was to gender arrangements for largely white and relatively affluent (i.e., housewifely) women. 1990 also marked the moment at which the concept of popular feminism found expression. Andrea Stuart considered the wider circulation of feminist values across the landscape of popular culture, in particular magazines, where quite suddenly issues which had been central to the formation of the women's movement (e.g., domestic violence, equal pay, workplace harrassment) were now addressed to a vast readership (Stuart 1990). The wider dissemination of feminist issues was also a key concern in my own writing at this time. Not just the immanent textual processes of popularization but also the contextual intersection of these new representations with the daily lives of young women who, as subjects (called into being) of popular feminism, might then be expected to embody more emboldened (though also of course "failed") identities. Interested in the dynamics of social change in gender relations, I was also concerned that both academic and activist feminism, worried by these popular and commercial forces, too easily veered toward censoriousness and didacticism, and thus missed the opportunity of at least considering how feminism was achieving, admittedly with a good deal of revision, some degree of effectivity among a wider and younger section of the female population (McRobbie 1994, 1999a).

Thus we have a field of transformation in which feminist values come to be engaged with, and to some extent incorporated across, civil society in institutional practices, in education, in the work environment, and in the media. This is what I mean by "feminism taken into account", a phrase which is retained throughout this chapter. This process has so far been described only sporadically in, for example, accounts of feminist success in education (see Arnot et al. 1999; Harris 2003). In media studies both Brunsdon and I considered how, with feminism as part of the academic curriculum (i.e., canonized), it is not surprising that it might also be countered. That is, feminism must face up to the consequences of its own claims to representation and power, and not be so surprised when young women students decline the invitation to identify as a "we" with their feminist teachers and scholars (Brunsdon 1997; McRobbie 1999a, b). In the United States there have been extended debates in relation to questions of feminist "failure" and the declining numbers of students enrolling in Women's Studies courses (Brown 1997).

In the early 1990s, and following Butler, I saw this moment of contestation, and what I would call "distance from feminism," as one of potential, where a lively dialogue about how feminism might develop would commence (Butler 1992; McRobbie 1994). Notwithstanding the debate inside the academy about women and gender studies and their future, it seems now, a decade later, that this space of "distance from feminism" and those utterances of forceful nonidentity with feminism have consolidated into something closer to repudiation than ambivalence, and it is this vehemently denunciatory stance which is manifest across the field of popular gender debate. This is the cultural space of postfeminism. Its expansiveness is a mark of just how much is at stake in relation to the gender regime. The active, sustained, and repetitive repudiation or repression of feminism also marks its (still fearful) presence or even longevity (as afterlife). The denunciation of feminism coexists, however, with the visibility of a gendered, generational fault line, where young women are championed as a metaphor for social change. And with this there also comes into view, particularly on the pages of (huge circulation, right-wing U.K. daily newspaper) *The Daily Mail*, something akin to a free market feminism embodied in the figure of the ambitious TV blonde (McRobbie 1999b).[2]

Nor are these phenomena exclusive to the changing representations of young women in the countries of the affluent West. As Spivak has argued, in the impoverished zones of the world, governments and NGOs also look to the minds and bodies of young women for whom education comes to promise enormous economic and demographic rewards (Spivak 2000). What is consistent is the overshadowing—indeed, displacement—of feminism as a political movement. It is this displacement which reflects Butler's sorrowful account of Antigone's life after death. Her shadowy, lonely existence suggests a modality of feminist effectivity as spectral; she has to be cast out—indeed, entombed—for social organization once again to become intelligible. One means by which this is enacted, is through the unfolding of televisual and other popular narratives, where a field of new gender norms emerges (e.g., *Sex and the City, Ally McBeal*) in which female freedom and ambition appear to be taken for granted, unreliant on any past struggle (an antiquated word), and certainly not requiring any new, fresh political understanding, but instead merely a state into which young women appear to have been thrown, or in which they find themselves, giving rise to ambivalence and misgiving.

The media have become the critical site for defining emergent sexual codes of conduct. They pass judgment and establish the rules of play. Across these many channels of communication feminism is routinely disparaged. This is another Butler point: Why is feminism so hated? Why do young women recoil in horror at the very idea of the feminist? To count as a girl today appears to require this kind of ritualistic denunciation, which in turn suggests that one strategy in the disempowering of feminism includes its being historicized and generationalized, and thus easily rendered out-of-date. It would be far too simplistic to trace a pattern in media from popular feminism (or prime-time feminism, including TV programs like *LA Law*) in the early 1990s, to niche feminism (BBC Radio 4's *Women's Hour*, and the women's page of *The Guardian* newspaper) in the mid-1990s, and then to overtly unpopular feminism (new century), as though these charted a chronological "great moving right show," as Stuart Hall might put it (Hall 1989). We would need a more developed conceptual schema to account for the simultaneous feminization of popular media with this accumulation of ambivalent, fearful responses. We would certainly need to signal the full enfranchisement of women of all ages as audiences; as active consumers of media and the many products they promote; and, by virtue of education, earning power, and consumer identity, a sizable block of the target market. We would also need to be able to theorize female achievement predicated not on feminism, but on female individualism, on success which seems to be based on the invitation to young women by various governments that they might now consider themselves free to compete in education and in work as privileged subjects of the new meritocracy.

There are various sites within popular culture where this work of undoing feminism with some subtlety becomes visible. Indeed, in some cases it involves utilizing the language of feminist cultural studies against itself. The Wonderbra ad showing the model Eva Herzigova looking down admiringly at her substantial cleavage enhanced by the lacy pyrotechnics of the Wonderbra, was through the mid-1990s positioned in major main street locations in the United Kingdom on full-size billboards. The composition of the image had such a textbook sexist ad dimension that one could be forgiven for supposing some familiarity with both cultural studies and feminist critiques of advertising (Williamson 1987). It was, in a sense, taking feminism into account by showing it to be a thing of the past, by provocatively enacting sexism while at the same time playing with those debates in film theory about women as the object of the gaze (Mulvey 1975), and even with female desire (De Lauretis 1988; Coward 1994). The picture is in noirish black-and-white and refers explicitly through its captions (from "Hello, Boys" to "Or Are You Just Pleased To See Me?") to Hollywood and the famous lines of the actress Mae West.

Here is an advertisement which plays back to its viewers well-known aspects of feminist media studies, film theory, and semiotics; indeed, it almost offers (albeit crudely) the viewer or passing driver Laura Mulvey's theory of women as object of the gaze projected as cityscape within the frame of the billboard. Also mobilized in this ad is the familiarity of the term "political correctness," the efficacy of which resides in its warranting and unleashing such energetic reactions against the seemingly tyrannical regime of feminist puritanism. Everyone, and especially young people, can give a sigh of relief. Thank goodness it's permissible, once again, to enjoy looking at the bodies of beautiful women. At the same time the advertisement also hopes to provoke feminist condemnation as a means of generating publicity. Thus, within hailing distance of the Wonderbra advertisement generational differences are also generated; the younger female viewer, along with her male counterparts, educated in irony and visually literate, is not made angry by such a repertoire. She appreciates its layers of meaning, she gets the joke.

When in a TV advertisement (1998/1999) another supermodel, Claudia Schiffer, takes off her clothes as she descends a flight of stairs in a luxury mansion on her way out the door toward her new Citroen car, a similar rhetoric is at work. This ad appears to suggest that yes, this is a self-consciously "sexist ad," and feminist critiques of it are deliberately evoked. Feminism is "taken into account," but only to be shown to be no longer necessary. Why? Because there is no exploitation here, there is nothing remotely naïve about this striptease. Schiffer seems to be doing it out of choice, and for her own enjoyment; the ad works on the basis of its audience knowing Claudia to be one of the world's most famous and highly paid supermodels. Once again the shadow of disapproval is evoked (the striptease as site of female exploitation), only instantly to be dismissed as belonging to the past, to a time when feminists used to object to such imagery. To make such an objection nowadays would run the risk of ridicule. Objection is preempted with irony.

A similar strategy can be seen in another advertisement. In a magazine advertisement for Volkswagen cars, the image again appears to quote the history of what came to be known as sexism in advertising by repeating the kind of crude association between the female body and the bodywork of a car. The line along the bottom of the image of a beautiful young woman in a swimsuit emerging from a pool runs "Wouldn't It Be Great If All Bodies Were Guaranteed To Last So Long?"

These three images were part of expensive campaigns looking for audiences in the twenty-five to thirty-five age range. In each case a specter of feminism is invoked so that it might be undone; indeed, one could be so bold as to suggest that for old-fashioned (young and old) male viewers unversed in media theory, tradition is restored or, as Beck puts it, there is "constructed certitude." For the girls, what is proposed is a movement beyond feminism, to a more comfortable zone where women are now free to choose for themselves (Beck 1992).

If we turn attention to some of the participatory dynamics in leisure and everyday life which see young women endorse (or refuse to condemn) the ironic normalization of pornography, where they indicate their approval of and desire to be pinup girls for the centerfolds of the soft porn lad mags, where it is not at all unusual to pass young women in the street who are wearing T-shirts bearing phrases such as Porn Queen or Pay To Touch across the breasts, and where (in the United Kingdom, at least) young women quite happily attend lap dancing clubs (perhaps as a test of their sophistication and cool), we are witness to a hyperculture of commercial sexuality, one aspect of which is the repudiation of a feminism invoked only to be summarily dismissed. As a mark of a postfeminist identity, young women journalists refuse to condemn the enormous growth of lap dancing clubs despite the opportunities available for them to do so across the media. They know of the existence of the feminist critiques and debates (or at least this is my claim) through their education; as Shelley Budgeon has described the girls in her study, they are "gender aware" (Budgeon 2001). Thus the new female subject is, despite her freedom, called upon to be silent, to withhold critique in order to count as a modern, sophisticated girl. There is quietude and complicity in the manners of generationally specific notions of cool, and more precisely an uncritical relation to dominant commercially produced sexual representations which actively invoke hostility to assumed feminist positions from the past in order to endorse a new regime of sexual meanings based on female consent, equality, participation, and pleasure, free of politics.[3]

There are countless examples of these kinds of activities which have become staple titillating content providers for the media (both quality and tabloid). Young women have license now to be badly behaved (drunk, disorderly, and undressed on any number of TV programs about females on holiday in Spanish resorts), while at the same time they also reinhabit tradition (with some barely perceptible ironic inflection) by rediscovering with delight, rituals and customs which feminism had dispensed with, including "hen nights," lavish white weddings, and the adoption of the male surname on marriage.[4] But what marks out all of these cultural practices is the boldness of the activity, and the strong sense of female consent and participation, the idea that these are all personal choices. This would suggest that these young women have learned some lessons from feminism, in particular, sexual openness and the entitlement to female pleasure. As emancipated female subjects living in a relatively affluent Western democracy, they are discouraged from considering the need for a new sexual politics for themselves. Instead, so liberated are they, that they can, again with a touch of irony, reexplore tradition or else adventure into fields of female taboo by frequenting lap dancing clubs, where their presence as customers boldly disrupts the traditional relations between sex workers and clients.

Female Individualization

We are, it seems, confronted with a dilemma: feminist media and cultural studies resist a move into social theory, which means that there has been little critical engagement with either the reflexive modernization work of Beck et al. (1994) or with the more Foucaultian work of Nikolas Rose (2000). We could say that each of these perspectives provides the most substantial account of social transformation to date in regard to processes of individualization, and thus potentially to female individualization. We have little space here to embark on such an interrogation, but it is possible to lay out the ground for such an undertaking by showing how well equipped Beck et al. are for dealing with the new conditions of female emergence, through independence to individualization. But we might also remark on the dangers of endorsing this analysis, and look rather to Rose for his account of the means by which power now works so successfully, through constant, seductive, and productive incitements to self-organization. How, then, does the idea of "feminism taken into account" register in the theory of social transformation of Beck et al.? What, exactly, do I mean by the dangers of this work? At a quite basic level, Beck et al. themselves take feminism into account, acknowledging its achievements, but they treat it like a thing of the past, perhaps politely referencing some key texts of feminist scholarship; but otherwise they have moved on. This state of pastness is confirmed by their proposals regarding the emergence of a different kind of popular political formation, a shift away from emancipatory politics (of which feminism is one example) toward life politics or, in Beck's terms, subpolitics (single-interest groups, lobbies, lifestyle issues, etc.).

Precisely because feminism is located within a historical perspective, as belonging to the 70s and 80s, this new sociological work has the advantage of appearing to be up to date. This has the effect of either typecasting other feminist sociologists as outdated or else expecting of them that they shift their own vocabularies accordingly (see for example Beck and Beck 1997). With the notable exception of Adkins (2002) there has been little forceful feminist criticism of the reflexive modernization thesis. What is more this work is appealing to many young women students because it speaks directly to them as postfeminist individualized subjects. Notwithstanding their relative inattention to culture or media, these authors provide a broad conceptual sweep which encapsulates the posttraditional order in which young female subjects find themselves growing up. In short their work rings true. This is a world where the nation state is superceded by global flows and communicative networks, and where social relations are transformed by processes of individualization, part of which can be understood as stemming from women's desires (unleashed by past feminist struggles) for greater independence. However there is double failure (as well as danger) at the heart of this work. In its over-emphasis on agency and the apparent capacity to choose in a more individualized society, it has no way of showing how subject formation occurs by means of notions of choice *and* assumed gender equality coming together to actually ensure adherence to new unfolding norms of femininity (the new gender regime, a term I borrow from Walby 2002). That is, choice is a modality of constraint. Second, these writers have little sustained concern for the adverse consequences of new individualism, in relation to the decline of social structures, on new and as yet unaddressed gender inequities. That planning of a life of one's own with recourse to an array of self-help manuals, popular fictions, and advice columns is in itself a new coercive structure for "the shaping of being," and for "making experience happen," rather than a solution to the new dilemmas thrown up by de-traditionalization, is to invert the claims of Beck and Giddens and to emphasize by these means what Rose calls the "inculcation of a form of life" (Rose 2000). This raises the question of how we can understand the complex relation between those changes in the gender regime which feminism has helped to inaugurate, and the processes of female individualization which are a critical dynamic of reflexive modernization.

Can female individualization indeed be regarded as both one outcome of feminism and a reward for its abandonment? Is this a compensatory gesture on behalf of mainstream politics (in the United Kingdom, New Labour) and also popular culture (grateful for the wider repertoire of gender relations which it can now utilize)? This is the line of argument I want to pursue. To do this, it's necessary to show how this kind of sociology fits so well with current preoccupations, especially those which focus on young women as a metaphor for social change, and how this in turn gives rise to the danger of confirming the young female subject as one who has no need for feminist politics.

The film *Bridget Jones's Diary* allows such an initial inquiry for the reason that it draws together so many of these themes, playing them back to an audience in such a way as to endorse the celebration of a postfeminist condition. Aged thirty, living and working in London, Bridget is a free agent, single and childless and able to enjoy herself in pubs, bars, and restaurants; she is the product of modernity in that she has benefited from those institutions (education) which have loosened the ties of tradition and community for women, making it possible for them to be disembedded and relocated to the city to earn an independent living without shame or danger. However, this also gives rise to new anxieties; there is the fear of loneliness, for example, and the stigma of remaining single. In the film the opening sequence shows Bridget in her pajamas, worrying about being alone and on the shelf. The soundtrack is "All by Myself," by Jamie McNeal, and the audience laughs along with her in this moment of self-doubt. We immediately know what she is thinking. Bridget portrays the whole spectrum of attributes associated with the self-monitoring subject. She confides in her friends. She keeps a diary. She endlessly reflects on her fluctuating weight, noting her calorie intake. She plans, plots, and has projects. She is also deeply uncertain as to what the future holds for her.

Despite the choices she has, there are also any number of risks of which she is regularly reminded: the risk that she might let the right man slip from under her nose (hence she must always be on the lookout), the risk that not catching a man at the right time might mean she misses the chance of having children (her biological clock is ticking), and the risk that, partnerless, she will be isolated, marginalized from the world of happy couples. With the burden of self-management so apparent, Bridget fantasizes tradition. She sees herself in a white wedding dress and surrounded by bridesmaids. The audience laughs because they, like Bridget, know that this is not how young women these days are meant to think. Feminism has intervened to constrain these kinds of conventional desires. It is a relief, then, to escape this censorious politics and freely enjoy that which has been disapproved of.

Thus feminism is invoked in order that it can be relegated to the past. There are of course some dramatic differences between the various female characters of current popular culture, from Bridget Jones to the girls in *Sex and the City* and to *Ally McBeal,* and those found in girls' and women's magazines from a prefeminist era. They are confident enough to declare their anxieties about possible failure in regard to finding a husband; they avoid any aggressive or overtly traditional men; and they brazenly enjoy their sexuality, without fear of the sexual double standard. In addition they are more than capable of earning their own living, and the degree of suffering or shame they anticipate in the absence of finding a husband is countered by sexual self-confidence. Being without a husband does not mean they will go without men.

With such light entertainment as this, suffused with irony and dedicated to reinventing highly successful women's genres of film and TV, a bold and serious argument about feminism being so repudiated is admittedly difficult to sustain. Having set myself this task, let me conclude by reminding myself and readers that relations of power are indeed made and remade within texts of enjoyment and rituals of relaxation and abandonment. These women's genres are critical to the construction of a new gender regime, based on the double entanglement which I have described; they are predicated on what Rose calls "this ethic of freedom," and young women have come to the fore as the preeminent subjects of this new ethic. These popular texts normalize postfeminist gender anxieties so as to reregulate young women through recourse to administrations of freedom. But even well regulated liberty can backfire (the source of comic effect), and this in turn gives rise to demarcated pathologies (leaving it too late to have a baby, failing to find a good catch, etc.) which carefully define the parameters of what constitutes livable lives for young women without the occasion of reinvented feminism. By so effectively, through the trope of freedom, enacting generational differences and thus bringing them into being, these forms successfully drive a wedge between women, which sets off the mother, the teacher, and the feminist into the realms of a bygone age. By these means postfeminism undoes feminism, on the basis that it is "always already known."

Notes

1. *Bridget Jones's Diary* appeared first as a weekly column in *The* U.K. *Independent* newspaper in 1996; its author, Helen Fielding, then published the diaries in book form, and the film, *Bridget Jones's Diary,* directed by Sharon McGuire, was released in 2001.

2. The *Daily Mail* has the highest volume of female readers of all daily newspapers in the United Kingdom. Its most frequent efforts in regard to promoting a postfeminist sensibility involve commissioning (for very large fees) well-known former feminists to recant, and blame feminism for contemporary ills among women—for example, the issue of Saturday, August 23, 2003, has Fay Weldon on "Look What We've Done." The caption reads, "For years feminists campaigned for sexual liberation. But here, one of their leaders admits all they have created is a new generation of women for whom sex is utterly joyless and hollow" (pp. 12–13).

3. By the normalization of porn, or "ironic pornography," I am referring to the new popular mainstreaming of what in the past would have been soft-core pornography out of reach of the young on the top shelf. In a post-AIDS era, with sexual frankness as an imperative for prevention, the commercial U.K. youth media have produced vast quantities of explicit sexual material for the teenage audience in recent years; and as a strategy for being ahead of the competition, this has been incorporated into the language of cool. With irony as a trademark of knowingness, sexual cool entails "being up for it" (i.e., lap dancing clubs) without revealing any misgivings, never mind criticism, on the basis of the distance entailed in the ironic experience.

4. There is a whole genre of retraditionalization books of rules for young women, and also novels which are based on breaking "the rules" for catching and keeping a man; *Sex and the City* refers regularly to these same rules. There is also a new fashion for reinhabiting tradition with frequently expressed desires for diamond engagement rings (rocks), drunken hen nights as prewedding rituals, and the taking of the male surname on marriage.

References

Adkins, L. (2002). *Revisions: Gender and Sexuality in Late Modernity.* Milton Keynes: Open University Press.

Arnot, M., David, M., and Weiner, G. (1999). *Closing the Gender Gap.* Cambridge: Polity Press.

Beck, U. (1992). *Risk Society.* London: Sage.

Beck, U. (1997). *The Reinvention of Politics.* Cambridge: Polity Press.

Beck, U., and Beck, E. Gersheim. (1997). *The Normal Chaos of Love.* Cambridge: Polity Press.

Beck, U., Giddens, A., and Lash, S. (1994). *Reflexive Modernization.* Cambridge: Polity Press.

Brown, W. (1997). "The Impossibility of Women's Studies." *differences: A Journal of Feminist Cultural Studies* 9: 79–102. Providence: Brown University.

Brunsdon, C. (1997). *Screen Tastes: Soap Opera to Satellite Dishes.* London: Routledge.

Budgeon, S. (2001). "Emergent Feminist Identities." *European Journal of Women's Studies* 8 (1): 7–28.

Butler, J. (1990). *Gender Trouble.* New York: Routledge.

Butler, J. (1992). "Contingent Foundations: Feminism and the Question of Postmodernism." In J. Butler and J.W. Scott (eds.), *Feminists Theorize the Political.* New York: Routledge.

Butler, J. (1993). *Bodies That Matter.* New York: Routledge.

Butler, J. (1997). "Merely Cultural." *New Left Review* no. 227.

Butler, J. (2000). *Antigone's Claim: Kinship Between Life and Death.* New York: Columbia University Press.

Butler, J., Laclau, E., and Zizek, S. (eds.). (2000). *Contingency, Hegemony and Universality.* London: Verso.

Coward, R. (1984). *Female Desire.* London: Paladin.

De Lauretis, T. (1988). *Technologies of Gender: Essays on Theory, Film, and Fiction.* Indianapolis: Indiana University Press.

Faludi, S. (1992). *Backlash: The Undeclared War against Women.* London: Vintage.

Hall, S. (1989). *The Hard Road to Renewal.* London: Verso.

Haraway, D. (1991). *Simians, Cyborgs and Women.* London: Free Association Books.

Harris, A. (2003). *Future Girl.* New York and London: Routledge.

McRobbie, A. (1994). *Postmodernism and Popular Culture.* London: Routledge.

McRobbie, A. (1999a). *In the Culture Society.* London: Routledge.

McRobbie, A. (1999b). "Feminism v the TV Blondes." *Inaugural lecture,* Goldsmiths College, University of London.

McRobbie, A. (2003). "Mothers and Fathers, Who Needs Them? A Review Essay of Butler's Antigone." *Feminist Review* no. 73 (Autumn).

Mohanty, C.T. (1995). "Under Western Eyes." In B. Ashcroft, G. Griffiths, and H. Tiffin (eds.), *The Postcolonial Studies Reader.* London: Routledge.

Mulvey, L. (1975). "Visual Pleasure and Narrative Cinema." *Screen* 16 (3): 6–18.

Rose, N. (2000). *Powers of Freedom.* Cambridge: Cambridge University Press.

Spivak, G. (1988). "Can the Subaltern Speak." In C. Nelson and L. Grossberg (eds.), *Marxism and the Interpretation of Culture,* pp. 271–317. Urbana and Chicago: University of Illinois Press.

Spivak, G. (2000). *Lecture delivered at Goldsmiths College,* University of London.

Stuart, A. (1990). "Feminism Dead or Alive?" In J. Rutherford (ed.), *Identity.* London: Lawrence and Wishart.

Trinh, T.M. (1989). *Women Native Other.* Bloomington: Indiana University Press.

Walby, S. (2002). "Feminism in a Global Era." *Economy and Society* 31 (4): 533–558. Special issue edited by C. Lury and A. McRobbie.

Williamson, J. (1987). *Decoding Advertisements.* London: Marion Boyars.

CHAPTER 2

Women, Girls, and the Unfinished Work of Connection: A Critical Review of American Girls' Studies

JANIE VICTORIA WARD AND BETH COOPER BENJAMIN

> The joining of women and girls lies at the heart of our research. This joining symbolizes and encourages our belief that the future experiences of women need not be bound to the past, in a process of endless repetition, and that psychological understanding can contribute to change.
>
> (Taylor et al. 1995: 6)

Introduction

In this chapter we map a series of shifts in the study of girls' development in the United States since the 1990s. We begin with the publication in the early 1990s of a cluster of influential scholarly and popular works in the fields of psychology and education. This literature documented what was seen as a psychosocial (and subsequently academic) "crisis" faced by girls as they entered adolescence. These books and studies generated widespread public concern and led to a variety of reform and intervention efforts designed to address girls' developmental challenges. In the years since, there has been a marked expansion in both the study of girls' lives in the United States and in programs designed to serve girls' needs. But the mainstreaming of this "girls' movement" has brought with it significant changes in the intent, substance, and implications of more recent scholarly and popular study.

In reviewing this literature, we identify a central thread connecting multiple shifts in the field of Girls' Studies in the United States. Specifically, we find that the intergenerational discourse that defined the first wave of contemporary girls' studies—one which drew a connection between experiences in girls' psychosocial development and persistent issues in adult women's lives—is largely absent from more recent work. We are concerned that this absence represents a diminishment of the transformative political potential of Girls' Studies and the girls' movement. We conclude our analysis by considering what might account for this shift, and how the study of girls' development and the politics of girls' lives could be reengaged and reinvigorated by scholars and practitioners alike.

Breaking Ground: The First Wave of Contemporary American Girls' Studies

In the early 1990s a series of American research studies, scholarly books, and popular publications identified a "crisis" in girls' development. Expanding a research program begun in the mid-1980s (see Gilligan et al. 1990), the Harvard Project on Women's Psychology and Girls' Development conducted studies involving both girls and adult professionals at two prestigious private girls' schools. In *Meeting at the Crossroads: Women's Psychology and Girls' Development* (1992), Lyn Mikel Brown and Carol Gilligan reported their findings: at the edge of adolescence, girls begin to edit their feelings and desires out of their closest relationships, fearing that honesty will breed conflict, and that conflict will lead to isolation and abandonment. This "central paradox" of girls' development—"the giving up of relationship for the sake of 'Relationships'" (Brown and Gilligan 1992: 7)—marked the mass movement of adolescent girls' authentic voices "underground" into protected spaces (such as a private journal), a compromise state that over time made it harder for girls even to identify, much less express, their true feelings and opinions.

During the same period, the American Association of University Women (AAUW), in conjunction with scholars at the Wellesley College Center for Research on Women, published a groundbreaking study of nearly three thousand boys and girls in American public elementary and high schools. The AAUW report, *How Schools Shortchange Girls* (1992), was the first national survey to assert a link between girls' psychosocial experience and schooling, arguing that deficits in girls' academic performance and career aspirations were connected both to biased school practices and also to girls' pronounced losses in self-esteem at the threshold of adolescence (AAUW 1991: 4). The report generated enormous popular interest, and in many cases alarm, as psychologists, educators, and parents scrambled to create school environments that would better support girls' educational success.

Two major publications following on the heels of the AAUW's popular attention expanded the main findings of the original report. Myra and David Sadker's *Failing at Fairness: How America's Schools Cheat Girls* (1994) investigated the issue of gender equity in American classrooms and revealed extensive bias in common educational practices whereby teachers and administrators privileged and promoted boys at the expense of girls' learning. In *Schoolgirls: Young Women, Self-Esteem and the Confidence Gap* (1994), journalist Peggy Orenstein documented the often demoralizing psychosocial experience of schooling for White, African-American, and Latina girls in two northern California middle schools. Excerpted in the *New York Times Magazine* and *Glamour* magazine, *Schoolgirls* offered a wide public audience compelling illustrations of the central findings of the AAUW poll and became a powerful reflective tool for adult women in girls' lives to revisit their own psychosocial and educational losses.

At the same time another book, written by a Midwestern psychotherapist, came to dominate the national spotlight, far surpassing the commercial success of the previous publications. *Reviving Ophelia: Saving the Selves of Adolescent Girls* (1994) drew on author Mary Pipher's clinical casework, describing adolescence as a treacherous terrain for girls, who were more likely to succumb to depression, eating disorders, self-injury, and attempts at suicide. Pipher attributed these risks to a "girl-poisoning culture":

> ...Girls today are much more oppressed. They are coming of age in a more dangerous, sexualized, and media-saturated culture. They face incredible pressures to be beautiful and sophisticated, which in junior high means using chemicals and being sexual. As they navigate a more dangerous world, girls are less protected. (1994: 12)

She also identified strengths and skills (such as media literacy) that girls should develop (and parents should inculcate) to prepare them to negotiate the "dangerous world" of junior high and beyond. An instant hit, *Reviving Ophelia* spent three years on the *New York Times* nonfiction bestseller list, and has sold over 1.5 million copies.

This literature galvanized a powerful public response, particularly from adult women. Several of the publications identified connections between women and girls as a key means for promoting girls' healthy and safe adolescent development. This idea was endorsed in subsequent publications (e.g., Debold et al. 1994; Sullivan 1996; Debold et al. 1999), and was put into practice as numerous girls' programs responded to the public outcry (e.g., the Ms. Foundation's Take Our Daughters to Work Day, the Ophelia Project). The literature inspired women to reflect on their own adolescent experiences, including experiences of bias and limitation (both self-imposed and institutional), and to identify their own developmental losses. As Peggy Orenstein acknowledges in the Introduction to *Schoolgirls*:

> It was not until I began this project that I truly confronted my own conflicts and recognized their depths. It was not until I saw how these vibrant young

women were beginning to suppress themselves that I realized how thoroughly I, too, had learned the lessons of silence, how I had come to censor my own ideas and doubt the efficacy of my actions. At times, the pain of discovery was so acute that I wanted to turn away, to simply discontinue the work. But in the end, writing this book, and working with these young women, has helped me to begin mending those contradictions, as I hope it will for other adult readers. (pp. xxvii–xxviii).

Recognizing the connections between their own histories and the challenges faced by girls today, adult women were encouraged to commit themselves to providing a new generation of adolescents safe harbor from the painful losses weathered by their mothers, mentors, and teachers.

Mapping the Shifts

In the decade or so since the publication of these influential studies and reports, the scholarly field of (and popular interest in) girls' psychosocial development has expanded broadly in the United States. Along with this expansion, however, have come important shifts in the focus of research and the tone of the discourse. In this section, we identify and discuss six key shifts in the literature (particularly in psychology and education) on girls' development.

First, while Girls' Studies has continued to press an agenda addressing girls' developmental needs, the strategies that researchers recommend have, in many cases, been altered from work that implicated adults and institutions to work that centers on the individual girl as the site of change. The literature of the early 1990s called for personal reflection among adults who work with and care for girls, and equally for institutional and cultural changes intended to preserve younger girls' "voices" and strengths as they enter adolescence. Gender equity educators in this period focused on interrupting patterns of bias in teacher–student classroom interactions, on curricular reforms that would integrate more information about women and girls into course content, and on engaging girls in nontraditional courses of study, particularly math, science, and technology (Hanson et al. 2002). In *Reviving Ophelia*, Mary Pipher's preface introduced measures that individual parents and clinicians could take to protect individual girls, but it concluded with a more collectivist vision of change on behalf of girls:

What can we do to help them? We can strengthen girls so that they will be ready. We can encourage emotional toughness and self-protection. We can support and guide them. But most important, we can change our culture. We can work together to build a culture that is less complicated and more nurturing, less violent and sexualized and more growth-producing. Our daughters deserve a society in which all their gifts can be developed and appreciated. (1994: 13)

Girls were in trouble, this literature suggested, but responding to their needs would require the engagement of adults (particularly adult women) and a transformation of the institutions that shape girls' lives.

In more recent publications—particularly in the wildly popular new literature on girls' relational aggression (a.k.a. "mean girls")—the site of change has moved from the collective to the individual. Strategies now focus increasingly on changing the girl herself (or sometimes her parents), rather than changing the culture to accommodate her developmental needs. The social psychologist Carol Tavris, reviewing a spate of "mean girls" books for the *Chronicle of Higher Education,* laments this turn of events, citing in particular the conclusion of the best-seller *Odd Girl Out*:

> Unfortunately, the only solution [author] Simmons can think of is prohibition. Schools, she suggests, should prohibit not only "male" forms of bullying and aggression, such as physical assault, but also "female" forms, such as "rumor spreading, alliance building, secret telling, and severe episodes of nonverbal aggression."… Psychological and punitive solutions are appealing in today's conservative times, when people don't want to think much about what it would take to create a "tending society" or make schools more appealing places to attend. The psychologizing of social problems is so much easier, because psychology directs us to look inward, to personal solutions rather than institutional changes. People cannot control the fact that peers are powerfully important to adolescents, and parents cannot force a child to "fit in" to an unwelcoming peer group. But they can supervise and influence the kind of peer groups their child belongs to, help the child find groups in which he or she will thrive, and press for programs that foster cooperation rather than competition among groups. (2002: 9)

Tavris suggests that this "psychologizing" trend reflects a broader societal abdication of adults' shared responsibility for addressing the origins of children's developmental difficulties.

Second, the growth of the field of Girls' Studies in the United States has resulted in a marked increase in specialization among researchers and a narrowing of the focus of individual studies. Viewed one way, this diversification is a tribute to the field's vitality and generativity, allowing researchers to carve out manageable subjects for investigation and to establish a deeper knowledge of a more finite phenomenon. Such burgeoning subspecialities within Girls' Studies include eating disorders, teen pregnancy, girls in the juvenile justice system, gender equity and the achievement gap in education, parenting of girls, girls' sexuality and sexual development, and relational aggression.[1] At the same time, although such specialization is a natural consequence of an expanding area of study, it becomes problematic when it results in a narrowing of the knowledge base as subfields get reified and increasingly disconnected from each other (Kuhn 1962/1996). Often knowledge in one specialty does not get translated, nor does it become part of the conversation in another. For example, although both the relational aggression and juvenile justice literatures investigate girls' experiences and expressions of anger (and their consequences), these two specialties seem strangely unresponsive to each other's findings. At the very least, these two literatures should be holding each other's findings in check, responding to the implications each holds for the other (e.g., the relational aggression literature's assertion that our culture constrains girls' and women's opportunities to express anger, versus the juvenile justice literature's direct evidence of girls' [particularly girls of color] expression of anger through violent action).

Third, several of the earliest American girls' studies established their narratives of girls' psychosocial and academic development on predominately White, middle-class samples (e.g., Brown and Gilligan 1992). These studies met with harsh critique for over-generalizing the experience of girlhood in a multicultural America. In the years since, researchers have attempted to enact a corrective measure by increasing their study of girls from the largest minority populations in the United States. Such research has resulted in significant refinement of our initial understanding of the "crisis" in girls' development. Where early Harvard Project research suggested that adolescent girls' diminishing willingness to make their voices heard was a near universal experience, later research (including works by Harvard Project researchers themselves, e.g., Taylor et al. 1995, more explicitly acknowledged race/ethnicity and social class as key components of girls' developmental experiences and contexts. This more recent work revealed that some populations of girls have a qualitatively different experience of adolescence. For example, African-American girls have been described as better able to maintain a strong sense of self and high self-esteem throughout adolescence. They often appear more willing to advocate for their needs and to resist injurious definitions of womanhood and femininity (Robinson and Ward 1991; Ward 1996, 2000; Fordham 1993).

Though groundbreaking, this research on minority girls' developmental experiences was far from complete. Despite recognizing the importance of context in understanding girls' development, contemporary researchers often fail to engage the cultural variations and distinctions masked within aggregate racial and ethnic groupings. The term "Latinas," as a prime example, collapses important differences among divergent cultures from South America to the Caribbean, from "Nuyoricans" to "Tejanas."

Social science research in the United States has traditionally struggled, as well, to reckon with the meanings and significance of social class stratification. The "American Dream" is grounded in the promise of the transcendence of social class boundaries, as in the opportunity to enable one's children to climb the social ladder through educational and financial achievement. The mythology of upward mobility encourages Americans (including many in the academy) to pathologize poverty and disregard the influence of privilege (Swadner and Lubeck 1995). When researchers employ multiple lenses, as in studies of girls' development that engage racial/ethnic and class location in addition to gender, this work becomes all the more challenging. Oftentimes these categories become conflated within studies, and new terms (such as "urban" girls) seem to function as proxies, glossing over more politically sensitive cultural and economic categorizations (e.g., low-income, typically minority girls growing up in economically impoverished, typically minority neighborhoods).

The absence of attention to intersectionality in the study of girls' lives seems particularly glaring in the case of contemporary research on middle-class White girlhood. Although it can be argued that these girls are well represented—even overrepresented—in American girls' studies, the majority of this literature continues to treat the middle-class White girl as a sort of "universal" figure, without critical attention to the influence of her racial and social class location. Too often, researchers seem not to engage the complexity of this multidimensional thinking in investigating girls' lives.

Finally, it is important to acknowledge that some populations of girls are still missing from the mainstream research literature. These girls tend to come from communities less accessible to researchers, such as linguistic minority groups and rural populations. Girls with disabilities, as well, are typically absent from research studies (Hanson et al. 2002).

Fourth, previously we have presented an argument for the importance of recognizing the ways that girls' experiences differ. We are also concerned, however, that the focus on differences *between* girls also obscures the significance of commonalities *among* girls: gendered cultural and political experiences that cross lines of race/ethnicity, class, and sexuality. Since the mid-1990s, we have witnessed a pendulum swing from a discourse that depicts all girls as experiencing the same developmental crisis in the same way, to a discourse that depicts each girl's adolescence as her own unique hell, mediated or exacerbated by a host of social and demographic determinants. While the contexts of girls' lives vary by geography, economics, and sexual orientation, among other distinctions, what's lost in this argument is the recognition that all American girls are influenced by, and must negotiate, persistent gender bias in institutions (e.g., schools, health care systems, organized religion) and the ubiquity of American popular culture.

Fifth, popular press coverage of the early girls' studies depicted adolescence as a developmental crisis, issuing dire warnings of risk and trouble, and urging adult intervention to "save the selves of adolescent girls" (Pipher 1994). As concern about girls became more widespread, interest in marketing to girls (in the form of girls' programs, sports, Web sites, toys, pop idols, etc.) grew alongside it. Appealing to girls and their parents as consumers required a softer sell than the crisis literature provided. Soon the adult marketplace, too, was flooded with books and resources for parents and teachers celebrating everything girl (for example, the literally hundreds of parenting books on the market dispensing advice about raising girls, Web sites such as the United States Department of Health and

Human Services "Girl Power Initiative," the huge number of book clubs organized by and for mothers and daughters, etc.).

The danger here lies not in either of these messages per se—alarm versus celebration—but in the cultural schizophrenia that divides and polarizes them. Much as in the case of the multiple lenses of race, ethnicity, social class, and sexual orientation, researchers have struggled to hold these two aspects of experience together. If we want to faithfully represent girls' lived experiences, then this struggle is a necessary one. While girls do tend to exhibit sophisticated relational awareness and interpersonal skills (Brown and Gilligan 1992), they are also at higher risk for depression and declining self-esteem in adolescence (Basow and Rubin 1999). African-American girls, who seem better able than White and Latina girls to maintain healthy self-esteem through adolescence (Commonwealth Fund 1997), are nonetheless significantly more likely to engage in sexual intercourse by age thirteen (itself a risk factor for early pregnancy, sexual victimization, and sexually transmitted infection) or to become involved in the juvenile justice system (Ward et al. 2002).

Sixth, American girls' studies were grounded initially in connections between girls' development and women's psychological and professional lives. By identifying how issues in girls' development persisted as problems in women's adulthood, the connections drawn between the two were inherently political. But as interest in girls' educational equity and psychosocial development expanded, and as girls' programs proliferated in schools, community-based agencies, and religious groups, the discourse of serving girls' needs experienced a definite shift.

Harvard Project researchers' interest in girls' development grew initially from observations and emerging theory about the psychology of women. Feminist scholars in the 1970s and 1980s had raised troubling questions about the limits of the major "universal" theories of psychological development (e.g., Freud's psychosexual theory, Erikson's "Eight Stages of Man," and Kohlberg's stages of moral development), based as they were on the experiences of White, middle-class males (e.g., Gilligan 1982; Miller 1976/1986). Recognizing that women's outcomes and perspectives often did not fit these theories, researchers began to trace the genesis of women's psychology backward toward girlhood. This challenge to the canon of Western social science generated energy and enthusiasm well beyond the grounds of the academy.

Women's advocacy organizations also began to examine their constituents' concerns and interests in this new light. The AAUW's decision in the 1990s to campaign for equity in education is a powerful example of how women's self-reflection generated political action on behalf of girls. The AAUW survey (and a decade of subsequent research reports) began as a response to concerns about gender bias and discrimination, particularly from members working in nontraditional fields (such as science and technology), who had first-hand evidence of the "academic pipeline" running dry as few young women pursued these courses of study.

The attention brought to girls' concerns through the popularization of the early literature helped to marshal political will and focused effort to investigate and intervene in girls' development. Widespread publicity helped to frame a national agenda to dismantle barriers to girls' health and success, and inspired countless programs of reform and remediation. Yet, in another way, the creation of a public girls' movement was a Pyrrhic victory for American feminism, because the widespread popularity of girls' concerns required that the message itself be toned down, dethorned, and homogenized. The movement of women on behalf of girls, initially motivated by women's recognition of the connections between their individual developmental losses and common political context, has given way to a field that tends to address girls' concerns solely as concerns for and about girls. In our efforts to "save the selves of adolescent girls," we have lost sight of how these efforts were meant to save ourselves as well: how addressing girls' needs also served explicitly feminist ends, as the literature defined work with girls as a form of collective resistance to patriarchy (e.g., Gilligan 1991; Debold et al. 1994).

Research and practice alike have shifted from a focus on strengthening alliances between girls and women toward a tendency to address girls' needs as a separate entity. In the world of programming, resources and attention are directed increasingly toward the girl herself (e.g., the "girl-fixing" described earlier in this section), at the expense of preparing women leaders to work effectively with girls by creating spaces for women to engage in reflective work that could enable and sustain their intergenerational alliances (Bay-Cheng et al. 2001). Leaders in the academic community, meanwhile, are beginning to acknowledge a similar shift in research on girls' lives. Defining an agenda for the psychological study of adolescent girls in the new millennium, the American Psychological Association's Task Force on Adolescent Girls: Strengths and Stresses identified this same shift as a problem to be ameliorated by future research:

> Girls' struggles are rooted in systemic problems—such as poverty, racism, and sexism—that require a collective, rather than an individual, response. This suggests a need for a new concept of health and stress resistance that locates the struggle between the girl and her world, not within the individual girl, and that holds the adults in girls' environments accountable for providing girls with experiences and opportunities for them to understand, engage with, and potentially transform what limits and harms them. (Roberts 1999: 415)

The Task Force's agenda calls for adults to support girls' engagement in struggle at both the individual and the collective, social level: to empower them to respond to their own concerns, while recognizing that their concerns are rooted in larger systems of oppression that shape all our lives.

Conclusion: Completing the Work of Connection

As practice-based researchers, our evidence and conclusions in this paper are drawn equally from our reading of the literature and from our experiences studying, consulting, conferring, and commiserating with those in classrooms, programs, and the academy. In these contexts, we frequently find ourselves stirred and challenged by the questions raised by practitioners. How should we be preparing staff (women) to work effectively with adolescent girls? What do girls need most from us? Most of all, we are dogged by a teacher's question that first appeared in Brown and Gilligan's *Meeting at the Crossroads*: "How can we help girls learn to deal with disagreement in public ... when we cannot deal with disagreement in public ourselves?" (1992: 14). We believe that we have a responsibility to engage in research and writing that addresses the questions and concerns of these practitioners. We also believe that the shifts we have mapped in this chapter tend to make that work more difficult, that they undermine both practitioners' ability to do effective work with girls and also our ability to provide them with scholarship that can inform their practice.

Each of the six shifts we have identified has its own consequences for how we frame and intervene in girls' lives. In addition, each of these shifts is connected to our central concern about the decline of alliance-building between girls and adult women. Moreover, these shifts have contributed substantially to the de-politicization of the girls' movement, which in turn has undermined the effectiveness of the movement itself.

As the APA Task Force argued, when we focus on "fixing the girl" to the exclusion of "fixing the culture," we lose sight of the systemic problems underlying individual girls' developmental concerns. This problem has many roots: the predominance of psychology (with its focus on the individual) in theory-building about girls' development, the American propensity to view the individual as both problem and solution, and the toning down of the girls' movement's politics as the literature pursued a wider audience. Our reluctance to "name" the forces of social oppression—racism, poverty, sexism, homophobia, among others—hampers our ability to lead girls well: to provide them with the analytic tools and personal fortitude we adults know are needed to navigate and thrive in the shadow of cultural bias.

While increasing specialization in the scholarly study of girls' lives is an inevitable—and often profitable—result of growing interest in the field, it also creates a new set of cautions and dilemmas. Theories, perspectives, and knowledge about girls' lives are being increasingly segregated into rigidly defined academic domains. Girls, however, are more than the aggregation of their risks and experiences. When subfields fail to engage each other's frameworks and findings, our understanding of the complexity of girls' lived experience suffers. Meanwhile, though strides have been made in attending to the experiences of multiple populations of American girls, too many groups of girls remain uncounted, absent from the major research literature, while others, though frequently represented, are too often studied with an uncritical eye. Even so, we are concerned that privileging difference at the expense of commonality undermines our ability to build coalitions, to establish the grounds for a larger political and social movement on behalf of girls.

This same tendency toward imbalance is also evident in the polarity between risk and resilience in girls' studies. Bridging the perspectives of celebration (resilience) and alarm (risk) is particularly important for adults who study, work with, or live closely with girls. Celebrating girls' capacities without acknowledging the risks they face distracts adults from preparing them for the real challenges of adolescent and adult life. Sounding the alarms of treacherous adolescence without recognizing girls' inherent strengths, meanwhile, undermines adults' recognition of the very skills that will enable girls to navigate this period successfully. Risk and resilience, alarm and celebration persist as themes in popular girls' studies because they are real cultural contradictions in the lives of all girls and women. These issues are irresolvable in any individual life because they are not individual issues: they are systemic and will require systemic change to transform them.

Despite the problematic shifts we have mapped in the study of girls' development, despite an anti-feminist backlash that has sought to pit the needs of boys against those newly identified with girls (Sommers 2000), despite a downturn in the American economy in which funds for girls' programming are running dry, the work continues. Every day, as they navigate the shifting sands of politics, economics, and scholarly knowledge, parents and practitioners come to us with questions. In order to respond effectively to them, we are calling for renewed political engagement in the study of and work with adolescent girls. This engagement will require (1) a research agenda that brings, in our multicultural nation, practitioners' concerns into conversation with the production of knowledge in the academy; (2) acknowledgment that we, as women, share with girls the reality of living within a culture that perpetuates biases and prejudices that harm us and shape our identities and opportunities; (3) recognition that this common cultural experience carries the potential to unite women and girls as partners in the same struggle.

Note

1. It is worth noting that each of these subfields (with the possible exception of sexuality) is typically represented in the literature as risky, a problem for girls' development.

References

American Association of University Women (1991). *Shortchanging girls, shortchanging America: Executive Summary.* Washington, D.C.: American Association of University Women Educational Foundation.

American Association of University Women (1992). *How schools shortchange girls.* Washington, D.C.: American Association of University Women Educational Foundation and National Education Association.

Basow, S.A., and Rubin, L.R. (1999). "Gender influences on adolescent development." In N.G. Johnson, M.C. Roberts, and J. Worell (Eds.), *Beyond appearance: A new look at adolescent girls,* (pp. 25–50). Washington, D.C.: APA Books.

Bay-Cheng, L.Y., Lewis, A.E., and Malley, J.E. (2001). *Gender socialization in early adolescence: Complexities of feminist interventions.* Paper presented before the Annual Convention of the American Psychological Association, August 26, 2001.

Brown, L.M. and Gilligan, C. (1992). *Meeting at the Crossroads: Women's Psychology and Girls' Development.* New York: Ballantine.

Commonwealth Fund. (1997). *The Commonwealth Fund Report on the Health of Adolescent Girls.* New York: Commonwealth Fund.

Debold, E., Brown, L.M., Weseen, S., and Brookins, G.K. (1999). "Cultivating Relational Hardiness Zones for Adolescent Girls: A Reconceptualization of Resilience in Relationships with Caring Adults." In N.G. Johnson, M.C. Roberts, and J. Worell (eds.), *Beyond Appearance: A New Look at Adolescent Girls,* pp. 181–204. Washington, D.C.: APA Books.

Debold, E., Wilson, M., and Malavé, I. (1994). *Mother Daughter Revolution: From Good Girls to Great Women.* New York: Bantam.

Fordham, S. (1993). "'Those Loud Black Girls': (Black) Women, Silence, and Gender 'Passing' in the Academy." *Anthropology and Education Quarterly* 24 (1): 3–32.

Gilligan, C. (1982). *In a Different Voice: Psychological Theory and Women's Development.* Cambridge, Mass.: Harvard University Press.

Gilligan, C. (1991). "Joining the Resistance: Psychology, Politics, Girls, and Women." *Michigan Quarterly Review* 29 (4): 501–536.

Gilligan, C., Lyons, N.P., and Hanmer, T.J. (eds.). (1990). *Making Connections: The Relational Worlds of Adolescent Girls at the Emma Willard School.* Cambridge, Mass.: Harvard University Press.

Hanson, K., Smith, S.J., and Kapur, A. (2002). "Does *All* Mean *All?* Education for Girls and Women." *Women's Studies Quarterly* 28 (3/4): 249–286.

Kuhn, T.S. (1962/1996). *The Structure of Scientific Revolutions,* 3rd ed. Chicago: University of Chicago Press.

Miller, J.B. (1976/1986). *Toward a New Psychology of Women.* Boston: Beacon Press.

Orenstein, P. (1994). *Schoolgirls: Young Women, Self-esteem and the Confidence Gap.* New York: Doubleday.

Pipher, M. (1994). *Reviving Ophelia: Saving the Selves of Adolescent Girls.* New York: Ballantine.

Roberts, M.C. (ed., with Clune, G.). (1999). "A New Look at Adolescent Girls: Strengths and Stresses. Research Agenda." In N.G. Johnson, M.C. Roberts, and J. Worell (eds.), *Beyond Appearance: A New Look at Adolescent Girls,* pp. 405–432. Washington, D.C.: APA Books.

Robinson, T., and Ward, J.V. (1991). "'A Belief in Self Far Greater Than Anyone's Disbelief': Cultivating Healthy Resistance Among African American Female Adolescents." In C. Gilligan, A.G. Rogers, and D.L. Tolman (eds.), *Women, Girls, and Psychotherapy: Reframing Resistance,* pp. 87–103. Binghamton, N.Y.: Harrington Park Press.

Sadker, M., and Sadker, D. (1994). *Failing at Fairness: How America's Schools Cheat Girls.* New York: Touchstone.

Simmons, R. (2002). *Odd Girl Out: The Hidden Culture of Aggression in Girls.* New York: Harcourt.

Sommers, C.H. (2000). *The War Against Boys: How Misguided Feminism Is Harming Our Young Men.* New York: Simon and Schuster.

Sullivan, A.M. (1996). "From Mentor to Muse: Recasting the Role of Women in Relationship with Early Adolescent Girls." In B.R. Leadbetter and N. Way (eds.), *Urban Girls: Resisting Stereotypes, Creating Identities,* pp. 226–249. New York: New York University Press.

Swadner, B., and Lubeck, S. (1995). *Children and Families "at Risk."* Albany: State University of New York Press.

Taylor, J.M., Gilligan, C., and Sullivan, A.M. (1995). *Between Voice and Silence: Women and Girls, Race and Relationship.* Cambridge, Mass.: Harvard University Press.

Tavris, C. (2002). "Are Girls Really as Mean as Books Say They Are?" *Chronicle of Higher Education* 48 (43). Online. Available at HTTP: <http://80-search.epnet.com.ezpl.harvard.edu/direct.asp?an=6966201&db=aph> (accessed August 26, 2003).

Ward, J.V. (1996). "Raising Resisters: The Role of Truth Telling in the Psychological Development of African American Girls." In J.B. Leadbeater and N. Way (eds.), *Urban Girls: Resisting Stereotypes, Creating Identities*, pp. 85–99. New York: New York University Press.

Ward, J.V. (2000). *The Skin We're In: Teaching Our Children to Be Emotionally Strong, Socially Smart, and Spiritually Connected.* New York: Free Press.

Ward, J.V., Rothenberg, M., Benjamin, B.C., and Feigenberg, L.F. (2002). "Gender Equity Issues: A Literature Review." Unpublished report to the Schott Foundation Strategic Planning Group. Cambridge, Mass.: Harvard University Graduate School of Education.

CHAPTER 3

Good Girls, Bad Girls: Anglocentrism and Diversity in the Constitution of Contemporary Girlhood

CHRISTINE GRIFFIN

In this chapter I aim to trace some of the key moves in the representation of girls and young women in academic research since the mid-1950s, in particular the contradictory ways in which girls and young women are constituted in contemporary First World societies, and the difficulties involved in living with, against, and through these contradictions. I argue that it is important to avoid adopting an Anglocentric perspective on the constitution of girlhood and the lives of girls and young women in contemporary societies, and also to acknowledge the diversity of girls' lives, and the cultural dimension of that diversity.

Valerie Walkerdine has challenged the taken-for-granted narratives of traditional developmental psychology that represent girls as constituted through the process of socialization (Walkerdine 1993, 1997). She drew on feminist poststructuralism, psychoanalysis, and cultural analysis to argue that girls are constituted as objects at the intersection of a number of competing claims to truth. In other words, there is nothing "essential" about girlhood; it is always produced and negotiated (by us all, but especially by girls) in particular historical and political moments. "Normal" femininity is constituted in part through a series of contradictions, especially around tensions between "good girls" and "bad girls," that tend to be played out with respect to representations of femininity and sexuality.

Lesley Johnson has also challenged essentialist narratives of girlhood in her important study on the social definitions of girlhood and growing up in Australia during the 1950s and early 1960s (Johnson 1993). Like many feminists involved in interrogations of girlhood, Johnson focuses her work on the complex series of contradictions involved in growing up as a girl. She challenges the traditional construction of girls as deficient in developmental terms when judged according to a masculine norm. Her text repeatedly returns to the important question of what it means to "grow up" for women, arguing that the constitution of "girlhood" has implications for the constitution of "womanhood." I would add that girlhood, womanhood, and the tension between "good" and "bad" girls are also constituted through dimensions of race, ethnicity, class, age, and dis/ability, and the impossibility of being (or becoming) a successfully "grown-up" female subject (Griffin 1993).

From Boyology to Teenyboppers: Looking at the "Modern Girl" in the Academic and Popular Domains

Contemporary academic and popular interest in girlhood must be understood in the context of a focus on "youth" that has tended to ignore girls and young women altogether, or to treat them as marginal beings at best (Fine 1988; Hey 1997). The attitudes and behaviors of boys have long been the primary focus of concern in what was initially termed "boyology" during the early twentieth century. Where young women and girls did appear, this usually took the form of texts displaying a combination of anxiety and fascination over sexuality, especially young women's involvement in prostitution.

By the mid-1980s, feminist researchers working with girls and young women began to reconfigure girls as visible, central, and valued in youth studies and the popular domain, aiming to understand the lives of girls and young women in their own terms and as located in wider political and historical contexts. British and U.S. youth research around girls and girlhood focused on difference and challenge: the distinctiveness of girls' lives posed a challenge to the taken-for-granted assumptions on which most theories about youth had been constructed (Griffin 1988; Lees 1996; MacPherson and Fine 1995). An important group of Black researchers argued that the lives of girls and young women of color (to use the U.S. terminology) in and outside of First World contexts did not necessarily fit the Western feminist perspectives on girlhood, and criticized the Anglocentric approach of much youth research, including the growing field of Girls' Studies (Ladner 1971; Amos and Parmar 1981).

If girls and young women have been and remain relatively invisible in most youth research, then some girls and young women have been more invisible than others. Most youth research has focused on young White men and women in First World contexts, and attempts to theorize their experiences have produced a set of theoretical perspectives and debates which revolve around the lives of Anglo-European (especially English) and Anglo-American young men and women (Mirza 1992; Phoenix 1991). This Anglocentric perspective remains pervasive in contemporary academic and popular representations of girlhood, though this is seldom acknowledged. As it is put into practice, this Anglocentric perspective does not reflect the diversity of girls' lives, the complexity of the contemporary constitution of girlhood, or the ways in which such a construction of girlhood works to "manage" or handle that diversity. Relatively few studies have examined the complex meanings associated with "difference" (or "sameness") for diverse groups of young women, although one notable exception is a project by Pat MacPherson and Michelle Fine (1995).

Looking at the "Traditional Girl": Anglocentrism and Girls' Studies

The focus on representations of girlhood in First World contexts allows one to look at the process of ethnocentrism as it is played out in the constitution of girlhood in the "developing" world, but with an awareness that such cultural contexts do not have neat boundaries. The First, Second, and Third Worlds are inextricably interconnected, yet each has a degree of cultural, economic, and political autonomy. If the "modern girl" is represented in predominantly Anglocentric terms, she is constituted in contrast to "traditional" girlhood, or the condition of girls and young women living in "traditional" cultures. "Modern" girlhood is located in the First World, associated with Anglo, Western cultures, and is seen as civilized and progressive for women, while "traditional" girlhood is associated with Third World contexts, with girls and young women of color, and is seen as anti-feminist and restrictive for women. Contemporary feminist approaches to the study of girlhood can still reflect a tendency to represent Third World cultures and the position of young women of color in First World societies as more "traditional" or sexist as far as the position of girls and women is concerned. For example, some texts continue to constitute the position of girls in "non-Western countries" as somehow *more* contradictory than that of girls in Western societies (de Ras and Lunenberg 1993). This tendency to associate "traditional" girlhood with Third World societies serves to marginalize young women of color from First World societies, even if they have been born and brought up in Britain, the United States, Australia, or Europe.

I want to interrogate this distinction between "modern" and "traditional" girlhood, using the example of Fauzia Ahmad's recent research on the complex meanings of "tradition" for a group of young British Muslim women of South Asian origin studying in British universities (Ahmad 2001). Ahmad's work challenges a number of assumptions about young South Asian and Muslim women.[1] In particular, her work questions the notion of young Muslim women "as 'victims' and recipients of oppression in patriarchal family relations, or as women with fixed religious identities"

(Ahmad 2001: 138). Ahmad interviewed a relatively small group of these women (N=15), but argues that they were "far more culturally and religiously aware *as a result of and despite* their educational experiences" (2001: 139; original emphasis). Ahmad's work is confirmed by a number of similar studies in the British context, notably those challenging the use of a simplistic distinction between "traditional" and "modern"/"Westernized" subjectivities in representations of young South Asian women, and especially young Muslim women (cf. Basit 1996; Afshar 1989; Brah 1993). Ahmad argues that among this group of primarily Sunni Muslim young women, higher education is not viewed as incompatible with the "Muslim way of being," and their parents view higher education and careers as absolutely necessary for their daughters.

Such a study poses something of a challenge to the construction of (all) Asian and/or Islamic cultures as inherently more patriarchal and sexist than (all) Western/Christian cultures, and as antipathetic to the education of girls (Brah 1993). It also works to unsettle the boundary between girls and young women in "Western" and "non-Western" societies. The work of Fauzia Ahmad and other researchers indicates that many young Asian women in Britain locate themselves not so much between two cultures as within and in relation to two (or more) cultures simultaneously, and do not necessarily see Asian and White cultures as so distinct and starkly opposed. For these and many other young South Asian women in the United Kingdom and elsewhere in the world, it is possible to value cultural and religious "tradition" and educational achievement simultaneously. Indeed, Ahmad discusses the diverse meanings of "tradition" for the group of young Muslim women she interviewed, challenging the dominant Western construction of "tradition" in this context as synonymous with "backward" and "primitive" ways of being, compared to the more "enlightened" West.

This is not to deny that many young Muslim women experience extremely restrictive lives in Islamic societies, but to recognize that many young White women in Western/Christian countries experience subordination and exploitation. Such restrictions take different forms, depending on the cultural and religious context in which they operate, and it is important to recognize the diversity of young women's lives, to appreciate the specific localized conditions in which young women live. Girlhood is constituted through multiple and frequently competing discourses, which position girls and young women in different ways, and are shaped by class and "race" as well as gender and sexuality (Reay 2001). While it would be foolish to constitute all young women as oppressed in an undifferentiated way, it would be equally mistaken to represent all young women in particular groups (e.g., young Muslim women) as living unrelievedly restricted lives.

Contemporary Representations of Girls, Young Women, and Girlhood: "Postfeminism" and the Discourse of "Girl Power"

Partly as a consequence of the impact of second-wave Western feminism, it became harder to ignore girls and young women quite so comprehensively by the 1990s. As (some) feminist ideas and practices entered mainstream culture, adult concern over girls and young women took on new forms. Angela McRobbie has identified these changes as reflected in the world of girls' and women's magazines (McRobbie 1997a). She uses the concept of "new sexualities" to refer to "images and texts which break discursively with the conventions of feminine behaviour by representing girls as crudely lustful, desiring young women" (1997a: 196). I want to shift feminist discussions of such discourses beyond the limitations of the Anglocentric perspective that tends to pervade these debates.

In affluent First World societies, the 1990s brought what is generally hailed as a "new" discourse to the arena of girlhood: that of Girl Power (Harris 2000; Cowman and Kaloski 1998/1999). Like so many discourses around girlhood, Girl Power is characterized by profound contradiction (Dibben 1999). In its most popular and pervasive form, as articulated around the manufactured British pop group the Spice Girls, "girlpower" appeared to endorse and value female friendships, even over and above the pressure to get (and bother about) boyfriends. Girl Power appeared to promise an all-female world of fun, sassiness, and dressing up to please your (girl) self. While the discourse of Girl Power clearly draws on and rearticulates elements of earlier feminist discourse, in so doing, it is also located as "postfeminist"; indeed, it constitutes the world as inherently "postfeminist" (Wilkinson 1999). The discourse of Girl Power takes it as self-evident that girls and women are "equal" to boys and men, and should be treated as such, eliding this into the assumption that girls and women are already equal to boys and men. As such, the world is instantly constituted as postfeminist; feminism (in whatever form) can be represented as irrelevant and old-fashioned; and there is no need for girls or women to challenge boys/men or any form of patriarchal system in an overtly politicized way (Sharpe 2001). It is not so much a question of whether Girl Power is or is not feminist, but that the discourse(s) through which "girl power" is constituted operates to represent feminism as simultaneously self-evident and redundant, thereby silencing feminist voices through a discourse that appears as "pro-feminist" (Griffin 2001).

Feminist critiques of Girl Power have seldom examined the ways in which this powerful discourse is racialized, nor the implications of this racialization for different groups of girls and young women. I want to look at Girl Power from a perspective that questions that usual distinction between "modern" and "traditional" girlhood. In practice (and discourses always involve practices), Girl Power has/had a style, and that involved lots of makeup and glitter and wearing tight clothes: raiding the wardrobe of your older sister rather than your mum. Wearing tight T-shirts and crop tops meant that a girl's flesh would always be visible, in a way that would be excluding for many of the young women interviewed by Fauzia Ahmad (2001), for example. The style of Girl Power is also excluding for any girl who feels at all self-conscious about the size and shape of her body, which is likely to be a majority of young women (Grogan 1999). Popular representations of Girl Power are overwhelmingly associated with young White women and girls, despite (or even because of) the token presence of Black girls.

Cowman and Kaloski have discussed the racist connotations of Mel B's name, "Scary Spice," and examined the ways in which different groups of girls relate to the individual Spice Girls (Cowman and Kaloski 1998/ 1999). Nicola Dibben's study of representations of femininity in popular music includes an analysis of the Spice Girls' music video *Say You'll Be There* (1997), and she comments on the use of Mel B (as the only Black Spice) and Mel C (as the White working-class Spice) to sing sections of the song using soul, funk, and rap-style voice-overs. As Dibben puts it: "a particular story is being told about the acceptability of different types of femininity according to class and race" (1999: 345). What little research there is on girls' and young women's uses of the discourse of Girl Power indicates that the latter is constructed as predominantly about and for White girls, although young women of color may use, negotiate, and/or subvert this discourse (cf. Reay 2001). Feminist critiques of Girl Power have seldom examined the ways in which this powerful discourse is racialized, or the implications of this racialization for different groups of girls and young women.

"Get Everything You Want (Now)": Girlhood, Consumption, and Feminism

The discursive context in which Girl Power has emerged focuses on an important domain in which the constitution of girlhood is played out: that of consumption, linked to the arenas of leisure and the domestic sphere. If we see consumption practices as part of the circuits of consumption, distribution, production, and reproduction (Brah et al. 1997), then these two sets of discourses (i.e., around girlhood and consumption) are likely to be connected in fundamental ways. It is now commonplace to argue that women have played a key role in the development of "consumer culture" and consumption practices, as have young people, especially since the emergence of the "teenage consumer" market following World War II. In First World markets, young people constitute (and are constituted as) an increasingly significant group of consumers, with girls and young women comprising an important segment of that population (Stearns 2001). However, girls' relation to consumption will be shaped in part by their financial position and access to money, but also by the availability (or lack) of subject positions in contemporary discourses around consumption that resonate with their everyday lives (Skeggs 1997).

Rather than considering the position of young women in diverse consumer markets, I want to focus here on the discursive role of consumption in constructing contemporary notions of girlhood. "Girlhood," and the bodies of girls and young women, are frequently represented both as consuming subjects and as objects of consumption, especially as objects of male heterosexual consumption and desire (Griffin et al. 1982). The tension between these two positions is evident in recent media representations of so-called "tweenies," prepubertal girls who are seen to constitute a novel and distinct set of targeted consumers (Brown 2001; Ellen 2000). Located in an uneasy position between teenager and child, "tweenies" have provided the focus for considerable adult (especially parental) anxiety since the late 1990s in a number of First World societies.

The discourse of Girl Power is frequently cited in anxious debates about "tweenies" and the consuming girl subject. This illustrates a fundamental tension in the constitution of the female consumer. On the one hand, women are positioned as ideal consumers, since femininity is seen as particularly well suited to the practices of consumption, that is, shopping (McRobbie 1997b). On the other hand, consumption is tied to notions of desire, and especially wanting material goods and services that one does not "need" in a strictly material sense (Stearns 2001). The consuming subject is therefore constituted as a subject with active wishes and desires (Bauman 2001). Patriarchal cultures are relatively comfortable with the notion that female consumers are shopping for their families, but are likely to be more unsettled by the image of the consuming female subject, expressing and acting on her own wishes and desires. Girls and young women are generally assumed to be shopping for themselves, but the challenge posed by girls' consumption for themselves is undermined if they can be represented preparing their (girl) selves for a (male) other: the actual or potential "boyf(riend)." In the media panic over "tweenies," however, the latter are represented as prepubertal and therefore seen as "too young" for boyfriends. They are represented as voracious consumers and as inappropriately (hetero)sexualized for their age (Ellen 2000). So their consumption is even more likely to be constituted as for themselves and their female friends, rather than for the purposes of attracting a boyfriend. This is one of several unsettling aspects of the young consuming female subject.

One of the Spice Girls' early hits, which is frequently cited as a key text of Girl Power, is immortalized in the words of their song "Wannabe," with the refs in, "Tell me what you want, what you really, really want." While the discourse of Girl Power is constituted in part as feminist (or, rather, post-feminist), it is also represented as fundamentally about the power of the girl as consumer, with a never-ending string of desired objects that she "really, really wants." I am not arguing here that the consuming girl is a subject of straightforward resistance, but noting the ambiguous quality of this subject position. As Nicola Dibben (1999) has argued, the Spice Girls' video *Say You'll Be There* can be read as both subversive of patriarchal constructions of femininity and as reinscribing them by offering the female body as the object of the male gaze. Dibben argues that the Spice Girls, like other popular texts, offer "the power of evasion (the evasion of social discipline and ideological control through exaggeration and fun, thereby disrupting the power of social norms) and the power of resistance (resistance by appropriating the forms of the dominant ideology, ... and using them in the construction of oppositional meanings)" (1999: 349).

Both strategies are problematic, Dibben argues, since "evasion occurs by finding pleasure in the cultural products of the dominant ideology, and thus sustaining such forms and practices; [and] resistance because it uses the forms provided by the dominant ideology and hence is always bound by its terms" (1999: 349). In addition, the subject position of the consuming girl is not of equivalent relevance for all girls and young women: it is profoundly shaped by class, ethnicity, sexuality, and disability. What are the resonances of the Spice Girls and Girl Power for the young women interviewed by Fauzia Ahmad, for example? My sense is that the discourse of Girl Power, for all the ambiguity of the subject positions that it appears to offer girls, has very different levels of connection with the lives of many girls and young women. An Anglocentric perspective would miss these diverse forms of connection, ensuring a double marginalization for girls and young women of color.

"Mad About Boys" and the Consuming Girl Subject

In the First World, anxieties over the context in which girls may act as desiring subjects tell us a great deal about the constitution of girlhood. Research on girls' and women's magazines has long argued that such texts "constitute powerful ideological instruments" (Ostermann and Keller-Cohen 1998: 531; cf. McRobbie 1997a). In their study of quizzes in American and Brazilian teenage girls' magazines, Ostermann and Keller-Cohen (1998) argue that girls' magazines naturalize heterosexuality as a "normal" part of young women's lives. The launch of a new magazine in Britain during 2001, *Mad About Boys,* aimed at girls in their pre- and early teen years, triggered something of a media panic related to the category of "tweenies" and the constitution of girls as active desiring agents (see Figure 3.1). The adult anxiety over *Mad About Boys* did not revolve primarily around the magazine's focus on heterosexual desire as an obligatory part of femininity, but concentrated on the construction of (hetero)sexual desire as a fundamental part of girlhood, especially of prepubescent girlhood. The relationship between girls and boys was seen to be (hetero)sexualized at an inappropriately young age, through the pictures of girls in face makeup and the representation of boys as potential boyfriends and as objects of girls' sexual desire. Although *Mad About Boys* ceased

Fig. 3.1. *Mad About Boys* magazine front cover, April 2001, no. 3. Reprinted with permission of Planet Three Publishing Network, Ltd.

publication after four issues due to poor sales,[2] I want to devote some attention to this text, since it brings together several key elements of the contemporary constitution of girlhood in British society.

Mad About Boys adapted the format and content of magazines aimed at older teenage girls into the preteen market—in other words, onto the borderlands of puberty and into the pre-pubertal zone of "girlhood." For example, the "makeover" carried out on eleven-year-old cover girl Sophia aimed to turn her into a "slick '50s chick" with makeup and smooth, sleek, curled-up hair (see Figure 3.2). This narrative of transformation begins with Sophia's apparent dissatisfaction with her "wild hair," and takes readers through a labor-intensive lesson in hair straightening and makeup application which would involve purchasing a range of hair and beauty products. There are some obvious confusions here that would probably be apparent only to readers over the age of (at least) forty. In the British context, the era most closely associated with the term "slick chicks" is the 1960s, and Sophia's made-over style, with its slicked-up, glossy, straightened hair and hoop earrings, is also more characteristic of the 1960s than the 1950s.

What interests me more in relation to Sophia's transformation "from wild child to slick chick" is the narrative of hair straightening around which it revolves. The narrative of straightening the "wild hair" of a young White girl will have resonances with the notion of disciplining the wildness associated with childhood and femininity. This story also has a racialized dimension relating to the practice of straightening "nappy" hair in women (and men) of African origin or descent, in order to conform to dominant constructions of "attractive" and desirable hair as smooth and glossy (Mercer 1994). My argument here is that an Anglocentric reading of Sophia's makeover story would miss the racialized dimension of this narrative about disciplining the "wild" girl child and her hair, and miss the potential resonances for African-Caribbean girl readers of this text, for example. Magazines such as *Mad About Boys* (and, indeed, all magazines of this kind) operate in dialogue with specific youth cultural practices, in this case those of girls and young women. Youth researchers have considered the ways in which such texts marginalize or render invisible certain female subjects (e.g., young lesbians), but have paid relatively less attention to the cultural resonances of such magazines for young women of color.

Mad About Boys also contains examples of that other staple feature of girls' comics and magazines: the quiz. Ostermann and Keller-Cohen (1998) have argued that the quiz genre is not so playful as it appears at first glance. Quizzes encourage girls in the practice of self-scrutiny, working as "disciplinary instruments" aimed at the heterosexist socialization of teenage girls. Their very informality marks quizzes out as part of a sustained and pervasive project that revolves around disciplining girls to be good. Ostermann and Keller-Cohen's detailed analysis demonstrates that such quizzes operate as "disciplinary instruments" in the Foucaultian sense.

Fig. 3.2. "Be a Slick Chick" makeover, *Mad About Boys*, April 2001, no. 3, pp. 10–11. Reprinted with permission of Planet Three Publishing Network, Ltd.

However, they have less to say about the cultural, ethnic, and racialized dimensions of the constitution of "good" and "bad" girls in these quizzes, or the implications of such processes for different groups of readers.

The *Mad About Boys* quiz "Mates or Lads?" is designed to test readers' loyalty to their girlfriends or "boyfs" (see Figure 3.3). The low scorers are represented as too loyal and supportive of their girlfriends at the expense of potential "boyfs." High scorers are represented as "more desperate for a man than Albert Square's Kat Slater" (a White, working-class female character in the long-running British soap *EastEnders*). In the middle are the "fine example(s) of girl power" who have "a really good balance going on" between their "girlie mates" and "fitting in your fair share of roman-cin'"(2001: 13). Those readers in this middle category are characterized as having girlfriends who "know they can depend on you" and a boyfriend who "knows that you rate him and won't drop everything the minute he calls" (2001: 13). This constitutes Girl Power as a heterosexual phenomenon, but also constructs the modern girl as located between the competing pressures and demands of girlfriends ("mates") and boyfriends ("roman-cin'"). The ideal modern girl (even at age eleven) must learn to juggle both sets of demands, which are constituted as in competition with one another, and fit in her own needs as well. There is no obvious right way to be a girl here: the girl subject is constituted in an uneasy and shifting location between competing external demands and pressures, and the obligatory expression of internal desires. This has something in common with Nicola Dibben's point about the ambiguity of the subject positions available to girls in the key texts of Girl Power (Dibben, 1999).

In *Mad About Boys*, Girl Power is marked as culturally and sexually specific, relevant only to girls who are interested in getting a boyfriend and in the practices of dating. The cartoon image of a girl caught between the competing demands of her male "boyf" and her female "mate" at the start of the "Mates or Lads?" quiz represents the girl in the center as an indeterminate light brown color with blue eyes; her "boyf" as White with blue eyes, ginger hair, and freckles; and her "mate" as brown-skinned with brown eyes. The "boyf" is racially marked as unambiguously White, and the (girl) "mate" as unambiguously Black, but the girl in the middle (who is located as the girl reader by the text) is marked as both (light) brown and White (with blue eyes). Once again, my argument is that an Anglocentric reading of this type of quiz as a text might focus on the work it does in the disciplining of girls as respectable heterosexual subjects, and miss the racialized dimension to this project.

One of the starkest aspects of these contemporary representations of British girlhood is the overwhelming Whiteness and slimness of the girls and young women depicted in the visual images. Only a minority of the young women represented in these magazines are "Black," and these are usually of African-Caribbean or mixed parentage, frequently with pale skins. There are very few images of Asian girls, and all the girls on the

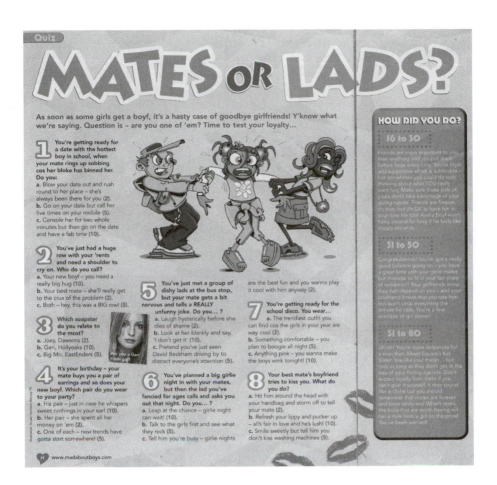

Fig. 3.3. "Mates or Lads?" quiz, *Mad About Boys*, April 2001, no. 3, pp. 12–13. Reprinted with permission of Planet Three Publishing Network, Ltd.

magazines' covers are slim, able-bodied and conventionally attractive White girls and young women. The magazines also revolve around a set of specific cultural resonances that presume their readers will share an interest in actual or potential "boyfs," "looking good," and the lives of celebrities in the worlds of TV, sports, pop music, and film. The magazines also make few or no references to the existence of young women who identify as lesbian or bisexual or to young women with disabilities.

My aim in this chapter has been to illustrate some of the limitations involved in adopting an Anglocentric perspective to examine the constitution of girlhood in contemporary societies, and the importance of recognizing the ethnic, racial, and cultural diversity of girls' lives as well as the racialization of the constitution of "modern" girlhood. Gender and sexuality remain an important element in this project, but they seldom if ever tell the whole story. I am primarily calling for a greater attention to diversity and difference in relation to how girls' lives and the constitution of girlhood are understood. Contemporary representations of girlhood also operate to marginalize or render invisible many other possible ways of being a girl, through their lack of resonance with the full diversity of girls' lives. This last point is not simply concerned with which groups of girls are absent from contemporary discourses of girlhood, but also with how girlhood itself is constituted as ambiguous in a way that renders certain "girl" subject positions as unsupportable, incomprehensible, or incompatible with "normal" girlhood. Dominant constructions of girlhood are constituted through a series of contradictions that operate to render the girl herself as an impossible subject. Girls and young women are generally represented as having (or being) too little or too much; as too fat or too thin, too clever or too stupid, too free or too restricted. The desiring subject is also a dissatisfied subject (Bauman 2001), and in the case of femininity, the primary focus of that dissatisfaction is constituted as within the self. Contemporary girlhood appears to be an impossible project, caught between competing forces, in a permanent state of dissatisfaction or desire, surrounded by idealized representations of itself, and simultaneously invisible. And yet, of course, the lives of girls and young women frequently belie the pessimism of such representations.

Notes

1. I originally wrote this paper before the attack on the World Trade Center in New York City in September 2001, and the subsequent military actions by U.S. and British forces in Afghanistan. I decided to leave this part of the text as it stands: if anything, such arguments against an overly simplistic view of Islamic cultures have increased their resonance in the current situation.

2. One of the reasons for the commercial failure of *Mad About Boys* may well have been the issue that would be likely to concern most potential purchasers: the price. At £1.50 a month for thirty-two pages, *Mad About Boys* represents far worse value for money than some of its main rivals. *Mizz* magazine, for example, costs £1.40 each fortnight and contains eighty-four pages.

References

Afshar, H. (1989). "Education: Hopes, Expectations and Achievements of Muslim Women in West Yorkshire." *Gender and Education* 1: 261–272.
Ahmad, F. (2001). "Modern Traditions? British Muslim Women and Academic Achievement." *Gender and Education* 13 (2): 137–152.
Amos, V., and Parmar, P. (1981). "Resistances and Responses: The Experiences of Black Girls in Britain." In A. McRobbie and T. McCabe (eds.), *Feminism for Girls: An Adventure Story.* London: Routledge and Kegan Paul.
Basit, T. (1997). *Eastern Values, Western Milieu: Identities and Aspirations of Adolescent British Muslim Girls.* Aldershot: Ashgate.
Bauman, Z. (2001). "Consuming Life." *Journal of Consumer Culture* 1 (1): 9–30.
Brah, A. (1993). "'Race' and 'Culture' in the Gendering of Labour Markets." *New Community* 29: 441–458.
Brah, A., Coombes, A., Lewis, R., and Phoenix, A. (eds.). (1997). "Editorial: Consuming Cultures." *Feminist Review* 55: 1–3.
Brown, D.K. (2001). "Lack of Girls' Comics Reduces Role Models." *Independent* 3, p. 4 (June).

Cowman, K. and Kaloski, A. (1998/1999). "Spicing Up Girls' Lives." *Trouble and Strife* 38: 3–11.

de Ras, M., and Lunenberg, M. (eds.). (1993). *Girls, Girlhood and Girls' Studies in Transition.* Amsterdam: Het Spinhuis.

Dibben, N. (1999). "Representations of Femininity in Popular Music." *Popular Music* 18 (3): 331–355.

Ellen, B. (2000). "8 Going on 18." *Life* magazine, *Observer* color supp., December 3, 28–30.

Fine, M. (1988). "Sexuality, Schooling and Adolescent Females: The Missing Discourse of Desire." *Harvard Educational Review* 58: 29–53.

Griffin, C. (1988). "Youth Research: Young Women and the 'Gang of Lads' Model." In J. Hazekamp, W. Meeus, and Y. te Poel (eds.), *European Contributions to Youth Research.* Amsterdam: Free University Press.

Griffin, C. (1993). *Representations of Youth: The Study of Youth and Adolescence in Britain and America.* Cambridge: Polity Press.

Griffin, C. (1997). "Troubled Teens: Managing Disorders of Transition and Consumption." *Feminist Review* 55: 4–21.

Griffin, C. (2001). "'The Young Women Are Having a Great Time': Representations of Young Women and Feminism." *Feminism and Psychology* 11 (2): 182–186.

Griffin, C., Hobson, D., MacIntosh, S., and McCabe, T. (1982). "Women and Leisure." In J. Hargreaves (ed.), *Sport, Culture and Ideology.* London: Routledge and Kegan Paul.

Grogan, S. (1999). *Body Image: Understanding Body Dissatisfaction in Men, Women and Children.* London: Routledge.

Harris, A. (2000). "Gurl Scenes and Grrl Zines: Young Women Making Political Networks." Paper presented at ESRC Seminar on Interdisciplinary Youth Research, Birmingham University, November.

Hey, V. (1997). *The Company She Keeps: An Ethnography of Girls' Friendships.* Buckingham: Open University Press.

Johnson, L. (1993). *The Modern Girl: Girlhood and Growing Up.* Buckingham: Open University Press.

Ladner, J. (1971). *Tomorrow's Tomorrow: The Black Woman.* New York: Doubleday.

Lees, S. (1996). *Sugar and Spice: Sexuality and Adolescent Girls.* Harmondsworth: Penguin.

MacPherson, P., and Fine, M. (1995). "Hungry for an Us: Adolescent Girls and Adult Women Negotiating Territories of Race, Gender and Class Difference." *Feminism and Psychology* 5 (2): 181–200.

McRobbie, A. (1997a). "*More!* New Sexualities in Girls' and Women's Magazines." In A. McRobbie (ed.), *Back to Reality? Social Experience and Cultural Studies.* Manchester: Manchester University Press.

McRobbie, A. (1997b). "Bridging the Gap: Feminism, Fashion and Consumption." *Feminist Review* 55: 73–89.

Mercer, K. (1994). *Welcome to the Jungle: New Positions in Black Cultural Studies.* London: Routledge.

Mirza, H.S. (1992). *Young, Female and Black.* London: Routledge.

Ostermann, A.C., and Keller-Cohen, D. (1998). "Good Girls Go to Heaven; Bad Girls … Learn to Be Good: Quizzes in American and Brazilian Teenage Girls' Magazines." *Discourse and Society* 9 (4): 531–558.

Phoenix, A. (1991). *Young Mothers?* Cambridge: Polity Press.

Reay, D. (2001). "'Spice Girls,' 'Nice Girls,' 'Girlies,' and 'Tomboys': Gender Discourses and Femininities in the Primary Classroom." *Gender and Education* 13 (2): 153–166.

Sharpe, S. (2001). "Going for It: Young Women Face the Future." *Feminism and Psychology* 11 (2): 177–181.

Skeggs, B. (1997). *Formations of Class and Gender: Becoming Respectable.* London: Sage.

Stearns, P.N. (2001). *Consumerism in World History: The Global Transformation of Desire.* London: Routledge.

Walkerdine, V. (1993). "Girlhood Through the Looking Glass." In M. de Ras and M. Lunenberg (eds.), *Girls, Girlhood and Girls' Studies in Transition.* Amsterdam: Het Spinhuis.

Walkerdine, V. (1997). *Daddy's Girl: Young Girls and Popular Culture.* London: Macmillan.

Wilkinson, H. (1999). "The Thatcher Legacy: Power Feminism and the Birth of Girl Power." In N. Walter (ed.), *On the Move: Feminism for a New Generation.* London: Virago.

CHAPTER 4

From Badness to Meanness: Popular Constructions of Contemporary Girlhood

MEDA CHESNEY-LIND AND KATHERINE IRWIN

Introduction

It is Monday morning and you decide to wear jeans to school instead of a skirt. The consequence of this seemingly innocuous action? You are kicked out of the clique and forced to eat lunch alone. Welcome to girl world, where the rules of popularity are rigidly enforced by a pack of mean girls, also called queen bees. The petty, mean, and manipulative side of girls' peer groups became a popular subject in the United States after the publication of a spate of best-selling books on the subject of mean girls with such titles as *The Secret Lives of Girls*, *Odd Girl Out*, and *Queen Bees and Wannabes*. Following suit, American television and print media in the early 2000s diffused the message that, contrary to traditional stereotypes, girls were far from being sugar and spice and everything nice.

For example, in a *New York Times Magazine* article titled "Girls Just Want to Be Mean," journalist Margaret Talbot (2002: 24) wrote, "it is not just boys who can bully." In contrast to boys' physical aggression, girls, according to Talbot, practice "relational aggression" that is intended to damage girls' social status and relationships. In addition to practicing ostracism, female bullies spread rumors about, leave incriminating phone messages for the parents of, and hurl insults at their victims. The negative effects of this type of aggression were said to be as damaging as, or even more damaging than, boys' physical violence. The not so subtle message was that these clique-oriented girls are just as bad as or worse than boys.

The United States has always had "bad girls" and a collection of media eager to showcase their waywardness. In the 1990s, U.S. news reports featured female gang members who, like their male counterparts, carried guns, killed people, and practiced brutal initiation rituals (Chesney-Lind 1997). In the 1960s and 1970s, American bad girls were female revolutionary figures such as Patti Hearst, Friederike Krabbe, and Angela Davis who brandished guns and fought alongside their rebellious male counterparts (Klemesrud 1978). Given this history, it seems that queen bees are just the American bad girl flavor of the month.

In this chapter, we trace the shifting imagery of the Black and Latina bad girls from the 1990s to the middle-class White queen bees of the early 2000s. While on the surface the shift in media representations of bad girls seemed to offer a more egalitarian view of bad girls, we demonstrate that images of mean girls in the United States had severe consequences for lower-class girls of color. We first focus attention on the bad girl of the 1990s and highlight the media's claims about violent female gang members. Next, we outline some of the recent arguments made in media accounts and popular books about mean, clique-oriented girls and note that bad girl constructions, although focusing on a more privileged group, remained heavily laden with class- and race-based stereotypes. Finally, we conclude by outlining trends regarding girls in the U.S. criminal justice system in the early 2000s and offering some hypotheses regarding why we continued to see poor girls of color disproportionately represented in formal mechanisms of social control in the early 2000s.

Violent Girls

The media's attention to the subject of violent girls in the 1990s comprised a response to the explosion of youth violence in the United States from the 1980s to the 1990s. From 1983 to 1994 the United States experienced a tripling of homicide victimization rates for Black males between the ages of thirteen and seventeen (Cook and Laub 1998), an approximately 70 percent increase in youth arrest rates for violent offenses, and a nearly 300 percent growth in youth homicide arrest rates (Snyder and Sickmund 1999). Once these statistics became public, the media were drawn to what some were calling an "epidemic of youth violence" (Cook and Laub 1998).

The vast majority of perpetrators and victims during the youth violence epidemic were boys and young men of color, and media coverage of the "epidemic" was also largely focused on boys. However, while boys and men were the primary individuals driving the violence arrest statistics, girls' arrest rates were increasing faster than boys' arrest rates—a fact that was not lost on the media. Between 1991 and 2000 in the United States, girls' arrests increased 25.3 percent while arrests of boys actually decreased by 3.2 percent (Federal Bureau of Investigation 2001: 221). Concomitant with these arrest increases were increases in girls' referrals to juvenile courts; between 1990 and 1999, the number of delinquency cases involving girls increased by 75 percent, compared to a 42 percent increase for boys (Stahl 2003). Arrests of girls for serious violent offenses increased by 27.9 percent between 1991 and 2000; arrests of girls for "other assaults" increased by even more: 77.9 percent (Federal Bureau of Investigation 2001: 221).

These statistics piqued the media's interest. The dominant explanation offered by the media accounts was that girls were being arrested more often because they were increasingly behaving like boys. In essence, the claims were that girls were selling drugs, joining gangs, carrying weapons, and engaging in violence as often as boys were. On August 2, 1993, for example, in a feature spread on teen violence, *Newsweek* had a box titled "Girls Will Be Girls" which noted that "some girls now carry guns. Others hide razor blades in their mouths" (Leslie et al. 1993: 44). Explaining this trend, the article noted that "The plague of teen violence is an equal-opportunity scourge. Crime by girls is on the rise, or so various jurisdictions report" (Leslie et al. 1993: 44). Exactly a year earlier, a short subject appeared on a CBS program titled *Street Stories.* "Girls in the Hood," which was a rebroadcast of a story that first appeared in January 1992, opened with this voice-over:

> Some of the politicians like to call this the Year of the Woman. The women you are about to meet probably aren't what they had in mind. These women are active, they're independent, and they're exercising power in a field dominated by men. In January, Harold Dowe first took us to the streets of Los Angeles to meet two uncommon women who are members of street gangs. (CBS 1992)

Years later, the theme was still quite popular. On November 5, 1997, ABC's *Primetime Live* aired two segments on Chicanas involved in gangs, also titled "Girls in the Hood" (ABC 1997), that followed two young women into their barrio for four months. The series opened with Sam Donaldson noting that "There are over six hundred thousand gang members in the United States. What might surprise you is that many of them are young women." Warning viewers that "some of the scenes you may see are quite graphic and violent," the segment featured dramatic shots of young women with large tattoos on their stomachs, youths carrying weapons and making gang signs, young women selling dope and talking about being violent, and distant shots of the covered bodies of drive-by shooting victims.

One of the underlying messages in these media accounts was that girls were achieving equality in male-dominated crime worlds. The *Washington Post,* for example, ran a story titled "Delinquent Girls Achieving a Violent Equality in D.C." on December 23, 1992 (Lewis 1992); the *Boston Globe Magazine* published an article that proclaimed on its cover, over huge red letters that said BAD GIRLS, "girls are moving into the world of violence that once belonged to boys" (Ford 1998); and from the *San Jose Mercury* (Guido 1998) came a story titled "In a New Twist on Equality, Girls' Crimes Resemble Boys'" that featured an opening paragraph that argued:

> Juvenile crime experts have spotted a disturbing pattern of teenage girls becoming more sophisticated and independent criminals. In the past, girls would almost always commit crimes with boys or men. But now, more than ever, they're calling the shots. (Guido 1998: 1B)

Girls, Gangs, Guns, and Emancipation?

Interestingly, while the imagery in the U.S. girls and gangs media hype of the 1990s implied that girls were breaking into boys' domains, research regarding gangs, violence, and inner-city drug markets suggested that this was not the case. As Bourgois (1996) illustrated, male drug dealers living in impoverished communities were left with few legitimate means to establish masculine identities. Not only did they turn to drug sales to establish positive identities, but they often used partner abuse and rape to announce their tough, masculine personas. Gang researchers consistently revealed that girls had very limited power vis-à-vis male gang members (Joe and Chesney-Lind 1995; Portillos 1999; Miller 2001), and although they were more violent than nonfemale gang members, they were less violent than male gang members (Miller 2001; Hagedorn and Devitt 1999; Deschanes and Esbensen 1999). In addition, research demonstrates that male gang members sometimes used rape or the threat of rape to control female gangsters (Miller 2001). Drug researchers also consistently noted that drug markets, even the exploding crack market with seemingly limitless sales opportunities in the 1980s and early 1990s (Bourgois 1989), tend to be locations in which women were seen as too weak to compete in the masculine world of drug dealing (Maher and Daly 1996).

Thus, crime worlds, and certainly the world of underground crack markets, were far from being locations in which women and girls achieved emancipation. In fact, as gang and drug research indicated, large-scale problems, such as those described by Wilson (1996), not only left men scrambling for ways to achieve positive identities in many U.S. urban centers, but also placed girls and women in precarious positions. Girls and women did not have access to legitimate or illegitimate economic opportunities, *and* they confronted hypermasculine cultural norms, what Anderson (1999) calls the "code of the streets," that were frequently leveled against them.

Queen Bees as Bad Girls

By 1995, the U.S. violence epidemic waned significantly. Attention to the subject of youth violence, however, did not abate. The collection of sensationalized school shootings, the most notorious being the Columbine High School massacre, piqued the media's attention such that by the late

1990s in the United States, the gangs, guns, and drugs story was replaced with stories of White suburban teens seeking revenge against their classmates. Violence prevention legislation and programming also shifted. By the early 2000s, anti-bullying programs, which promised to improve school climates and increase students' and teachers' feelings of safety (Olweus et al. 1998), became a favorite violence prevention strategy among U.S. school districts. In fact, by May 2003, thirty-three U.S. states had passed anti-bullying laws, most of which required school districts to adopt anti-bullying policies. This suggests that the initiative to combat the youth violence epidemic of the 1980s and early 1990s translated into an effort to do something about bullying by the early 2000s.

One of the claims in the bullying research was that girls practice a subtle form of bullying. Although not kicking, punching, or threatening to physically hurt their victims, girls practice "relationship" or more broadly indirect aggression against other girls. The basis for these claims came from the psychological literature on adolescent aggression (Bjorkqvist and Niemela 1992; Crick and Grotpeter 1995). The discovery of girls' aggression in the psychological literature became popularized in a series of highly celebrated books, such as *Queen Bees and Wannabes*, *Odd Girl Out*, and *The Secret Lives of Girls*. The best-selling *Odd Girl Out* claimed that mean girls destroyed their victims' self-esteem and made going to school a painful event for many girls. These claims also came, in part, as a backlash to years of feminist research claiming that women are more nurturing, caring, and relationship-oriented than men (Gilligan 1982; Taylor et al.1995).

TV and print media further diffused the constructions of mean girls found in popular books on girls' aggression. Wiseman, author of *Queen Bees and Wannabees*, made a guest appearance on *Oprah*. Simmons's work became the focus of a *Dateline* story titled "Fighting with Friends." In addition, the mean girl story was told in a series of newspaper and magazine articles with titles such as "Girls Just Want to Be Mean" (Talbot 2002), "Girl Bullies Don't Leave Black Eyes, Just Agony" (Elizabeth 2002), "She Devils" (Metcalf 2002), and "Just Between Us Girls: Not Enough Sugar, Too Much Spite" (*Pittsburgh Post-Gazette* 2002). The primary claim in these reports, like claims in popular books, was that girls are socially competitive creatures and that, in their efforts to be popular and powerful, they inflict lifelong damages on their victims.

The hazing incident at Glenbrook High School, located in a middle-class suburb of Chicago, on May 4, 2003, breathed new life into the contemporary constructions of mean girls. According to witness Nick Babb, quoted in an article in the *Glenview Announcements* newspaper (Leavitt 2003: 2), the hazing event turned violent when "a few individuals in the senior class decided they hated some of the juniors. Certain people decided they wanted to turn this whole thing into something personal." The violence reportedly included placing buckets over the heads of girls and beating the buckets with bats, as well as pushing and kicking. This is all in addition to smearing feces, pig intestines, fish guts, paint, and coffee grounds on girls while a collection of students looked on, cheered, and drank beer. After the event, five girls required medical attention; one had a concussion, one had a broken ankle, and another required stitches.

Although the media consistently noted that girls are not likely to be physically violent, the Glenbrook High hazing incident provided an exception to this rule. The ensuing attention on bullying problems also communicated a not so subtle message that female bullies can be just as dangerous as male bullies. In a *Morning Sun* article (Sullivan 2003: 24), for example, bullying was defined as "anything from teasing to fistfights. In short, it's considered any repeated behavior that has a negative impact on the students involved." This echoed the language of anti-bullying programs, noting that bullying destroys a school climate and makes the classroom and halls "unsafe" places to be. The safety discussed was both social and physical, and thus the clique behaviors of girls were symbolically placed on par with the boys' physical aggression.

Mean Girls in Perspective

As the media stories of mean girls and bullying exemplify, in the early 2000s we had a new type of bad girl. In contrast to the Latina or African-American gang member growing up in the hood, the bad girl of the early 2000s was White, middle-class, and suburban, and had a promising future. The shifting imagery of bad girls says something about social power and especially about the intersection of gender-, race-, and class-based power. Wiseman, the author of *Queen Bees and Wannabes*, through her Empower Program encouraged popular girls to understand their privilege and to stop the cycle of exclusion that keeps many students on the social margins. She noted in an interview that "the comments by the popular students [comments like "There are different groups in school, but we all get along"] reveal how those who have privilege are so accustomed to their power that they don't recognize when they are dominating and silencing others" (Talbot 2002: 40). Talbot (2002: 40) argued that, in this way, Wiseman's program deconstructs the claims made by social elites by "using analytic tools familiar from the sociology of privilege and from academic discourse on racism." Here, social marginalization and even racism in school were linked to the behavior of powerful groups. In this case, the powerful group was the pack of queen bees, and the solution was to make them aware of and step down from their privilege.

The move from the image of the gun-toting gangbanger to the back-stabbing queen bee, therefore, arguably has placed a much more powerful group into the spotlight, though queen bees are hardly the power elite. By arguing that girls were becoming as violent as boys in the 1990s, the media suggested that Latina and African-American girls were being liberated from traditional gender norms and consequently participating in the violent gang world on equal footing with boys. As we have seen, this was certainly not the case. So, too, were the media wrong when they positioned White, middle-class girls who wield relationship aggression against others as the culprits of school-based marginalization. Alternative aggressions are, fundamentally, weapons of the weak. As such, they are as reflective of girls' powerlessness as they are of girls' meanness. Women and other oppressed groups have not, historically, been permitted direct aggression (without terrible consequences). As a result, in certain contexts, and against certain individuals, relational aggressions were ways the powerless punished the bad behavior of the powerful. This was, after all, how slaves and indentured servants—female and male—got back at abusive masters, women before legal divorce dealt with violent husbands, and working women today combat abusive bosses.

Controlling Bad Girls

While media constructions of bad girls and the national and local attention that it brought to problems such as hazing, bullying, and gossip provided one means of containing bad behaviors, the ultimate system of social control in the United States is arguably the criminal justice system. Given this, any discussion regarding bad girls begs for an analysis of girls' status in these formal systems of social control. Indeed, once we examine the trends among girls in the U.S. juvenile justice system from the 1990s to the early 2000s, we see that girls' increasing arrest rates had more to do with increased social control over girls than it did with increasing rates of girls' violent offending.

Girls' Violent Offending

One of the more interesting U.S. criminal justice trends during the peak of the youth violence epidemic was that girls' violence looked nothing like the image presented in the media. Where the media suggested that girls were becoming like boys, the truth was that girls' violence dramatically differed from boys' violence. For example, a Girls Incorporated (1996) study demonstrated that about a third of girls reported having been in a physical fight in the last year, whereas over half of the boys in the study reported being in a fight. In addition, girls were far more likely to fight with a parent or sibling (34 percent compared to 9 percent), whereas boys were more likely to fight with friends or strangers. Finally, boys were twice to three times more likely than girls to report carrying a weapon in the past month (Girls Incorporated 1996: 13). Therefore, girls did not fight or carry weapons as often as boys, and were more likely to fight with a family member than boys were.

Furthermore, while girls' arrest rates for all forms of assault skyrocketed in the 1990s, girls' arrests for robbery fell by 45.3 percent, and for murder by 1.4 percent, between 1991 and 2000. In addition, several self-report data sources and official statistics revealed that boys' and girls' violence decreased dramatically in the late 1990s, thus indicating that the youth violence epidemic had waned significantly. What is most interesting is that self-report studies indicated that girls' violence rates decreased more dramatically than boys' rates (see Brener et al. 1999). Although girls' self-reported violent offending seemed to decline dramatically in the late 1990s, girls' arrest rates for violent offenses continued to increase. Arrests of girls for serious violent offenses increased by 27.9 percent between 1991 and 2000; arrests of girls for "other assaults" increased by even more: 77.9 percent (Federal Bureau of Investigation 2001: 221). Thus, girls' decreased involvement in violence seemed to have no effect on arrests, especially on arrests for "other assaults."

Of even greater concern, U.S. national data indicated that between 1989 and 1998, detentions involving girls increased by 56 percent, compared to a 20 percent increase in boys' detentions (Harms 2002: 1). This same national study attributed the "large increase" in the detention of girls to "the growth in the number of delinquency cases involving females charged with person offenses" (Harms 2002: 1). A study by the American Bar Association and the National Bar Association (2001) reported that half of the girls in secure detention in the United States were African-American and 13 percent were Latina. White girls accounted for only one-third of the girls in secure detention although they made up 65 percent of those in the at-risk population.

Given these trends, there is a need to generate some hypotheses regarding why, given girls' decreasing involvement in violence, girls' arrest rates and detention rates, especially arrest rates for Blacks and Latinas, are continuing to increase in the early 2000s. Looking at the social construction of bad girls in the media provides only a partial answer. By the late 1990s, the media construction of the violent Black and Latina gangbangers had disappeared. Instead, petty and mean White girls became the target of media attention. Thus, the arrest rates for girls of color in the 1990s cannot be explained simply as the result of a media-led moral panic about the behaviors of minority girls. Something more subtle seemed to be occurring in regard to increasing public concern about middle-class White girls' behaviors and the type of female offender most likely to end up in the U.S. juvenile justice system.

Enforcement Practices, Arrest, and Incarceration Trends

Girls' increasing arrest statistics can be explained partially by examining the anti-youth violence movement in the United States from the 1990s to the early 2000s. The efforts to control youth violence began as initiatives to stem the youth violence epidemic. By the end of the 1990s, however, the focus shifted to school violence and especially to increasing students' and teachers' feelings of safety after several horrific school shootings. We suggest that, given this history, criminal justice agencies changed their practices in two ways that ended in increasing arrests of girls, especially Black girls and Latinas. The first is a practice that we call "relabeling," and includes recategorizing offenses that were once considered status offenses (noncriminal offenses like "runaway" and "person in need of supervision") into violent offenses. The second is the process of "up-criming" in which youths were being arrested for behaviors committed in school or at home that would have been ignored a decade ago.

There is some evidence that relabeling has been one of the driving forces behind girls' increased arrest rates in some U.S. states. For example, a review of the over two thousand cases of girls referred to Maryland's juvenile justice system for "person-to-person" offenses revealed that virtually all of these offenses (97.9 percent) involved "assault." A further examination of these records revealed that about half were "family centered" and involved such activities as "a girl hitting her mother and her mother subsequently pressing charges" (Mayer 1994). This finding has been corroborated in other studies (see Acoca 1999; Bureau of Criminal Information and Analysis 1999). Relabeling of girls' arguments with parents from status offenses (like "incorrigible" or "person in need of supervision") to assault was a form of "bootstrapping" that was particularly pronounced in the official reports of delinquency among African-American girls (Robinson 1990; Bartollas 1993). This practice also facilitated the incarceration of girls in detention facilities and training schools—something that would not have been possible if girls were arrested for noncriminal status offenses.

Evidence for "up-criming" also exists. It has long been known that arrests of youths for minor or "other" assaults ranged from schoolyard tussles to relatively serious, but not life-threatening, assaults (Steffensmeier and Steffensmeier 1980). Currie (1998) added to this the fact that these "simple assaults without injury" were often "attempted," "threatened," or "not completed." At a time when official concern about youth violence was almost unparalleled and school principals were increasingly likely to call police onto their campuses, it should come as no surprise that youths' arrests in this area were up. It is noteworthy that this is largely due to zero tolerance and other anti-violence policies implemented after school violence incidents perpetrated almost exclusively by boys.

Youth Violence, Moral Panics, and Real Consequences

It is now more or less clear that the media hype about bad and mean girls, while not grounded in real increases in youth violence, had dramatic consequences for girls, and particularly for girls of color. Given that public attention cracked down on the bullying behaviors of White girls, this trend seems particularly ironic. While the media were focused on the behaviors of mean girls and the ways that they damaged the social climate of schools, the formal system of social control in the United States was engaged in relabeling and up-criming. Girls' increased arrest rates came because girls were bearing the brunt of this intensified system of social control at a faster rate than boys in the United States. Therefore, girls who were "acting out" in school or in the home were being punished formally. While it is likely that all girls were at risk for coming into contact with the criminal justice system at a faster rate than boys, it is clear that girls of color were unable to slip out of the purview of formal social control mechanisms. Taking a closer look at two U.S. school violence cases in the late 1990s and early 2000s illustrates why youth of color were particularly vulnerable to criminal justice sanctions at that time.

In the Glenbrook High School hazing incident on May 4, 2003, in which several girls and a few boys beat and kicked other girls, thirty-two students were suspended, and twelve girls and three boys confronted misdemeanor battery charges; if found guilty, they could have faced maximum penalties of 364 days in jail and $2000 in fines. Students, however, secured lawyers and fought these charges. Two students, in fact, filed a federal lawsuit to lift their suspensions and recover monetary damages from the school, though this was eventually denied. Parents, who provided the resources for these lawyers, stood by their children and made repeated claims, when interviewed by newspaper reporters, that their daughter or son was a good kid who was only marginally involved in the event. In the end, the school offered students the chance to graduate on time if they agreed, in writing, to forgo movie, book, or television deals.

Contrast this case with similar high-profile suspensions in another Illinois neighborhood, Decatur. There, a seventeen-second fight between seven African-American boys attending a high school football game resulted in the boys being expelled from school for two years. This despite the fact that the fight involved no weapons and none of the youths was injured. Until the intervention of Jesse Jackson, none of these youth were allowed counsel, and the two seniors, with less than four credits to go to graduation, would have lost the chance to graduate (Wing and Keleher 2000: 1). Though zero tolerance anti-violence policies in the Decatur school kept students from returning to school, Jesse Jackson coaxed the school district into allowing two of the boys to transfer to a reform school in the area and graduate on time.

Here we have examples of the effects of a decade of crackdown on youth violence. Through zero tolerance policies and an increased sensitivity to all forms of youthful "acting out," more U.S. youths were coming into contact with the criminal justice system in the 1990s and early 2000s. With the financial support of family members, middle-class, White girls and boys were likely to wiggle out from under these stiffening sanctions more often than youths of color. In fact, as the violence arrest rates for girls during the 1990s and early 2000s illustrate, girls were likely to be arrested for assaults committed in the home. Thus, for many youths, parents were not protectors from the criminal justice system and, instead, were the instigators of official sanctions.

In short, it appears that as the public fear of the "superpredator" youth subsided in the case of boys, its female version—the bad girl—was alive and kicking in the new millennium. Of even greater concern was the disproportionate effect this had on girls of color, whose families and communities did not necessarily have the resources to challenge the criminalization of minor forms of youthful misbehavior. As a consequence, minority youth, and particularly girls of color, were being brought into the U.S. criminal justice system for offenses that a decade earlier would have been ignored.

References

ABC Primetime Live. (1997). "Girls in the Hood." November 5.

Acoca, L. (1999). "Investing in Girls: A 21st Century Challenge." *Juvenile Justice* 6 (1): 3 13.

American Bar Association and the National Bar Association. (2001). *Justice by Gender: The Lack of Appropriate Prevention, Diversion and Treatment Alternatives for Girls in the Justice System.* Washington, D.C.: American Bar Association.

Anderson, E. (1999). *Code of the Street: Decency, Violence, and the Moral Life of the Inner City.* New York: W.W. Norton.

Bartollas, C. (1993). "Little Girls Grown Up: The Perils of Institutionalization." In C. Culliver (ed.), *Female Criminality: The State of the Art,* 469 482. New York: Garland Press.

Bjorkqvist, K., and Niemela, P. (eds.). (1992). *Of Mice and Women: Aspects of Female Aggression,* 1 16. San Diego: Academic Press.

Bourgois, P. (1989). "In Search of Horatio Alger: Culture and Ideology in the Crack Economy." *Contemporary Drug Problems* 16: 619 649.

Bourgois, P. (1996). "In Search of Masculinity: Violence, Respect and Sexuality Among Puerto Rican Crack Dealers in East Harlem." *British Journal of Criminology* 36: 412 427.

Brener, N.D., Simon, T.R., Krug, E.G., and Lowry, R. (1999). "Recent Trends in Violence-Related Behaviors Among High School Students in the United States." *Journal of the American Medical Association* 282 (5): 330 446.

Bureau of Criminal Information and Analysis. (1999). *Report on Arrests for Domestic Violence in California, 1998.* Sacramento: State of California, Criminal Justice Statistics Center.

CBS. (1992). "Girls in the Hood." *Street Stories.* August 6.

Chesney-Lind, M. (1997). *The Female Offender: Girls, Women and Crime.* Thousand Oaks, Calif.: Sage.

Cook, P.J., and Laub, J.H. (1998). "The Unprecedented Epidemic in Youth Violence." In M. Tonry and M.H. Moore (eds.), *Youth Violence. Crime and Justice: A Review of Research,* 27 64. Chicago: University of Chicago Press.

Crick, N.R., and Grotpeter, J.K. (1995). "Relational Aggression, Gender, and Social-Psychological Adjustment." *Child Development* 66: 710 722.

Currie, E. 1998. *Crime and Punishment in America.* New York: Metropolitan Books.

Deschanes, E., and Esbensen, F.-A. (1999). "Violence Among Girls: Does Gang Membership Make a Difference?" In Meda Chesney-Lind and John Martin Hagedorn (eds)., *Female Gangs in America: Essays on Gender and Gangs,* 277 294. Lakeview Press: Chicago.

Elizabeth, J. (2002). "Girl Bullies Don't Leave Black Eyes, Just Agony." *Pittsburgh Post-Gazette,* April 10, p. A1.

Federal Bureau of Investigation. (2001). *Crime in the United States 2000.* Washington, D.C.: Government Printing Office.

Ford, R. (1998). "The Razor's Edge." *Boston Globe Magazine,* May 24, pp. 13, 22 28.

Gilligan, C. (1982). *In a Different Voice.* Cambridge, Mass.: Harvard University Press.

Girls Incorporated. (1996). *Prevention and Parity: Girls in Juvenile Justice.* Indianapolis: Girls Incorporated National Resource Center.

Guido, M. (1998). "In a New Twist on Equality, Girls' Crimes Resemble Boys.'" *San Jose Mercury,* June 4, pp. 1B 4B.

Hagedorn, J., and Devitt, M. (1999). "Fighting Female: The Social Construction of Female Gangs." In Meda Chesney-Lind and John Martin Hagedorn (eds.), *Female Gangs in America: Essays on Gender and Gangs,* 256 276. Chicago: Lakeview Press.

Harms, P. (2002). *Detention in Delinquency Cases, 1989–1998.* OJJDP Fact Sheet no. 1. Washington, D.C.: U.S. Department of Justice.

Joe, K., and Chesney-Lind, M. (1995). "Just Every Mother's Angel: An Analysis of Ethnic and Gender Variations in Youth Gang Membership." *Gender and Society* 9 (4): 409 431.

Klemesrud, J. (1978). "Women Terrorists, Sisters in Crime." N.Y.T. News Service. *Honolulu Star Bulletin,* January 16, p. C1.

Lamb, S. (2001). *The Secret Lives of Girls: What Good Girls Really Do—Sex Play, Aggression, and Their Guilt.* New York: The Free Press.

Leavitt, I. (2003). "Hazing's Horror Related." *Glenview Announcements,* May 8.

Leslie, C., Biddle, N., Rosenberg, D., and Wayne, J. (1993). "Girls Will Be Girls." *Newsweek.* August 2, p. 44.

Lewis, N. (1992). "Delinquent Girls Achieving a Violent Equality in D.C." *Washington Post,* December 23, pp. A1, A14.

Maher, L., and Daly, K. (1996). "Women in the Street Level Drug Economy: Continuity or Change?" *Criminology* 34: 465 491.

Mayer, J. (1994). "Girls in the Maryland Juvenile Justice System: Findings of the Female Population Taskforce." Presentation to the Gender Specific Services Training Group, Minneapolis, Minn.

Metcalf, F. (2002). "She Devils." *Courier Mail,* Queensland, Australia, June 22, p. L 06.

Miller, J. (2001). *One of the Guys: Girls, Gangs, and Gender.* New York: Oxford University Press.

Olweus, D., Limber, S., and Mihalic, S. (1998). *Book Nine: Bullying Prevention Program.* Boulder: Center for the Study and Prevention of Violence, Institute for Behavioral Sciences, University of Colorado.

Pittsburgh Post-Gazette. (2002). "Just Between Us Girls: Not Enough Sugar, Too Much Spite." June 5, pp. S3.

Portillos, E. (1999). "Women, Men and Gangs: The Social Construction of Gender in the Barrio." In Meda Chesney-Lind and John Martin Hagedorn (eds.), *Female Gangs in America: Essays on Gender and Gangs,* 232 244. Chicago: Lakeview Press.

Robinson, R. (1990). "Violations of Girlhood: A Qualitative Study of Female Delinquents and Children in Need of Services in Massachusetts." Ph.D. dissertation, Brandeis University.

Simmons, R. (2002). *Odd Girl Out: The Hidden Culture of Aggression in Girls.* New York: Harcourt.

Snyder, H.N., and Sickmund, M. (1999). *Juvenile Offenders and Victims: 1999 National Report.* NCJ 178257. Washington, D.C.: U.S. Department of Justice, Office of Justice Programs, Office of Juvenile Justice and Delinquency Prevention.

Stahl, Anne (2003). "Delinquency Cases in Juvenile Courts." *OJJDP Fact Sheet* #31 (September). Washington, D. C.: U.S. Department of Justice.

Steffensmeier, D.J., and Steffensmeier, R.H. (1980). "Trends in Female Delinquency: An Examination of Arrest, Juvenile Court, Self-report, and Field Data." *Criminology* 18: 62 85.

Sullivan, O.L. (2003). "Respect the Key Ingredient in Pittsburg Middle School Initiative." *Morning Sun,* January 24, p. 24.

Talbot, M. (2002). "Girls Just Want to Be Mean." *New York Times Magazine,* February 24, pp. 24– 64.

Taylor, J.M, Gilligan, C., and Sullivan, A.M. (1995). *Between Voice and Silence: Women and Girls, Race and Relationship.* Cambridge, Mass.: Harvard University Press.

Wilson, W.J. (1996). *When Work Disappears: The World of the New Urban Poor.* New York: Alfred A. Knopf.

Wing, B., and Keleher, T. (2000). "Zero Tolerance: An Interview with Jesse Jackson on Race and School Discipline." *Colorlines* 3 (1): 1 3.

Wiseman, R. (2002). *Queen Bees and Wannabees: Helping Your Daugher Survive Cliques, Gossip, Boyfriends and Other Realities of Adolesence.* New York: Crown.

PART 2
Feminism for Girls

CHAPTER **5**

Feminism and Femininity: Or How We Learned to Stop Worrying and Love the Thong

JENNIFER BAUMGARDNER AND AMY RICHARDS

The Second Wave wasn't funny. There was no humor. It was an earlier stage of feminism. We were breaking barriers. It was so new. I actually think that there's going to be a much more profound feminist movement. I think it's going to be very different—very mystical and not fearing the feminine. [It won't be] repressing but really inviting the feminine.

—Eve Ensler, author of *The Vagina Monologues*

For the last decade, young girls in the United States have been told by the advocacy organization Girls, Inc., to be "Strong, smart and bold." Meanwhile, sneaker giant Nike's memorable ad campaign tells girls and women to "Just do it." And most girls raised in the wake of the 1976 bestseller *Free to Be...You and Me* were told by parents and teachers, "You can be whatever you want." These sound bites challenged girls to rise to their potential—which girls certainly did, as witnessed by how many of them play sports and say they want to be president when they grow up. But it also left them confused. Confused because these messages boiled down to integrating themselves into a male world and proving they could do masculine things. We argue that it is a progression of feminism that younger "third-wave" women (and men) are embracing girlieness as well as power.

In part, these slogans were responding to second-wave feminists, who presumed that girls needed a self-esteem boost. The second-wave feminists based their presumption on their memory of what it was like to be a girl in the 1940s, 1950s, and 1960s. In marked contrast to today's girls, these girls of yesteryear were protected rather than challenged, and restricted rather than encouraged. The world in which they grew up deprived them of access to male things and enforced their participation in female things. This left them to assume, and thus promote, the notion that to be a "good girl" you had to master "boy things." That girls should do this while rejecting femininity. *Go to work, play sports, be tough, but don't do it while wearing nail polish, pink uniforms, or crying.* Prizing work, sports, and strength are good and essential messages for girls—we need to have access to what is characterized as boy stuff—but as feminists we have to address the other half of this message: What does it mean to be a girl today? And, more narrowly, what message are we sending to girls and boys about the value of femininity?

Before we can answer that question, though, we have to ask, How are we defining "girl"? Do we mean those preadolescents who are climbing trees and playing with Barbie? Or do we mean those grown women on *Sex in the City* who in their independence, their bonds with female friends, and their love of feminine fashion invoke a sense of eternal girlhood? We mean both. Further, as we will discuss later, both challenge second-wave feminists in ways that have distorted feminist theory (or just feminist received wisdom) on the topic of girls and girlies. There is a jealousy when it comes to the lives of young girls because they are so radically different from what older women experienced. Meanwhile, the vamping that goes on among the Carrie Bradshaws and Bridget Joneses in popular culture and the real women who call themselves "girl" is threatening because female power still gets translated as how well we can attract men. It isn't a specific constituency that we need to address, but the essence of what it means to be a girl—or girlish or girlie—not the person possessing it.

As we wrote in our book *Manifesta: Young Women, Feminism, and the Future* (2000), what we are calling "girlie" is this intersection of feminism with feminine culture. "Girlie says we're not broken, that our desires aren't simply booby traps set by the patriarchy. Girlie encompasses the tabooed symbols of women's feminine enculturation—Barbie dolls, makeup, fashion magazines, high heels—and says using them isn't shorthand for 'we've been duped.' Using makeup isn't a sign of our sway to the marketplace and the male gaze; it can be sexy, campy, ironic, or simply decorating ourselves without the loaded issues. Also, what we loved as girls was good and, because of feminism, we know how to make girl stuff work for us. Our Barbies had jobs and sex lives and complicated relationships with friends and family. Sticker collections were no more trivial than stamp collections; both pursuits cultivated the connoisseur in a young person.

"While it's true that embracing the pink things of stereotypical girlhood isn't a radical gesture meant to overturn the way society is structured, it can be a confident gesture. When young women wearing 'Girls Rule' T-shirts and carrying 'Hello Kitty' lunch boxes dust off the Le Sportsacs from junior high and fill them with black lipstick and green nail polish, it is not a totem to an infantilized culture but a nod to our joyous youth. Young women are emphasizing our real personal lives in contrast to what some feminist fore-mothers anticipated their lives would—or should—be: that the way to equality was to reject Barbie and all forms of pink-packaged femininity. In holding tight to that which once symbolized their oppression, girlies' moti-vations are along the lines of gay men in Chelsea calling each other "queer" or black men and women using the term 'nigga.'"

Girlhood, like the singlehood embraced by these girlies (and their fore-mothers, such as former *Cosmopolitan* editor Helen Gurley Brown), is more a state of being than an age. The writer Strawberry Saroyan invokes this sense when describing her friendship with Natasha: "I now believe, when I recall not only the years of our friendship but our friendship itself, there's one thing that keeps springing to my mind, and it's the idea of girl-hood. Yes, the *idea* of it: the sense that I believe that both Natasha and I had that we were living out some time in our lives—our twenties—and trying to become some person who was almost mythical in our own heads."[1] When we're feeling girlie, it's because we feel independent, irrever-ent, and free from judgment—and this could happen at nine or ninety. When little girls sing Spice Girls songs and adult women throw parties to celebrate this season's premier of *Sex in the City* or host Madonna parties, it's this fierce, fun independence they are tapping into. Prizing, acknowl-edging, or valuing the "feminine"—be it the domestic sphere, being a mom, or a talent for adornment—is within the scope of feminist history and future.

Given that girlie is associated with qualities feminists are arguing for—why, then, is it so often interpreted as such a rejection of feminism? In part, this is because older feminists fought for women not to be lured by feminine trappings. They created an analysis of beauty culture which sug-gested that fulfillment most likely does not lie solely in one's vacuum cleaner, and proved themselves worthy of male colleagues, whether as gui-tarists or astronauts. The feminist movement from the 1960s until today did a very good job of ensuring that females of all ages could be valued in society for more than our sex appeal. Feminists proved that we weren't hardwired to be good at housekeeping, but what they overlooked in this process of ensuring that women were "taken seriously" is that some women—and men—are drawn to feminine things (i.e., "unserious" things). Beyond that, feminine things weren't truly the problem; being forced to adopt them was. Second-wave feminists fought so hard for all women not to be *reduced* to a "girl"—they didn't lay claim to the good in being a girl. (The women of the time who did fill that niche tended to be anti-feminists like Phyllis Schlafly, preaching the joys of home and hearth from her executive office.) Inadvertently, feminists and nonfeminists alike have been left with a mixed message: Girls might have the potential to be powerful, but girl things assuredly do not.

Older feminists have identified this degrading of feminine and female traits, of course. Cultural feminists of the 1970s even tried to create a gynocentric alternative lifestyle, glorifying women's ways of doing everything from talking to sex. Why, then, is there such resistance to accepting girlies and girlishness as part of feminism? (For the moment, we will limit our analysis to girlie feminists and address the issues and conflict prompted by "real" girls later.) This brings us to the real nerve that girlie exposes: one of young women rebelling against mothers. As we wrote in *Manifesta*: "In the same way that Betty Friedan's insistence on professional seriousness was a response to every woman in the office being called a girl, this Third Wave generation is predestined to fight against the equally rigid stereotype of being too serious, too political, and seemingly asexual. Girlie culture is a rebellion against the false impression that since women don't want to be sexually exploited, they don't want to be sexual; against the necessity of brass-buttoned, red-suited seriousness to infiltrate a man's world; against the anachronistic belief that because women could be dehumanized by porn, they must be; and the idea that girls and power don't mix. The problem with this rebellion is that it further concretizes the myth that older feminists hated sex and men."

The consumerism inherent in girlie doesn't help the situation, either. For so many second wavers, feminism was linked to socialism—or at least to critiquing capitalism. They were fighting a patriarchal system that maintained itself off the backs of women. They were also adopting the politics of the time to incorporate women. Many of the influential second-wave feminists were "red diaper babies," meaning their parents were Communists. Today Communism is a humbled force and women participate in that capitalist system as much as men do. Younger women, who have grown up with increased access to the "good" parts of capitalism, have begun to ponder the fact that asking women to opt out is essentially asking them to choose to be marginalized. Young feminists came of age in a much more disposable and capitalistic time than did their second-wave predecessors. Many young feminists do not take rejecting consumerism as their major organizing principle, which is often read as rejecting feminism. (Not so. People tend to fly now rather than take the bus; it's not a rejection of middle-class or working-class values. It is simply what people do now.) We are not arguing that capitalism and clothing can't be political. Who makes your clothes and under what conditions is highly political. But when there is a critique of girlie-feminists and their clothes, the point is rarely the plight of sweatshop laborers. The butt of the critique is usually the young women espousing feminism while wearing Gucci. Defining girlie is too often expressed by what young women wear (miniskirts! lipstick!), and thus what gets focused on is the accessory, not the content of the person wearing it.

The ascent of the "girl" as a strong and distinct feminist identity is probably one of best examples of what differentiates third-wave feminists from second-wave feminists. We see third wave not as a specific set of assumptions or theories, but as an evolution of feminism building on previous generations. And where does that leave us? We have riot grrrl, Spice Girls, Indigo Girls, Girl Power, gURL.com, Rockrgrl, cybergrrl, Bamboo Girl, indiegrrrl, "New Girl Order," and even this collection, *All About the Girl,* to name just a few examples of third wavers appropriating the word "girl" within a feminist context. Although these terms have come into common usage, there is still a need for clarity about this girl stuff and, even more broadly, why there is a need for a third wave of feminism.

Younger women grew up in a feminist-influenced time. We grew up not just with feminism, but also with critiques of feminism—from within and without (the proverbial backlash). Because of when we were born, younger women can take certain freedoms for granted—namely, the right to choose whether to have a child, the freedom to play sports, and access to many formerly male-only institutions such as the Supreme Court and the U.S. Army. This is our birthright, and though older feminist are chagrined at our sense of blithe entitlement, they want us to have access to abortion and sports, and that is in fact what they fought so hard for. Nonetheless, they don't understand that our entitlement is a mark of their success. If we can play sports, why don't we? In other words, why be a girl if you don't have to?

One of the first third-wave feminists to theorize formally about girlie was Debbie Stoller, a founder of *Bust* magazine and author of a forthcoming book about knitting. Stoller's theory is all over the pages of *Bust,* in its vibrator pushing and its do-it-yourself bikini pattern, and can be simplified as "girl is good." Stoller believed that you shouldn't have to make something masculine in order to make it valued by society. In fact, we should bring feminine things into masculine spaces. This might mean painting one's nails during the coffee break in the board meeting. We also need to value traditionally female skills like knitting and canning vegetables or decorating. Furthermore, Stoller did not believe in preserving these feminine traits just for women, but also in opening up the girlie space for men's girlie aspect. *Bust* regularly features men in sensitive or domestic arenas. One weakness of Stoller's theory is that it can be prescriptive, too, leaving one with the impression that the only way to be a good third-wave feminist is to be superfeminine—the reverse of what women felt in the early 1970s. We can't replace one set of rules (glorifying male roles) with another (glorifying traditional femininity). The third-wave goal is to present a range from which feminists can feel comfortable to express themselves.

People often question whether "girlie" isn't just an American phenomenon or further proof that feminism really *is* about only White, middle-class women. Or, rather, they will ask if worrying about Manolo Blahnik's and vibrators could possibly have relevance to a woman escaping genital mutilation in Kenya or an illiterate girl in Afghanistan. "Is it *really* something you can take to other parts of the world?" we are often asked, as if the two of us are trying to sell Aboriginal women baby doll tees. Girlie certainly has its limitations, but there is proof of its appeal and power around the world and in many disparate communities. Remember the women in Afghanistan sneaking lipstick, something forbidden to them under the Taliban? Another example of girlie being international is the acceptance of *The Vagina Monologues* as a cultural event in countries as contrasting as Kenya and Afghanistan, as well as on hundreds of college campuses in the United States.

Within the United States, *The Vagina Monologues* has magnetized younger women toward the women's movement and is a great vehicle for getting at the complexity of the third wave. The play simultaneously calls for sexual freedom and satisfaction for women (Eros and equality), and advocates for women not to be silent about the sexual violence in their lives (human rights and safety). During the show, women wear miniskirts (and look fabulous and happy, sexy and proud) and simultaneously claim it as something they own—they say "no" as a girlie stance. They say "no" without the armor of masculine or conservative clothing that women have been told they need. Women who perform *The Vagina Monologues* understand that feminine things, such as feather boas, hearts for Valentine's Day, and fancy dresses, aren't political in and of themselves, but the girl wearing them can be. And the girls doing *The Vagina Monologues* certainly are politically active: they raise money to fund local anti-violence projects, speak out about taboo subjects, and say "vagina" in polite company—a radical act in itself.

A third-wave feminist approach to girls and girlies takes into account sexism and a second-wave feminist critique. The third-wave analysis of girls and girlies acknowledges that four decades of feminism have altered the prescription to "be a good girl" into the philosophy that "girl is good." This girlie-girl is still entitled to critique beauty standards and consumerism. Feminine accoutrements do not disqualify her. Too frequently, many of the young women we meet on our travels to college campuses might be attracted to these articles of femininity or consumerism, but they analyze that desire from the perspective of others: as a conflict and a potential compromise of their feminism. They make their desires suspect for the sake of a popular feminist critique. They render invisible their own example as a feminist who happens to be attracted to girlie things, or consider themselves the exception to the rule, and everyone else a Britney Spears wanna-be.

While the manifestations of girlie theory have momentum now, its roots go deeper than Stoller, just as girlies were once girls. In the early 1980s, Carol Gilligan, one of the mainstays of the girls' movement focusing on girls ages nine to fifteen and a leader of second-wave feminism, attempted to address how she herself could politically argue that women were equal to men, but have her own emotional biases against them.

Gilligan, a Harvard psychologist, was specifically reacting to the lack of women's voices in her field. She noticed that even when women were in what she called a human conversation, it was still a male discourse. She identified this problem and acknowledged that she herself perpetuated it. Once Gilligan realized that she was helping to socialize women toward the patriarchy, she set out to make the conversation one in which women's and men's voices could be equally valued, rather than asking women to conform to an approved male dictate.

In other words, long before Stoller was saying girl is good, Gilligan was saying it's no better to teach girls to take on male values than it is to force them into stereotypical female roles; in fact, it's the same hijacking of selfhood and autonomy. And when Girlies claim Barbies, pink, eye shadow, and knitting to be as valid as trucks, blue, combat boots, and sports, that's all part of the resistance, too. Both are attempting to put girls' "voices"—broadly defined as what girls like, think about, talk about, and what moves them—into the human conversation.

The initial response to Gilligan's research, which was detailed in her best-selling book, *In a Different Voice*, mostly accentuated the negative aspects of not being a boy. This was the case of a second-wave analysis being applied to third-wave girls. The second-wave approach identifies sexism and the ways boys are given more freedom. A third-wave approach would include the power that girls have today, not extrapolate so much from a context of the past. Girls went from being invisible to being vulnerable. In a way, the girls' movement that shot up in the wake of Gilligan's research mirrored some of the feminist reaction to theories like Stoller's: in both instances, there was no confidence that the individual girl or girlie knew what she was doing. Thus, under the guise of helping girls and women keep their voices, the women's movement inadvertently mutes them.

This left the third-wave generation conflicted about who they were supposed to be or, more important, what feminists would "allow" them to be. The barrier to individuality and individual expression was no longer "the patriarchy" that hobbled the second wave, but *feminism* (and, too often, older feminists who didn't understand young women's midriff-baring tops or thong underwear). Gilligan's solution to the loss of "voice" (which we interpret as self-knowledge, creativity, and self-worth) was to form strong relationships with other women. When women are sounding boards for one another, affirming their interior monologues, she argued, they will gain the confidence and centrality to eventually change what society values. This is exactly what happens when women come together to perform *The Vagina Monologues,* or when women feel like they have found a friend while reading the pages of *Bust*.

Today we see the girlie/feminist conflict play out mostly among college-age women and young professional women. Many of the young women we meet (or exchange E-mails with) as we travel around the country are into the ideals and goals of the women's movement, but they fear that they can't be both themselves and a feminist. They assume that having any "weakness" for femininity disqualifies them from being a feminist. The personal decisions they make—having boyfriends, shaving, Brazilian bikini waxes, getting married, wanting to have a body like Gwyneth Paltrow, being into fashion—leave others to assume that they are dupes of the patriarchy. Aren't these the trappings of femininity that their mothers (or Women's Studies' professors) rejected? But the fact is that beyond these personal dilemmas, these young women are organizing the Take Back the Night marches, they are demanding that they be able to play sports with the boys and they are being whatever they want to be.

Our book *Manifesta* was written in part to address exactly that crowd, the ones who say "I took the Women in Mass Media class—why do I still feel the need to wear high heels? Am I weak?" This question is clearly on the minds of young feminists. We have no doubt that younger women connect to feminism's ideals. We see them living feminist lives exemplified by their righteousness and sense of entitlement. Similarly, they are inspired by feminism's history when they have the opportunity to learn about it. What they often don't have, however, is a sense of *how* to be a feminist. They aren't clear about what feminism requires from them. Is it about how many petitions one signs? Or showing up for marches? Or reading the feminist classics? Often, too, they perceive that their personal lives undermine their political convictions. To top it off, they often think of feminism as what they can't do (Don't be boy-crazy! Don't shave!), rather than a philosophy that shows them the potential for what they can do.

Many of these young women are like Brooke, whom we met at the University of North Carolina at Chapel Hill. Brooke, after noting the dearth of baby-sitting services on campus for employees and students and the abundance of potential student worker bees, wanted to form a baby-sitting service through the university. She saw a barrier and thought: "What can I do? Am I allowed to make these things a feminist issue without the approval of the 'feminists'?" In other words, if it was such a good idea, wouldn't the real feminists—the ones who invented V-Day or coined sexual harassment or wrote the books she was reading—wouldn't they have already thought of it? In *Manifesta*, Kathleen Hanna (co-creator of the movement known as riot grrrl) calls this nagging, nay-saying voice "The Phantom." The Phantom says, "Somebody already thought of that. Somebody already wrote that book. Just glom onto someone else's plan."

The feminist Phantom is the "feminist mystique." If the feminine mystique (coined by Betty Friedan) is enforced satisfaction with child rearing and domesticity, the feminist mystique is the attitude that made us feel guilty for embellishing ourselves with girlie things. Worse, the feminist mystique leaves us to assume that the feminist label belongs only to those who have sorted out all their issues and are no longer conflicted about men, sex, their bodies, their incomes, or fashion.

The reason the Phantom has so much power isn't just about sexism and low self-esteem. It's also that we spend so much time talking about what feminism was and not enough about what it can be. Because we learn so much more from what people do than what they say, we need to take a step back from rhetoric and put the focus on acts. When we look around at what young women are doing rather than what they are wearing, it's clear that there is a feminist continuum. Young women are creating zines (just like the second wave created *Ms.* and *Off Our Backs*), they are protesting hate crimes (just as their foremothers withheld income tax so as not to support the Vietnam War), and they have flooded every profession (moving beyond the access provided by the second wave, which gave us the first female Supreme Court justice and the first female astronaut).

What this leads us to is the fact that girls today—both the ten-year-old with skinned knees and the thirty-five-year-old with the vibrator—possess a freedom and fierceness that women in the 1960s could hardly imagine. That is a poignant reality for the freedom-fighting feminists of the 1960s and 1970s, and there is a spine of pain to their critique that girls are weak or girlies are naïve. It hurts to see the manifestations in future generations of what one has longed for for oneself. The feminists who implored girls to be "strong, smart, and bold" got what they wished for. Some still need to recognize that the wish came true. And perhaps younger women need to share some of their entitlement with older women, imploring them to "just do it" and be "strong, smart, and bold."

Notes

1. Strawberry Saroyan, *Girl Walks into a Bar: A Memoir* (New York: Random House, 2003), 182.

CHAPTER 6

Girl Power Politics: Pop-Culture Barriers and Organizational Resistance

JESSICA K. TAFT

There has been a great deal of feminist debate over the idea of "Girl Power," its relation to feminism, and whether or not Girl Power is good for girls and young women.[1] This chapter intervenes in this debate by focusing specifically on how the discourse of Girl Power relates to girls' political subjectivity.[2] With its origination in the riot grrrl movement and third-wave feminism, Girl Power began as an explicitly political concept. By the 1990s, the discourse of Girl Power had also been deployed by various elements of popular culture and the mainstream media in a way that constructed a version of girlhood that excludes girls' political selves. However, even as some versions of Girl Power discourse were creating barriers to girls' politics, organizations for girls were constructing their own meanings of Girl Power and challenging these barriers to girls' social and political engagement.

Stuart Hall defines discourse as "a group of statements which provide a language for talking about—i.e., a way of representing—a particular kind of knowledge about a topic" (1996: 201). The discourse of Girl Power, then, is made up of all those statements that use this phrase and therefore create meanings of girls' power. It is created in the discursive practices of a wide range of individuals and institutions with a variety of interests and agendas, and is therefore both power-charged and diverse. Its meaning is not fixed, and remains open to a multitude of possibilities.

In the first part of this chapter, I explore four meanings or versions of Girl Power (and the popular culture institutions that produce them) that construct barriers to both girls' activism in general and girls' engagement with feminist politics in particular, and define girlhood as a non-political space. These four meanings are Girl Power as anti-feminism, Girl Power as postfeminism, Girl Power as individual power, and Girl Power as consumer power.[3] The discursive practices that prevent girls' political action are not necessarily organized around a hegemonic master plan with this goal in mind. Each has a specific purpose and localized use, but they do indeed join together to define girls as noncritical, nonactive subjects. Thus, rather than implying a conspiracy of advertisers, pop stars, and journalists working to prevent girls' politics, I would like to show that the discursive practices that produce these meanings of Girl Power each construct Girl Power in a manner whose implications could serve to inhibit girls' political engagement.

In the second part of the chapter, I discuss how two girls' organizations redefine Girl Power to challenge the depoliticizing versions of Girl Power and the barriers to girls' politics that such meanings create. Based on field research at two sites,[4] I will address the ways that these two programs respond to depoliticizing meanings of Girl Power and attempt to empower girls as sociopolitical actors. Analyzing the discourse of Girl Power from these two angles makes visible how its messages for girls' political engagement are contested. However, it is crucial to note that the two sides of this conflict do not have equal social and cultural power, and the depoliticizing meanings of Girl Power are more visible due to their location in dominant media institutions. This makes them potentially more influential than the meanings produced by the girls' organizations discussed. However, girls do not passively accept the discursive practices of either popular culture or girls' organizations, but produce their own readings from these practices. Unfortunately, due to space limitations, this chapter does not explore girls' interpretations. Therefore, my argument is not about how Girl Power discourses impact girls' political selves, but rather that meanings and versions of Girl Power offered by the mainstream media could produce barriers to girls' active citizenship, and that these depoliticizing meanings of Girl Power are and can be challenged by girls' organizations.

Anti-Feminism

Anti-feminism, as I use it here, refers to those meanings of Girl Power that actively distinguish the phrase from feminism and/or put forth a negative portrayal of feminism, discouraging girls from feminist politics. The Spice Girls are among the most discussed promoters of Girl Power, and their relationship to feminism has been a contentious topic for commentators (Lemish 1998; Davies 1999; Driscoll 1999, 2002). The group has been described as everything from "tools of patriarchy" to "performing affirmative race, gender and class-based politics" (Brabazon and Evans 1998: 41). What I want to suggest here is that while their version of Girl Power may indeed be empowering, celebratory, and affirmative of girls' strength, it also contains anti-feminist messages. Namely, the Spice Girls present Girl Power as the nonpolitical and nonthreatening alternative to feminism.

In their book *Girl Power*, the Spice Girls proclaim in large pink block letters that "feminism has become a dirty word. Girl Power is just a nineties way of saying it. We can give feminism a kick up the arse" (Spice Girls 1997: 49). Even as they invoke some type of connection to feminism, they make clear that Girl Power *is not* feminism, but instead is going to be a new way of being girls/women, one that kicks feminism, not embraces or extends it. As Whelehan notes, this quote easily plays into anti-feminist backlash and a negative image of feminism instead of challenging those who have made feminism a dirty word (2000: 45). This claim by the Spice Girls is positioned above a picture of the band members in sleepwear, lying on a bed.

This association implies that Girl Power is softer, sexier, less active than feminism and that Girl Power gives feminism a "kick up the arse" by emphasizing beauty and appearance. Additionally, the Spice Girls' descriptions of why they have Girl Power have nothing to do with changing power relationships, but only developing new personal qualities like "playing girls' football" and "appreciating my roots" (1997: 5–7). The Spice Girls are not kicking feminism to a new level of political action or expanding it to address their needs. Instead, these quotes and images suggest that they are replacing feminism with an alternative, and make no indication that this alternative is a project for social or political change.

Similarly, in U.S. news coverage of the 1999 Women's World Cup soccer tournament, the players, as role models of Girl Power, are clearly distinguished from feminists. In an article in *USA Today*, Jill Lieber writes, "There is not a … rebel in the bunch." She celebrates that "it is girl power, not feminism that inspires these young women and girls" (1999: 1A). For Lieber, Girl Power is not rebellion, but a contained expression of strength and athleticism on the soccer field. Both the Spice Girls and promoters of Women's World Cup soccer dissociate Girl Power from feminism. Both these groups want and need to make Girl Power palatable and marketable, and a too-close connection with feminism could reduce their success.

This anti-feminism presents girls with a negative image of feminist politics, thus discouraging involvement in this particular movement. Lieber and the Spice Girls both offer Girl Power as the safe, friendly, and "best" way for girls to express their girl pride. The Spice Girls and many who wrote about the 1999 U.S. women's soccer team claim that a fashion-focused and sports-oriented Girl Power is more appropriate than feminism's outdated political rebellion. Thus, girls are encouraged to identify their girl-positive feelings with a nonpolitical rather than a politicized discourse, and to think about girlhood in these purely cultural ways, rather than as a space for social and political action.

Postfeminism

Postfeminism, as I use it here, is the argument that girls and women are doing fine, feminism is unnecessary, and the movement is over. The deployment of Girl Power discourse to make these postfeminist claims plays an important role in the disconnection of Girl Power and feminism by dismissing the need for feminist action. Some journalists have used the language of Girl Power to claim that girls have attained all the power they could ever want, and there is nothing left to be done. These assertions that feminism is unnecessary promote the idea that girls should be satisfied and content with the current social order, potentially obstructing their attempts and desires to create social change.

Journalist Susan Orlean, in an article titled "Girl Power: Has Sabrina the Teenage Witch Worked Her Magic on a Generation?" celebrates how great things are for girls today. She writes that the television character Sabrina the Teenage Witch is an empowered girl who lives life "in the way that only girls who have grown up taking feminism for granted are able" (1998: 54). According to Orlean, Sabrina doesn't need feminism; her life is great as it is. In this article, Girl Power comes to symbolize girls having achieved power and equality in the world.

Going even further than the celebration of girls having made it to equality are those writers who mobilize the discourse of Girl Power to suggest that girls and women now have too much power in the world. The *New York Times* article "How Boys Lost Out to Girl Power" is one example of this use and meaning of Girl Power. In it, journalist Tamar Lewin suggests that feminism and the focus on girls are excessive. Additionally, this article creates an opposition between Girl Power/feminism and issues of race and racism. Lewin writes that the "myth that schools shortchange girls has diverted policy attention from African-American boys, a group at genuine education risk," and "boys-versus-girls bean-counting has gone too far, especially when measured against very large racial differences in educational achievement" (1998: sec. 4, p. 3). Girls' racial identities are made invisible, and, because they are not named, are normalized as White (Kenny 2000). There are no within-gender or within-race comparisons, and both White boys and African-American girls are hidden from view. This not only fails to enact an analysis of the intersecting forces of race and gender but also describes feminism as a movement that is only about gender issues and cannot speak to the needs of African-American boys.

In these uses of the discourse of Girl Power, the phrase comes to mean that girls are powerful and that gender equality exists, or even that girls are dominant. While this is certainly not the true state of gendered power dynamics, these meanings of Girl Power also imply that feminism is only about gender issues. This version of Girl Power portrays girls as having achieved gender equality, without ever noting the way that this is tied to racial, sexual, and class politics. Girls cannot be discussed as a racially neutral, classless group; to do so is to normalize White, middle-class, heterosexual girls and to make invisible girls of color, working-class girls, and queer youth (Bettie 2003). The question of whether or not girls have achieved "equality" must be asked in the context of their racial, sexual, and class identities. Further, to assume that girlhood, Girl Power, and feminism are only about gender issues ignores the substantial contributions of Black, Chicana, non-Western, and queer feminists, and erases their claims about the intersectionality of race, class, gender, sexuality, nation, and ability.

The claims that equality exists, and the use of Girl Power to signify girls' equality (or dominance) in the world, not only make gender oppression invisible but also hide the social forces of racism, classism, and homophobia. In doing so, they alienate girls and young women who are experiencing multiple oppressions, leading them to believe that feminism does not address their own needs and concerns. By presenting a world with no need for social change, this use of the Girl Power discourse fails to provide girls with tools to understand and challenge situations where they experience sexism and other forms of oppression. Thus, girls are discouraged from seeing inequality and from engaging in challenges to such inequalities.

Individual Power

Closely related to Girl Power's postfeminist meanings is its invocation to describe the world as a meritocracy void of sexism, racism, classism, ableism, and heterosexism. Magazines and advertisements aimed at girls use the discourse of Girl Power in a way that reflects the ideologies of individualism and personal responsibility, and has a noticeable disregard for social systems and institutions. Power relationships are glossed over or ignored as articles and ads in girls' magazines claim that girls can do or be anything, so long as they work for it. While Girl Power as "girls can be anything" can give girls a sense of power and esteem, it hides both the material and the discursive forces shaping identity and the ways that these gendered, raced, classed, and sexualized identities may give girls privileges or pose challenges.

An article in *Girl's Life*, a magazine aimed at girls between the ages of ten and fourteen, claims, "You too can be a celebrity." The article gives two "easy" steps to achieving any and all goals. Step one is to "create a new you [because] making a little external change is a great motivator." The second step revolves around having helpers—an "agent to help you review what steps you've taken toward your goal and plan what to do next" and a "publicist" to tell others about how much you have done. And abracadabra, you have made yourself a success! ("You Too Can" 1999: 56–59). Other articles and ads may be a little less outrageous, but have the same emphasis on individual achievements through a combination of looks, work, and support. For example, another issue of the same magazine features a story about a young woman who has her own dance company. How did she get there? Through hard work, standing up for what she believed in, and following her dreams ("One Girl" 2000: 75). An advertisement for Barbie and space camp claims "you can be a leader, you can be strong, you can be confident. Girls can do it all." These sorts of claims of Girl Power as individual power are fairly common in media for girls, with Girl Power being presented as an attribute of women scientists, athletes, and other success-story figures.

These examples, on the positive side, emphasize girls as potentially powerful people and encourage them to try new things and believe in themselves. However, in failing to address the social factors of race, class, gender, sexuality, and physical ability, the ads and articles mobilize Girl Power discourse to hide current injustices rather than helping girls to analyze oppression or even acknowledge social problems. Instead, they place the responsibility for achievement on the shoulders of each individual girl. Not only can this lead to feelings of inadequacy and low self-esteem, but this meaning of Girl Power as individual power could serve to inhibit girls' connections with one another, reduce the possibilities for social analysis and critical thinking, and thus hinder girls' social and political engagement. Like traditional liberal feminism, which "ignores the existence of other social and cultural factors which might make it impossible for an individual to acquire the means to realize such potential" (Whelehan 1995: 37), this meaning of Girl Power clouds girls' vision of current injustices, places blame for all problems on their own shoulders, and encourages their acceptance of the status quo.

Consumer Power

Marketers and those with products to sell use the discourse of Girl Power to produce and circulate one of the most pervasive images of girlhood: that of the girl as consumer. Girl Power as defined by marketing executives and corporate interests often confines girls' social power to their purchasing power. In an article titled "Girl Power," marketers and those working in retail can learn about getting "tween girls" (seven to twelve years old) to buy their products (1999: 54). The December 8, 1997, issue of *Fortune* magazine featured a six-page article on Girl Power and marketing. The piece celebrates the conspicuous consumption of teenage girls, reporting that 88 percent of girls between thirteen and seventeen "just love to shop." A large portion of the article centers on the success of catalog companies peddling trendy clothes for girls.

> Airshop knows about girl power. Its catalogue runs pictures and poems sent in by its creative customers. It publishes mini-profiles of teenage girls—girls who are kicking butt in male-dominated fields.... Is Airshop a hip, shoestring literary magazine or a catalogue for adolescent consumers? It's both. If you want to sell to the girl-power crowd, you have to pretend that they're running things, that they're in charge. *(Munk 1997: 136)*

This emphasis on consumption suggests that without these commodities a girl is not powerful, thus making Girl Power seem like the possession of only those girls who can afford these products. Additionally, even for those who have the power to buy, this discourse limits their power only to the commercial realm. Girls' power does not include the power to create, to think, and to act. We need to be concerned about the fact that girlhood is produced as a space of consumption at the expense of girlhood as a space of cultural production (Kearney 1998) or social and political engagement.

Program Responses: Camp Ashema

Girl Power as anti-feminism, postfeminism, individual power, and consumer power all write girls' sociopolitical power out of the language of Girl Power. This poses a challenge to those programs that aim to empower girls in the sociopolitical arena. However, some girls' organizations are responding to these versions of the Girl Power discourse, reconstructing and creating new meanings of Girl Power and imagining a definition of girlhood that includes girls' social and political selves. While I focus here on the oppositional aspects of two groups, I would like to make clear that these organizations also reinscribe some of the barriers mentioned above and are constructing their own nonauthentic versions of girlhood and Girl Power. In short, these organizations are not without elements to be critiqued.

Gender analysis and group decision-making are two techniques used by Camp Ashema, a Girl Scout camp in rural New England. The camp serves primarily White, rural girls between the ages of ten and thirteen from a variety of class backgrounds. It utilizes a discourse of Girl Power in its promotional materials, and seeks to encourage campers to "discover the power of being a girl." The camp's mission and vision statement state a commitment to "building strong girls," which includes "developing self-esteem, encouraging personal growth, recognizing and addressing gender bias, appreciating diversity [and] fostering shared values."

The camp actively tries to incorporate an analysis of gendered social relations and power structures into its daily practices, countering Girl Power as anti-feminism and individual power. The staff's training manual states, "Campers will have the opportunity to acknowledge society's barriers which limit girls' achievement and teach/learn tools to overcome those barriers." This is accomplished through daily "cool chats." These are consistent small group conversations between one staff member and approximately six girls. Staff members are given lesson plans for these discussions, which address gender bias, gender stereotyping, and other "girl-focused" issues, and which encourage girls to think critically about the ways social forces influence their own lives.

The second manner in which Camp Ashema tries to challenge versions of Girl Power that construct barriers to girls' activism is its emphasis on collective girl-decision-making. By giving girls the power to make choices about their camp program as a group, the camp effectively positions girls as capable and active decision-makers rather than passive consumers of the camp experience. Girl Power here often means girls and women working together toward some sort of group goal. The page in the staff manual titled "Girl Planning: What Makes Us Different" states that it is the camp's intent to "help girls develop into independent decision makers, while participating in the group process." The camp encourages girls to make decisions through a progressive approach that starts from the very beginning of camp with staff allowing girls to make basic daily-life choices, and progresses to girls developing their own goals for their time at camp and planning most of the program, while the adults serve mostly as "facilitator[s] and guide[s] in the program planning." This emphasis on decision-making provides girls with a space to be active agents, thus challenging meanings of Girl Power that position girls only as passive consumers.

Program Responses: Teen Women's Action Program

Unlike these somewhat indirect, but still potentially effective, techniques of gender analysis and group decision-making, the Teen Women's Action Program (TWAP) directly encourages girls to become community change agents and empowered citizens. TWAP is an after-school and summer program in a large mid-Atlantic city that works primarily with African-American, Latina, and Vietnamese-American teen women (ages fourteen to eighteen) from middle-class, working-class, and poor neighborhoods. It is, according to its mission statement, "a multi-cultural organization that builds and supports teen women and girl leaders so that they can improve their own lives and transform their communities." Participants are encouraged to move through a program progression that begins at the level of the personal and then develops into group and community problem-solving and action. The after-school program begins with training and discussions on self-advocacy skills like communication, problem-solving, decision-making, conflict resolution, and self-assessment.

These skills encourage teens in the program to share their personal experiences with one another and to support each other in their individual struggles to improve their own lives. The program then shifts to a series of topical trainings on reproductive health, violence, stress, and oppression during which the teens continue to take on greater leadership roles within their groups. These serve to help the group move from understanding their individual experiences to a broader social analysis. This is where the challenge to meanings of Girl Power as postfeminism and individual power is most direct.

After completing this phase of the program, the teens focus on a problem in their school community of their own choosing. They design and conduct community needs assessments so that they have an informed understanding of the problem. Then, with these assessments complete, they plan a project that attempts to contribute to solving the problem. Previous projects have included workshops on pregnancy, eating disorders, and mental health; zines on stress, dating violence, and sexual harassment; and a festival addressing segregation among teen women in the school. The teens can then work with the organization in the summer on larger, citywide action campaigns. One long-term campaign has worked to improve access and quality of life for teen women in the foster care system by creating new residential group home regulations, conducting leadership and self-advocacy workshops, and increasing foster teen involvement in group home governance through organizing. Another has written a new sexual harassment policy for the public schools, presented it to the school board, and actively campaigned for its approval and implementation. This emphasis on group-oriented community projects for social justice counters those meanings of Girl Power that claim that change is unnecessary, that are devoid of structural analysis, and that position girls as consumers rather than active citizens. For TWAP, Girl Power is the power to create community change.

Conclusion

In conclusion, I would like to discuss some of the broader implications of the discursive barriers to girls' activism and how girls' programs can empower girls in the sociopolitical realm. First, it seems obvious that both scholars and professionals interested in girls' political agency need to be cautious about our use of the language of Girl Power, since we do not wish to invoke some of the more widespread meanings discussed in this chapter. We need to recognize this term as a contested one, and be clear about how we are using it. This does not mean giving up on the discourse of Girl Power, but seeing that it has meanings that may be counter to the project of encouraging girls' political activity. Second, I would like to suggest that girls' programs need to develop even more ways of challenging the depoliticizing meanings of Girl Power and further encourage girls as agents of social change. Too often, girls' programs aim to psychologize and individualize the experiences of girls, deemphasizing social forces and collective action. The emphasis on improving the self-esteem of individual girls reinscribes the mainstream media's versions of Girl Power by continuing to keep discussions of girlhood focused on the individual girl and her path to success. A more radical, sociological, and feminist approach would call for social analysis and collective response to the many forces that shape girls' lives. It is my hope that this chapter has demonstrated some of the cultural and discursive barriers to such an approach so that we may attempt to rethink both our understandings of girls' power and the practices of programs that aim to "empower girls."

Notes

1. See, for example, Budgeon 1998; Whelehan 2000.
2. I am following Bhavnani's argument that politics, when discussed in relation to youth, must be broadly defined, and utilize her definition: "the means by which human beings regulate, attempt to regulate and challenge with a view to changing unequal power relationships" (1991: 52).
3. The analysis in this first section is based on extensive document searches conducted between September 1999 and March 2000, and the detailed discourse and content analysis of these articles and advertisements.
4. Conducted in 1999, 2001, and the summer of 2002.

References

"Barbie and Space Camp." (1999). *Girls' Life*, April/May, p. 10. Advertisement.

Bettie, J. (2003). *Women Without Class: Girls, Race and Identity*. Berkeley: University of California Press.

Bhavnani, K.-K. (1991). *Talking Politics: A Psychological Framing for Views from Youth in Britain*. Cambridge: Cambridge University Press.

Brabazon, T., and Evans, A. (1998). "'I'll Never Be Your Woman': The Spice Girls and New Flavours of Feminism." *Social Alternatives* 17: 39–42.

Budgeon, S. (1998). "'I'll Tell You What I Really Really Want': Girl Power and Self-Identity in Britain." In S. Inness (ed.), *Millennium Girls: Today's Girls Around the World*. Lanham, Md.: Rowman & Littlefield.

Davies, J. (1999). "'It's like Feminism, but You Don't Have to Burn Your Bra': Girl Power and the Spice Girls' Breakthrough 1997." In A. Blake (ed.), *Living Through Pop*. New York: Routledge.

Driscoll, C. (1999). "Girl Culture, Revenge and Global Capitalism: Cybergurls, Riot Grrls, Spice Girls." *Australian Feminist Studies* 14: 173–193.

Driscoll, C. (2002). *Girls: Feminine Adolescence in Popular Culture and Cultural Theory*. New York: Columbia University Press.

"Girl Power." (1999). *Chain Store Age*, September 1, p. 54.

Hall, S. (1996). "The West and the Rest: Discourse and Power." In S. Hall, D. Held, D. Hubert, and K. Thompson (eds.), *Modernity: An Introduction to Modern Societies*. Cambridge, Mass.: Blackwell.

Kearney, M.C. (1998). "Producing Girls: Rethinking the Study of Female Youth Culture." In S. Inness (ed.), *Delinquents and Debutantes: Twentieth-Century American Girls' Cultures*, New York: New York University Press.

Kenny, L.D. (2000). *Daughters of Suburbia: Growing Up White, Middle Class and Female*. New Brunswick, N.J.: Rutgers University Press.

Lemish, D. (1998). "Spice Girls' Talk: A Case Study in the Development of Gendered Identity." In S. Inness (ed.), *Millennium Girls: Today's Girls Around the World*. Lanham, Md.: Rowman & Littlefield.

Lewin, T. (1998). "How Boys Lost Out to Girl Power." *New York Times*, December 13, sec. 4, p.3.

Lieber, J. (1999). "Changing Face of Sports: World Cup Women Hear High-pitched Sound of Girl Power." *USA Today*, June 21, p. 1A.

Munk, N. (1997). "Girl Power." *Fortune*, December 8, pp. 133–139.

"One Girl." (2000). *Girls' Life*, February/March, p. 75.

Orlean, S. (1998). "Girl Power: Has Sabrina the Teenage Witch Worked Her Magic on a Generation?" *The New Yorker*, May 18, pp. 54–59.

Spice Girls. (1997). *Girl Power*. Secaucus, N.J.: Carol Publishing Group.

Whelehan, I. (1995). *Modern Feminist Thought: From the Second Wave to "Post Feminism."* New York: New York University Press.

Whelehan, I. (2000). *Overloaded: Popular Culture and the Future of Feminism*. London: The Women's Press.

"You Too Can Be a Celebrity." (1999). *Girls' Life*, April/May, pp. 56–59.

CHAPTER 7

Mythic Figures and Lived Identities: Locating the "Girl" in Feminist Discourse

JENNIFER EISENHAUER

I'm Not Just a Girl! (Figure 7.1) is the work of one of my former sixth grade art students. When asked to create a work about a border significant to her own life, Brooke identified language as the border she wanted to explore in her work. Specifically, her work centered on the idea of how language labels and positions girls. She searched magazines, locating words that she felt defined "girls." Through her work, she articulated a fairly complex idea about language. She was not simply saying, "These are names that hurt my feelings, these words *never* describe me"; rather, she was identifying how language orders her possibilities and demarcates invisible limits as *normal* and *natural*. Her work identified how discourses of girlhood constituted her own subjectivity and what it meant to be a "girl."

Brooke's work has contributed to my own asking *What is a girl?* in this chapter. Her work pointed to an understanding of the "girl" not simply as something that someone *is* (a question of being and ontology), but as something that one is discursively constituted *as*. At the time that she created this work, I was investigating in my own research feminist punk music and zine communities. I was interested in these sites particularly in regard to their complication of assumptions regarding young women's lack of interest in feminism.[1] Brooke's work made me reflect on my inability to address "girls'" cultures and/or subcultures as well as "girls" in

---

*I am very grateful to Brooke for allowing me to include her artwork, *I'm Not Just a Girl!*, in this chapter.

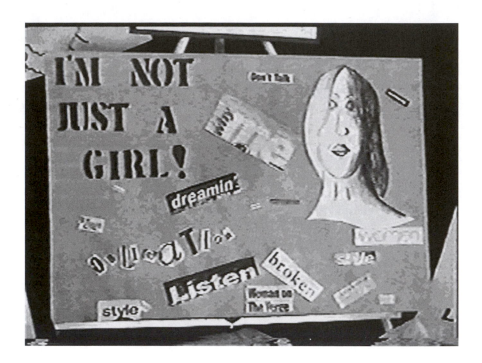

Fig. 7.1. Brooke R., I'm Not Just a Girl! Collage, 1999. Reprinted with permission.

education without first addressing how the very language through which I speak of "girls" constitutes "girls" as subjects (Jones 1993).

It is to this regard that my question changed from being *Where are the "feminist girls"?* to *How has feminism constituted the "girl"?* The question of the "girl" becomes a question of feminism's subject. Rather than focusing in this investigation upon an examination of what feminism means for "girls" and analyzing what attributes to "girls" interest or lack of interest in feminism, I explore the construction of the "girl" as a repeatedly othered subject within feminisms. What does the "girl" mean for the construction of feminisms when she becomes an/other subject rather than an object of study, woman's "other," or a state of becoming? Particularly, I am interested in how "girl" subjects are constituted within discourses of feminisms' futures, discourses constructed through the tropes of awakening, growing up, and becoming. To this regard, I propose that the "girl" emerges as a disruptive potentiality that questions and complicates assumptions regarding the subject of feminism.

In writing the word g-i-r-l as "girl" rather than girl, I am already suggesting a shift from normative definitions and a problematizing of "girl." I am framing this inquiry not as a search for original or foundational definitions, or biological truisms, nor am I proposing a teleological investigation in which a presumed present or future understanding of the "girl" is seen as the result of a linear historical progression. Rather, I am interested in, as Valerie Walkerdine suggests, how the "girl" functions as a sign and how categories produced as signs "'catch up' the subjects, position them, and in positioning, create a truth" (Walkerdine 1987: 65).

In what follows, I would like to examine more closely how the sign "girl" functions in feminisms constructed through tropes of linear becoming that construct, as Lesley Johnson identifies in *The Modern Girl* (1993), feminism as the growing up and awakening of women (Johnson 1993: 15). As well, I suggest that feminisms of growing up, becoming, and awakening may challenge a man/woman binary while maintaining a binary of woman/girl. When the discussion of the "girl" or the representation and analysis of subjects identified as "girls" is rationalized as necessary for the *future* of feminism, or for the *women* these "girls" become, the "girl" remains defined in relation to the woman, her differences unacknowledged and the complexity of the "girl's" construction oversimplified. Take, for example, a possible reading of Simone de Beauvoir's commonly quoted statement that "One is not born, but rather becomes a woman." What is one born when one has not yet *become* a woman? Is someone who has not yet "become" a woman a "girl"? *Is girl to woman as nature is to culture?*[2]

Awakening, Growing Up, and Becoming: Constructing the Future Feminist

When exploring the National Women's Association Web site in the summer of 2001, I encountered an advertisement for a "future feminist" T-shirt. The future feminist T-shirt was available only in children's sizes. While either a girl or a boy could wear the T-shirt, the juxtaposition between the label "future" and the child raises many questions. Who can be a "feminist" as reflected within the construction of the future feminist T-shirt? Can a young girl or boy be a feminist? What is the subject of feminism? I am not suggesting that this shirt reflects a universal or singular interpretation, but rather that its meaning is different, depending upon how these signifiers function in varying feminist discourses. I would like to explore possible readings of the "future feminist" as constituted within feminist discourses constructed through generational metaphors. In my conclusion, I will offer another possible reading of the "future feminist" as an ironic myth and potentially disruptive and critical site with important implications within the ongoing critical discussion of feminism's subject.

I see the defining of the "third wave" within feminist discourses as an important site for examining those assumptions impacting the constitution of "girl" subjects within feminisms. While Heywood and Drake identify one of the earliest uses of the term "third wave" as being found in the edited anthology *The Third Wave: Feminist Perspectives on Racism,* the texts that instigated numerous "third-wave" cartographies were Rebecca

Walker's *To Be Real: Telling the Truth and Changing the Face of Feminism* (1995) and Barbara Findlen's *Listen Up: Voices from the Next Feminist Generation* (1995).[3] In writings that attempt to define and map feminism's third wave (Bailey 1997; Drake 1997; Orr 1997; Siegel 1997), the third wave is most often characterized broadly as a feminist politics emerging from a generation of people born into feminism, as the project of feminist "daughters," and somewhere along the way the third wave, a term initially used to characterize the critique of racial homogeneity and Western bias in feminist theorizing, came to be specifically associated with a "young" feminist generation.

Heywood and Drake raise an important and often overlooked question in *Third Wave Agenda: Being Feminist, Doing Feminism* (1997) when they inquire as to what the relationship is between the "self-named U.S. third world feminism of *This Bridge Called My Back* (1981) and the third wave feminism of the 'next generation'" (Heywood and Drake 1997: 9). Their discussion of third-wave feminists' identification of *contradiction* as a "fundamental definitional strategy, a necessary, lived, embodied strategy" creates connections between these seemingly different articulations of third waves (Heywood and Drake 1997: 8). This shared exploration of contradictory subjects reflects a critique of definitional practices and the recognition of the relationship between the politics of language and subjectivity, particularly as they relate to discussions of feminisms and feminisms' subjects.

Likewise, when the "girl" is understood as a contradictory rather than a coherent subject, discussions that situate the "girl" as "young feminist" shift from articulating narratives of the replication and continuation of feminist constructions across linear time, to understanding the "girl" as well as the "young feminist" as critical sites for problematizing the definition of feminism as the growing up and awakening of women. What does it mean, as Chilla Bulbeck observes, that "Second wavers dismiss the intellectual interests and contributions of third wavers as naïve, merely because young feminists have not lived long enough to have anything profound to say. Younger feminists, too, are frozen—if not in time, in a stereotype of inexperience" (Bulbeck 1999: 5)? When being "young" is discursively linked with inexperience, the critiques issued by those identified as "young" become constructed as naïve, disrespectful, and historically uninformed. Rather than naturalizing a conflict between generations assumed to have coherent and recognizable borders, I propose focusing upon investigating how the language of generational and wave metaphors perpetuates a divisive coherency that represents history as a teleological legacy and that forecloses upon the critical potential of a contradictory, multiple, and layered understanding of feminisms' subjects.

The definition of the third wave presumes a feminist history characterized by three separate moments. What separates the second and third waves of feminism is located within the intersection of generation and a perceived shift in feminist goals. Generational differences understood as differences in age become one way of differentiating between a second and a third wave of feminism. As Ann Kaplan states, "While I would not claim that any of us are culturally fixed by any generational location, I would claim that such historical passings-through, which are named 'aging,' make a difference in the questions that different feminists think to ask, and in the conceptualizing of problems" (Kaplan 1997: 13). Constructing differences between second and third waves of feminism within the parameters of age results in defining a third wave as the project of "young feminists."

The very concept of the "wave" as a way of organizing and explaining feminisms reflects multiple metaphors. More typically uses of the term "wave" are linked to generation and reflect oceanic metaphors described in relation to evolutionary processes and the family. As Cathryn Bailey states in "Making Waves and Drawing Lines: The Politics of Defining the Vicissitudes of Feminisms":

> When we speak of a wave, we typically mean "one among others." "Wave" just doesn't sound like the right word for the lone occurrence of something. Waves that arise in social and political milieus, like waves that arise in water, become defined only in context, relative to the waves that have come and gone before. Furthermore, to call something a wave implies that it is one among others in some sort of succession, both similar to and different from the other occurrences. For waves in water, the similarities are temporal and proximal…the differences that distinguish waves in water are also temporal and proximal ones, variations in amplitude, duration, intensity and volume. (*Bailey, 1997: 18*)

Deborah Siegel presents a similar use of the wave metaphor in "The Legacy of the Personal: Generating Theory in Feminism's Third Wave": "Just as the same water reforms itself into ever new waves, so the second wave circulates in the third, reproducing itself through a cyclical movement" (Siegel 1997: 46–81).

Reflected in both Bailey's and Siegel's use of the wave metaphor is an acknowledgment of variation and differences between feminist waves as well as constructing waves as connected, "reproducing," and "relative." Ultimately, while these waves offer variety, both authors' use of the wave metaphor maintains a continuity among waves. What does it mean for the "future feminist" when differences between waves are defined as "temporal and proximal" and the second wave is understood as "reproducing itself" in the third? As well, while Siegel emphasizes that feminism is "a political movement without the fixity of a single feminist agenda in view," she also states:

> Regardless of how, when, and under what circumstances one becomes a part of the current wave of feminist activism and scholarship, what unites practitioners in a third wave of praxis is a *pledge* to expand on the groundwork laid during waves one and two: a commitment to continue the *feminist legacy* of assessing

foundational concepts, particularly the category "women"; and the courage to
embrace the challenge of moving feminism ... into the next millennium. (*Siegel
1997: 56; emphasis mine*)

What I find particularly interesting and relevant to the question of the
discursive constitution of the "young feminist" is how the construction of
the wave metaphor references a comparison to both military and family.
When Siegel speaks of the unity of the third wave as located in their
"pledge" as well as describing their "challenge as moving feminism into the
next millennium," I am reminded of the use of the wave metaphor as a
battle strategy, as in *waves of attacking troops*. The "future feminist"
becomes a recruit and/or a volunteer who continues to fight a war on
patriarchy.

Leila Rupp makes a similar observation in "Is Feminism the Province of
Old (Middle-Aged) Women?" While discussing the third-wave position
questions of age as a contemporary feminist question, Rupp's account
reveals an ongoing issue related to age within feminisms. Her historical
investigation highlights a feminist contradiction between a distrust of
younger feminists and the simultaneous construction of the young feminist as the future of feminism as well as its obligatory member. Rupp
describes the formation of the NWP Student Action Committee in 1969 as
a primary goal outlined by the NWP (National Women's Party). As Rupp
highlights, the NWP described the Student Action Committee as designed
"to bring young hands and energies to the front to relieve shoulders too
long burdened with responsibilities others refused to help them carry" and
to "utilize the training and talents given them by past feminist[s] so their
sacrifices shall not have been in vain" (Rupp 2001: 167). Interestingly, the
language informing this 1969 *call to order* of the younger generation
included in Rupp's investigation also reflects military metaphors within its
discussion of "training" and bringing younger members to the "front to
relieve...past feminist[s]" (Rupp 2001: 167). While this example does not
specifically use the term "wave," it describes an understanding of generations within feminism through appeals to a military wave metaphor and
defines feminism as an obligation and duty of the "young."

In addition, third-wave discourses of contradictory subjects and feminisms complicate generational and wave metaphors that construct feminism as a linear and progressive history. Judith Roof's critique of the
"generation" metaphor in "Generational Difficulties; or, The Fear of a Barren History" suggests that the use of the term "generation" is caught up in
a discourse of progress defined by the "assuring [of] feminist pioneers that
they are indeed part of a trajectory—a passionate journey—that has
always been leading somewhere" (Roof 1997: 70). Roof critiques the generational and familial narrative as relying on a "patriarchal understanding
of history" that assumes "a linear, chronological time where the elements
that come first appear to cause elements that come later" (Roof 1997: 71).
Her critique of ordering a feminist history through linear narratives of

progress is particularly useful in critically examining the construction of the young feminist as disruptive daughter. Roof identifies how generational constructions foster an "understanding of the past's products as both legacy and property." This legacy and property are given as a gift to the next generation. However, this giving remains one-directional. As Chilla Bulbeck identifies, "Generational feminism is constructed in terms of a 'gift' from the older generation to the younger; rarely is reciprocal gift giving identified" (Bulbeck 1999: 5).

It remains that uses of the wave metaphor reflecting familial and generational ordering within feminisms suggest that while waves may appear different on the surface, beyond these differences waves ultimately emerge from the same water. If a "feminist legacy" is constructed as the normative basis and underlying, unifying principle of feminist difference, then a critique of the very assumption of a "feminist legacy" becomes a defiance of the "family" itself. This construction of defiance is particularly relevant to those critiques articulated by the "young" and/or "future" feminists when problematizing the legacy can ultimately result in situating the "young" feminists' critiques as abject, other, nonwave, and nonfeminist.

What I would like to propose by building upon the extensive work done by women of color, Third World feminists, and queer theorists is that the metaphors supporting feminisms' constructions symbolically constitute the subject of feminism as a particular ideation of "woman."[4] To this critique I would also like to trace what these series of metaphors mean, particularly for those constructed as "girl" and/or "young" within feminist discourses. This question points to the need to complicate the category of "woman" not only in regard to its cultural, racial, and sexual assumptions, but also in regard to age. Appeals to a "feminist legacy" should also recognize a feminist history repeatedly critiqued by its "others"—a feminist history as teleological becoming that inadequately addressed the complexity of subjects as defined through race, sexuality, class, age, and culture.

A connection that I view as integral to understanding the complexity of the "girl's" position within feminist discourse is found within the contradiction that emerges between the "girl's" own subjectivity and the very displacement of her subjectivity in her role as "future." The complication of the "girl" as constituted within feminist discourses identifies that an additive revision, for example, from now on referring to the subject of feminism as being "the woman *and* the girl," would fail to adequately address the discursive constitution of the "girl" as other. Rather, I identify the "girl" as addressing the need to formulate a critical language of difference, by which I mean the continued complication of the subject of feminism as well as troubling the construction of feminism as a *community of sameness* (Johnson 1993: 154).

"Girl" as Ironic Myth: What Is the Subject of Feminism?

The construction of the woman as one who has *become* and the girl as one who is on her way has direct bearing on the questions *What is the subject of feminism?* as well as *What is the subject of feminist pedagogy?* In *Gender Trouble: Feminism and the Subversion of Identity* (Butler 2nd Ed. 1999), Judith Butler questions ordering feminism in relation to the subject of women. Butler argues that feminism has assumed "that there is some existing identity, understood through the category of women, who not only initiates feminist interests and goals within discourse, but constitutes the subject for whom political representation is pursued" (Butler 2nd Ed. 1999: 4).

I would like to suggest that Girls' Studies becomes an integral site not only for complicating definitions of girlhood, and through these critical investigations advocating for social change, but for also complicating the very assumptions informing the constitution of subjects within feminisms. Girls' Studies becomes a site of othered feminist subjects when feminism is constituted as the growing up, awakening, and teleological becoming of particular women. In this regard, the girl as an ambiguous feminist subject functions much like Donna Haraway's ironic myth of the cyborg.

Haraway disrupts assumptions surrounding the presumed construction of a universal feminist subject in her "Cyborg Manifesto" (1991). She defines a cyborg as a "cybernetic organism, a hybrid of machine and organism, a creature of social reality as well as a creature of fiction" (Haraway 1991: 149). When Haraway proposes the cyborg as the subject of feminism, she works to disrupt the borders of what defines "women's experience" within feminisms (Haraway 1991: 149). Haraway's cyborg troubles the ability to maintain the subject of feminism as a unitary category of women. Haraway references Sandoval's discussion of oppositional consciousness as a means of locating how the subject "woman" has never meant *all* women (Haraway 1991: 155). She cites Sandoval as a means of raising the question "What would another political myth for socialist-feminism look like? What kind of politics could embrace partial, contradictory, permanently unclosed constructions of personal and collective selves and still be faithful, effective and, ironically, socialist-feminism?" (Haraway 1991: 157).

Haraway describes the cyborg as an ironic myth. The idea of irony as a kind of retelling or re-presentation as reflected in Haraway's cyborgian myth points to an understanding of language as unstable, shifting, and constructed. Haraway's ironic myth, the cyborg, troubles constructions that result in exclusion by locating the cyborg's inability to clearly reside on either side of a binary as a disruptive potential. Her cyborg troubles the vehicles of its own exclusion while being "nature" and being "culture," being "woman" and not being "woman," simultaneously. Haraway calls these exclusionary practices into question through the creation of a myth that cannot simply be dismissed as inapplicable or false.

In suggesting that the "girl" is an ironic myth, I identify the "girl," like Haraway's cyborg, as "a creature of social reality as well as a creature of fiction" (Haraway 1991: 149). The hybridity, ambiguity, and contradictory characteristics of the "girl" as feminist subject critiques the woman as feminism's subject. The "girl" becomes an important site for critiquing normative assumptions within feminisms and shifting inquiry from *Why should the "girl" be considered a feminist subject?* to *What assumptions have resulted in her exclusion?*

Within constructions of feminism as a kind of growing up, awakening, and teleological becoming of women, the girl becomes woman's other through the binary of woman/girl. While feminisms have extensively critiqued how the binary man/woman hierarchically constructs women's subjectivities as relational to the man's position as subject, the girl's position as subject defined only through her becoming a woman translates as well the woman/girl divide as effective/ineffective, real/imaginary, agent/victim, and whole/divided.[5] My concern relates to how this opposition privileges the position of the woman in relation to that of the girl, and in so doing, places the girl on the side of that which we can all overcome through "enlightenment," "progress," or "awakening." I am interested in what it would mean for feminisms and feminist pedagogies if the girl were not understood as a place from which women come, and not as a moment that we need to protect in order to protect the future of "women." I wonder what it would mean for feminisms and feminist pedagogies to understand the "girl" not as a singular state defined by age or behavior, but as a constantly shifting, discursively constituted sign that comes to mean and represent many things besides "young female."

In conclusion, I would like to return once again to the artwork, *I'm Not Just a Girl*. In reflecting upon this work, I am reminded of Hélène Cixous's statement "I don't 'begin' by 'writing': I don't write. Life becomes text starting out from my own body. I am already text" (Cixous 1991: 52). Brooke acknowledges that she is as well "already text" when she represents herself through the very language that she identifies as limiting her as a "girl" subject (Cixous 1991: 52). Her contradictory and ironic subjectivity is evident in that her critique and the object of her critique do not form neatly into an opposition. Rather, the language she critiques is the very language that simultaneously constitutes her as a "girl." As a subject and cultural producer in an art classroom, I am reminded as well that she did not *become* a subject by learning to write, learning the skills and techniques of an artist. She did not *become* a subject by learning a language of critique or feminism. As well, her work does not represent "girls." She is already text. She is already subject. Her work performs her contradictions and her multiplicity. She is not JUST a girl! Her work is not JUST a "girl's" work.

This student understands how categories presumed to be natural and normal are confining and exclusionary. She understands how sameness serves to exclude difference. She understands that gender is not simply "what is," but what is performed and constructed through her daily lived experiences. However, in order for her not to remain "just a girl" within feminist and educational discourses, we must develop a critical language of difference. A language that can construct *the girl as not just...*

Notes

1. For a discussion of feminist punk and/or zine communities, see Kathy Bail, *DIY Feminism* (St. Leonards, U.K.: Allen and Unwin, 1996); Anita Harris, "Revisiting Bedroom Culture: New Spaces for Young Women's Politics," *Hecate* 27 (2001): 128–137; and M. Leonard, "Paper Planes: Traveling the New Grrrl Geographies," in T. Skelton and G. Valentine (eds.), *Cool Places: Geographies of Youth Cultures* (London: Routledge, 1998), 101–118.

2. I am thinking here especially of Sherry Ortner's important work, "Is Female to Male as Nature Is to Culture?," in J. Landes (ed.), *Feminism: The Public and the Private* (Oxford: Oxford University Press, 1974).

3. Heywood and Drake discuss as well the anthology *The Third Wave: Feminist Perspectives on Racism* as having a "difficult road to publication":

   > This book, unlike the work of conservative white feminists, has seen a difficult road to publication. Perhaps because this book challenges easily assimilated feminist stereotypes and because it is published by a small, independent house, the book's production has seen problems that rarely occur in the large, mainstream publishing houses to which conservative feminism has easier access. (L. Heywood and J. Drake (eds.), *Third Wave Agenda* (Minneapolis: University of Minnesota Press, 1997: 1).

4. Questioning the subject of feminism has been extensively undertaken by women of color, Third World feminists, and queer theorists. Alice Walker's (1983) use of the term "womanism" to articulate a "black feminism or feminism of color" surfaces perceived biases in the term "feminism" itself (quoted in Heywood and Drake 1997: 62). Likewise, bell hooks, in *Feminist Theory: From Margin to Center* (Cambridge, Mass.: South End Press, 2000: 46), criticizes the construction of feminism's subject as sharing a "common oppression" and argues that the idea of "sisterhood" was "informed by racist and classist assumptions about White womanhood. Martin and Mohanty criticize feminism's subject as a Western vision of feminism, a bias that is unsuccessfully addressed through additive solutions. They state that "A failure to recognize difference except through additive and binary structures continues to situate feminism as a Western enterprise" ("Feminist Politics," in T. de Lauretis, ed., *Feminist Studies/Critical Studies*, Bloomington: Indiana University Press, 2000: 193). Gayatari Chakravorty Spivak in "Can the Subaltern Speak" addresses how the positioning of Third World women in feminist discourses served to "obscure their subjectivity while promoting the interests of the authors of the texts" (see A. Jaggar, "Globalizing Feminist Ethics," in U. Narayan and S. Harding, eds., *Decentering the Center*, Bloomington: Indiana University Press, 2000: 5).

5. See also Hélène Cixous's discussion of the binary of man/woman in her "Sorties," in S. Kemp and J. Squires (eds.), *Feminisms* (Oxford: Oxford University Press, 1997), 231–234.

References

Bail, K. (ed.). (1996). *DIY Feminism*. St. Leonards, U.K.: Allen and Unwin.

Bailey, C. (1997). "Making Waves and Drawing Lines: The Politics of Defining the Vicissitudes of Feminism." *Hypatia* 12 (3): 17–27.

Bulbeck, C. (1999). "Simone de Beauvoir and Generations of Feminists." *Hecate* 25 (5): 5–22.

Butler, J. (1990, 1999). *Gender Trouble: Feminism and the Subversion of Identity*. New York: Routledge.

Cixous, H. (1991). *Coming to Writing and Other Essays*. Cambridge, Mass.: Harvard University Press.

Cixous, H. (1997). "Sorties." In S. Kemp and J. Squires (eds.), *Feminisms*. Oxford: Oxford University Press.

Drake, J. (1997). "Third Wave Feminisms." *Feminist Studies* 23 (1): 97–108.

Findlen, B. (ed.). (1995). *Listen Up: Voices from the Next Feminist Generation*. Seattle: Seal.

Haraway, D. (1991). *Simians, Cyborgs, and Women: The Reinvention of Nature*. New York: Routledge.

Harris, A. (2001). "Revisiting Bedroom Culture: New Spaces for Young Women's Politics." *Hecate* 27 (1): 128–137.

Heywood, L., and Drake, J. (eds.). (1997). *Third Wave Agenda: Being Feminist, Doing Feminism*. Minneapolis: University of Minnesota Press.

hooks, b. (1984). *Feminist Theory: From Margin to Center*. Cambridge, Mass.: South End Press.

Jaggar, A. (2000). "Globalizing Feminist Ethics." In U. Narayan and S. Harding (eds.), *Decentering the Center: Philosophy for a Multicultural, Postcolonial, and Feminist World*. Bloomington: Indiana University Press.

Johnson, L. (1993). *The Modern Girl: Girlhood and Growing Up*. Bristol, U.K.: Open University Press.

Jones, A. (1993). "Becoming a Girl: Post-structuralist Suggestions for Educational Research." *Gender and Education* 5 (2): 157–166.

Kaplan, E.A. (1997). "Feminism, Aging, and Changing Paradigms." In D. Looser and E.A. Kaplan (eds.), *Generations: Academic Feminists in Dialogue*. Minneapolis: University of Minnesota Press.

Leonard, M. (1998). "Paper Planes: Traveling the New Grrrl Geographies." In T. Skelton and G. Valentine (eds.), *Cool Places: Geographies of Youth Cultures*. London: Routledge.

Martin, B., and Mohanty, C.T. (1986). "Feminist Politics: What's Home Got to Do with It?" In T. de Lauretis (ed.), *Feminist Studies/Critical Studies*. Bloomington: Indiana University Press.

Orr, C. (1997). "Charting the Currents of the Third Wave." *Hypatia* 12 (3): 29–47.

Ortner, S. (1974). "Is Female to Male as Nature Is to Culture?" In J. Landes (ed.), *Feminism: The Public and the Private*. Oxford: Oxford University Press.

Roof, J. (1997). "Generational Difficulties; or, The Fear of a Barren History." In D. Looser and E.A. Kaplan (eds.), *Generations: Academic Feminists in Dialogue*. Minneapolis: University of Minnesota Press.

Rupp, L. (2001). "Is Feminism the Province of Old (or Middle-aged) Women?" *Journal of Women's History* 12 (4): 164–173.

Siegel, D. (1997). "The Legacy of the Personal: Generating Theory in Feminism's Third Wave." *Hypatia* 12 (3): 46–81.

Spivak, G.C. (1988). "Can the Subaltern Speak." In C. Nelson and L. Grossberg (eds.), *Marxism and the Interpretation of Culture*. Urbana: University of Illinois Press.

Walker, R. (ed.). (1995). *To Be Real: Telling the Truth and Changing the Face of Feminism*. New York: Doubleday.

Walkerdine, V. (1987). "Femininity as Performance." In L. Stone (ed.), *The Education Feminism Reader*. New York, Routledge.

CHAPTER **8**

"I Don't See Feminists as You See Feminists": Young Women Negotiating Feminism in Contemporary Britain

MADELEINE JOWETT[1]

Introduction: Young British Women and Feminism

This chapter explores young British women's relationships to the category "feminism."[2] In particular, I seek here to complicate the commonly held belief that young British women invest in feminist ideas while disclaiming a feminist identity, a notion effectively articulated by Jane Pilcher as the "I'm not a feminist, but ..." phenomenon (Pilcher 1993). This notion rests on two specific understandings that I wish to call into question here: first, the implicit idea that young women can easily and expeditiously draw on the ideas of feminism in order to evaluate them accordingly, and second, the explicit claim made by many academics that young women refuse a personal affiliation with the category through negative cultural understandings of what it means to be a feminist, which are generally seen to be connected to persistently unfavorable media coverage (Pilcher 1993, 1998; Griffin 1989).

I want to suggest that processes of (dis)investment in feminist ideas and identities are far more complex, and that for contemporary young British women, they have a specific relationship to a particular period in British history. It is my argument that the British cultural imagery is currently filled with powerful discourses of progress, achievement, and optimism—produced through the millennial moment of reflective celebration and the futuristic rhetoric of the New Labour government most particularly—which are impacting young women's assessments of feminism as an (ir)relevant politics for the twenty-first century. Drawing on detailed empirical research, this chapter will seek to demonstrate the ways in which novel understandings of feminism are being generated, occupied, and resisted by young women as they negotiate the competing discourses available through which they can understand their world and their future.

Before I begin to elaborate on these points, I need to say a few words about the background to the empirical research on which the claims of this chapter are based. During 2000/2001, I conducted a series of loosely structured focus groups with twenty-six British White and British Asian women aged between sixteen and twenty-eight, on the themes of (in)equality, Girl Power, and feminism. This varied cohort included students and secretaries, homemakers and care workers, saleswomen and engineers; it attended to differences of parental and marital status, sexuality, and (dis)ability. While social class is notoriously difficult to categorize, I would assert that these women were essentially working-class or lower middle-class by education, reflective of the constituency of the town in which they were located, which was mainly made up of skilled and semi-skilled manual, administrative, and agricultural workers, with few professionals and no rolling student population (see Jowett 2003).

I selected the focus group as my chief research method because it offered a window through which to witness the dynamic negotiation of meaning in dialogue, through which contested categories such as feminism come to be made and challenged. This method afforded an opportunity to trace the path within such processes—to witness not just what was discussed but also how it was discussed. In this sense, the structure of the conversations constitutes material, a point this chapter attempts to reflect upon by paying attention to the direction of common discussion trajectories in its analysis.

Equality Britain

Indeed, the cross-group similarities of conversational paths was both remarkable and revealing. Most notably, all groups responded to my opening request for thoughts on the idea of equality by retrospectively reflecting on the freedoms and opportunities enjoyed by contemporary British women compared with previous generations. Many participants gave accounts of how they "knew" things had changed for women; how they could now choose from a wider variety of jobs and careers, pursue courses of education and training, live alone and support themselves and their children. High-profile examples of British female success were cited, including former Prime Minister Margaret Thatcher; the lawyer (and wife of current Prime Minister Tony Blair) Cherie Booth, Q.C.; and the pop band the Spice Girls. The existence of formal equality legislation and systems of regulation such as the Equal Opportunities Commission were taken to be axiomatic evidence of the eradication of discrimination. Crucially, these conversations often referred to wider cultural themes and political developments, particularly the new millennium and the policies of the New Labour Government, which were very much in their minds at this time and which were clearly seen as connected to ideas of equality and progress:

> Jenny: We're coming to a new century now....

> Anna: Yeah. Because, like, years ago, I wouldn't have been able to go into engi- neering. But now there's new ways in from this government. We're very aware of that in our future line of work.

> Emma: I suppose it's important to remember just how far we've come. In the next century, women are just going to be able to take equality for granted.

That opportunities for young British women have improved greatly since the 1970s is difficult to deny; their life courses have become detradi- tionalized as they continue into higher education, delay or decline mar- riage and motherhood, and exhibit a new attitude toward female power which Angela McRobbie has termed "common sense assertiveness" (McRobbie 2000: 210). Indeed, researchers have documented the develop- ment of a new assurance among young British women which can be seen in their indubitable belief in their right to equality. In the latter 1990s Skeggs identified a discourse of entitlement in Britain, which she attrib- uted to a combination of increasing consumerism and the language of cit- izenship developed under the long period of Conservative rule in the 1980s and 1990s (Skeggs 1995).

I would argue that these discourses have become more pronounced in recent years, as the New Labour government has consolidated ideas of individual initiative, diligence, and entrepreneurship into its populist rhet- oric. This administration has arguably had a seismic impact on the texture of British culture, replacing as it did a long period of Conservative rule (which had begun before the birth of many of these participants), and receiving as it has a massive amount of media attention. Crucially, much of this attention has centered upon New Labour's claim to personify the hopes of a new generation: to be the vanguard of a national program of regeneration and social improvement.[3] Such ideas have certainly filtered into popular consciousness; Rachel Thomson and colleagues have recently argued that "Discourses of social mobility are particularly strong at the moment, both in social policy in New Labour Britain and in the informal cultures of young people" (Thompson et al. 2003: 34). That the idea of national and generational renewal—which Helen Wilkinson has termed "the making of a young country" (Wilkinson 1996: 226)— has been linked to an evident investment in the idea of social progress among young women in particular has not gone unremarked. Jeremy Gilbert has gen- dered this evident mood of national optimism, asserting: "This belief in the future...most specifically belongs to young women at the present time" (Gilbert 1998: 84). Gilbert argues that it is the project's echoes of personal and social improvement which ensure that: "all that is best about New Labour chimes with the needs and desires of young women in Britain today" (Gilbert 1998: 85).

This relationship has deeper levels, however. It is not only that young women feel an affiliation with the New Labour rhetoric of social improvement because it fits with what Gilbert terms their "openness to the future" (Gilbert 1998: 85). Rather, as Angela McRobbie has recently argued, young women have in some sense become emblematic of, and responsible for, the "new Britain" heralded by New Labour:

> Since New Labour came to power in May 1997 young women have become a "metaphor for social change"…in this capacity they are charged with the not insignificant task of, in effect, delivering the new meritocracy by means of female achievement. (*McRobbie 2001: 361*)

In this sense, young women's grasping of the equality they assume is a responsibility which reaches further than the individual success which they see as their right; it is part of their duty to demonstrate and make the new meritocracy on which evidently potent ideas of New Britain depend.

Voicing Inequality

Given these puissant ideas of female progress, together with evidently dominant ideas about female opportunity and potential, it is perhaps easy to see how young women could smoothly articulate what might be seen as a rather uncritical view of their power and imagined futures when immediately asked to describe their world. Crucially, however, this culture makes the acknowledgment of continuing inequality very difficult indeed. I witnessed a keen reluctance among these young women to discuss the possibility that gendered inequity might be both extant and resistant to change:

> Kelly [pauses, then takes a deep breath]: I suppose there is still a bit of, in certain areas like, erm, I don't know, erm…[drifts]. But you, you should be able to do it. But I must admit, I think there probably would still be a little bit of, erm, discrimination.

The confessional nature of Kelly's comment—evidenced in the phrase "I must admit"—indicates clearly the cultural proscription which surrounds such assertions of inequity. Pat MacPherson and Michelle Fine have observed a similar reluctance to speak about issues of continuing inequality and discrimination among young American women, describing such knowledges as "the great unsayables" within young female experience (MacPherson and Fine 1995: 181). Thus even when anecdotal examples of gendered discrimination were aired, they were evidently discomforting, and were often resisted and denied:

> Maddy: Is it that maybe women should be treated equally but they're not? [silence] Or is it that they are….

Alex [interrupting]: No, we are. [Indistinguishable voices say, "Yeah, we are."]

Rebecca: But I work for my dad, he has a car business, and when men ring up, and I answer, because I'm the secretary, they say, "No, I want to speak to a man." [silence]

Maddy: So is the assumption there that you're not equal….

Rebecca [interrupting]: Yeah.

Maddy: You're not treated equally?

Rebecca: Yeah.

Emma: Suppose so. [Indistinguishable quiet voices say "Yeah."]

Alex: We should be.

Valerie Walkerdine and colleagues have recently suggested that the potent idea of individual freedom and the synchronous claim for classlessness currently evident within Britain ensures that people no longer have the space to feel a sense of social injustice or frailty, much less to speak of it. They state that there are "difficulties in trying to speak about class … at the turn of the century. The confusion and frustration in … attempts to do so is palpable…," and that individuals "are no longer entitled to harbour a sense of unfairness (Walkerdine et al. 2001: 52). The idea of entitlement to participate in a supposedly "equal" and classless society then removes the entitlement to feel encumbered by it, let alone to speak about it. The belief in this generic equality precisely silences the articulation of experiences of inequality. Anna's quiet observation—"I know we've got equality, but you still get problems, don't you?"—therefore constitutes an attempt to reconcile the apparently incongruous and disconcerting understandings of Britain which simultaneously spoke to, and contradicted, different knowledges.

However, even when inequity was voiced, it was dismissed as simply a residual and temporary problem. A sense of cheery inevitability pervaded the conversations, as Emma, echoing many of her peers, simply stated, "The next generation'll be able to take it for granted." She could not explain how this would be accomplished, nor could she visualize any obstructions—the intoxicating belief was that equality would now be easily seized by individual women, empowered by the achievements of previous generations. The idea of resilient inequality was then rendered superfluous by concurrent investments in this kind of fatalistic optimism; the inexorable nature of positive progress. Moreover, such developments were inevitably seen as gender-free, a factor which was clearly linked to contextually specific ideas about governmental policy and social progress.

Shameen: The thing is, this is a new century. And with the government's Human Rights Act, it's for everybody; its not sex discrimination anymore. I think everything's being incorporated into that, it includes us all….

Kelly: Yeah, so why do we still need feminists?

Negotiating Feminism(s)

Kelly's rhetorical question here hints at the impact of such ideas upon feminism. Without doubt, this understanding of Britain as on a guaranteed evolutionary trajectory had profound consequences for feminism, which was, at an initial level at least, almost universally viewed as a once vital but now redundant politics. Thus Melanie explained, "Years and years ago this feminist thing was really big and people did fight for women's rights, and that was good. But we're equal now, so there's not that need." Feminism was thus seen as something which had contributed to female progress in the past, but was no longer relevant. Significantly, feminists today were certainly not understood as man-hating, activist, anti-feminine harridans, the associated negative characteristics which have been asserted as the chief reason behind young women's rejection of feminist identities. Indeed, while such images may remain in the distant cultural memory, they are certainly not understood as contemporaneous and do not feature heavily in young women's own understandings of feminism:

> Kelly: If someone had said to me: "Describe what the word 'feminist' means," I would maybe say a load of weirdos that are burning their bras, but that happened years ago and doesn't really exist anymore. You don't really hear the word "feminist" anymore, do you?

> Andrea: You, like, think of the sixties, and burning bras, when you think of feminists. Its a very stereotyped thing, and I think of it as something in the past, not that's happening now. I mean, it was before we were born!

> Hayley: My mum used to be a feminist, she went to Greenham Common[4] in the 1980s. She hated men then; she was put upon, so she was a feminist then. [Sounds of agreement from peers.] She's not like that now, she's got a good life, she just doesn't worry about it now. I don't think feminism's relevant today.

> Karen: Well, it happened years ago, things like that, didn't it? In my generation you don't … feminism's not really talked about. I mean, we've never really heard of feminism. But I definitely don't see, I don't see feminists today as women that go round and hate men, and I don't see that as bad at all. It's a different generation who think like that about feminism.

Hayley's and Karen's points are perhaps particularly telling, for they reveal deeper layers to the relationship between young British women and feminism. It is not that young women recognize merit in feminist ideas but disclaim feminist identities through persistently negative understandings of man-hating, activist feminists. Indeed, such individuals are in some sense now rehabilitated; Hayley's mother, who is positioned as a perfect example of this feminist, is accepted as having acted in a sensible and legitimate fashion given the lack of freedom she is understood to have experienced. Thus the very kind of feminist whose press vilification was said to have been decisive in turning young women away from the category is today rationalized and valorized; she is understood as a woman living in a time before the notion of entitlement to equality and self-determination which they all enjoy, and who therefore took necessarily "radical" action such as joining a women-centered communal space and distancing herself from oppressive men. Feminism is then justified through its historicity. Crucially, as Karen suggests, it is an earlier generation who sees those associations with feminism as both negative and primary; while her generation does not see such historic actions as without justification, they generally do not see feminism as contemporaneous at all.

However, this dismissal of feminism as obsolete does not mean that actively negative understandings of feminists are now absent. Indeed, in the discussions I witnessed, a novel but equally pejorative notion of the feminist emerged which could have done so only if the ideas that I have outlined were in place. For assumptions of inevitable equality ensured that feminisms which were understood to be continuing to argue that discrimination toward women as a group is endemic or resistant were seen as melodramatic and redundant. Those who were understood to be relentlessly protesting about "oppression" in a modern society—a society which was improving, and in which women could bring about changes for themselves—were necessarily viewed as irrelevant. Such feminists were seen as ludicrous, at best pitiable or comical; described by Hayley as "still complaining," and by Shameen as those who "think it's all still against them." Although these understandings work from an established lineage, it is important to recognize that they are related to historically specific understandings of the positive inevitability of social progress. Popular understandings of feminism have then altered to form a new set of loaded associations, supporting Hilary Hinds and Jackie Stacey's recent assertion that the negative figure of the feminist in British culture is "thoroughly sedimented … and yet endlessly mutable" (Hinds and Stacey 2001: 156).

"Going Against the Tide"— Owning Feminism

Yet as I noted at the outset of this chapter, the focus group method provides space for contestation. Thus, reacting to ideas of feminists as passé and ludicrous, Kirsten stated to her group: "I don't see feminists as you see feminists." She voiced her own feelings both about the contemporary ideas of progress and equality that were being articulated, and about their impact on those who, like herself, considered themselves feminists:

> Kirsten: I think we get a bit complacent, because things are …[pause] now it's not as bad as it was, is it? I mean, we're a lot better off than we were thirty years ago, but we're not equal. But it's like if you say you're a feminist at the moment, everybody goes "What? A feminist?!" [Mimics sharp intake of breath and overemphasizes shocked facial expression to group laughter.] Because I was talking to my boyfriend, and I was going "Oh, I'm going to Maddy's on Friday," and he

said, "What's all that about, then?" And I went, "Oh, about feminism," and he
went, "Well, you're not a feminist, are you?!" And I went, "I AM!"

Despite the keen awareness of the associated cultural censure, Kirsten's
enthusiastic self-identification with feminism was not unique; several of
the young women in this project articulated similar affiliations with the
category in the face of genial, but nonetheless real, ridicule from their
research peers. Significantly however, such affiliations were often made
with direct reference to the culture of assumed progress which these young
feminists wished to resist. Thus, as seventeen-year-old Leena commented,
"Because people think women know where they are now, feminism is a
taboo subject, it's boring, and being a feminist is seen as embarrassing. So
I say I'm a feminist, and proud." Leena's deployment of "so" is, I think,
worthy of note, signaling as it does her knowledge that her opinion is in
opposition to an established cultural consensus. In a different group, Clare
asserted that it was precisely the contemporary positioning of feminism as
irrelevant that pushed her to vocalize her identification with the category
more vigorously. She explained, "Because that's the way feminism is seen, I
say [I'm a feminist]. I say it anyway."

Leena told me that in her opinion, "Oppression hasn't gone away, it's just
become more subtle." Her response, like that of several of the young women
in this project, was to make her feminism rather less than ambiguous. The
existence of new pejorative understandings of outmoded feminisms certainly led to surprise and wonderment among those listening to such confident self-identifications. Yet it is an interesting point to note that common
reactions included awe and applause as much as shock and derision:

> Alex: I suppose, now I've thought about it, you have to be quite brave to be a
> feminist don't you?
>
> Andrea: I think feminists today must be pretty strong women.
>
> Karen: It's a taboo subject, feminism, isn't it? Because people think that we're all
> equal. I mean, we wouldn't be sat here having this discussion if we were all equal.
> But I can imagine that feminists have to be like "I hold my head up and say, 'I'm
> a feminist, I'm not bothered.'"
>
> Anna: I think feminists must be especially brave, because they're going against
> the tide.

Such responses serve to underscore young women's own acknowledgment of the prohibitions on feminism within contemporary British culture. But they also demonstrate a commitment to a category with which
they have not generally been allied. Crucially, they suggest that given the
space, young women will act as highly critical agents, challenging and contesting the discourses which they clearly imbibe in a nonetheless discriminating fashion. These dialogues illuminated the restrictive discourses
which help preclude positive relationships to feminism, but they also

provided space for the generation of burgeoning resistant discourses through which these young women began to rearticulate and reassess their lives and opinions, and to form new relationships to feminism.

Conclusions

By their very nature, the persuasive ideas of accomplished female emancipation and future female power witnessed in this project hinder the critical engagement of young British women with feminism as a body of thought which believes in highlighting and challenging continuing power imbalances. Such ideas also assist in the creation of new understandings of persistent feminists as passé and preposterous, encouraging further disinvestment. It is not simply that young women recognize value in feminist arguments yet reject the idea of being a feminist through traditional media-inspired stereotypes, then, but rather that the very idea of feminism as relevant is culturally proscribed. However, it is also essential to note that many young women resist such proscription, and desire feminism for themselves. That they are prepared to assert their affinity with the category while aware of the way it could incur social losses is all the more extraordinary and courageous.

While they may buy into some erroneous ideas about female freedom, these young women are certainly not ideological dupes. As the accounts here suggest, they are engaged in a process of negotiation as they endeavor to comprehend potent discourses which simultaneously speak to and contradict their own experiences and understandings, and which impact on their readings of their world and of the place of feminism within it. When they find space to do so, they place available discourses into contestation, resulting in the production of their own questions and, in some cases, their own feminisms. Crucially, I would argue that attention to the dialogic processes through which such alliances were made and articulated—processes which illuminate the discourses available to young women as they seek to comprehend and make their lives—is extremely informative for academic understandings both of the ways in which inequality is perpetuated and resisted, and of the novel relationships with feminism that young British women are forging for themselves.

Notes

1. I would like to thank all those who have contributed to the development of this chapter, especially Sara Ahmed, Louise Bainbridge, Bela Chatterjee, Lynne Jowett, and Jackie Stacey. I'd also like to thank all those who organized and attended the New Girl conference, Kings College, London, in November 2001 and the Institute for Women's Studies Open Seminar series in March 2002, at which I gave earlier drafts of this chapter.

2. While I talk here of "young British women" as a group, I do not wish to imply that their attitudes are undifferentiated with regard to class, "race," age, religion, sexuality, (dis)ability, or geographical location. Indeed, the thesis upon which this chapter is based reflects precisely upon the particular ways in which these identities, contexts, and structural constraints impact upon relationships to feminism. In this short piece, however, I am concerned less to examine individual relationships than I am to illuminate the kinds of

discourses around feminism that are generally available in contemporary Britain. For more on this, see Jowett (2003).

3. For more on the New Labour and Blairite projects and their impact on British culture, see Fairclough (2000); Driver and Martell (2002). For work which particularly addresses the gendered politics of New Labour, see McRobbie (2001); Franklin (2000).

4. Greenham Common was a peace camp in Berkshire, England, populated by women in the 1980s. Press denigration of the camp formed the basis for many press caricatures of feminism at the time. For more on this, see Roseneil (1995).

References

Driver, S., and Martell, L. (2002). *Blair's Britain.* London: Polity.

Fairclough, N. (2000). *New Labour, New Language?* London: Routledge.

Franklin, J. (2000). "What's Wrong with New Labour Politics?" *Feminist Review* no. 65, Autumn pp. 138–142.

Gilbert, J. (1998). "Blurred Vision: Pop, Populism and Politics.'" In A. Coddington and M. Perryman (eds.), *The Moderniser's Dilemma: Radical Politics in the Age of Blair.* London: Lawrence and Wishart.

Griffin, C. (1989). "'I'm Not a Women's Libber, but....'" In S. Skevington and D. Baker (eds.), *Feminism, Consciousness and Identity: The Social Identity of Women.* London: Sage.

Hinds, H., and Stacey, J. (2001). "Imaging Feminism, Imaging Femininity: The Bra-Burner, Diana, and the Woman Who Kills." *Feminist Media Studies* 1 (2): 153–177.

Jowett, M. (2000). "New Feminism in Contemporary Britain." *Politics Review* 9 (3): 12–14.

Jowett, M. (2001). "Is Feminism Still Important?" *Sociology Review* 11 (1): 16–18.

Jowett, M. (2003). "Negotiating Feminism: Young Women's Changing Relationships to Feminism in the Context(s) of Contemporary Britain." Ph.D. thesis, Lancaster University, U.K.

Jowett, M. (forthcoming). "Young Women and Feminist Politics in the Twenty-first Century." To be published at: http://thefword.co.uk.

MacPherson, P. and Fine, M. (1995) "Hungry for an Us: Adolescent Girls and Adult Women Negotiating Territories of Race, Gender, Class and Difference." In *Feminism and Psychology* Vol.5, No.2.

McRobbie, A. (2000). *Feminism and Youth Culture.* London: Macmillan.

McRobbie, A. (2001). "Good Girls, Bad Girls: Female Success and the New Meritocracy." In D. Morley and K. Robins (eds.), *British Cultural Studies.* Oxford: Oxford University Press.

Pilcher, J. (1993). "'I'm Not a Feminist, But...'": Understanding Feminism." *Sociology Review* 3 (2): 2–6.

Pilcher, J. (1998). *Women of Their Time: Generation, Gender Issues and Feminism.* Aldershot, U.K.: Ashgate.

Roseneil, S. (1995). *Disarming Patriarchy.* Buckingham: Open University Press.

Skeggs, B. (1995). "Women's Studies in Britain in the 1990's—Entitlement Cultures and Institutional Constraints." *Women's Studies International Forum* 18 (4): 475–485.

Thomson, R., Henderson, S., and Holland, J. (2003). "Making the Most of What You've Got? Resources, Values and Inequalities in Young Women's Transitions to Adulthood." *Educational Review* 55 (1): 33–46.

Walkerdine, V., Lucey, H., and Melody, J. (2001). *Growing Up Girl: Psychosexual Explorations of Gender and Class.* Basingstoke: Palgrave.

Wilkinson, H. (1996). "The Making of a Young Country." In M. Perryman (ed.), *The Blair Agenda.* London: Lawrence and Wishart.

PART 3

Sexuality

CHAPTER 9

Pretty in Pink: Young Women Presenting Mature Sexual Identities

KATE GLEESON AND HANNAH FRITH

In this chapter we explore some of the tensions and the power struggles we experienced when, as adult researchers, we interviewed young women. We begin by providing a brief analysis of eighteen in-depth interviews with young women aged between twelve and sixteen from Bristol and Cardiff.[1] These young women were from homes with average to low incomes, and all of them volunteered to be interviewed in their own schools. Initially we set out to explore young women's consumption practices and the ways in which they use consumer products and shopping practices (such as trying on clothes with their friends) to construct identities. We did not set out explicitly to focus on the use of clothing to signal mature sexual identities. However, we soon began to hear a whisper through the data where girls hinted at the sexual significance of particular types of clothing. We began to feel that clothing might be one of the few opportunities for young women to explore and publicly present their sexuality.

This chapter will explore the shifting power relations between ourselves and our participants, and their attempts to resist our reading of them and their clothing practices. In particular, although we wanted to argue that young women were hinting at sexualized identities, our participants resisted this characterization of themselves and we became frustrated at not being able to pin down the meaning of the sartorial practices they described. We came to realize that such ambiguity is an important resource for young women in a context where being explicit about sexual intentions is inherently fraught. We will conclude by exploring how this conflict over meaning is indicative of shifting power dynamics within the research process, and consider the implications for feminist researchers.

Our Analysis of Sartorial Identities

In reviewing our transcripts of the data we had collected about young women's clothing practices, we became aware of an almost intangible sexualized gloss to many parts of the interviews. These shifted in and out of focus, and we found it difficult to identify and pin down exactly what it was within the interviews that was giving us this impression. Were we reading into the transcripts too deeply, going beyond what our participants had actually said? To illustrate our emerging understanding, we will briefly identify three aspects of the data which we thought alluded to the sexual significance of clothing for our young, female participants: (1) the distancing from "pink" clothing, which was seen to represent immature, asexual femininity; (2) the use of sexualized descriptions of items of clothing; and (3) the use of clothing to attract the heterosexual male gaze.

Rejecting Pink

Others have noted that dress is one of the most significant markers of gender identity (Barnes and Eicher 1992), and that colors and styles of clothing, even for very young children, are culturally coded as masculine or feminine (Pomerleau et al. 1990; Renzetti and Curran 1995). Probably the first thing that we became aware of as we started to explore the data was the reference to the color pink as a code for describing clothing associated with immature feminine identities—the color and style of apparel are not used to distinguish only between masculinity and femininity, but also between different forms of femininities.

As with other researchers (for example, Freitas et al. 1997), our participants found it easier to talk about what they were not, rather than to lay claim to particular identities. It seemed to be easier for these young women to talk about the immature identities that they rejected than to describe the sexually mature look that they were trying to achieve. The older girls, in particular, rejected pink as symbolizing a childish femininity. For example, Sarah (nearly fifteen), who now prefers baggy clothes in blue and black, talks about an item of clothing that she had owned in the past that she particularly dislikes.

EXTRACT 1

> Sarah: Not really. Or I've got a dress with flowers on now, and that's ha; that's like, aha—Yeah, ok, I'm not gonna wear that ever, sort of thing again. Pink clothes, ha.
>
> Kate: Pink clothes, so you used to wear it but you wouldn't wear it now?
>
> Sarah: Yeah. I wouldn't wear pink or anything like that now.

Kate: Why is that?

Sarah: I've just gone off pink, I just don't like it anymore. It's too feminine, right; it's just, I think, 'cause pink's a more a feminine color.

Emma (age sixteen): ... they're so girly and all, like, flowers and stuff like that; there's nothing just plain and something, they got to be something on them and everything.

Kate: Right, lots of detail.

Emma: Yeah, ... it's all flowery and girly and pink and stuff like that.

Pink does not just represent femininity; it represents a particular kind of femininity—one which is passive, innocent, asexual, and immature (that is, girly and feminine). Others have noted the symbolic representation of normative femininity through pink, and the ways in which pink is rejected (usually in favor of black) by women who are attempting to negotiate alternative versions of femininity, such as punks and goths[2] (Williamson 2001). The rejection of feminine pink is complex. At one moment girls might reject pink in favor of a more boyish self-presentation, but in another they reject it in favor of a more overtly sexualized self-presentation, both of which challenge a particular version of femininity.

Sexualized Clothes

In contrast to the pink and flowery clothes rejected by our participants, the clothes they liked to wear were often described as short, tight-fitting, low-cut, revealing dresses, and high heels. As listeners to these descriptions, we heard these young women talking about clothing that is highly sexualized in British society. According to Entwistle (2000: 187), "The fashion system's obsession with the sexuality of the body is articulated through particular commodities which are constructed as sexual." Although the exact nature of these sexualized commodities changes, some garments (such as short skirts and high heels) are widely recognized as stereotypically associated with (a particular version of) female sexuality. In describing their preferred clothing, these young women seemed to us to be describing the presentation of sexual selves.

Hannah: ... you said the words "tight tops" about three or four times. Why do I get the feeling that these are important? Are those some a ... do you have quite a lot of tight tops?

Pippa (age twelve): Yes.

Hannah: What ... why are they tight [laughs] rather than ....

Pippa: Well, they're like fine, thin straps and....

Hannah: What, like little vests [undershirts]?

Pippa: Yes.

Hannah: And why particularly those kinds of tops rather than shirts or jumpers [sweaters] or T-shirts?

Pippa: ... some, like when you're younger, you're more likely to show off your body, but when you're older, you cover up.

Hannah: So when you're looking for clothes, are you looking for clothes that are going to show off your body?

Pippa: Well, most of the time.

The visibility of the body and flesh is subject to order, surveillance, and regulation, and yet the exposure of the body is fundamental to femininity and social order (Eicher 2001). Women (especially adolescent girls) are both encouraged to cover up, be modest, and conceal their flesh, and yet at the same time to reveal their bodies (through certain styles of clothing). One example of this tendency for clothing to both conceal and reveal is the use of slits (see Davis, 1992, for further discussion of this). In the following extract, Jane (age fourteen) describes some of the "party" dresses she wears to go clubbing[3]:

EXTRACT 4

Kate: So what sort of thing is nightclub clothes, what sort of thing would you like to wear?

Jane: I've got loads of dresses, I've got a black dress [inaudible] with a slit there.

Kate: Yeah, oh, I....

Jane: I've got, um, a purple dress with a slit there [material omitted]. I got a nice dress with all patterned flowers on it, like black things on it. It's been painted black on it, and it goes down like that.

Kate: So it's, like, slashed across from the hip to across the knee ...

Although our participants rarely talked about dressing in order to look or feel "sexy," these descriptions of clothing seemed to us to be very different from the jeans, jumpers [sweaters], and T-shirts they discussed at other times. They hinted at a desire to adopt an identity as a sexual actor.

Being Seen

For these young women, part of the pleasure associated with particular styles of clothing is the pleasure of being seen and of attracting attention—typically attention from boys! Emily (sixteen) was asked about clothes that have special meaning for her:

EXTRACT 5

> Kate: And did that give you a good memory attached to that top?
>
> Emily: Yeah, it was fun, ha ha. Um, I got quite a few looks [laughing] from some boys with it on.
>
> Kate: Oh, right.
>
> Emily: Um, that's now my pulling top[4] [laughs].
>
> Kate: Oh, right, so it got you some attention.
>
> Emily: Yeah, yeah [laughs].

The young women expressed pleasure in the use of clothing to attract attention in contexts where they were available to a male gaze. However, they often denied the deliberateness of this act.

EXTRACT 6

> Kate: You slipped something in there very quickly then; you said, "That's because that's the kind of boys I like." Is that part of what it's about, choosing the style?
>
> Jodie (age fifteen): I don't know, er … probably er … I su … ppose … I might do, but I haven't consciously gone "Ooh, I could get these boys if I dress…."

Although young women talked about relishing attention, they stopped short of saying that they were deliberately courting attention from the opposite sex.

Taken together, these three things (rejection of childish, asexual, pink clothes; the sexualized descriptions of clothing; and the wearing of clothes to attract attention) seemed to us to hint at links between clothing and sexual expression. Our initial approach to the data was to recognize that young women were in a process of transition from girlhood to womanhood, from immature feminine identities to sexually mature identities. However, as we reviewed the interview transcripts in order to establish this analysis, we began to notice the ways in which the young women themselves resisted our attempts to characterize them in this way. This led us to reexamine the interviews, our own role within these conversations, and the intricate power dynamics that were at play.

Reflecting on the Research Process

In reading through the interviewer transcripts, we became increasingly frustrated in our attempts to pin down the exact meaning of these young women's sartorial practices. Although the data seemed to hint at the importance of clothing in presenting mature and sexual identities, we had difficulty finding direct evidence to support this hunch. We began to realize that the interpretations of the data we were making now as analysts, were also the interpretations we had begun to make as interviewers. As interviewers we had picked up on the sexualized language of our participants and had (as good interviewers should!) tried to probe these responses further. However, the girls resisted our attempts to characterize them in this way, and we were frustrated by the lack of clarity and directness in their responses. Here are some examples of how we tried to pin things down, and encourage our interviewees to be explicit. In the first, Nicola (fifteen) is happy to describe a favorite top to Kate but is not prepared? not able? not willing? to say exactly what it is about the top that she likes.

EXTRACT 7

Nicola: It's, er, a top which goes down there. It's a halter neck and it's almost see-through.

Kate: It's a halter neck, it's almost see-through, and it's quite short. It's kind of like....

Nicola: And it's very short, yeah. I ... I like short tops. People don't reckon they suit me, I just like 'em.

Kate: ... So think about this top in particular, this short halter top. What is it about it that you really love?

Nicola: Um, not exactly sure. I just really like what it looks like, cos....

Kate: Uh-hum.

Nicola: I seem to think it's very me.

Kate: It's very you.

Nicola: Yeah.

Kate: Ok, what's that mean, what's you about it?

Nicola: I don't know.

Kate: I know it's hard to describe just ...

Nicola: Um ... huh [long pause]. [laughs.]

Kate: It's too difficult to describe? [Laughs.] Don't worry. It's very difficult to explain that....

[material omitted]

Kate: Are you aware of what other people are thinking when you wear it?

Nicola: Um, no.

Nicola describes a short, see-through, halter top. After quite a sexualized description Kate tries to establish exactly what it is about this top that Nicola likes, and (eventually) whether she thinks about how she appears to others when wearing it. In the second example Lizzy (twelve) describes a favorite top to Hannah:

EXTRACT 8

Lizzy: It's like a cute gypsy top, and it's got three-quarter-length arms.

Hannah: Right.

Lizzy: And it … it … it's got, like, little ties here; you tie 'em up, and little tie there.

Hannah: So it's quite … is it like quite gathered around there?

Lizzy: Yeah.

Hannah: Its got a big scoop.

Lizzy: Yeah, and you put it on, it's like…. [inaudible]

Hannah: And it, yeah ….

Lizzy: Tightens up round there.

Hannah: And what is it about that, that you particularly like?

Lizzy: I don't know. I just really like it.

Hannah: [laughs]

Faced with our attempts to encourage them to be explicit about their understanding of these garments, Lizzy and Nicola prefer to use the rhetoric of personal taste—"I just really like it." Taste is not something we can question, but reference to personal preferences dismisses the idea that items of clothing can be meaningful in and of themselves and independent of the wearer. There are a number of ways of reading this apparent mismatch between our own reading of these clothes as sexual, and our participants' reading of these clothes as simply reflecting personal preferences. Perhaps we are mistaken in thinking that these clothes are sexualized; perhaps we are reading too much into our interviews. Alternatively, perhaps the clothes hold those cultural meanings, but our participants are unaware and ignorant of this. But we feel that there is more going on here—that these young women have a good understanding of the codes for displaying mature sexual identities and they have the cultural capital to "do" mature identities, but they choose not to share that knowledge with us. For example, earlier Jane (fourteen) described a series of dresses with slits in various places (see extract 4). When Kate tries to home in on what it is about those dresses that she likes, Jane accepts her definition of the clothes as sexual but denies her own agency in presenting herself as sexual.

Extract 4 (Cont.)

Kate: So it's, like, slashed across from the hip to the … across the knee. So those things are quite revealing, showing your legs…. Do you like to be noticed? Is that what you're kind of…

Jane: No.

Kate: No? No.

Jane: I don't like to be noticed. But when I wears like skirts and things like that, when I walk down the street with a skirt on, all the men are pervs,[5] aren't they? They all beep the horn and that.

Kate: Yeah.

Jane: And I don't like that.

Kate: You don't like that?

Jane: No, I just ignore them....

Kate: So you're not wearing it for them to look at?

Jane: No.

Kate: But you are wearing things that are ...

Jane: I am wearing it because I likes to wear it.

Kate: Right, ok.

Jane: But I don't wear it for attention.

Kate identifies the clothes as sexual and attempts to position Jane as actively seeking male attention and/or actively presenting a sexualized identity by wearing sexualized clothing. Jane doesn't deny that the clothes are sexual, or at least that they could be seen as sexualized by others (for example, salacious men), but she presents the fact that her clothes reveal parts of her body as incidental—she doesn't wear them to deliberately attract attention, and sometimes the attention she attracts is problematic. The reason that she dresses this way is down to personal preference— again this mitigates a broader social reading of her clothing practices in which the clothes themselves have meaning and denies that by adopting these clothing styles she can be seen to embody that meaning. Our attempts to "read off" meaning from their descriptions of clothing are resisted by these young women, who wish to hold on to the ambiguity which clothing affords them.

Unlike researchers who attempt to identify an unambiguous "language" of clothes (for example, Lurie 2000) or a semiotics of style (Hebdige 1979), we recognize that ambiguity in clothing gives young women opportunities to negotiate just exactly how "mature" and/or "sexual" they want to appear in particular situations and in relation to particular people, and to renegotiate these when necessary. Not only may this ambiguity be negotiated within the embodied presentation of the self in clothing (that is, when women are actually engaged in clothing practices), but this ambiguity extends into their accounts of their clothing practices with us as researchers. We saw this ambiguity as problematic for us as researchers because we saw our primary purpose as to get beyond the ambiguity to gain a clear picture of what exactly is going on.

However, the meanings of the clothing that they describe are not fixed, but are constantly negotiated between us during the course of the interview. These meanings are not neutral, but have implications for the positioning of the research participants (and ourselves as researchers) both by us as researchers and by themselves as participants (see Frith 1998). We wanted to know what they knew, we wanted to understand young women's constructions of identity. We didn't feel this was a particularly problematic mission, having vague ideas that somehow understanding young women was a good thing. To make their voices heard, to make their positions clear and their knowledge shared, was a noble thing to do. We had positioned ourselves as being "on the same side" as these young women. We were sympathetic to their attempts to adopt mature identities. We were not interested in being part of the surveillance that helped constrain and delimit their self-presentation.

We did not realize that by trying to make them be explicit about sexual codes and how they linked to clothing, we were engaged in a negotiation of power. In an attempt not to introduce our own agendas, we often avoided explicitly asking about or naming certain clothing practices as sexually relevant, hoping that our participants would do this for us. However, the onus is really on us to introduce the sometimes uncomfortable and dangerous topics in order to clarify our willingness to speak about them. Given that it is often difficult for young women to acknowledge their own serprality, it is unfair of us to let these women take the risk of intoducing their sexual intentions into the discussion. Maybe it is not surprising that their talk is so ambiguous, because we didn't license talk about sexuality—we didn't give permission to discuss this difficult area.

But even if we make it more comfortable for our participants to speak about sexual identity, it doesn't mean that they will be willing to discuss these matters with us explicitly. They may still not choose to give up the powerful position as "knowers" in order to make things clear to us (see also Harris 2001). For us to understand the communications of these young women would mean gaining still further power as adults. For them to share their knowledge with us would of course mean sharing, or even giving up, the power invested in their knowledge. As McClean Taylor, Gilligan, and Sullivan (1996) illustrate, there are a number of ways in which our participants can resist our attempts to understand them without actually refusing to take part in the study. They can resist by remaining silent or by answering our questions in ways which do not allow us to understand their experiences and their practices. Like these researchers, we found that the dynamic between the researcher and the researched was far more complex than we originally suspected. Like most researchers, we felt that it might be difficult for us to communicate in a sufficiently clear way so that we could really understand our participants. *It did not occur to us that our participants might choose not to be understood and that ambiguity might be essential to their complex presentations of self and identity.* We have positioned young women as knowable, but they may choose not to be known. We have positioned young women as people to be empowered by us through a process of making their voices heard, their positions understood. They may resist this positioning—by resisting our moves to empower them or by taking up powerful positions with no regard to our intervention.

Our reexamination of the research process has shown us that ambiguity is key not only to the negotiation of power within the interview (in that participants decide when to let us in and when to deflect our questions and leave their responses unintelligible), but also to the negotiation of identity through clothing practices and talk about clothing practices. It should come as no surprise that young women find negotiating a sartorial identity simultaneously a source of anxiety and of pleasure, given the close interconnections among clothing, femininity, and sexuality. It should also come as no surprise that, as researchers, we find it difficult to pin down what identities women are trying to achieve with their clothing choices when ambiguity is a crucial means for women to negotiate their way through contradictory identities as women who are attractive without actively seeking admiring glances, who are sexual but not too sexual, and who are clothed without deliberately creating a look.

We began by thinking that our role was to empower our participants, to understand, and to ensure that their viewpoints were heard. They did not necessarily accept this positioning, and used ambiguity in dress and language to retain for themselves a more powerful position. Ambiguity may not reflect a lack of clarity, but it may be a powerful resource which allows women to negotiate meaning and position.

Notes

1. Both Bristol and Cardiff are large, multicultural cities. Bristol is in the southwest of England; Cardiff is in South Wales and is the capital city of Wales.
2. In Britain punks tend to dress in shocking and sexually explicit clothing which makes reference to anti-consumption and to culturally embedded sexual icons. Goths tend to wear dramatic, dark-colored clothing which evokes Victorian period dress. Hair color is often black; makeup is usually vivid, with much use of white face makeup, and black eye makeup and lipstick.
3. When our interviewees talk about going "clubbing," they are referring to going dancing in nightclubs, which they are not legally allowed to enter until eighteen years old.
4. "Pulling" or being "on the pull" can be understood as a slang term for going out with the intention of meeting, "picking up," or attracting attention from (in this case) men.
5. By using the term "pervs," Jane is referring to men who show an inappropriate, salacious, and voyeuristic interest in her.

References

Barnes, R., and Eicher, J.B. (eds.). (1992). *Dress and Gender: Making and Meaning*. Oxford: Berg.
Davis, F. (1992). *Fashion, Culture and Identity*. London: University of Chicago Press.
Eicher, J.B. (2001). "Dress, Gender and the Public Display of Skin." In J. Entwistle and E. Wilson (eds.), *Body Dressing*. Oxford: Berg.
Entwistle, J. (2000). *The Fashioned Body: Fashion, Dress and Modern Social Theory*. Cambridge: Polity Press.
Fine, M. (1992). *Disruptive Voices: The Possibilities of Feminist Research*. Ann Arbor: University of Michigan Press.
Fine, M. (1994). "Working the Hyphens: Reinventing Self and Other in Qualitative Research." In N.K. Denzin and Y.S. Lincoln (eds.), *Handbook of Qualitative Research*. London: Sage.
Freitas, A., Kaiser, S., Chandler, J., Hall, C., Kim, J.-W., and Hammidid, T. (1997). "Appearance Management as Border Construction: Least Favorite Clothing, Group Distancing and Identity...Not!" *Sociological Inquiry* 67 (3): 323–335.
Frith, H. (1998). "Constructing the 'Other' Through Talk." *Feminism and Psychology* 8 (4): 530–536.

Harris, A. (2001). "Revisiting Bedroom Culture: New Spaces for Young Women's Politics." *Hecate* 27 (1): 128–138.

Hebdige, D. (1979). *Subculture: The Meaning of Style*. London: Methuen.

Lurie, A. (2000). *The Language of Clothes*. New York: Holt and Company.

McClean Taylor, J., Gilligan, C., and Sullivan, A. (1996). "Missing Voices, Changing Meanings: Developing a Voice-centred, Relational Method and Creating an Interpretive Community." In S. Wilkinson (ed.), *Feminist Social Psychologies*. Buckingham: Open University Press.

Opie, A. (1992). "Qualitative Research, Appropriation of the 'Other' and Empowerment." *Feminist Review* 40: 52–69.

Pomerleau, A., Bolduc, D., Malcuit, C., and Cossette, C. (1990). "Pink or Blue: Gender Stereotypes in the First Two Years of Life." *Sex Roles* 22: 359–367.

Renzetti, C.M., and Curran, D.J. (1995). *Women, Men and Society*. Boston: Allyn and Bacon.

Williamson, M. (2001). "Vampires and Goths: Fandom, Gender and Cult Dress." In W.J.F. Keenan (ed.), *Dressed to Impress: Looking the Part*. Oxford: Berg.

CHAPTER **10**

Talking Sexuality Through an Insider's Lens: The Samoan Experience

ANNE-MARIE TUPUOLA

We are required to walk our own road—and then stop, assess what we have learned, and share it with others. It is only in this way that the next generation can learn from those who have walked before them.... We can do no more than tell our story. They must do with it what they will.

(Sisulu 1995, cited in Ramphele 1995: xi)

Popular images and narratives of the sensuous Polynesian female danger-ously obscure and mask the unspoken challenges and complexities of female sexuality in Pacific contexts (Sua'ali'i 2000). The common and somewhat dated associations of the South Pacific as a place of "free love" and the South Pacific female as promiscuous, exotic, and erotic minimize the stringent codes of conduct many of these females face as they develop their sexualities (Tupuola 1994, 2000). I am mindful of the plethora of lit-erature and studies about the Samoan female and the impressions they give, whether intentional or not, of ongoing perceptions and assumptions about sexuality in Samoan societies. The sexual development of the young Samoan female is commonly discussed within the context of universal adolescent theories, while Mead's portrayal of the Samoan girl as sexually free and permissive remains a popular narrative and stereotype of the Samoan female adolescent and sexuality (Côté 1994; Freeman 1983; Holmes 1987; Mageo 1998; Mead 1943; Schoeffel 1995; Shore 1981). While a lot of literature about the Samoan female has been useful in mak-ing sense of the Samoan culture and the complexities of sexuality for the

Samoan female, very few of the works ask the Samoan women themselves or include the voices of the Samoan female in their arguments and perspectives. Furthermore, it is not very often that literature or texts about Samoan female sexuality are written about or discussed publicly by the Samoan female (Tupuola 1994, 1998).

During my own undergraduate and graduate years studying adolescent development, I was introduced to texts that discussed Western and, in many instances, American adolescent experiences. These texts referred to universal adolescent processes that were far removed from my own developmental process as a young Samoan woman (Adelson 1980; Bernard 1969; Clarke-Stewart et al. 1988; Lerner 1986; Santrock 1987; Sebald 1984). Many of the common academic perceptions about American female sexuality seemed to emphasize personal and social independence, sexual experimentation, and sexual maturity. This led me to ask: Are adolescent stages of development, in particular sexual experimentation and sexual maturity, attainable stages of development for young Samoan women? Are Western and American models of adolescent sexuality useful in understanding the experiences of the young Samoan female? This cross-cultural approach to female sexuality proved challenging because of the taboo nature of the topic in Samoan contexts as well as the reluctance of Samoans in general to speak publicly about their private realities.

My postdoctoral research in the United States has enabled me to meet and converse with American youth as well as gain access to diverse texts and narratives by these youth themselves. These narratives are critical because they challenge my own reliance on popular adolescent textbooks to understand American female sexuality. Thus, my journey as researcher is complex and challenging as I revisit my own stereotypes about adolescent American female sexual development and begin to make sense of Samoan female sexuality within global contexts.

This chapter explores the complexities of Samoan female sexuality within global contexts. It does so by first examining Western narratives of female sexuality with specific attention to the United States. What do these narratives convey about sexuality, and do they relate to the realities of the young Samoan female? Second, this chapter will discuss the way young Samoan women make sense of their own sexuality. Is sexuality openly discussed in Samoan contexts? Are young Samoan women encouraged to explore their own sexualities? The third objective is to analyze Samoan female sexuality through a global lens. Are the master narratives of adolescent female sexuality commonly associated with American adolescents useful in making sense of the Samoan female sexual experience? Do the experiences of the American and the Samoan female overlap, or are there significant differences?

I approach this discussion through a personal lens, reflecting on my own complex journey in researching Samoan female sexuality. The reference I make to "insider" in the title is reflective of my fluid and transient identities and "homelands." As a New Zealand Samoan I view female sexuality in diverse contexts, mindful of the increasingly shifting identities of young Samoan women. My current location in the United States enables me to move beyond the textbook to make sense of, on many levels, the complex experiences of the American female adolescent as she reaches sexual maturity. Therefore, "insider," in this context, is not used to essentialize young Samoan and American female sexual developments but, rather, to establish the context from which my observations and insights stem.

I begin my discussion of Samoan female sexuality with a small selection of narratives by American female adolescents. How do they perceive female sexuality? Are they as sexually independent as I assume them to be? Following this, I turn to the voices of young Samoan women as they talk about their sexuality. Do their experiences relate to those of their American female peers? How do both groups make sense of their own sexualities? Finally, I reflect on my own challenges as an "insider" researcher as I continue to make sense of Samoan female sexuality within contemporary contexts:

> Social science should indeed go out into the world but with only a desire to listen and participate. One must bracket one's former understanding about particular social phenomena and attempt to understand these processes from the point of view of the experiencer. (*Kellehear 1993: 27*)

Talking Sexuality in U.S. Contexts

Sexuality can have a variety of meanings, depending largely on the cultural context (Hammonds 1999; Price and Shildrick 1999; Rose 2001). In many popular Western developmental texts, sexuality and sexual identity are considered universal phases of adolescence marked by physiological changes, sexual curiosity, sexual engagement, and sexual experimentation (Adelson 1980; Lerner and Spanier 1980; Matteson 1975; Santrock 1987). These theories seem to reflect the sociocultural conditions of the young Western male and fail to acknowledge the different experiences of the female adolescent (Gilligan 1988, 1990, 1993). Consequently, an increasing number of feminist theories of adolescence have emerged in the United States, drawing clear differences between male and female adolescent sexual development. While they do make critical contributions to the body of adolescent literature, some seem to essentialize female sexuality and assume sexual maturity to be a universal stage, attainable for all young women. The following narratives are taken from texts that were recommended to me by American teenagers in New York. The comments are by American female adolescents themselves, and relate specifically to female sexuality and the different cultural boundaries surrounding this. These narratives are from only a small selection of a multitude of texts by American youth and are not meant to speak for all American adolescent females. The following excerpts are by young women of varied cultural backgrounds (Caucasian, Chinese, Latino) as a way of de-essentializing the American female adolescent experience.

According to Danitcat (1997), it is important for young people to express their realities in a form comfortable to them. In her view, it seems imperative that youth "break the silence" that surrounds them, examine their lives closely, and "invite others to do the same" (Danticat 1997: xii). The first young woman I refer to is Latrice Davis, a seventeen-year-old who writes about her sexuality in the text *Starting with I.* Latrice associates sexuality with risk-taking behavior, having a boyfriend, and pregnancy. The dilemma that Latrice faces is the ongoing pressure for her to have a boyfriend and the ongoing social and cultural expectation for her to be dating at her age. Latrice says, "My mother, for example, is always bugging me about it. On any particular Saturday night she'll say, 'Tricey, when I was your age, I used to have boyfriends galore'" (Davis, cited in Estepa and Kay 1997: 104).

This experience contrasts with that of a young woman who relates sexuality to sexual experimentation. Her story refers to the "prom" as a sexual rite of passage. She says, "It was a crazy night...others lost their virginity like me. I look back on it and I remember how special it was...I don't regret it" (anonymous, cited in Best 2000: 66). In the book *The Freedom Writers Diary* a young woman alludes to the cultural boundaries associated with sexuality. This fourteen-year-old talks candidly about her intimate relationship with her boyfriend, her parents' anger, and the age specificity associated with female sexuality. In her words:

> They [her parents] kept telling me that I couldn't see my boyfriend ever again. They put me on restriction.... Finally, my parents decided that I could be with my boyfriend under one condition. That my boyfriend and I waited until I turned fifteen (this is a tradition from my culture, indicating that when a girl turns fifteen, she is a woman and mature enough to take serious responsibilities). **(Diary 17, cited in The Freedom Writers 1999: 37–38)**

Loretta Chang, eighteen years of age, further elaborates on the cultural boundaries of sexuality. Her experience points to cultural and gender misinterpretations of female sensuality:

> Some jerk threw a Snapple bottle at me while I was crossing a Manhattan street ... all I saw was a group of guys standing around, smiling and saying, "Look at her, look at her."... At home that night I told my mother about what happened. I was expecting her to comfort me. Instead ... she said to me, in her Chinese accent,...'Because of what you wearing. It's too sexy.'" (*Chang, cited in Estepa and Kay 1997: 110–111*)

These diverse views associate sexuality with sexual experimentation, sensuality, risk-taking behavior, and sex and intimacy within heterosexual contexts. The following comment captures the reality of a young gay female, the challenges of coming out, as well as the risks of going against the "normative" perceptions of adolescent sexuality. Gina Trapani, seventeen years old, explains:

> I didn't know of anyone else in the world who was gay or had even questioned herself...I felt very left out because I didn't have a boyfriend.... It was and still is very frustrating for me to have to live a lie out of fear of other people's reactions (*Trapani, cited in Estepa and Kay 1997: 127–128*)

A similar view is shared by another young teenager as she comes to terms with her lesbianism. She says, "I realized I was a lesbian recently.... After coming to terms with who I am, I had so many questions.... Would we still be welcomed in our little social group? What will our families do when they find out?" (Diary 127, cited in The Freedom Writers 1999: 244–245).

These young women's experiences capture sociocultural expectations associated with being an adolescent as well as the different ways the individual female makes sense of her sexual identity. Many of the young women speak candidly about their sexual experiences and share their private worlds as they search for their sexual identity. Some are openly critical of the sociocultural norms and familial expectations they need to adhere to, and are mindful of the challenges they face if they do not conform. These narratives begin to challenge my own stereotypes of the American female adolescent. The stories remind me that young women in American societies face cultural and social restrictions and the pressure to conform to prescribed stages of sexual development commonly found in Western and American adolescent textbooks. As I begin to listen to these youth, my own tendencies to homogenize the American female sexual experience and to draw binaries between the Samoan and American female adolescent reality become questionable.

In revisiting and challenging my own theoretical assumptions and preconceptions of sexuality and the young American female adolescent, it is also necessary to reflect on my own studies of young Samoan women. In particular, it seems critical to self-reflect on the complexities and challenges of researching female sexuality within Samoan contexts.

Making Sense of Sexuality: Samoan Contexts

> Samoa is a group of Pacific Islands located in the heart of Polynesia. It comprises ... two main islands and is situated approximately halfway between Hawaii and New Zealand.... The total population is 182,000 of which 35,000 live in and around Apia ... the administrative and commercial capital on the island of Upolu.... When it gained its independence in 1962, Samoa earned the distinction of being the first independent sovereign state in the South Pacific.
>
> (See Lemisio 2000)

The Samoa that Lemisio refers to does not capture the ongoing migratory flow of Samoans to New Zealand. According to the 2001 census, the Samoan population of 115,017 accounted for over 50 percent of the

Pacific Islands population in New Zealand, and over 50 percent of Samoan youth were born in New Zealand (Statistics New Zealand 2001). The shifting identities of this predominantly youthful diasporic Samoan population in New Zealand are shaped by local New Zealand, indigenous Samoan, and global popular and youth cultures (MacPherson 1996; Tupuola 1999).

This section provides a glimpse of the Samoan culture and the experiences of the young Samoan female, and cannot be generalized for all Samoan societies or young Samoan women. For the purpose of this chapter I refer to a small selection of narratives that reflect the shifting identities of my research participants and their diverse experiences. It is my intention to identify the pivotal role of the *aiga* (family, both immediate and extended) and *fa'aSamoa* (the Samoan culture) as the young women make sense of their sexualities in different Samoan contexts.

Talking about sexuality in traditional Samoan societies is generally taboo. The discussion of one's private life is not always encouraged for fear of tarnishing the honor and name of the *aiga*. The role of the young woman is especially intricate and important in some traditional Samoan communities because her demeanor, behavior, and sexuality tend to reflect upon the honor of her family. It is common for some women to have male relatives protect them and to ensure that the opportunity to experiment sexually before marriage is minimized. The young woman is usually also expected to accept certain cultural codes of conduct, and seems obligated to do so with reverence, honor, and respect (see Tupuola 2000). My own writing and talking about Samoan female sexuality are challenging. I risk being ostracized from the Samoan community and face possible reprimand from some *aiga* members for not adhering to certain Samoan codes of conduct and for providing the space for young Samoan women to talk about their private worlds in confidence.

The young Samoan women I refer to here were participants in my master's and doctoral studies (Tupuola 1993, 1998). They range in age from fourteen to thirty years, are born in Samoa or New Zealand/Aotearoa, and come from a mix of traditional extended family households, urban single-parent homes, and nuclear family settings. Irrespective of their differing backgrounds, many were apprehensive about discussing anything related to sex for fear of reprimand, and were concerned about being recognized by their families and Samoan peers. Thus, unlike some of their American peers earlier in this chapter, all women asked to remain anonymous, and while many of them were willing to share their experiences, they were still mindful of the taboo nature of our conversations. Thus every effort was made to mask the true identity of these women so their stories can be shared publicly:

> I think I was a little reluctant to talk about sex at first … but it was neat how we could look at the text … to make sure our ideas weren't misinterpreted.… I felt

privileged participating in this research ... it was well prepared and sensitive to my and other women's needs. (*Sixteen-year-old New Zealand Samoan*)

When I asked the participants about their sexual developmental processes, some of the women from traditional Samoan households and societies had difficulty making sense of their own sexuality. These women, who were either born in Samoa in rural districts or raised in New Zealand in extended family households, seemed to associate sexuality with the expectations of their families at the expense of their own needs. One participant, born in Samoa, says: "I don't know what sexuality means ... I've just learned what a period is ... I got it recently and had no clue what was happening to me. Um, my *aiga* never talked about sex, and everything I do is shaped by my *aiga* (fifteen-year-old Samoan). An eighteen-year-old participant, born and raised in New Zealand, elaborates on this view. She says:

If you're a Samoan girl, you don't have any control of your feelings and behavio[r] ... my sexual feelings were there but I couldn't express it.... I kept it hidden and it was driving me crazy, but it was better than getting a hiding or embarrassing the name of my parents.

What these comments briefly capture are some of the sociocultural, psychological, and emotional constraints some participants face as they try to negotiate their sexuality within the context of their family (see Tupuola 2000). While these experiences may not be true for all young Samoan women, the little knowledge some of these participants had about their own bodies was concerning, as was their need to mask their sexual feelings. One twenty-eight-year-old New Zealand Samoan concurs: "So, even though you ... get these sexual feelings ... *fa'aSamoa* [Samoan culture] ... can determine when it's permissible for the girl to explore sexually or to become sexually active. For me that wasn't until I got married and twenty-eight years of age." Some of these perspectives seem to reiterate the sociocultural constraints shared by their American peers earlier in this chapter. Both groups seemed to face pressure from their families as well as an expectation to conform to societal "norms" of adolescence. For some of the American young women there appeared to be pressure from family and peers to have a boyfriend and to experiment sexually. Interestingly, while some young Samoan women also faced pressure from their families (both immediate and extended), the reasons were somewhat different. Many families expected some participants, irrespective of their age, not to date or to have sexual experiences before marriage.

What about participants who had little Samoan influence in their lives and who lived predominantly Westernized lifestyles? Many participants in my doctoral pilot study talked about their desire to be sexually independent and were openly critical of Samoan expectations. Some participants used words like "I felt exploited," "unfair," and "claustrophobic," and considered these cultural constraints damaging to the psyche of the young Samoan female: "... you cannot control female sexuality, it's no longer a realistic expectation. For me to get away, I had to disgrace them [*aiga*]. I had to break the cycle …" (twenty-one-year-old born in Samoa). Similar critical sentiments were expressed by some of their American female peers in their comments. While some of the American female narrators were very confident about speaking out and venting their feelings to peers and family, some of the young Samoan participants "talked back" in a different way. Some young Samoan women considered suicide and pregnancy as ways to escape from their family expectations:

> I am twenty-seven years old, and I was not allowed a boyfriend … I would sneak out behind my parents' back and, yeah, I fell pregnant and that was my escape. I lost my *aiga* but I am a lot happier and I'm surviving without all the pressure. (*twenty-seven-year-old New Zealand Samoan*)

A twenty-year-old participant concurs:

> I did everything for my parents…. when I asked to go on one date recently, they went berserk and called me hurtful names. I couldn't take it anymore and ran away and tried to kill myself…. I didn't care about their hono[r] anymore…. I wanted to punish them. (*twenty-year-old born in Samoa*)

Interestingly, a lot of the participants defined sexuality within the confines of their families and the Samoan culture. Very few, unlike their American female peers, talked about sexuality in relation to their friends, leading me to ask how they viewed sexuality within the context of their own peer groups. Some participants wanted to be, in their own words, "sexually independent" and "sexually liberated" as their *papalagi* (European) female friends appeared to be: "I watch my *palagi* friends at school and they are just so lucky … their parents allow them to date, to have a boyfriend and they seem so happy and independent" (sixteen-year-old New Zealand Samoan). Others, who had, in their words, "liberal views of female sexuality" supported friends who dated and did not consider sexuality to be a big issue: "I don't think sexuality is such an issue with my friends, some of us date, some don't and it's no big deal" (seventeen-year-old New Zealand Samoan).

This open-mindedness was tested when I showed these participants a video clip from a documentary aired on New Zealand television. This specific clip was of a young Samoan woman discussing her lesbian identity. Her experiences of coming out were similar to those of her lesbian American peers in this chapter, especially the labeling she faced from the wider community. The responses by the research participants were not as supportive as those made toward their heterosexual peers and their comments became judgmental, as seen in the following:

> The video was cool, but I was put off by that one of the Samoan girl talking about a lesbian—I thought that was really rude, her talking about that stuff on camera. I personally don't think it's normal, it's against my religious beliefs, and

I found her offensive ... seeing a Samoan lesbian was really strange. (*seventeen-year-old New Zealand Samoan*)

How disgusting, this Samoan woman is giving a bad name to all Samoans, and anyway there's no such thing as a Samoan lesbian, it's just so unnatural and evil, I'm just so disgusted with this whole sexuality thing, it's evil, unnatural, and she will get punished. (*eighteen-year-old New Zealand Samoan*)

These homophobic comments seem to capture the negative responses both young American women feared and talked about in their narratives. How will they come out to their families and peers? Will they be accepted in wider society? What these comments also reiterate are the limiting ways some Samoan and American youth define sexuality. Why do most narratives about adolescent sexuality emphasize heterosexuality? Is there room for young gay women to talk about their sexual identity in both Samoan and American contexts? These questions deserve further exploration so that young gay women feel safe and comfortable enough to come out and speak out about their own sexual identities with confidence.

In reflecting upon my own attempt to make sense of female sexuality, I cannot ignore the shifting position and stances I need to take as researcher. My own skepticism about adolescent development textbooks in my graduate years led me to explore the realities of American female adolescents further. This process was fruitful as I began to challenge my own stereotypes of the young American female. When I continue to compare their realities with those of the young Samoan female, my approach needs to move beyond simplified cross-cultural binaries to acknowledge the heterogeneous makeup of both groups. Therefore, as I begin to make sense of Samoan female sexuality in the new millennium, it is essential to acknowledge the increasingly global and transient identities of young Samoan women and the seeming overlap (of the sociocultural and developmental expectations associated with heterosexuality) between the American female adolescent and the young New Zealand Samoan female realities. Thus it seems necessary to research Samoan female sexuality in less isolation and within theoretical and methodological frameworks that are mindful of female experiences globally.

My journey as an insider researcher has been complex and challenging as I attempt to make sense of female sexuality in this current era. The excerpts that I include from both the young American and the young Samoan females are only a snapshot of the diverse ways both groups search for their sexual identity. Their responses are not intended to speak for all American and Samoan women, but rather to show how my own assumptions and biases regarding these groups have been disrupted. Through my own self-reflective voyage I hope that my own generation and those to come have the courage to speak out so that sexuality is defined and shaped by the individual woman. Future research about Samoan female sexuality (both heterosexual and homosexual) can no longer be conducted out of context, and must begin with the voice of women themselves. Furthermore, it seems critical that dialogue about female sexuality is not made in isolation but, rather, in collaboration with local, cross-cultural, and global contexts and female populations.

References

Adelson, J. (ed.). (1980). *Handbook of Adolescent Psychology.* New York: John Wiley.

Bernard, H. W. (1969). *Readings in Adolescent Development.* Scranton, Penn: International Textbook Co. Inc.

Best, A.L. (2000). *Prom Night: Youth, Schools, and Popular Culture.* New York: Routledge.

Chan, L. (1999). "Tired of Being a Target." In A. Estepa and P. Kay (eds.), *Starting with I: Personal Essays by Teenagers,* 110–113. New York: Persea Books.

Clarke-Stewart, A., Perlmutter, M., and Friedman, S. (1988). *Life Long Human Development.* New York: John Wiley & Sons, Inc.

Côté, J. (1994). *Adolescent Storm and Stress: An Evaluation of the Mead–Freeman Controversy.* Hillsdale, N.J.: Lawrence Erlbaum Associates.

Danticat, E. (1997). "Foreword: In the Face of Silence." In A. Estepa and P. Kay (eds.), *Starting with I: Personal Essays by Teenagers,* xi–xiv. New York: Persea Books.

Davis, L. (1997). "Single and Lovin' It." In A. Estepa and P. Kay (eds.), *Starting with I: Personal Essays by Teenagers,* 103–105. New York: Persea Books.

Desetta, A., and Wolin, S. (eds.). (2000). *The Struggle to Be Strong: True Stories by Teens About Overcoming Tough Times.* Minneapolis: Free Spirit.

Estepa, A., and Kay, P. (eds.). (1997). *Starting with I: Personal Essays by Teenagers.* New York: Persea Books.

The Freedom Writers. (1999). *The Freedom Writers Diary: How a Teacher and 150 Teens Used Writing to Change Themselves and the World Around Them.* New York: Main Street Books.

Freeman, D. (1983). *Margaret Mead and Samoa: The Making and Unmaking of an Anthropological Myth.* Canberra: Australian University Press.

Gilligan, C. (1988). *Mapping the Moral Domain: A Contribution of Women's Thinking to Psychological Theory and Education.* Cambridge, Mass.: Harvard University Press.

Gilligan, C. (ed.). (1990). *Making Connections: The Relational Worlds of Adolescent Girls at Emma Willard School.* Cambridge, Mass.: Harvard University Press.

Gilligan, C. (1993). *In a Different Voice: Psychological Theory and Women's Development.* Cambridge, Mass.: Harvard University Press.

Hammonds, E.M. (1999). "Towards a Genealogy of Black Female Sexuality: The Problematic of Silence." In J. Price and M. Shildrick (eds.), *Feminist Theory and the Body: A Reader,* 93–104. New York: Routledge.

Holmes, L.D. (1987). *Quest for the Real Samoan: The Mead/Freeman Controversy and Beyond.* South Hadley, Mass.: Bergin & Garvey.

Kellehear, A. (1993). *The Unobtrusive Researcher: A Guide to Methods.* Sydney: Allen & Unwin.

Lemisio, T.I. (2000). "General Information About Samoa." www.samoa.ws/govtsamoapress.

Lerner, R.M. (1986). *Concepts and Theories of Human Development.* 2nd edn. New York: Random House.

Lerner, R.M., and Spanier, G.B. (1980). *Adolescent Development: A Life-Span Perspective.* New York: McGraw-Hill.

MacPherson, C. (1996). "Pacific Islands Identity and Community." In P. Spoonley, C. MacPherson, and D. Pearson (eds.). (1996). *Nga Patai: Racism and Ethnicity in Aotearoa New Zealand.* Palmerston North: Dunmore Press.

Mageo, J. (1998). *Theorizing Self in Samoa: Emotions, Genders and Sexualities.* Ann Arbor: University of Michigan Press.

Matteson, D.R. (1975). *Adolescence Today: Sex Roles and the Search for Identity.* Homewood, Ill.: Dorsey Press.

Mead, M. (1943). *Coming of Age in Samoa: A Study of Adolescence and Sex in Primitive Societies.* Harmondsworth: Penguin.

Price, J., and Shildrick, M. (eds.). (1999). *Feminist Theory and The Body: A Reader.* New York: Routledge.

Ramphele, M. (1995). *Across Boundaries: The Journey of a South African Woman Leader.* New York: Feminist Press/City University of New York.

Rose, T. (2001). "'Two Inches or a Yard': Silencing Black Women's Sexual Expression." In E. Shohat (ed.), *Talking Visions: Multicultural Feminism in a Transnational Age,* 315–324. Cambridge, Mass.: MIT Press, 2001.

Santrock, J.W. (1987). *Adolescence: An Introduction.* Dubuque, Iowa: Wm. C. Brown.

Schoeffel, P. (1995). "The Samoan Concept of *Feagaiga* and Its Transformation." In J. Huntsman (ed.), *Tonga and Samoa: Images of Gender and Policy,* 85–105. Christchurch: Macmillan Brown Centre for Pacific Studies.

Sebald, H. (1984). *Adolescence: A Social Psychological Analysis.* 3rd edn. Englewood Cliffs, NJ: Prentice-Hall, Inc.

Shore, B. (1981). "Sexuality and Gender in Samoa: Conceptions and Missed Conceptions." In S.B. Ortner and H. Whitehead (eds.), *Sexual Meanings: The Cultural Construction of Gender and Sexuality,* 192–215. Cambridge: Cambridge University Press.

Statistics New Zealand. (2002). *2001 Census of Population and Dwellings.* Wellington: Statistics New Zealand.

Sua'ali'i, S. (2000). "Deconstructing the 'Exotic' Female Beauty of the Pacific Islands." In A. Jones, P. Herda, and T.M. Sua'ali'i (eds.), *Bitter Sweet: Indigenous Women in the Pacific,* 93–108. Dunedin: University of Otago Press.

Trapani, G. (1997). "What Would You Do if I Was Gay?" In A. Estepa and P. Kay (eds.), *Starting with I: Personal Essays by Teenagers,* 126–128. New York: Persea Books.

Tupuola, A. (1993). "Critical Analysis of Adolescent Development: A Samoan Women's Perspective." Master of Arts thesis, Victoria University of Wellington.

Tupuola, A. (1994). "Who's Educating Whom? Complexities of Doing Innovative Research." Paper presented at Victoria University of Wellington Postgraduate Conference, Wellington, New Zealand.

Tupuola, A. (1998). "Adolescence: Myth or Reality for Samoan Women? Beyond the Stage-like Toward the Shifting Boundaries and Identities." Doctoral thesis, Victoria University of Wellington.

Tupuola, A. (1999). "Shifting Identities for Pacific Diasporic Youth in New Zealand: Research and Methodological Implications into the Twenty-first Century." In PIERC Education (eds.), *Educating Pasefika Positively.* Auckland: PIERC Education.

Tupuola, A. (2000). "Learning Sexuality: Young Samoan Women." In A. Jones, P. Herda, and T.M. Sua'ali'i (eds.), *Bitter Sweet: Indigenous Women in the Pacific,* 61–72. Dunedin: University of Otago Press.

CHAPTER **11**

Shifting Desires: Discourses of Accountability in Abstinence-only Education in the United States

APRIL BURNS AND MARÍA ELENA TORRE

Under the guise of protection from the "life-threatening" consequences of desire and sexuality, conservative and Christian Right movements in the United States have successfully set a national "abstinence-only-until-marriage" agenda under which school-based comprehensive sex education programs are evaporating while abstinence-only programs flourish. Unprecedented funding by the Bush administration (up 3000 per cent since 1996—the year federal funding for all comprehensive sex education ceased) currently supports over 700 abstinence programs that preach the "sex can wait" gospel across all fifty U.S. states, and more than a third of U.S. high schools teach abstinence until marriage (Dailard 2000; Corinna and Blank 1997/2003; Rosenberg 2002). Each of these programs must adhere to a strict eight-point definition that requires teaching that "sexual activity outside of the context of marriage is likely to have harmful psychological and physical effects" and "bearing children out of wedlock is likely to have harmful consequences for the child, the child's parents and society."[1]

Abstinence-only programs must promote abstinence as the only sure way to prevent pregnancy and disease, and mention condoms and contraception only in the context of their potential for failure; they are forbidden by federal law to promote or endorse condom use. While the focus of this conservative agenda is largely domestic, the impact reaches far beyond U.S. borders as abstinence and anti-abortion policies also

127

shape international reproductive health services offered to teenagers that are supported by U.S. dollars (Sengupta 2002). According to the *Washington Post* (June 29, 2003), a third of President Bush's $15 billion Global AIDS Bill is earmarked for the promotion of abstinence.

The current attack on comprehensive sexuality education programs in the United States, and the simultaneous shift to abstinence-only curricula, threaten the development of young women's political self-determination, self-efficacy, and ability to effect meaningful social change, in part through the impoverishment of intellectual and sexual desire (Burns and Torre 2003). The harsh educational policy and practice that increasingly characterize schooling in the United States provide a fertile context for the growing abstinence-only movement. In fact, the discourses surrounding public education—those of accountability, standards, excellence (Mitchell 2003), and increasingly choice—have proliferated, and threaten to eclipse discourses of intellectual engagement. These same discourses of accountability, standards, excellence, and choice are also strategically deployed by the abstinence-only movement, most consequentially for young people of color and poor and working-class youth.

In the following pages we consider the ways in which the rhetoric of abstinence-only curricula is supported and co-elaborated by current educational discourse in general, focusing specific attention on the ways in which such discursive technologies contribute to a schooling process that is increasingly subtractive as it grows ever more regulated. The spreading dominance of discourses of moral standards and personal accountability are increasingly stratifying young people by race and class, and continuing to fuel a "missing discourse of desire" within public education (Fine 1988). Like Fine, we understand "missing" as an insufficiency or inadequacy of current discourses of girls' desire, rather than as absence or lack thereof. Indeed, as Anita Harris (2003) has argued, the popular discourse of girls' desire has proliferated, becoming ever more commercial and commodified—a shifting discourse that remains more a tool of discipline and control than one of liberation.

To explore these issues, we conducted focus groups with young women in New York City who work as teen advocates for a feminist reproductive health organization and community researchers, all actively engaged in the debates concerning young women's lives and sexuality education.[2] In addition, we analyzed empirical data from a large-scale participatory study on the achievement/educational opportunity gap, specifically individual interviews and a survey co-produced by youth, taken by 3799 young people in twelve racially integrated school districts in New York and New Jersey.[3]

In our initial conversations with young women, we found that a discourse of girls' sexual desire was not so much missing as it had become, in the words of poet Langston Hughes (1951/2001), "a dream deferred." Contrary to dominant stereotypes of poor and working-class girls of color as oversexed and promiscuous (Tolman 1996; Rios-Moore et al. 2003), in our discussions explicit comments about sexual desire were subordinated to desires for achieving immediate practical goals such as graduating from high school, finding "a good job," and securing "a nice home." Desire was understood to be a dangerous luxury, described by one group as "gravy"—a separate condiment that might enhance their lives, but with so little on their plates, who has time to worry over taste? And who can afford the steep price constantly threatened by abstinence groups—pregnancy, sexually transmitted infections, emotional scars, a life in ruins? As one young woman explained, "For most of us, because we are facing other challenges, that's not our top priority."

Desiring Excellence

The young women of color whom we spoke with repeatedly expressed their desires for success, relying heavily on a strong sense of personal responsibility and delayed gratification (of all desires) as strategies for personal and social success. Given their lived realities of limited social privilege, these strategies were experienced as the most available and seemingly viable. Further, many of the young women held extremely high standards of success for themselves. For example, the girls of color surveyed reported the desire to earn an advanced college or professional degree twice as often as their counterparts (male or female) did. Witness Sequoia, a young African-American woman, representative of many of the young women in our groups, in her tremendous sense of responsibility not only for her own well-being and success but also for that of her family and community, and in her faith that education will provide the tools she will need.

María: What do you desire?

Sequoia: One of my desires is to get an education, and to do something with my life, to be somebody and be able to take care of my family, you understand? To have money in the bank for my kids when I pass away. So even when I leave, I can know that my family is being taken care of. So one of my desires is to go to school and get my education and to do right, so that I can have all those things for my family, so when I think about desire in school, and work, it's all on the same level, because a job and my education are two things I need to fulfill my desire.

Sequoia's comments illustrate a deep coupling of responsibility and accountability, whereby her desires, no longer solely about her own pleasure, lash her to an increasing accountability to and for family, teachers, and community. This high-pressure combination increases the stakes of achievement and success, holding young women to nearly impossible standards of responsibility perceived to extend beyond their own lives and mortality. This experience is all too common for girls of color who reported the strongest commitment to school and community, with nearly 54 percent identifying their grades as a "very important" priority and nearly 62 percent identifying being socially conscious as important in their lives. Such "hyperresponsibility" carries with it consequences that can reach into adulthood, whereby many high-achieving young people are so accustomed to fulfilling the expectations of others that they sometimes become unpracticed at examining their own motivations and desires (Arnold 1995).

We hear a similar discourse of responsibility being laid on the world-weary shoulders of young women of color in educational discourse of academic standards and student accountability. Creating an "accountable" education system is the main priority of the 2001 No Child Left Behind Act. This federal legislation mandates that states establish standards of excellence, and then implement standardized tests as a means of making schools accountable for improving student achievement across race, ethnicity, and social class. Accountability is enforced by making federal funding directly contingent on test-based levels of achievement. Unfortunately, these punitive measures at the school level (for example, larger class sizes, lowered levels of teacher education/certification/experience, fewer resources, and lowered morale) are then passed on to students, with the most dire of consequences felt by those students in schools with the highest needs (Darling-Hammond 2001; Fine and Powell 2001).

The stakes that are increasingly attached to such test results (such as a diploma, grade or academic level, and, increasingly, school funding and teacher evaluation) have consistently been associated with increased drop-out rates (Fair Test/Mass.Care 2001; New York City Board of Education 2001), particularly for students of color, whereby more students are dropping out in earlier grades and during the year just prior to the high-stakes test (see Fine and Powell 2001; Haney 2001; Lee 2001; Mizell 2002). The young women we spoke with expressed a keen awareness of all that is riding on their individual success that was coupled with a profound understanding that their few opportunities to "do right" remain ever contingent and that their sexual desire can put them in jeopardy with just one slip. This multilevel consciousness produces what we've called "anxious achievement." Family and community investment, in terms of resources and emotional and material support, are often consciously, vicariously, and strategically allocated, adding further to the pressure of such achievement desires. The resultant high stakes fuel a heightened interest in working hard and getting good grades, creating a passionate desire to succeed academically—one flush with a potent mixture of hope and anxiety, fear and excitement—suggesting the creation of what might be referred to as an "erotics of achievement."

Inundated by "true life" stories of how easy it is to "lose everything" (see contest below), working-class girls and girls of color are constantly reminded of the fragility of their success. Dipping into the waters of sexual desire, they are repeatedly warned, will only lead them off-track and into disaster. Abstinence-only programs exploit these feelings of anxious achievement by capitalizing on the danger and extreme consequences of knowing and/or acting on sexual desire (Tolman 2002). They purposely create a climate of fear and anxiety so that youth can recognize the "safety" in "making the right choice" of disengaging their sexual desire. Take, for example, the Abstinence Essay Contest sponsored by the annual Healthy Mothers, Healthy Babies teen health fair at Eastside High School in Paterson, New Jersey, which offered prizes for artwork and essays that advised teens about the benefits of "avoiding sex" (Washburn 2002). That two of the three winners were pregnant suggests that not only were they headline fodder, but also ideal spokespersons to "save" other teens from a similar fate. Alicia Wilson, a pregnant junior and third-place winner, submitted a "searingly honest essay" in which she described how disappointed her family was "because I was the only one from my family who wanted to go to college to make something of myself, and they were counting on me" (Washburn 2002).

This is not to suggest that all the young women we spoke with were fully convinced of the dangers of sexuality. When one young woman described a poster in her school that warns, "Desire Is the Root of All Evil," she and her peers were deeply ambivalent, even critical, about the truth of such messages. However, all reported having been steeped in the terrifying consequences of engaging sexuality and desire. *Sex Respect* and government pamphlets like *Saving Sex for Marriage—Abstinence Is a Choice Worth Making* rely on dramatic "true stories" of "ruined lives" and graphic pictures of sexually transmitted infections in order to scare youth away from all forms of sexual activity—from "petting" to intercourse, and everything in between. Whether or not young women agree with the moral messages, the horror-filled images and portrayals of dire life outcomes have a lasting impact, as described in the following exchange:

> Martina: I was freaked out by it ... I had nightmares about having um, um, a parasite in my stomach ... like growing. I was, like, a baby's gonna suck the life out of me ... that would be the end of [my] life.... A lot of people are telling you it is, you believe it.... I remember seeing pictures of infested penises, and, like, vaginas that looked [like] there were mushrooms growing out of it ... and I was, like—ah,. the joys of pleasure, you know?! I was, like, no thanks, I'll pass ... that stuff works, it really does work.

> April: Do you think they do that [use scare tactics to teach] in other subjects?

> Terraneisha: They do that with testing, you must pass this or you won't graduate ... specifically in subjects when you have to pass a big test.... They pressure you into passing it, [you feel like] I have to do this, I have to do that—it doesn't help.

Terraneisha's concern is echoed in the data from the Educational Opportunity Study in which one in two of all the students of color surveyed worried that standardized tests could prevent them from graduating high school. The scare tactics deployed by the abstinence-only movement to limit girls' desire, ostensibly to prevent teenage sex, tend to mirror the punitive discourse and practices around high-stakes testing and zero-tolerance discipline policies—a connection that was not lost on the young women in our focus groups. And just as desire and sexuality are framed as inherently dangerous and "risky," so risk-taking in all its forms becomes generalized as unhealthy and danger-filled. This reframing of risk represents yet another loss for young women, as risk is an important element of innovation, the development of creativity as well as critique, and the ability to provide a basis with which young people can come to establish a sense of self-efficacy and trust in themselves.

Beyond the classroom, the abstinence-only agenda, like test-driven educational policies, comes with a different set of consequences for youth of color and poor and working-class youth, wherein the consequences for White, middle-class youth are not as damning, weighty, or long-lasting. The abstinence-only lobby actually structures specific kinds of risk-taking for differently positioned youth, by constricting the type, quality, and accuracy of the information that youth have access to about sexuality and reproduction (as is federally mandated) and by reducing the number of safe spaces where young people can practice negotiating and advocating for themselves sexually.

Attending a failing high school now means being placed "at risk"—of dropping or being pushed out of school, of enforced poverty, and of an increased likelihood of being involved with the criminal justice system (Fine et al. 2001; Poe-Yamagata and Jones 2000). Similarly, the absence of comprehensive sex education structures sexual risk-taking by facilitating sexual ignorance and naïveté in young people, most devastatingly for young people lacking the resources to ameliorate negative or unwanted outcomes. As Valerie Walkerdine and colleagues (2001) point out, working-class girls attempting to move out of their class position face tremendous, although perhaps unconscious, anxiety around their uncertain futures, highlighting the fact that these border crossers will have to go it alone and pay extremely high prices for their mobility. Ironically, then, the demonized and loudly trumpeted "consequences" of sexual risk-taking—getting pregnant, having a child—can sometimes offer up the safety of community and family. But, as demonstrated in the Healthy Mothers example, too often the trade-off is the dream of academic achievement, a career, and financial independence.

Accounting for Desire?

Inherent in the teachings of abstinence-only programs is an emphasis on individual responsibility and self-control. The coupling of moral standards and personal accountability in education operates in tandem with the agenda of the abstinence-only movement to establish desire as always unhealthy and inherently dangerous. Consider the flame-filled proclamations of *Sex Respect*, which caution youth to "Cool down the fire of your sexual desire—Wait for your permanent mate," and warn that "Sex before marriage—A quick way to lose at the game of life" (Mast 2001). Through the use of terror tactics and the withholding of accurate and pertinent information, young women are told by abstinence-only curricula that they alone are accountable for their choices—even in the absence of any real alternative or viable options. Consequently, when things "go wrong," the prescribed treatment for the ensuing shame and self-blame is "individual rehabilitation," which can be seen in the likes of "born-again virgins" and repenting young mothers (see truelovecanwait.org). Further, as public attention and responsibility are diverted away from the material, economic, and social conditions in which young women of color live, a spirit of individual change rather than social change is reinforced, and the potential for social activism is defused.

It appears, yet again, to be the troubling case that some youth are in fact held more accountable than others. Young women of color reported suspension rates nearly four times higher than their White and Asian peers, a disturbing finding, given the punishing trends in the larger U.S. context, wherein women of color are among the fastest-growing prison populations (Camp and Camp 2000). Consequently, pregnancy, disease, and the lack of academic success for youth with the fewest options all become coded in the public imagination as individual failures rather than as the social and political abandonment of young people. Indulging in desire (actively or not) is understood to be the reason for their failure, not the organization of schools, the absence of accurate information and presence of misinformation, the ideologies of merit and deservingness, or the distribution of human and material resources.

The structuring of anxious achievement—via high-stakes investment in success; hyper-responsibilization for self, family, and community; and self-blame—results in a reordering of the erotic, away from an erotics of the body as a site of pleasure and the self as sexually desiring, to an erotics of achievement and material success. Once again young women, particularly those of color and those who are poor or working-class, are made much more vulnerable than their White and middle-class peers. Only now, the irresistible smiling face that whispers promises in the dark is not so much the cute and cunning football player (though he still very much exists) as it is the seductive lie of equal opportunity and meritocracy perpetuated by a rigged educational system that takes it all back in the morning (see Fine and Burns 2003).

Leaving Something to be Desired

The long reach of the abstinence-only legislation is frighteningly illustrated by a recent lawsuit in Texas. Students, with the backing of the American Civil Liberties Union, sued their Houston high school for the right to hold Gay–Straight Alliance (GSA) meetings, having been denied permission to do so by the school administration (ACLU 2003). When the youth initially approached the school for permission to hold such meetings, they were told that they would have to conform to a newly created set of rules governing the establishment of new clubs that differed from the regulations for other noncurricular clubs. After resubmitting their "conforming" application, they were simply put on hold by school officials for months, a common tactic by schools discouraging the establishment of such groups.

The GSA was finally allowed to meet, but there were significant restrictions. As part of the settlement, youth are allowed to participate in GSA meetings only with their parents' permission, and they are not allowed to discuss sex at all. In fact, in order for the school to maintain its government funding, all discussion around sexuality must comply with the restrictive eight-point abstinence-only-until-marriage definition. In this instance, the abstinence-only agenda stretches far beyond a sex-education program implemented in public schools for the health of young people—it lands us squarely in Margaret Atwood's (1986) Gilead, where "gender-treachery" carries heavy costs. Forcing a gay-positive student group to forward the notion that sex outside of marriage is harmful to self and society, constitutes an actual harm to youth who identify as queer, who question their sexual orientation and/or gender roles, or challenge the institution of marriage. And this is an additional harm exacted on an already vulnerable school population.[4]

Gay–straight alliances can serve as educationally productive spaces by providing low-stakes environments for self-exploration—alternative spaces where youth can safely try on identities, challenge gender roles, question heterosexuality and traditional patriarchal values. They are places in which youth can take risks and reflect on their sexuality—what it means, how it shapes them, who they are, what they want and don't want. As Martina narrates below, these spaces are necessary but all too rare in public schools.

> Martina: I think that the fact that we had no place for people to discuss [sexuality] in a mature and open fashion, led to a lot of misunderstandings on the part of kids ... because adults are too afraid. Oh, "You can talk about it, but you can't talk about this, this, and this; you can't mention that, and you can't give them that." So that leaves out 75 percent of the conversation. Having half the conversation is sometimes worse than no conversation at all.

As publicly funded spaces for comprehensive conversations about sexuality and desire are increasingly shut down by the abstinence-only movement, many young people themselves have taken on the responsibility for creating such spaces for youth through peer education, Web sites (see http://sexetc.org), and zines (Harris 2001), often with the help and resources of women's health and community-based organizations. Having detailed the costs of deferring desire (Burns and Torre 2003), and described here the very local form of terrorism exacted by high-stakes educational policies and abstinence-only curricula on youth who dare to engage their sexual and intellectual desire, we raise now a site of possibility in a growing youth movement that is quietly moving through high schools across the United States: gay–straight alliances.

In our work in public schools, GSAs have proved to be fertile spaces for the development of social and political youth work, even beyond issues relating to sexuality. Hothousing the political/social consciousness of many of their members, GSAs are often the most diverse and political groups on campus. At one high school in New York state, GSA members, in this case mostly high-achieving young White women, organized the school's first diversity event, one that went beyond the generally benign cultural exchange around food and dance characterizing most diversity events. This event included student discussions on a broad range of issues, and featured speakers presenting on such topics such as the political context of U.S./Afghanistan relations, homophobia, and indigenous peoples' rights in the United States.

The vital activity of this GSA illustrates precisely the kind of social and political cross-pollination feared most by the abstinence-only movement. However, while GSAs offer a site of hope, we remain cautious as the political "victory" in Texas bears out Michelle Fine's (2003) recent warning: "When a progressive idea is paired, for 'political expedience' with a Right-wing agenda, the progressive element typically becomes the recessive gene (the maiden name?) and evaporates, over time, to a shell of itself." Indeed, the Texas GSA won its right to meet, forcing the school, and the nation at large, to acknowledge youth desire and sexuality; however, the abstinence-only agenda also won with its eight-point definition reframing these expressions of desire as harmful and something to protect youth from. We must hold, then, the worry that, when muzzled, the radical potential of GSAs, currently numbering 1000 in the United States alone, may shift from a means of subverting and destabilizing institutions such as marriage and heterosexuality, to a powerful means of protecting them.

We close with a call for action. While the conservative and Christian Right movements work hard to contain and eradicate spaces where desire and sexuality are acknowledged and embraced, those of us concerned with nurturing the sense of self-direction and intellectual and political initiative that emerges in these contexts, must work equally hard to protect and sustain them. As an extension of high-stakes educational policy, abstinence-only is not just an attack on desire—it is also a threat to critical intellectual engagement that supports young women's sense of entitlement, encourages self-advocacy, and informs potential political action.

Notes

The authors wish to thank Michelle Fine and Anita Harris for their helpful comments, and to acknowledge the generous support of the Rockefeller Foundation, the Spencer Foundation's Disciplinary Studies in Education grant at The Graduate Center, and the Leslie Glass Institute.

1. Welfare Reform Act of 1996 (P.L. 104-193).

2. The young women in the focus groups were African-American, Latina, Asian, and biracial, and ranged in age from sixteen to twenty-two.

3. The Achievement/Educational Opportunity Gap Study is a large-scale participatory action research project conducted with youth and researchers from the City University of New York, including Michelle Fine, Janice Bloom, April Burns, Lori Chajet, Monique Guishard, Yasser Payne, Tiffany Perkins-Munn, Kersha Smith, and María Elena Torre, with funding from the Rockefeller Foundation.

4. Students who describe themselves as gay, lesbian, or bisexual are more likely than their peers to report verbal and physical attacks and are also more than three times as likely to miss school because of feeling unsafe (Massachusetts Youth Risk Behavior Survey 1999. <http://www.state.ma.us/gcgly/yrbsf199.html>.)

References

American Civil Liberties Union (ACLU) "Texas School District Settles ACLU Lawsuit By Allowing Gay-Straight Alliance" March 5, 2003. Retrieved May 11, 2004, from the World Wide Web: http://www.aclu.org/news/NewsPrint.cfm?ID=12027.

Arnold, K. D. (1995). *Lives of promise: What becomes of high school valedictorians.* San Francisco: Jossey-Bass Publishers.

Atwood, M. (1986). *The Handmaid's Tale.* Boston: Houghton Mifflin.

Burns, A., and Torre, M.E. (2003). "Revolutionary Sexualities: Discourses of Desire in the Context of Abstinence-only Sex Education." *Feminism and Psychology.*

Camp, C.G., and Camp, G.M. (2000). *The Corrections Yearbook 2000: Adult Corrections.* Middletown, Conn.: Criminal Justice Institute.

Corinna, H., and Blank, H.(1994/2003). *A Calm View from the Eye of the Storm.* Scarlett Letters Online. Available at <http://www.scarletletters.com/current/041102_nf_hchb.shtml> (accessed May 26, 2003).

Dailard, C. (2000). 'Fueled by campaign promises, drive intensifies to boost abstinence-only education funds', *The Guttmacher Report on Public Policy* 3 (2). Retrieved May 11, 2004, from the World Wide Web: http://www.guttmacher.org/pubs/journals/gr030201.html

Darling-Hammond, L. (2001). Apartheid in American education: How opportunity is rationed to children of color in the United States, *Racial Profiling and Punishing in US Public Schools* (pp. 39–44): Applied Research Center.

FairTest: The National Center for Fair & open Testing. *Dropout Crisis Developing in Boston Middle Schools* (2002). Retrieved May 11, 2004, from the World Wide Web: http://www.fairtest.org/care/boston%20dropouts.html

Fine, M. (1988). "Sexuality, Schooling and Adolescent Females: The Missing Discourse of Desire." *Harvard Educational Review 58* (1): 29–53.

Fine, M. (forthcoming). "Desire: The Morning (or 15 Years) After." *Feminism and Psychology.*

Fine, M., and Burns, A. (2003). "Class Notes: Toward a Critical Psychology of Class and Schooling." *Journal of Social Issues, 59*(4).

Fine, M., and Powell, L. (2001). "Small Schools as an Anti-racist Intervention." In *Racial Profiling and Punishment in U.S. Public Schools,* 45–50. Oakland, Calif.: Applied Research Center. Available at <http://www.arc.org/erase/profiling_nr.html> (accessed March 14, 2003).

Fine, M., Torre, M.E., Boudin, K., Bowen, I., Clark, J., Hylton, D., Martinez, M., Missy, Roberts, R.A., Smart, P., and Upegui, D. (2001). *Changing Minds.* New York: The Graduate Center of the City University of New York.

Haney, W. (2002). "Ensuring Failure: How a State's Achievement Test May Be Designed to Do Just That." *Education Week:* July 10, 2002, 56–58.

Harris, A. (2001). "Dodging and Weaving: Young Women Countering the Stories of Youth Citizenship." *International Journal of Critical Psychology* , 4: 183–199.

Harris, A. (2003). "Forthcoming of Desire as Governmentality: Young Women, Sexuality and the Significance of Safe Spaces." *Feminism and Psychology.*

Hughes, L. (1951/2001). "A Montage of a Dream Deferred." In A. Rampersad (ed.), *The Poems: 1951–1967 (Collected Works of Langston Hughes)*. Columbia: University of Missouri Press.

Lee, V. E. (2001). *Restructuring high schools for equity and excellence: What works*. New York: Teachers College Press.

Massachusetts Youth Risk Behavior Survey. (1999). <http://www.state.ma.us/gegly/yrbsf1999.html.>

Mast, C.K. (2001). *Sex Respect: The Option of True Sexual Freedom*. A Public Health Workbook for Students. Homer Glen, Ill.: Respect, Inc.

Mitchell, K. (2003). "Educating the National Citizen in Neoliberal Times: From the Multicultural Self to the Strategic Cosmopolitan" *Transactions of the Institute of British Geographers. 28* (4): 387–403.

Mizell, L. (2001). Horace had it right: The stakes are still high for students of color. In T. Johnson & J. Emiko Boyden & W.J., Pittz (Eds.), *Racial profiling and punishment in U.S. public schools* (pp. 27–38). Oakland, CA: Applied Research Center. Retrieved May 11, 2004, from the World Wide Web: http://www.arc.org/erase/profiling.html

Poe-Yamagata, E., and Jones, S. (2000). *And Justice for Some*. Building Blocks for Youth Report. Washington, D.C.: Youth Law Center.

Rios-Moore, I., Allen, S., Arenas, E., Contreras, J., Jiang, N. and Threatts, T., with Cahill, C. (2003). *Makes Me Mad: Stereotypes of Young Urban Womyn of Color*. New York: Center for Human Environments, The Graduate Center of the City University of New York.

Rosenberg, D. (2002). "The Battle over Abstinence." *Newsweek,* December 9, 2002, p. 68.

Sengupta, S. (2002). "U.N. Forum Stalls on Sex Education and Abortion Rights." *New York Times,* p. A3.

Sex, Etc.: A Web Site by Teens for Teens. Available at <http://sexetc.org> (Accessed on June 30, 2003).

Stuever, H. (2003). "Viva Las Virgins!: Elvis Does the Abstinence Convention, but Only from the Waist Up." *Washington Post,* June 29.

Stuever, H. June 29, 2003 "Viva Las Virgins!: Elvis Does the Abstinence Convention, but Only From the Waist Up" *The Washington Post*. Retrieved May 11, 2004, from the World Wide Web: http://www.hankstuever.com/virgins.html.

Tolman, D.L. (2002). *Dilemmas of Desire: Teenage Girls Talk about Sexuality*. Cambridge, MA: Harvard University Press.

Tolman, D.L. (1996). "Adolescent Girls' Sexuality: Debunking the Myth of the Urban Girl." In Bonnie J. Leadbeater and Niobe Way (eds.), *Urban Girls: Resisting Stereotypes, Creating Identities,* 255–271. New York: New York University Press.

Walkerdine, V., Lucey, H., and Melody, J. (2001). *Growing Up Girl*. Houndmills, U.K.: Palgrave.

Washburn, L. (2002) '2 Pregnant Teens Win Abstinence Essay Contest', *The Record* (Bergen County, NJ) May 2, 2002, p. 103.

PART **4**
Popular and Virtual Cultures

Where My Girls At? Black Girls and the Construction of the Sexual

DEBBIE WEEKES

You talking so much sex But you nah tell the youts 'bout AIDS And you tell them 'bout consequence? No.... Tell me who you wants 2 know What, when, who, where Or how you do your ho?

(Ms Dynamite 2002)

Music has been a site of struggle and empowerment for women for many years, while simultaneously acting as an arena of degradation and oppression (Hollows 2000). Subcultural work from the 1970s onward has pointed to music, and the cultural groupings which emerge from it, as providing an important space for young people, particularly in their teenage years, although the relationship between young women and music has often been the focus (Hebdige 1979; McRobbie 1991; Thornton 1995). Not only has it acted as a medium for providing distance between young people and their parents, but it can also be used as a political tool and a voice for the dispossessed, in addition to the pleasurable escapism of modern-day pop. However, young African-Caribbean women, like many women, are engaged in an ambiguous relationship with the music they consume, and, with the increasing relevance and popularity of music videos, the sexualized images they view. This discussion will explore the way Black women negotiate the spaces created for them within certain musical forms and question why they continue to listen to, enjoy, and actively promote songs which portray them ambiguously. Importantly, through acknowledging the variety of both celebratory and derogatory imagery embedded within Jamaican ragga and African-American hip-hop and R'n'B, it will suggest that such musical effects on the construction of young female sexual selves enable Black girls to resist where they are placed in hierarchies of femininity. However, it will also be suggested that such resistance may only be temporary, limited to specific representations of Black girlhood.

Music has been theorized as deeply central to the identities and politics of African people throughout the diaspora (Gilroy 1993; Back 1996), and has been noted as an important means of understanding the political consciousness of Black women in America (Davis 1992). Music therefore can help young Black women and men come to a sense of their racial, gendered, and sexual selves, particularly in view of the variety of genres stemming from the Caribbean, America, and Africa. Since it is such an important medium, its construction of Black women as at once sexual and also oversexualized requires interrogation not least because of its importance to young teenage women, but also to preteenage women who occupy that ambiguous space between childhood and adolescence, and for whom sexualized imagery is partnered with teenage consumerism—beauty, fashion—and their attendant images of maturity and sexuality (McRobbie 1991).

The musical forms which are explored in this discussion do not conform to the dichotomy between rock and pop which characterized much feminist cultural criticism (McRobbie and Garber 1976), and neither are the ways that African-Caribbean young women consume hip-hop/ragga similar to the way fandom has been theorized in feminist research (Lewis 1992; Hollows 2000). Popular and other forms of modern music are central in the construction of the sexual, and hip-hop and ragga celebrate both the identities and the sexualities of African-American and African-Caribbean people. However, the positions taken up by young women in these sexual discourses are often problematic. Music which congratulates Black women for their sexual prowess creates a false sense of security for young girls exploring their sexual selves and, as is attested to here through research with a group of African-Caribbean young women, can expose the contradictions embedded within the relationship between masculinity and popular culture.

Research Method

This discussion is based upon an ethnographic study in the East Midlands, an area within the United Kingdom which, though consisting of a number of urban regions, is one of the more rural parts of England. Just under 40 percent of the population in the East Midlands live in small towns and villages of less than 10,000 people. The research upon which this discussion is based was an exploration of Black female subjectivity through a series of interviews with twenty-nine African-Caribbean girls aged twelve to sixteen. The city within which the girls lived and went to school was not heavily multicultural; people of Black Caribbean descent constituted only 3.4 percent of the local population. Indeed, fourteen out of the twenty-nine young women were selected from a small, mixed, voluntary aided (Church of England) school, and at the time of interviewing, they constituted the majority of Black females on the school roll.

The research explored the nature of Black female identity across a variety of social locations—in their roles as school pupils, youth club attenders, sound crew members,[1] and, in three cases, as young mothers—and both group discussions and face-to-face interviews were conducted in youth clubs, schools, and educational institutions for young mothers and mothers-to-be of compulsory school age. Data collection involved taped semi-structured and open-ended interviews, questionnaires, and field notes in order to explore the sorts of discourses within which the participants' identities were constituted, or which ideas around sexuality and music were fairly prominent. The way that these young Black women tended to inhabit masculine spaces, such as youth clubs and sound crews, was also explored through periods of participant observation. This provided a stark contrast to the way "traditional" femininities were experienced—as young mothers and through the representation of Black womanhood in music.

Ragga "Gyals" and Hip-hop B-Girls

The young African-Caribbean women who participated in my research were developing identities constituted out of the heterosexual scripts embedded within wider educational and relational discourses, and found themselves placed at the bottom of hierarchies of femininitiy which privileged Whiteness and derogated Blackness (Weekes 1997). The musical and other Black popular cultural forms that they drew on instead centered Blackness, in view of the importance of the Black rapper/DJ and the nature of the (Black) audience with whom they engaged in dialogue. Ragga music, a recent construction linked to more "melodious" reggae and emerging out of the rebelliousness of the ghetto DJ and/or "raggamuffin" (Noble 2000), is a cultural product which has permeated geographical boundaries between its original location (Jamaica) and those of its wider audience throughout the African diaspora.[2] In its representation of local identities, ragga reflects the class-specific tensions which exist between Jamaican (high) culture and (ghettoized) slackness, illuminating the processes through which ghetto culture has become imbued with sexual depravity.

Within this cultural context, respectability—morality/passivity/femininity—has an oppositional relationship to reputation— sexual virility/subversion/masculinity—and ragga, and the ghetto identitiy it speaks to, reflect (masculine) reputation through emphasis on sexuality (Cooper 1993; Noble 2000). Its lyrics often refer specifically to sexual boasting and the desire/derogation of the Black female body, causing concern both among the local Jamaican middle classes and across diasporic locations. This concern is quite specifically related to the historical associations between Blackness and deviance that both ragga and African-American hip-hop seem to promote (West 1993).

Hip-hop or rap, like ragga music, gives primacy to Black masculinized discourse and speaks to a largely masculine audience. Its messages oscillate between the crises which occur between young urban Black youth and police and the importance of remaining authentic and "real" lyrically in the face of popular commercialism (Boyd 1997). Rap has provided economic opportunity for many African-American young males, and as a result reflects not only the competitive toasting and boasting between artists which dominated early hip-hop, but also the economic disadvantage and nihilism which currently frame Black masculinities. However, rap is a broad genre, and West Coast gangsta rap[3] embraces discourses of sex and sexuality which have been criticized for their misogyny.

The academic response to this imagery has been diverse. The misogyny within some rap has been linked to the cultural conservatism of nationalism, elements of which are reflected in the music of artists such as Ice Cube (West 1993); as legitimizing violence against women (Ransby and Matthews 1993); and as adding to the Black male nihilism it claims to represent (Williams 1992). Alternatively, the lyrical abilities of rappers have been theorized as relatively harmless, where it has been suggested that they simply reaffirm historical Black oral practices of teasing, parody, or "signifying" (Dyson 1993; Lusane 1993); or that they reflect wider patriarchal gender relations (Rose 1992). However, the primacy of sexual conquest in older gangsta rap and in more modern, commercially successful rap[4] may rid the genre of its "emancipatory potential" (Back 1996: 207), evoking instead complex relationships between Black masculinity and femininity which, as will be shown below, can have problematic implications for young Black women.

Rationalizing Images of Sexuality

Noble (2000) has noted the discomfort Black women experience through their consumption of ragga music, which gives central space to Black female sexuality. Though there are historical associations between Blackness and sexuality, discourses of silence and shame surround the expression of Black female sexuality (Skeggs 1997; Noble 2000), which is linked as much to the tension between respectability and deviance (Weekes 2002) as it is to the contradictions between lived Black female experience and public imagery. Noble (2000) notes that the emphasis on respectability within images of Black womanhood arose precisely as a reaction to the oversexualized Black femininity within Eurocentric discourse. However, this places restrictions on Black female sexual expression and makes it increasingly difficult for Black women to create sexual spaces outside of both sets of stereotypes.

For younger Black women, the ability to create safe spaces outside of sexual stereotype is particularly hazardous. Sexual expression through musical consumption for some of these young women takes on a resonance similar to the way the female fans of popular boy bands were theorized as fantasizing sexual moments with objects of desire (McRobbie 1991). However, this process combines with the more sexualized discourses surrounding adolescence to which young Black women are subject within schools, youth clubs, and the street (Weekes 2002). The contradictions are revealed in the way they feel they are celebrated within music while censoring the consumptive responses of those women who are over-sexual and "slack."[5]

Bianca and Justine (both age fifteen) are members of the Supremes' sound crew, a group of individuals all enacting the role of the DJ, and they enjoy the lyrical content of ragga music despite the gendered ambiguities within it.

> Bianca: I said I don't mind about slack lyrics, I don't really listen to them, it's the ones what apply to me.
>
> [Justine starts singing a song to demonstrate.]
>
> Justine: Your body good!
>
> Bianca: [laughing] Yeah, them kind of songs, because my body's good! My body is good. It's not run-down.
>
> Justine: Because what they're chatting about is reality, 'cause it does happen. Say if they're cussing down people in the songs, how they're slack and they're dirty, sometimes it's true, 'cause you do meet people like that. Some of the songs relate to the slack women, some of the songs relate to the people with big … [vaginas] and all that … it is dirty-like, but I think it's true.
>
> DW: Some people say that slack lyrics degrade all women, so it makes all women look bad.
>
> Justine: No!
>
> Bianca: Women that say that are … the song probably applies to them, and they don't like it.

A hierarchy of femininities has been constructed by these young women in the way they have interpreted the messages within this music. Bianca is flattered by the way the male DJs congratulate her on the shape, size, and appearance of her body. The relevance of these constructions of Black womanhood relates to the gendered and racialized spaces Black women occupy in relation to White women and the dominant definitions of beauty which impinge upon their subjectivities. Bianca's reference to the nature of her body echoes the emphasis within ragga on the sizes of Black female bodies which subverts dominant beauty definitions of women who are both fair and slim (Noble 1996). Rose (1994) argues that rappers (and DJs) who construct gendered imagery around Black female bodies are redefining the notion of female beauty through a specific emphasis on, for example, Black women's behinds. This subverts dominant ideas of beauty which do not include Black women in relation to the color of skin or the shapes of their bodies.

These girls have also created a hierarchy of Black femininities as they recognize and are drawn into the madonna/whore discourse which lies at the heart of this lyrical construction of Black female sexuality, arguing that there are some women who are oversexual and deviant, and thus should be subject to censure. In creating such moral distances within this hierarchy, Black girls are positioned as attractive/desirable against those who cross the boundaries between alluring and animalistc sexualities. Interestingly, however, though within ragga the audience is Black and female, the targets of derision for the girls as consumers of this product are "raceless,"[6] in that the racial background of the sexually deviant woman is not made explicit.

However, the celebratory emphasis on the Black female body is tempered by the way Black bodies are lyrically dismembered in ragga music, through reference to the buttocks and genitalia (Noble 2000). In musically constructing Black female sexuality as animalistic and exotic, these lyrics then reinforce a stereotypical association that these young women may feel they have escaped. More important, it is the male gaze within which this music is situated which underlines the ambivalent relationship that these young women have to it. If we consider the way gender politics is played out within gangsta rap music, for example, where women are referred to as "hoes" and "bitches"[7]—derogatory terms which are again heavily sexualized—the message and its ownership appear clearer than the celebratory aspects of ragga. The response of the young women, however, is the same, as Francine and Rochelle, both fifteen reveal:

DW: Well, what about the way that some ragga artists talk about women, for example?

Francine: I don't think it's right, but then again, it don't bother me 'cause I know I'm not like that.

Rochelle: It depends how you take it; if you take it personally, then you won't like no music at all then, but … I mean, I know they call us bitches and everything, but I know I'm not a bitch, and you've just got to hope that if you meet somebody that they'll appreciate who you are and not what you are.

Nia, also fifteen, had similar views:

Nia: That's *bad,* that is, when you use them kinda language ..." you bitch and a ho" …not bad as in terrible, but I like it. It livens it up, when you're talking about your bitch and your ho. I only like it on the songs, but if they was calling me a bitch, I'd tell 'em that their mum's a sorry bitch for having them. No.

They've never said that to me. Kevin said it to us lot, but he just says it for a joke, he's just joking. He goes, "What you bitches and ho's saying?" I goes, "I'm not answering him cos he can't be talking to me."

Celebrations of female sexuality need to be placed within a context where the female is constructed as spectator (hooks 1994). Male ownership of these sexualized messages problematizes the role of female music consumers, as well as the female DJs and rappers who attempt to respond to the way female sexuality is musically portrayed. Young women may indeed feel that they are taking control over their own definitions of female sexual expression through rejecting parental and other authoritative discourses around appropriate feminine behavior, yet the lyrical celebration of female sexuality within the music they consume may still be constructed through a male gaze. Nevertheless, despite the psychic discomfort felt by these young women around their own investment in these lyrical constructions, there appears to be a sense of linkage between them and the Black male rappers and, indeed, fans on the basis of race. This can be explored through the relationship between female and male rappers/DJs.

Reconstructing the Sexual

Female rappers and ragga DJs are able to create responses to the ambiguous positioning of Black women within music within the public arena, and the nature of these responses varies. Some can make a distinction between sexual expression both in music and visually in music videos and open sexual invitations to males. Since they are clearly the owners and producers of these messages, the distinction is clear. However, women who appear as "side dressings" to the main musical message, such as the music video "booty queens," are not producing the messages and are "expendable" to male (either as rappers or as fans) desire (Rose 1994). Lil' Kim, a female rapper who writes her own music, does, however, also send out open invitations to males through her sexualization in song, yet at the same time makes the male viewer the sexual object. Lady Saw and Patra, female ragga DJs prominent in the 1990s, also drew heavily on objectifying their male audience.

These responses to masculinized containing of femininity in music have been problematized as simply reinforcing pornographic male fantasies, but Skeggs (1994) argues that sexuality is one of the few resources that can be used by working-class women, giving them self-worth and highlighting the power relations that restrain women.

In a similar vein, rappers such as BWP (Bytches with Problems)[8] and, more recently, Missy Elliot's 1999 single "I'm a Bitch," reappropriated the derogatory term applied to women, engaging in a discursive shift. But this reappropriation has not been completely successful as the take-up by women of the "bitch" discourse has been curtailed while its negative connotations persist within male rap lyrics. Many female rappers also address the complexities embedded within male and female relationships which can also reinforce the dominance of heterosexuality (Rose 1994). Black female rappers, however, acknowledge that if Black women choose heterosexual relationships, they as artists must address gendered issues on the basis of that choice (Skeggs 1994). Yet even those messages of sexual independence expressed by some female artists are at times interspersed with their financial demands on their partners, privileging male economic abilities over those of women.

The music of female rappers has been constructed as anti-sexist through the voice it gives to young women, but this implies there is sexism in all male rap. Rose (1994) acknowledges the hesitancy expressed by some female rappers to accept the label "feminist," especially in view of the complex interweaving of race and gender which links them as much to their male rap counterparts as to other women. The responsibility for contesting the public spaces so frequently dominated by men is readily achieved by the simple presence of female rappers, and their ability both to challenge perceptions of women in rap as well as to engage in dialogue with both male rappers and fans is important.

There do, however, remain important issues about the nature of these messages to very young and adolescent women and the extent to which they are able to subvert them. Here a group of much younger African-Caribbean women are subverting in their anger the imagery of Black women they have witnessed in the music around them. In their relative immaturity in comparison to Rochelle, Francine, and Nia quoted above, these young women show their wider understanding of the way they are positioned within sexist and oversexualized lyrics written and performed by male artists. Not only this, but there is the added factor of their inexperience with boys, and their apparent refusal at this stage in their lives to view boys as at all important to their identities.

Chantel, a thirteen-year-old member of a youth club's netball team, responded to an old ragga track by General TK (1993):

I spy

What do you spy?

Pretty little brown girl with a tight needle eye

I spy

What do you spy?

P-U-S-S-Y with a tight needle eye

DW: Chantel, how do you feel about them, slack lyrics?

Chantel: Well I don't really listen to it anyway ... I hear it ... because ... at home it's on, and I listen to that all the time. And it really gets on my nerves because I don't know why they have to sing songs like that. I mean, they can just sing some different songs .... Although me and my friend made up one.

DW: What's it about?

Chantel: [singing] I spy, what do I spy, B-U-D-D-Y about two inches high!

Chantel's reponse to General TK's desire for sexual intercourse with girls who are still virgins is to subvert his desire through referring to "buddy"—an old rap slang word for penis. In constructing "buddy" as small and inadequate, she both subverts male desire by replacing it with her own, while also rejecting it through parody. In response to the lyrical content of some of the ragga songs they had heard played on radios, these young women also recognized the problems embedded within the moral distancing displayed by some of the older girls previously quoted.

Chantel: Some of the songs are good and some of 'em are like criticizing Black women.

DW: In what way?

Chantel: Sexual ways.

DW: Would you dance to that music if you went to a party?

Chantel: Probably dance to it, but I wouldn't play it at home.

Nisha: It's degrading.

DW: Some of the girls in the [other group], when I asked them, said they think there are some slack women out there and it applies to them. Do you agree?

Chantel: What kind of slack women are they talking about?

DW: You know, they make songs [saying] girls shouldn't be promiscuous, sleep around.

Chantel: Well, if they're all sleeping around, they're not going to get a chance to listen to it, are they?

Nisha: I think there is [women who sleep around] but there's men who sleep around, and they don't do songs about men who sleep around.

Chantel: … it's usually the men who do the songs; you never see women doing them kind of songs. (youth club netball team members Chantel, thirteen, and Nisha, fifteen)

That their recognition of the dangers embedded in assuming oversexualized lyrics enables women to celebrate their sexualities is both refreshing and important, because they have linked themselves to the other young women who are positioned in this way, rather than enjoying their construction by men. Importantly, these comments illustrate the subversive relationship that young women can have with the music they consume, but it is also necessary to situate the responses of young women to the age period they inhabit. The diverse responses of some of the older girls presented here are clearly spoken within an age period where sexual activity among women of their ages is subject to parental, educational, and societal censure due to high rates of sexually transmitted infection and teenage pregnancy among their Black female peers. Thus the uncomfortable relationship between Black women and their sexuality which Noble (2000) describes clearly takes root in adolescence through girls inhabiting ambivalent sexual spaces where their power to define sexual identity through relating to cultural products is contested.

Conclusions

With the increasing popularity of music videos as one of the main ways of promoting music to audiences, the ability of Black women to ignore, subvert, or indeed simply enjoy the lyrics within the musical genres highlighted is made complex. These visual constructions of licentious, animalistic Black women complicate the distance young women can place between themselves as respectable music consumers and the sexually deviant/aggressive women whom they feel require censure in hip-hop and ragga. Clearly, however, though many issues are raised by the way the young women I have spoken to respond to these processes of sexualization, the relationship they have to the cultural product they consume is an active one. Indeed, there is a danger in promoting the idea that women consume simply and unquestioningly. The consumption of services and products has historically been gendered in the form of the female and placed both oppositionally and unequally against the notion of production as masculine (Hollows 2000). As consumers of both ragga and hip-hop, Black women, however, have a powerful position in the creation of musical cultures—the clothes they wear to reveal their bodies and the dances they create, particularly within ragga, subvert the power afforded to the male producers of the form. The male gaze within which their identities are constructed is thus gullible, played with by women on dance floors who simulate intercourse with invisible partners. Importantly, within such heterosexual spheres these invisible objects of desire can be either male or female (Noble 2000).

However, for the young women whose voices have been represented in this discussion, their lyrical construction as (over)sexual objects of male desire remain problematic. The possibilities of celebrating female sexual knowledges in the face of rising teenage pregnancy rates are hampered by the ambiguous messages about girlhood, objectification, sexuality, deviancy, and censure embedded within popular culture. Further, the subjectivities of Black males—especially the young Black males who listen to and buy the music, as well as the Black male artists themselves—need to be set within wider discourses in order to avoid pathologizing their construction. As hooks (1994) has argued, the sexism contained within gangsta rap is a reflection of values sustained within patriarchy. Though the musical discourses presented above were those most consumed by the young women in the sample, it is important to recognize that other musical forms produce gendered (sexual) subjectivities to similar degrees— the sexism portrayed within forms of British and American rock music has also been subject to media scrutiny (McRobbie and Frith 1991)—and these cultural productions are in no way unique in the imagery they portray. Neither is it the case that listening to rap and ragga is the preoccupation of all young African-Caribbean women. The rate at which certain forms of rap and R'n'B, and indeed ragga, which give primacy to the oversexual, have begun to dominate the British music pop charts, demonstrates that these debates are now as important to the subjectivities of White and Asian female fans as those of African-Caribbean girls. We also need to interrogate how the dichotomy of sexualization and innocence portrayed by teen pop music divas such as Britney Spears compares with the use of pole dancers and porn stars in music videos by rap veterans such as Snoop Doggy Dogg and Dr Dre.

The young women in this discussion continue to engage with contentious musical imagery because they are involved in a complex process of being constructed as sexual objects while "othering" and objectifying in order to create moral and psychic distance between themselves and the more questionable lyrics they listen to. It is clear that as music consumers, young women are as able as other music fans to select material from these musical discourses, while simultaneously discarding that which they feel to be irrelevant. This may be in the more problematic guise of othering those women whom they feel require the sexual censure within these musical lyrics, yet in so doing, these Black girls have placed themselves more positively within the dichotomy of good/attractive/sexually alluring women versus undesirable/oversexual women. It is therefore as important to interrogate the processes which alienate young Black women from discourses of sexuality—both in the shaming and silencing of Black female sexuality and in the way Black girls are excluded from definitions of desirable, appropriate womanhood (Weekes 2002)—as it is to critically assess the construction of Black female bodies as sexually expendable within popular culture.

Alternatively, other young women refuse to engage with particular musical forms, not finding the music relevant to their subjectivities, although, as discussed previously, there may be a link between young developing sexual selves and the sexual undertones of music they choose to consume. Though the subversion of these younger women who rejected the images of Black womanhood within certain lyrics appears to compare more favorably to the responses of the older and in some cases sexually active girls, it is important to acknowledge the identification this latter group makes with Black males as well as with their female counterparts. The empowering, often political, but strengthening effects of music have been documented—in its power to unify across racial boundaries (Back 1996), for example. The global appeal of urban music produced in both America and the Caribbean continues to exert local influences on young Black fans, reinforcing links between Black individuals throughout the diaspora, which has binding and communal effects (Weekes 2003). The young Black women in this discussion who have expressed preference for rap and ragga music, despite the gendered imagery embedded within specific aspects of it, are thus as influenced by these binding processes as other either older and/or male fans. However, subverting music's more complex gendered messages for the female MTV generation becomes increasingly hazardous the easier it is for these images to enter the public consciousness.

Notes

1. The sound crew or sound system developed out of the popularity of reggae music among African- Caribbean people in the late 1970s/early 1980s in urban aeas and involves the playing of pre-recorded music, usually at functions such as parties and weddings. The "crew" was traditionally all male, consisting of those playing the records, those directing the crowd via the microphone, and those who were needed to move the equipment (mixers, speakers, etc). The involvement of women in these spaces continues to be small, and the development of such groups among young African-Caribbean women in my research was useful in exploring the relationship between males as producers and women as consumers of music (Hollows 2000).

2. The mass appeal of both ragga and hip-hop illustrates that they do not simply reflect internal dialogues about Jamaican or American national identities, and their diasporic appeal spreads across Europe, America, Canada, and the Caribbean, and throughout what Gilroy (1993) has called the Black Atlantic. Also see Back (1996).

3. This music, which dominated the early 1990s, was by artists such as Snoop Doggy Dogg and The 2 Live Crew, who were subject to legal censorship for their pornographic and violently sexual lyrics. However, though many rappers now lyricize less about social crises, violence against the police, and women, instead promoting the "playa" lifestyle— pool parties, expensive cars, and jewelry—the degradation of women in lyrics is continuous, as is evidenced by Eminen, Dr Dre, and Snoop Dogg.

4. Popular rappers such as Ludicris and Jay Z boast of sexual conquest, but do so under the guise of equal, though often sexually explicit, relationships with women.

5. "Slack" and "slackness" here refer to the ways that behavior was deemed to be licentious by the young women researched, and reflect a particular form of ragga prevalent at the time of interview which was known popularly as "slack lyrics"—music which both congratulated and derogated Black women for their tendencies to participate in lengthy sexual marathons, and censured women for the size and shape of genitalia. Interestingly, young African-Caribbean women aged beween fourteen and twenty were among the largest consumers of "slack lyrics" (Brinkworth 1992).

6. Whereas the comparison between respectability and deviancy for these young women is usually those afforded with traditionally defined beauty— young White women. See Weekes (2002).

7. The discourse of the "bitch" commonly used in rap and some R'n'B songs was employed by artists as a means of controlling the way that women used their sexuality to gain access to them, and also to complain about the (sexualized) hysteria of female fans (Rose 1994). The term, and the way it is employed within certain forms of music, have been reacted against not only by feminist critics but also by African-American conservative politicians who argue that this discourse creates an environment within which violence against women is perpetrated. That the term is also used by men to describe other men in a derogatory fashion highlights that its usage is intended to feminize the identities of males, further adding to the ambiguity surrounding the constructing of women within the music.

8. BWP engaged in gangsta revenge fantasies, drawing on the violence of male rappers and turning it against them.

References

Back, L. (1996). *New Ethnicities and Urban Culture: Racisms and Multiculture in Young Lives.* London: UCL Press.

Bayton, M. (1992). "Out on the Margins: Feminism and the Study of Popular Music." *Women: A Cultural Review* 3 (1): 51–59.

Boyd, T. (1997). *Am I Black Enough for You? Popular Culture from the 'Hood and Beyond.* Bloomington: Indiana University Press.

Brinkworth, L. (1992). "Why Are the Sisters Taking Up the Slack?" *The Guardian*, June 25, p. 21.

Cooper, C. (1993). *Noises in the Blood: Orality, Gender and the "Vulgar" Body of Jamaican Culture.* London: Macmillan.

Davis, A. (1992). "Black Nationalism: The Sixties and the Nineties." In G. Dent (ed.), *Black Popular Culture.* Seattle: Bay Press.

Dyson, M. (1993). *Reflecting Black: African-American Cultural Criticism.* Minneapolis: University of Minnesota Press.

General TK. (1993). *I Spy.* Dubplate music/Greensleeves Records.

Gilroy, P. (1993). *The Black Atlantic: Modernity and Double Consciousness.* London: Verso.

Hebdige, D. (1979). *Subculture: The Meaning of Style.* London: Methuen.

Hollows, J. (2000). *Feminism, Femininity and Popular Culture.* Manchester: Manchester University Press.

hooks, b. (1994). *Outlaw Culture: Resisting Representations.* London: Routledge.

Lewis, L. (1992). *The Adoring Audience: Fan Culture and Popular Media.* London: Routledge.

Lusane, C. (1993). "Rap, Race and Politics." *Race and Class* 35 (1): 41–56.

McRobbie A. (1991). *Feminism and Youth Culture: From Jackie to Just Seventeen.* Basingstoke, U.K.: Macmillan.

McRobbie, A., and Frith, S. (1991). "Rock and Sexuality." In A. McRobbie (ed.), *Feminism and Youth Culture.* Basingstoke. U.K.: Macmillan.

McRobbie, A., and Garber, J. (1976). "Girls and Subcultures." In S. Hall and T. Jefferson (eds.), *Resistance Through Rituals.* London: Hutchinson.

Ms Dynamite. (2002). *A Little Deeper.* EMI Music Publishing, Ltd.

Noble, D. (1996). "Ragga Queens, Batty Men and the True Rastaman: Race, Sexuality and Gender in the Local and Global Narration of Diasporic Black Identities." Paper presented to British Sociological Association Conference, "Worlds of the Future," April.

Noble, D. (2000). "Ragga Music: Dis/Respecting Black Women and Dis/Reputable Sexualities." In B. Hesse (ed.), *Un/settled Multiculturalisms: Diasporas, Entanglements, Transruptions.* London: Zed Books.

Ransby, B., and Matthews, T. (1993). "Black Popular Culture and the Transcendence of Patriarchal Illusions." *Race and Class* 35 (1): 57–68.

Rose, T. (1992). "Black Texts/Black Contexts." In G. Dent (ed.), *Black Popular Culture.* Seattle: Bay Press.

Rose, T. (1994). *Black Noise: Rap Music and Black Culture in Contemporary America.* Hanover, N.H.: Wesleyan University Press.

Skeggs, B. (1994). "Refusing to Be Civilised: 'Race', Sexuality and Power." In H. Afshar and M. Maynard (eds.), *The Dynamics of "Race" and Gender: Some Feminist Interventions.* London: Taylor & Francis.

Skeggs, B. (1997). *Formations of Class and Gender.* London: Sage.

Thornton, S. (1995). *Club Cultures: Music, Media and Subcultural Capital.* Cambridge: Polity.

Weekes, D. (1997). "Shades of Blackness: Young Black Female Constructions of Beauty." In H. Mirza (ed.), *British Black Feminism: A Reader.* London: Routledge.

Weekes, D. (2002). "Get Your Freak On: How Black Girls Sexualize Identity." *Sex Education* 2 (3): 251–262.

Weekes, D. (2003). "Keeping It in the Community: Creating Spaces for Black Girlhood." *Journal of Community, Work and Family* 6 (1): 47–61.

West, C. (1993). *Race Matters.* Boston: Beacon: Press.

Williams, S.A. (1992). "Two Words on Music: Black Community." In G. Dent (ed.), *Black Popular Culture.* Seattle: Bay Press.

CHAPTER 13

Spicy Strategies:
Pop Feminist and Other Empowerments in Girl Culture

BETTINA FRITZSCHE

The phenomenal global success of the Spice Girls has, from its beginnings, been accompanied by probably as many haters of the group as fans. This is true not only for their predominantly preadolescent audience, but also for adult critics and academics. The story of the girl group is a prime example of modern stardom as it has been characterized by Lawrence Grossberg (1995: 373): the Spice Girls are a studio band, assembled according to marketing strategies. The girls are celebrities without a history, catapulted to a stardom which, so it seems, was there waiting for them all along. Consequently, the audience was set to discover their talents only *after* they had already become stars.

One of these "talents," their proclamation and embodiment of "Girl Power," has given rise to much controversy. For a number of reasons the notion of Girl Power has been especially criticized from a feminist viewpoint. The Spice Girls have been accused of presenting nothing more than a new halfhearted and commercialized version of a style which had been initiated by predecessors like Madonna and the Riot Grrrls. Whereas the Riot Grrrls were an explicit subcultural movement with explicit feminist intentions and aggressive displays of female sexuality, Madonna fascinated academics with her parodistic play on gender attributes, which could be celebrated as "empowered transvestism" (Garber 1993: 127). In comparison, the Spice Girls' version of Girl Power seems, as *Rolling Stone*

(1997: 83) put it, like "a co-optation more heinous than any Riot Grrrl's worst nightmare." Another criticism, put forward by Gayle Wald (1998: 588), warned that an uncritical celebration of girlhood could reinforce the patriarchal notion that women will be accepted in society as long as they're willing to behave like children. But the Spice Girls have also had their defenders. Angela McRobbie (1998) considers them a symptom of popular feminism, fighting in a playful way for self-assertion and sexual enjoyment, dissociating themselves from an older generation of tired, White, middle-class feminists.[1]

Despite this controversy, the girl group has been, especially in its successful beginnings, the target of the admiration of many enthusiastic young female fans. In this chapter I shall, using the results of an interview-based study, discuss the question of to what extent "pop feminist" phenomena like the Spice Girls can be considered a source of empowerment for young women and girls. An interest in this question is accompanied by the methodological problem that the fans' way of consuming the band obviously is different from the cognitive readings of the academics mentioned above. As many cultural studies scholars have pointed out, media consumption nowadays cannot be seen as an isolated process of encoding, but should be examined as a phenomenon embedded in daily life.[2] The media use of fans, exemplified by practices such as the collection of posters, is not just an act of interpretation; rather, it is an integral part of a popular culture. For this reason, my examination shall focus on the meaning Spice Girls fans make of the band within their particular fan culture.

In this sense, the interviews I conducted did not focus on the girls' reflections about the band, but rather on their actions as fans. At the beginning of the narrative interviews they were asked, "How did you become a fan and how did things develop until now?" The interviewees were then given the opportunity to narrate their biography as fans. The documentary method, following the tradition of the Chicago School and the "sociology of knowledge" as conceptualized by Karl Mannheim,[3] was chosen as the method of interpretation. The documentary method concentrates on narrations and on descriptions in the interview text which give information about the interviewees' actions and the constitution of experience which underlies their actions. The aim is not to discover underneath their narrative a latent level which remains closed to themselves, but to reconstruct experiences which often cannot be formulated directly. The experiences are nevertheless often documented in the interview, and allow the formulation of conclusions about central patterns of orientations. In this way, the documentary method makes it possible to analyze the fans' culture in the context of their experiences and orientations as adolescent girls. My sample consists of eight narrative interviews and one group discussion with fans and former fans of the Spice Girls, aged between ten and seventeen. The interviewees come from various social backgrounds and live in various cities and rural villages in Germany.[4]

Some of the typical aspects of fan culture which allow the fans to participate in practices of exchange within their peer group include the
collection of CDs and fan items, and an expert knowledge of their subject.
Sometimes these practices form part of established ritualized practices
within the girls' friendships (for example, a daily telephone conversation
with the girl's best friend can be used to exchange news about the band).
In the girl group fans' culture, the aspect of "imitation" also plays a crucial
role. It manifests itself in the establishment of a "mini Spice Girls gang,"
testing out the fashion styles represented by the stars, and also in the
formation of dance groups. The girls watch and imitate the band's dance
videos together, often creating their own new steps along the way. But in
spite of their determination to learn to dance, dress, and behave like their
idols, many fans assured me that they had no intention of simply aping the
band, but wanted to find their own personal style.

In this sense, this specific popular culture can be termed a mimetic
culture. According to cultural anthropologists Gunter Gebauer and
Christoph Wulf (1998: 11), mimetic acts are social physical acts which are
independent, but at the same time refer in some way to other actions.
Mimesis is always more than a simple, passive reproduction of existing
role models; it has its own creative potential. The ritualized and mimetic
character of certain practices typical of fan culture enables its participants
to take a careful and playful approach toward their new status as fans. The
subject position "fan" is always associated with other subject positions or
even replaces them. Each of the Spice Girls is perceived by their fans as a
very distinct individual, so they often imitate the band members by trying
out different ways of presenting themselves, which are linked to particular
qualities like being cute, self-confident, or sexy. The mimetic approach
toward the Spice Girls obviously allows them to negotiate social expectations about the ways girls are expected to move and display their bodies. In
this way, they can experiment with finding their own position between not
being fashionable enough and being too fashion-oriented, between being
too plain and too sexy, dressing too poorly or showing off, and so on.[5]

But the dance groups also serve a function dealing with needs that go
beyond simple matters of style. This is shown in the interview with fifteen-
year-old Julia. Julia, who was a Spice Girls fan at the age of thirteen, says
that she used to see herself as shy and incapable of fighting for her own
interests. So she was very taken by the self-assurance the girl group represented for her. She became part of fan culture when she was asked by some
friends to join their dance group. In the beginning, the role of Victoria
("Posh Spice") was the only one left for her, but later she was able to "work
her way up" to Mel B ("Scary Spice"), whom she admired for being the
tone-setter in the band.

Asked about the criteria for the distribution of roles in the dance group,
Julia explains:

Well, one was similar to them from the start and then, gradually, one grew into the role. We became more and more similar to them. And although Beate, who played Emma, was always the tiny, shy one on stage, in fact she was always the most self-confident one of us all. She was the one who always defended me, but on stage it was the other way round. In a way, we swapped our roles exactly on stage. I was then the one who said, well, I was the one who defended everyone, and otherwise it was her, even if she played the most shy one.

In terms of dance mimesis, Julia could playfully embody her ideal of a self-confident person and in this way prove to herself that she is able to do so. The exchange of roles she and her friend Beate carried out on stage enabled the girls to experience themselves in a completely different position in their peer group, without risking conflicts or feelings of competition. In associating shyness with being "tiny" and the inability to defend oneself, Julia characterizes her own "original role" as the position of a dependent child. Taking over the role of self-confident Mel B, she can make first experiences with the identity of an independent youth who already is able to defend herself. Meanwhile, her friend can allow herself during dance mimesis a short travel back into the sphere of protected childhood. In this respect the girls' Spice Girls mimesis can be described as a way of negotiating the passage from childhood to the position of youth.

A second important aspect of fan culture, as Julia experienced it, was the negotiation of her relationship with boys. She had been a tomboy as a child, and later fell in love with a member of the boy group Caught in the Act. This turned out to be a disappointing experience. The Spice Girls then represented for her the attitude "We need boys as lovers, but otherwise forget about them, don't run after them, find your own way instead." She found this opinion plausible, and it also made her curious. Now, two years later, she says:

The Spice Girls always conveyed the idea that boys are only interesting if you have fallen in love with them. And with Caught in the Act it was basically the same. At least you imagined you were in love with them. And later I realized that it was possible to be just friends with boys.

Meanwhile, after having tried out different attitudes toward the other sex within her fandom, Julia distances herself from both extreme positions which she supported in different phases during that time. From her current standpoint she criticizes the Spice Girls' attitude toward boys, as well as her own feelings for the boy group Caught in the Act, for reducing the relationships between the sexes to an erotic level. Where the thrill of romantic relationships between men and women typical for the world of pop music motivated Julia's interest in stars at the beginning, she now feels restricted by it and is beginning again to meet boys on a friendship basis. She presents herself as an enlightened young woman who has left the erotic confusions of adolescence behind and has now achieved a noncomplicated attitude toward the other sex.

A rather different meaning is attributed to the Spice Girls by seventeen-year-old Rebecca, who lives in a small town in the west of Germany. At the age of fifteen, while all her friends preferred boy groups, Rebecca was a Spice Girls fan. As a reason for becoming a fan she points out her interest in the notion of Girl Power. Her favorite remark of the Spice Girls was "A Spice Girl may well be mad, as long as there's a method behind her madness." Rebecca's negotiation of the notion of madness is a central aspect in the interview. She complains about the "very normal people" in her town who were no fun. In a mimetic approach toward the Spice Girls, she had herself pierced, and she delightfully describes other ways she and her best friend found to provoke her grandma into saying, "What will the neighbors think?" Rebecca's self-assertiveness in disregarding social norms becomes clear when I ask her why most girls go for boy groups and her answer is "I can't understand them, they are somehow queer." In naming the heterosexual setting of boy group fandom with a term which normally is used to discriminate against homosexuals, Rebecca playfully and ironically turns around the conventions of her surroundings.

Like Julia, her fandom is strongly related to society's expectation that during the phase of youth, first experiences are made in the field of heterosexuality. But where Julia used her fan culture in order to negotiate her new relationships with boys, Rebecca's interest in the girl group helped her to dissociate herself from this expectation. But she also associates unconventional behavior with the danger of being regarded as sick. Rebecca loves to draw and describes one of her pictures, saying, "It looks totally psychopathic. You'd think it was painted by someone who was completely out of their mind." But in spite of this, she wants to go to an art college:

> There are no prospects in art. You want to do it, but you don't know where it will lead. But the Spice Girls helped me to say, "I will do this and it will amount to something."

Coming back to my question, if the Spice Girls as a pop feminist phenomenon can be regarded as a source of empowerment for young girls, it would be possible to identify Rebecca—as opposed to Julia—as the prototype of an empowered fan. Thanks to the girl group, she succeeds in not caring about boys, in behaving out of the ordinary and provocatively, and in striving for a career as an artist. But this perspective is accompanied by certain problems. On the one hand, it concedes the Spice Girls more power in the lives of their fans than they actually have. The girls' various interpretations and applications of "Girl Power" and other messages embodied by the girl group make it clear that the Spice Girls do not initiate particular forms of behavior in their fans. Rather, their fans know how to use the girl group's media image as a toolbox which they use as they see fit in pursuing their own individual goals.[6] Also, a distinction between rebellious and conformist fan behavior is problematic insofar as it can result in ignoring the many aspects of the girls' fan culture which are not explicitly nonconformist but nevertheless very creative. For example, using dance mimesis in testing different ways of presenting oneself toward others is neither a simple case of conformity nor is it necessarily liberation. But it shows how clever Spice Girls fans can use their culture in learning to cope with the requirements of adolescence.

In her examination of Hollywood cinema and female spectatorship Jackie Stacey (1994: 234ff.) points out that since the expansion of consumerism in the 1950s, the relationship between self-image and star ideals has become increasingly interactive. The act of consuming gives us the chance to become similar to the star by means of mimetic self-transformation. In accordance with this development the Spice Girls are not distant idols for their audience, but rather a commodity in itself, which can be integrated into one's own consumer tactics. Many of the girls interviewed emphasized that they did not want to become like the stars, but rather to find their own style. They don't seem to feel restricted by a fashion dictate represented by the stars.

The idea that one has to be self-willed and choose from a diverse palette of fashion and style possibilities became a normative expectation in itself, which can be negotiated within a mimetic fan culture.[7] In this sense I agree with Abercrombie and Longhurst (1998), who point out that certain changes in the media landscape can no longer be adequately analyzed in the frame of a paradigm based on the question of whether the audience resists dominant ideology or, rather, incorporates it. The authors support the thesis that especially phenomena like the complex activities of fans and enthusiasts among the audience should be interpreted within a paradigm which focuses on questions of identity and identification.

In my study I found those reflections to be confirmed. I would argue that the Spice Girls can serve as a means of liberation for their young audience from restrictive gender norms. Also, the media image of the girl group can have a restrictive effect itself, as it maintains the ideology of the importance of appearance in female identity.[8]

But above all, an interpretation of the Spice Girls fans' narratives is useful in showing which normative expectations are important for teenage girls and how they find their own way in dealing with those expectations. Fan culture offers them the opportunity to take a playful approach toward questions of self-representation, self-confidence, and heterosexuality, which can be, but does not necessarily have to be, used for resistance. In this respect the Spice Girls can be regarded as a source of empowerment for their fans. They are very much associated with the subject position of a strong, self-confident, and successful female teenager, and offer an attractive point of reference for their cultural activities. The tremendous success of the girl group clarifies the continuous lack of such symbols in the lives of young women and the unbroken legitimacy of feminist demands for new media representations of femininity.

But it is not only from this perspective that I would argue that the Spice Girls should be taken seriously in the discussions of feminist academics. The creative tactics of the fans of the group teach us the many possible variants of empowerment for girls. And a recognition of the political potential of the empowerment conveyed by popular culture could be the precondition for a feminist strategy aiming to increase girls' possibilities in dealing with the demands of modern society. Feminism's aim to enlarge girls' (and women's) scopes of action cannot be achieved by explaining the word to them. Instead, it seems important to me to learn to understand the very common, playful, and body-centered ways that girls cope with society's scripts of identity. This would be a necessary precondition to encourage them to pursue aspects of their own identity which do not conform.

Notes

1. For detailed analyses of the Spice Girls as represented in their lyrics, music, videos, and other popular texts, see also Dibben (1999) and Lemish (2003).

2. See, for example Radway (1988), Ang (1990, 1996), and Abercrombie and Longhurst (1998).

3. For more on the documentary method, see Mannheim (1952) and Bohnsack et al. (2001).

4. These interviews were part of a larger empirical study about fans of boy groups and girl groups.

5. For an examination of dance as a practice girls use to negotiate social restrictions on the presentation of female bodies, see McRobbie (1984, 1994).

6. On this point I agree with John Fiske (1992), who considers fans as an especially discriminating and selective group of consumers.

7. Several authors reported an increasing pressure on youths to create a distinct, authentic identity. See, for example, Ganetz (1995).

8. This argument is fruitfully examined in Dafna Lemish's audience study; see Lemish (1998).

9. Such an understanding of empowerment corresponds with Lawrence Grossberg's definition. Grossberg (1992: 64) states that empowerment does not "guarantee any form of resistance to or evasion of existing structures of power, although it is a condition of the possibility of resistance.... Empowerment refers to the generation of energy and passion, to the construction of possibility."

References

Abercrombie, N., and Longhurst, B. (1998). *Audiences: A Sociological Theory of Performance and Imagination.* London: Sage.

Ang, I. (1990). "Culture and Communications: Towards an Ethnographic Critique of Media Consumption in the Transnational Media System." *European Journal of Communication* 5: 239–260.

Ang, I. (1996). "Ethnography and Radical Contextualism in Audience Studies." In Ang's Living Room Wars. *Rethinking Media Audiences for a Postmodern World*, 66–81. London: Routledge.

Bohnsack, R., Loos, P., and Przyborski, A. (2001). "'Male Honour': Towards an Understanding of the Construction of Gender Relations Among Youths of Turkish Origin." In H. Kotthoff and B. Baron (eds.), *Gender in Interaction: Perspectives on Femininity and Masculinity in Ethnography and Discourse.* Amsterdam: Benjamins Publishing Co.

Dibben, N. (1999). "Representations of Femininity in Popular Music." *Popular Music* 18: 331–355.

Fiske, J. (1992). "The Cultural Economy of Fandom." In L.E. Lewis (ed.), *Adoring Audience: Fan Culture and Popular Media*, 30–49. London: Routledge.

Ganetz, H. (1995). "The Shop, the Home and Femininity as a Masquerade." In J. Fornäs and
G. Bolin (eds.), *Youth Culture in Late Modernity*, 72–99. London: Sage.

Garber, M. (1993). *Vested Interests: Cross-dressing and Cultural Anxiety*. London: Routledge.

Gebauer, G., and Wulf, C. (1998). *Spiel Ritual Geste: Mimetisches Handeln in der sozialen Welt*.
Reinbek bei Hamburg: Rowohlt.

Grossberg, L. (1992). "Is There a Fan in the House?: The Affective Sensibility of Fandom." In
L.E. Lewis (ed.), *Adoring Audience: Fan Culture and Popular Media*, 50–65. London:
Routledge.

Grossberg, L. (1995). "MTV: Swinging on the (Postmodern) Star." In J. Munns and G. Rajan
(eds.), *A Cultural Studies Reader: History, Theory, Practice*, 369–376. London: Longman
Group.

Lemish, D. (1998). "Spice Girls' Talk: A Case Study in the Development of Gendered Identity." In
S.A. Inness (ed.), *Millennium Girls: Today's Girls Around the World*, 145–167. New York:
Rowman & Littlefield.

Lemish, D. (2003). "Spice World: Constructing Femininity the Popular Way." *Popular Music and
Society*. (forthcoming)

Lewis, L.E. (ed.) *Adoring Audience-Fan Culture and Popular Media*, pp. 50–65. London: Routledge.

Lewis, L.E. (1995). "MTV. Swinging on the (postmodern) Star." In: J. Munns; G. Rajan (eds) *A
Cultural Studies Reader. History, Theory, Practice*, pp. 369–376. London: Longman Group.

Mannheim, K. (1952). *Essays on the Sociology of Knowledge*. London: Routledge and Kegan Paul.

McRobbie, A. (1984). "Dance and Social Fantasy." In A. McRobbie and M. Nava (eds.), *Gender
and Generation*, 130–161. London: Macmillan.

McRobbie, A. (1994). "Shut Up and Dance: Youth Culture and Changing Modes of Femininity."
In McRobbie's *Postmodernism and Popular Culture*, 155–176. London: Routledge.

McRobbie, A. (1998). "Muskelpakete und Schwänze. Die Bedeutung von Girlie-Kultur." In
A. Baldauf and K. Weingartner (eds.), *Lips Tits Hits Power? Popkultur und Feminismus*,
274–284. Vienna: Bozen.

Radway, J. (1988). "Reception Study: Ethnography and the Problems of Dispersed Audiences and
Nomadic Subjects." *Cultural Studies* 2 (3): 359–376.

Rolling Stone. (1997). no. 156, March 20.

Stacey, J. (1994). *Star Gazing: Hollywood Cinema and Female Spectatorship*. London: Routledge.

Wald, G. (1998). "Just a Girl? Rock Music, Feminism, and the Cultural Construction of Female
Youth." Signs: *Journal of Women in Culture and Society* 23 (3): 585–610.

CHAPTER 14

Jamming Girl Culture: Young Women and Consumer Citizenship

ANITA HARRIS

> Well, I got my first credit card, and I was quite excited. Then I realised what it was I was excited about—oh yippeee, validation in the money world, that I can be trusted to spend, spend, spend!... Young Adults ... you are being welcomed into the privileged world of consumerism, and we hope you never leave! And why would you, you are SO comfortable. We just want you to spend!
>
> (Kylie, catpounce e-zine, Australia)

For young people in the twenty-first century, citizenship and participation are increasingly achieved through "validation in the money world." As the distinction between states and markets blurs, public spheres for community debate disappear, and global economic forces shape local youth experiences of rights and opportunities, citizenship for young people is being radically altered. The so-called "individualization and monetarisation of everyday life"[1] has meant that some key planks of citizenship, such as economic security and capacity for participation in civic life, are being eroded. Young people are newly obliged to create their own opportunities for livelihood, and civic engagement is difficult to operationalize in the absence of robust structures for participation. Consumption has come to stand in as a sign both of successfully secured social rights and of civic power. It is primarily as consumer citizens that youth are offered a place in contemporary social life, and it is girls above all who are held up as the exemplars of this new citizenship.

Here I look at changing modes of citizenship for young people in new times, and the ways in which young women are constructed as the ideal subjects for these new ways of enacting both social rights and participation through consumption. In the second part of the chapter I point to some examples of young women's resistance to these constructions. I suggest that some young women are developing creative strategies in response that temporarily disrupt connections between consumption and citizenship, and attempt to insert production and community-building back into youth participation.

Young People and Consumer Citizenship

Expectations of and opportunities for citizenship for youth have become increasingly complicated in the context of contemporary socioeconomic conditions. This is borne out in a number of ways. The collapse of the full-time youth job market has made economic circumstances precarious, and the new policy emphasis on education without the flow of adequate jobs for the newly skilled has seen the deferral of possibilities for an independent, financially secure life for many. The rollback of welfare has also radically redefined the role of the state in relation to youth, who are now required to make their way in a restructured economy without a social security safety net. Within the world of work for youth, competition is fierce and much stock is placed in personal effort, flexibility, and networking to secure employment. Social rights, that is, livelihoods, are no longer guaranteed, but become dependent on individual resources and capacity to create opportunities and make connections.

However, one of the most significant shifts in the construction of youth citizenship has been toward consumption. Young people's relationship to the resources in their communities, and their ability to speak out as members of these communities, are shaped through a broader reconceptualization of citizenship as consumer power.

As a consequence of the outsourcing and privatization of many of the services and utilities that were once provided, or at least monitored, by the state, community members are obliged to enter into contractual arrangements with profit-making providers to secure basic "life needs" such as electrical supply to their homes or emergency medical attention. Terms such as "customer," "client," and "consumer" have overwhelmingly taken the place of "citizen" in the areas of health, education, housing, and employment. The social rights of citizens are no longer ensured by the state, but must be negotiated on an individual level between consumer and corporation. The current generation of youth is the first to have experienced these circumstances as its only reality. It is also unique in having to negotiate this retreat of the state in a time of massive economic insecurity. Young people's capacity to enter into successful "customer relations" and make "consumer choices" among the new social rights service providers depends entirely on their economic circumstances. In other words, the new mode of enacting citizenship, that is, through empowered consumer choice, is in fact feasible only for those who have the financial capacity to take their custom elsewhere. Young people who are most vulnerable in the new economy are those least likely to be in this situation of empowered choice makers.

Citizenship is also narrowed down to this concept of consumer power in regard to active participation. Privatization and marketization have also resulted in a retraction of the public sphere. Places where people could gather to debate social issues are either disappearing or becoming corporatized. For example, Michelle Fine and Lois Weis document the ways in which community spaces have become either nonexistent or sites of surveillance.[2] For young people, the shopping mall has almost entirely replaced public spaces, such as the street or parks, and social services, such as drop-in centers, as the site for community. The commercialization of youth leisure has meant that free opportunities for assembly are far diminished. In order to participate in the new sites of community that are demarcated for youth, such as multiplex cinemas, shopping centers, and music festivals, young people must be able to pay. Further, as work diminishes as a mechanism of identity formation, self-presentation and lifestyle are becoming more important as resources for cultural capital. The global youth culture industry has been quick to respond to this situation, offering young people a vast array of products and styles to purchase as part of their identity work. Steven Miles describes this as the representation of young people as "fully-fledged citizens of a consumer society," rather than of a civil society; that is, a consumer identity operates in place of a citizenship based on secure economic and social foundations.[3] Naomi Klein notes the irony of the multinational corporations excluding some youth from the job market while generating exploitive work for others, but relying on all young people to consume their products.[4]

Girls as the New Consumer Citizens

The reinvention of youth citizenship as consumer power has been largely enacted through young women. Girls have become the emblem of this consumer citizen via a problematic knitting together of feminist and neoliberal ideology about power and opportunities, combined with some socioeconomic conditions that appear to have favored their rise in status over that of young (and older) men. All young people are expected to take increasing responsibility for their social rights, but it is young women in particular who are imagined as those best positioned to succeed in this endeavor. The so-called "feminization" of the labor market, whereby service and communication industries have expanded and manufacturing has contracted, along with a new value being placed on skills such as negotiation and close attention to presentation, is seen to have created many opportunities for young women in work. The phenomenon of feminization links success in securing social rights with success in consumption, and suggests that it is young women who are best able to make these connections. As social theorist Lisa Adkins notes, style, fashion, accessories, and presentation are the "essential preconditions for economic power."[5] Obtaining high-status work in the industries driving the new economy—lifestyle, marketing, and image—depends on consumption skills, and it is young women above all who are imagined to have this skill set. In this way, the new youth citizenship is enacted by girls, because they are apparently able to use consumption to secure their social rights.

Young women are also positioned as excellent choice makers, having taken the gains of feminism, such as increased freedoms, assertiveness, and economic independence, and applied them to the market. Their confidence and success are frequently measured by their purchasing power. In the words of one journalist, "Girl power is flexing its economic muscles" via the spending power of "single, professional, independent and confident young women."[6] Girls are imagined to have an enormous amount of control over family purchases, as well as considerable discretionary income of their own. For example, U.S. girls aged eight to eighteen are estimated to be worth $67 billion. For twelve-to-seventeen-year-old British girls, the figure is £1.3 billion, while the collective income of eleven-to-seventeen-year-old girls in Australia is AUS $4.6 billion.[7] Business magazines and market research companies report on young women's consumer patterns and habits with great excitement about the capacity and potential of this group as economic agents. Much stock is placed in girls to revitalize the economy, both in the deindustrialized West and the Asian "tiger" economies recovering from the crisis of the late 1990s. For example, Tom Holland of the *Far Eastern Economic Review* writes that "if consumer spending is to take over from U.S. demand as the locomotive of powering Asia's economic recovery, it will be hip, young women who are driving the process."[8] Young women are thereby constructed as powerful actors in the marketplace who enact their new opportunities for independence and control by purchasing products and displaying a consumer lifestyle.

The Girl Power market not only relies on young women as its key consumer group, but sells an image of savvy girlness to them in the process. An Australian marketing manager says, "Those who wish to tap into women's purchasing power need to develop an approach that recognises this audience as media-savvy, market-educated and cashed up for a carefully considered spend."[9] Part of this "recognition" is the construction of such an image in the first place, and this has occurred primarily by drawing on the enormous discursive clout of "Girl Power." The term "Girl Power" itself has been used in innumerable advertising campaigns for products such as clothing, accessories, cosmetics, and snacks. It is also frequently used in government and nongovernment services and programs for young women that relate to health, sexuality, education, sports, business knowledge, and self-esteem. Most of these programs construct Girl Power as a personal belief system that makes girls smart and confident: to be girl-powered is to make good choices and to be empowered as an individual. These uses of Girl Power position young women as creators of their own identities and life chances, and as liberated by their participation in the consumer culture that surrounds them. They both emphasize the positive opportunities for young women to invent themselves; to become, in Ulrich Beck's words, "choice biographers."[10]

In addition to the Girl Power message of self-invention and anti-collectivism, Angela McRobbie suggests that it disconnects feminism from politics and justice, and implies that strong and empowered girls are those who have and spend money.[11] Girl Power presents itself as a discourse of young women's citizenship status and entitlements; for example, it advocates autonomy, rights, independence, and power. However, it teaches that rights and power, that is, citizenship, are best enacted through individual choices in the market.

For many young women, this conflation of power with consumption is experienced as deeply problematic. As a consequence, much of youth activism and politics has shifted to addressing this very issue of the invention of female consumer citizenship as the last word in feminist success. Next I discuss some examples of this new kind of young feminist cultural activism that challenges these attempts to position girls as powerful citizens only when they consume. I use the examples of young women involved in alternative media, such as zines and Web sites, as well as those who participate in political art and activism, such as anti-corporate globalization protest. I suggest that the efforts of these young women to "jam" consumer culture and create new public spaces for debate and community indicate important ways that consumption is being resisted and citizenship re-visioned.

Jamming Girl Culture

[In] our time, feminism is a commercial product—like the Spice Girlz, cosmopolitan feminizm.... And "liberated" women are a sexy and a useful product for consumption as well.... we have the ... liberated sex objects and the cool fucked-up moneymakers.

(Yen, "Emancypunx" collective, Poland)

Young women such as the Polish "Emancypunx" collective are some of many who interrogate the ways "liberation" is sold to girls through the conflation of feminism and consumption. The purpose of these kinds of collectives and loose organizations is to create cultures of critique and to find other, especially anti-capitalist, sources of power and creativity for young women. In particular, they encourage girls to be active producers of their own cultures rather than passive consumers of what is mass-manufactured for them. They suggest that although consumption is represented as a new source of power for women, real capacity to make change remains at the level of production. Vina, of the Austrian collective "Nylon," says that it is still the case that "in the field of culture, men are more likely to be seen as cultural producers, whereas women are 'only' perceived as 'consumers.'"[12] To reinsert women into culture as producers, and to resist the seduction of consumption, these girls recommend active engagement with the culture industry. Accordingly, one of the most common protest strategies utilized by these young women is the culture jam.

"Culture jamming" refers to a number of techniques that use the very material of consumer culture to undermine its messages and power. Well-known elements of commercial culture, such as slogans and icons, are interfered with so that their meanings are changed and their inherent illogic is exposed. For example, hacktivists might subtly alter text on a corporation's Web site to point out its poor labor practices, or a graffiti artist might carefully add words to a billboard to make a statement about the health consequences of using that product. The objective is to use the commercial techniques to draw people into the product and then disrupt their reading of it. As Naomi Klein argues, "For a growing number of young activists, adbusting has presented itself as the perfect tool with which to register disapproval of the multinational corporations that have so aggressively stalked them as shoppers, and so unceremoniously dumped them as workers."[13] Unlike more overt political material, such as pamphlets or protest placards, culture jams use brand advertising strategies to reinterpellate a passive, consumer-oriented audience as critical thinkers.

For example, Carly Stasko, a Canadian girl culture jammer, makes zines and stickers, writes over billboards, performs street theater and "events," and conducts media literacy workshops and high school classes on street art and social change. One of her well-known collages depicts a supermarket checkout lane filled with "Girl Power" packages, but the slogan reads: "Warning: for best results don't buy girl power. Grow your own!" She argues that these techniques enable young women to resist the passive girl consumer position, and demonstrates how disrupting mass media "instead of constantly consuming spin" constitutes a new form of feminist activism that can respond to the oppression of a mediated girl culture.[14]

Consistent with this, Canadian anti-corporate globalization "girl activists" Kimberley Fry and Cheryl Lousley argue that these kinds of strategies are necessary in an age when protest discourse and social justice agendas themselves have become appropriated and commodified. They say:

> The response among many youth, including eco-grrrls, is to target the culture industry directly. They take on Nike and other corporations whose vulnerability lies in the integrity of their brands. They take on the media conglomerates and advertising culture which sustain the exploitative, consumer economy. But rather than aim for an anti-capitalist purity, this new generation of activists play

with cultural images and challenge them through a production of their own independent, consumer-free spaces.[15]

This play can, of course, be a dangerous game, since political agendas may be lost in the countercultural fun. For example, Verity Burgmann argues that these techniques are of limited value because they do not always connect with a broader political movement, and "on its own, culture jamming does not confront the power of those who produce the images parodied."[16] However, when these links are made—and for young women involved in anti-corporate globalization movements, they frequently are—the results can be powerful. These young women undermine the easy conflation of Girl Power with consumption, and at the same time campaign and protest against the corporations and practices of the global economy that separate young women into either mindless consumers or exploited workers—and, in doing so, divide them from each other. For example, speaking of the links between the two, Vina says, "In our recent issue [of *Nylon* zine] there's an article about the global fashion industry, that creates desires based on specific images of race and gender and sells to Western consumers—those fashion items are mostly produced by women in export processing zones and sweatshops in Asia, south Europe, and Latin America."[17] A critique of and intervention into the girl market is frequently accompanied by a broader theorization and activism around the forces and conditions of global capital that create this market in the first place, and that exploit other girls far more than the Western consumers they target. Culture jamming is but one incursion that links up with many others of a more confrontational nature.

Creating New Public Spheres

I want to support and encourage all women to be active participants in the dialogues happening in our society.

(Riika, Ladybomb distribution network, Finland)

Young women involved in anti-consumer politics acknowledge that protest itself has become a more complicated experience under corporate globalization. Resistance is more easily silenced where a public sphere has diminished, and the slogans and styles of protest are frequently absorbed by the advertising industries. Possibilities for public protest as well as civic engagement are curtailed for young women who do not wish to adopt the questionable power and voice of the consumer citizen. Searching for alternative ways to speak out under these conditions has generated efforts to create new kinds of communities and new places for debate and participation. Alternative media and the Internet are central to the creation of these sites. For example, Clodagh of Ireland says, "Zines are an amazing opportunity to participate and have a say in what is going on…,"[18] and an Italian girl activist, Veruska, concurs: "Zine making means people who take their own space to spread self-expression and build new bonds of communication … put yourself in discussion, inspiration, creativity, passion, activism."[19] The importance of generating covert modes of both self-expression and networked activism is even greater for young women in circumstances where corporate power is matched by state control. For example, Carol of the Malaysian zine *Grrrl:Rebel* says, "In countries like Malaysia and Singapore, you would get arrested if you write any articles that can be considered as threats to the government…. People have to be really 'underground' to run their activities … and this is where zines play an important role as a source of information and networking."[20] A similar concern is felt by many young women in many Western countries where "anti-terrorist" security policy has deeply affected their capacity to express critique.

Under these conditions of both corporate and state encroachment on youth political cultures, the Internet has flourished as a site where collectives and individuals can gather to share ideas, debate issues, and strategize about protest. These constitute "virtual communities" not simply because many of them exist only on the Internet, but also because they are not necessarily "real"; that is, there is no evidence of a formal social order, and membership is loose and transient. Many young women position themselves as outside their own societies and as, instead, citizens of these transnational "imagined communities"[21] precisely because they are amorphous and liminal. The communities are designed in these ways to evade the gaze of authority in order that they can accomplish political work; that is, in Riika's words, to "fight against the white supremacist capitalist patriarchy!"[22] As Veruska articulates it, "The most radical aspect [of this community] is the great underground artistic, political, literature, musical revolution we are building….A community where people support each other, get inspired, collaborate together."[23] However, sometimes the capacity to construct a space for self-expression in a world that feels wholly administered can be enough. For example, Lynette, of the Singaporean zine *There Are Not Enough Hours in the Day for All the Bitching I Have to Do!*, says that her driving force is "to create a space to escape to in this world."[24] The need for both a public forum and a haven is born of the singular interpellation of girls as consumer citizens. New media can operate as places for personal expression or political participation, but in either case they represent an urgent need on the part of young women to express themselves outside of the spaces currently available to them. This is regardless of their enduring effects as a politics, which remains an open question.

Jamming girl culture and creating new public spheres are but two ways that young female activists address the shaping of young women's "postfeminist" status around consumer citizenship. While some young women do constitute the revitalizing market for consumer products, it is many other girls who form the hidden, often informal labor force producing these goods in unregulated, outworked circumstances. The backdrop against which these new systems of consumption and production take place is the globalization of capitalism and the sharpening of class and race inequities between and among young women. Girl activists struggle with the problem that structural explanations for their differential circumstances are losing ground in the face of pervasive discourses of Girl Power, self-invention, and meritocracy. Young women's activism around consumer citizenship is therefore not limited to culture jamming or the attempted creation of new public spheres through alternative media and the Internet. Many are also involved in other kinds of political activities and movements that tackle the global political economy that has generated these limited opportunities for citizenship for young people in the first place. It is when these connections are made that the creative but often isolated techniques of the culture jammers and virtual community builders can develop solid foundations for a new girl citizen who does not merely consume commercial culture, but is an active producer and critic in her community.

Notes

1. Roberts et al. (2001).
2. Fine and Weis (2000), 1140.
3. Miles (2000), 125.
4. Klein (2001).
5. Adkins (2002), 65.
6. Lambert (2003).
7. See Barwick (2001) and Brown (2000) for U.K. figures; Nikas (1998) for Australia; and Cuneo (2002) for the United States.
8. Holland (2000), 62.
9. Quoted in Lambert (2003).
10. Beck (1992), 135.
11. McRobbie (2000).
12. Vina (2002). Thanks to Elke Zobl for her important resources at grrrlzines.net.
13. Klein (2001), 284.
14. Stasko (2001), 278.
15. Fry and Lousley (2001), 150.
16. Burgmann (2003), 306.
17. Vina (2002).
18. Clodagh (2002).
19. Veruska (2002).
20. Carol (2001).
21. Anderson (1991).
22. Riika (2002).
23. Veruska (2002).
24. Lynette (2002).

References

Adkins, Lisa. (2002). *Revisions: Gender and Sexuality in Late Modernity.* Buckingham: Open University Press.

Anderson, Benedict. (1991). *Imagined Communities: Reflections on the Origin and Spread of Nationalism.* London: Verso.

Barwick, Sandra. (2001). "Sex, Boys and Make-up: Is This What Tweenie Girls Want?" *Daily Telegraph,* February 8, p. 22.

Beck, Ulrich. (1992). *Risk Society: Towards a New Modernity.* London: Sage.

Brown, Maggie. (2000). "Give Us the Pocket Money." *The Guardian,* May 29, p. 36.

Burgmann, Verity. (2003). *Power, Profit and Protest.* Sydney: Allen and Unwin.

Carol. (2001). Quoted in Elke Zobl, "Stop Sexism with Style! *Grrrl:Rebel.* An Interview with Carol and Elise." http://grrrlzines.net/interviews/grrrlrebel.htm.

Clodagh. (2002). Quoted in Elke Zobl, "Lighting a Fire of Thought and Ideas: *Ideas Is Matches.* An Interview with Clodagh." http://grrrlzines.net/interviews/ideas.htm.

Cuneo, Alice. (2002). "Affiliation Targets Youngest Female Consumers." *AdAge,* August 27.

Fine, Michelle, and Weis, Lois. (2000). "Disappearing Acts: The State and Violence Against Women in the Twentieth Century." *Signs: Journal of Women in Culture and Society* 25 (4): 1139–1146.

Fry, Kimberley, and Lousley, Cheryl. (2001). "Green Grrrl Power." *Canadian Woman Studies: Young Women: Feminists, Activists, Grrrls* 20/21 (4/1): 148–151.

Holland, Tom. (2000). "Her Choice." *Far Eastern Economic Review* 163 (24): 62–65.

Klein, Naomi. (2001). *No Logo.* Flamingo. London: UK.

Kylie. (2001). http://catpounce.diaryland.com/credit.html.

Lambert, Catherine. (2003). "It's the Dawn of Girl Power." *Herald Sun,* April 13, Sydney.

Lynette. (2002). Quoted in Elke Zobl, "*There Are Not Enough Hours in the Day for All the Bitching I Have to Do!*: An Interview with Lynette, Singapore." http://grrrlzines.net/interviews/lynette.htm.

McRobbie, Angela. (2000). "Sweet Smell of Success? New Ways of Being Young Women." In McRobbie's *Feminism and Youth Culture.* London: Macmillan.

Miles, Steven. (2000). *Youth Lifestyles in a Changing World.* Buckingham: Open University Press.

Nikas, Catherine. (1998). "The Power of Girls." *Ragtrader,* April 3–16, pp. 20–21.

Riika. (2002). Quoted in Elke Zobl, "Challenge, Argue, Think, Define, Prove Your Points! Be Inspired and Encouraged by *Ladybomb* Distro: An Interview with Riika." http://grrrlzines.net/interviews/ladybomb.htm.

Roberts, Ken, et al. (2001). "The Monetarisation and Privatisation of Daily Life, and the Depoliticisation of Youth in Former Communist Countries." Paper presented at "Youth— Actor of Social Change?" Symposium, Council of Europe, Strasbourg, December 12–14.

Stasko, Carly. (2001). "Action Grrrls in the Dream Machine." In Allyson Mitchell, Lisa Bryn Rundle, and Lara Karaian (eds.), *Turbo Chicks: Talking Young Feminisms.* Toronto: Sumach Press.

Veruska. (2002). Quoted in Elke Zobl, "*Clit Rocket:* Queer Revolution. An Interview with Veruska Outlaw." http://grrrlzines.net/interviews/clitrocket.htm.

Vina. (2002). Quoted in Elke Zobl, "Girls, Keep on Getting the Word Out! The Austrian Zine *NYLON* Is Spreading the F-Word: An Interview with Sonja Eismann and Vina Yun from *NYLON.*" http://grrrlzines.net/interviews/nylon.htm.

Yen. (2002). Quoted in Elke Zobl, "*Emancypunx:* Creating Space for Women and Making Different Perspectives Visible in Poland. An Interview with Yen." http://grrrlzines.net/interviews/emancypunx.htm.

CHAPTER 15

Girls' Web Sites: A Virtual "Room of One's Own"?

JACQUELINE REID-WALSH AND CLAUDIA MITCHELL

It is a commonplace of media/technology research that there appears to be a "digital gender divide" between girls and boys and their voluntary engagement with computers and technological games. In turn, there is a concern that these play or leisure activities directly relate to the development of skills that are highly valued in today's society—for example, playing certain video games may prepare boys for future education with computer simulation and careers as pilots, engineers, computer programmers, and so on (Cassell and Jenkins 1998: 11; Buckingham 2000). Indeed, computer gaming culture as a whole seems to be a male-dominated domain (Kline 2002). Unwittingly, much of the discourse seems to repeat the "girls and math" illogic of the 1980s where girls were seen as "deficient" and had to catch up, as was pointed out by Walkerdine (1989). At the same time, the knowledge girls do acquire is perceived as being of little or no value because the activities girls engage in either on the screen or around the computer appear to reproduce established gender stereotypes of fashion doll play, shopping, chatting, and so on (Thomas and Walkerdine 2000). In the popular and academic literature there is much discussion addressing dangers for children, most particularly for girls, on the Web. Stemming from this, questions arise about how child and girl users might negotiate the unsafe space of the Web as a play space.

In this chapter, we briefly examine one small aspect of girls' computer play: their voluntary engagement with the World Wide Web in building home pages. We focus on the voluntary and nonschool use of digital

173

technology for a variety of reasons, not the least of which relates to, as Tobin observes (particularly of teen boys' home computer use), a shift to modes of learning about computer technology occurring outside formal learning settings (Tobin 1998: 127). This shift of learning may also be regarded as complementary to what Luke (2000: 80) observes as a shift in what constitutes "play" to a "whole new cultural realm of play and sociality which go beyond the phenomenal world of place and the linearity of analogue time." The link between the computer, popular culture, and the engagement occurring in a private or domestic space seems to appear most obviously during the age period of early adolescence. This is the age group in which girls begin to engage with a wide range of popular culture media, much of which is directed at them as a consumer group: films, television series, music, magazines, and romance fiction (as noted by Christian-Smith, Driscoll, McRobbie, Tapscott, and Walkerdine, among others). These girls may engage in a number of popular culture/popular media activities at once. They may be engaging in apparently "redundant" activities—such as logging on to a Web site and playing along while watching a game show. Or they may be engaging in disconnected activities at the same time, such as playing a computer game, talking on the telephone, and watching music videos on television. Instead of experiencing cognitive dissonance, it would appear that they are enacting their own version of "convergence!"

Like Tobin (1998), Walkerdine (1998), and Takayoshi et al. (1999), we are interested in the Web as a cultural space that blurs the boundaries between production and consumption, children and adults, and, as we also argue in *Researching Children's Popular Culture* (Mitchell and Reid-Walsh 2002), of girlhood itself. In North America the Internet and Web are relatively more accessible spaces for children than the often costly, elaborate computer games that are stand-alone commodities. Children rely on parental income to own a computer and modem, and pay for the connection, but these devices and computer access have multiple uses and can be used by the entire family. Moreover, Web sites constructed or designed by girls are one of the few spaces under their control. Indeed, our logic in some ways approximates that of Virginia Woolf in her famous essay *A Room of One's Own* (1929), where she links the history of English women's writing with the access by nonaristocratic women to a separate, private, and safe space. We would like to propose that by constructing a personal Web site, a girl can obtain a virtual "room of one's own," no matter how cramped her physical living conditions may be. Thus, analogous to their physical rooms, we consider these Web sites to be semiprivate places of creativity and sociality, and sites of "virtual bedroom culture."

The idea of girls' "bedroom culture" as a distinct cultural form was conceived of by McRobbie and Garber in 1976 to address the invisibility of girls as subjects in youth-based subculture studies. They considered girls to be "negotiating a different space" and to be "offering a different type of resistance" than the boys (McRobbie and Garber 1991: 221). Girls' subcultures, especially those of younger girls, tended to be based inside the home. These consisted of activities such as magazine reading, listening to music (Frith 1987), talking on the telephone, and so on. The location of these activities was largely the result of parental control, whereby girls' actions and activities were restricted more to the private sphere, while boys were allowed to roam more freely in the public space of the street (McRobbie and Garber 1991: 12; Nava 1992: 79–80). During the middle 1990s, however, especially after the Jamie Bulger murder in 1993, as Valentine (1997) and McNamee (2000) observe, parental concerns about public safety began to apply both to girls and to boys. Partly in response to the change of location of some boys, especially younger boys, the idea of a "digital bedroom" was conceived of by Julian Sefton-Green and David Buckingham (1998) to account for the physical location of many children's cyber play.

Textual Approaches to Web Sites

We are interested in ways of interpreting girls' Web sites, focusing on several preadolescent and young adolescent girls' personal home pages that are selected from publicly accessible search engines. Due to ethical issues we did not invade "girls only" or "children only" domains to gather information. We also viewed the publicly available descriptions of sites hosted by www.gURL.com. We selected only those sites that appear to be constructed, or at least designed, by the girls themselves. Adult roles appear to be advisory or, as in the case of young or disabled girls, physical aides. These sites appear to be constructed partly for their own pleasure but also as a way to project themselves in the domain of the Net and potentially to engage with others in communication (hence the omnipresence of the site counter and guest book). We consider these sites to be a popular cultural form, not a high cultural form. As virtual manifestations of the girls' bedrooms, these sites are partly repositories of images of popular culture in a manner analogous to how their rooms may be storehouses of popular artifacts (Mitchell and Reid-Walsh 2002). Popular culture images may even form the materials that the site is composed of. Our analysis has several components. First, we consider how these girls as builders compose or construct their sites in the domain of the free home page. Second, we examine how the personal home page appears to function not only as a personal space but also an idealized space for the girls. In our speculative discussion we focus specifically on the feature of the guest book.

In our work, we attempted to determine the age of the girls at the time of site construction by considering both explicit and implicit information. Although children wisely do not often give much personal information about themselves, sometimes they will provide specific information about grade or age. Other times, the use of language and focus of hobbies on a site may suggest a particular age. We tried to find pages by younger girls who are preadolescents or "tweens" because it appears that this is not only the time when they may be first engaging in "girl culture" in the physical world, but also that they are still in grade school and therefore may have more leisure time for working on a site. For example, the Canadian girl's page noted below (although it has probably been abandoned, because it has not been updated in a couple of years and some of the links are no longer working) is by "Heather." She was probably around ten at the time of the page's construction, for she tells us she is in grade five. We know that she lives on the West Coast of Canada, is Caucasian and blond; we know about her family size, her pets, and her hobbies, but not her exact location. She provides an E-mail address: http://www.geocities.com/EnchantedForest/Glade/9492/heather1.html.

In contrast to the other images on the page, which are static, the moving pages of her guest book are a prominent and attractive feature that invites the viewer to respond.

Sometimes, the age of the home page creator can be partly deduced by the topic or theme, such as the ones that are related to the "neopets" craze. There are numerous home pages devoted to these pets, and they tend to be by girls. Some girls have started "guilds," which are a type of virtual community based loosely upon the care of and play with these pets. Because http://www/neopet.com is a protected site, often you cannot E-mail the owners, or sometimes even enter their sites, without logging on and registering with neopets.com. For example, http://www.geocities.com/ash_choo/me.html is an anonymous site organized by a thirteen-year-old red-haired girl. She gives a photo of herself; tells about her pets; and has links to dolls, the Sims computer game, and virtual pets; but gives no information about herself.

With younger girls or disabled children who need aid, though siblings or parents serve as the literal builders, their site may be consider theirs because they reflect their passions and their interests. For instance, here is "Elizabeth's Snow White page" a Web site devoted to the Disney film *Snow White and the Seven Dwarfs*, http://www.ecn.bgu.edu/users/gjmuzzo/lizzie1.htm. The elaborate front page states that elder siblings actually constructed the page for her and that the Web travel she participates in while searching for Snow White sites is an alternative to physical travel, which is severely limited due to her multiple disabilities.

The Generic Construction of Web Sites: Digital Building Blocks and Guest Books

When girls engage in constructing their own Web sites or personal home pages, this activity often appears to be a virtual derivative of the logic and process of step-by-step building block construction popular with small children, continued in more elaborate construction by older children. While Buckingham and Sefton-Green label this type of creativity "Lego-creativity" (1998), we are interested in extending the Lego analogy to encompass Web site construction. Because no knowledge of HTML is required, even small girls/children can build Web sites. We argue that the popularity of building Web sites among small children could stem from the ability to apply skills learned from play with material objects to the virtual realm: not only the logic of building blocks, but also of drawing, making sticker albums, collecting trade cards, writing diaries, and so on—all activities associated with girls.

The guest book is a common feature of most Web sites. It is a program that allows outside users to log entries to a Web page, and has been used as a way for visitors to post comments about a Web site. Unlike a "Web forum," which is interactive, it is a linear listing of visitor comments, questions, and posts. It does not allow other visitors to post comments or reply directly to someone else's post. Each new message is simply posted to the top of the guestbook page. It provides a sense of control for the owner of a site, although authors of Web advice literature targeting children caution that a guest book is not completely safe for the user. In an article targeting schools, "Safety on the Internet," the authors explain that the user's comments can be viewed by the Web master as well as any other person who looks at the guest book on the site. They warn children to not give too much specific information. Also, they warn about going to the addresses of the signatures on one's Web page. They conclude that the benefits outweigh the worries because of the ability to engage in one-way communication: "Guestbooks are great for communicating with people without worrying about using E-mail...." (http://seahawk.scwms.mcps.k12.va.us/Curriculum/Soti/day6.htm).

It is interesting to think of how the guest book is seen as a way to engage with others. If the relation is understood in light of Paul Willis's idea of serial community being a feature of youth culture, then a type of interactivity is still present, but of a different, disengaged type. In *Common Culture* (1990) Willis discusses the notion of proto-communities which spring up from contingency or even accident. He defines these social groupings not as modes of direct communication but as an indirect form through the expression of shared interest, style, fashions, and so on. He states that metaphorically, a "serial" community is "a spaced-out queue of people rather than a talking circle" whereby the participants are placed randomly or chaotically in social and material place and time (p. 141). It seems that the indirect communication made possible by the technology of the guest book is an instance of this type of community. As noted above, this may also be a somewhat "safer" mode of interaction because the page owner remains apart from the viewer, and can read and respond to the comments on the page itself as opposed to using E-mail. In the following section we link this idea of a serial community being enabled by the guest book to the girls' home page being a type of ideal space under the girls' control.

Girls' Personal Home Pages as an Idealized Space

The personal home page with its guest book suggests the presence of a private, even domestic, space in cyberspace. As a type of nonrealistic, ideal space, the home page might be regarded as a utopia. It may also be understood not as utopia (which literally is a nowhere) but as more of a heterotopia, which, according to Foucault, has a "real place" but is set in opposition to most places (1986: 24). Our analysis of girls' Web sites in *Researching Children's Popular Culture* (2002) is partly inspired by Sarah McNamee's idea of considering the space of children's video game play in their bedrooms as a strategy for negotiating and resisting spatial boundaries (2000: 484) by considering this virtual play to exist in a kind of heterotopia. McNamee points out that children are located in a real place (their bedrooms) and engaging with real machines (the computers), but the space where they experience the adventure is not there but in one of Foucault's "other spaces" (2000: 484–485). In our discussion we summarize the ideas from Foucault's article "Of Other Spaces" (1986), where he theorizes his notions of utopia and heterotopia in light of the history of colonization by Western culture. We discuss how Foucault's representation of the history of space in the West seems to be reproduced in the act of exploring the Web and in the colonization of cyberspace. We apply aspects from Foucault's principles of heterotopia to girls' Web sites as both a concept that describes the home page as an entity and as a way to understand how home pages are structured.

Foucault outlines five principles in relation to heterotopias: In his first principle he states that heterotopias are present in all cultures in all periods, although they take different forms. In early or "primitive" societies there are "crisis heterotopias" which are "privileged or sacred or forbidden places" reserved for people in crisis, such as adolescents, menstruating women, pregnant women, and the elderly. In more complex societies there are "heterotopias of deviation," such as prisons, rest homes, psychiatric hospitals, and retirement homes (pp. 24–25). The second principle is that as a society changes, an extant heterotopia functions differently. Foucault's example is the cemetery, which until the end of the eighteenth century was located in the center of a town, next to the church, but then, to mirror changing views of death, was moved to the outskirts of town (p. 25). The third principle concerns how heterotopias can juxtapose in a single "real space" several sites that are themselves incompatible, such as in a cinema, which in a rectangular space has a two-dimensional screen on which three-dimensional space is projected, and a garden, the microcosm of the earth, and its representation, the carpet (1986: 25–26). The fourth principle concerns the ways that heterotopias are often linked to slices of time: either indefinitely accumulating time, such as in museums and libraries, or the obverse, transitory time, such as fairgrounds and vacation villages. The fifth principle concerns the paradoxes in heterotopias and how they seem to possess a system of "opening and closing that both isolates them and makes them penetrable." Foucault states that usually heterotopias are not "freely accessible, like a public place" such as barracks, prisons, and saunas. Particularly interesting to our analysis of virtual bedrooms is the example of the guest bedroom on South America farms that provides entry to travelers yet denies them access to the family:

> The entry door did not lead into the central room where the family lived, and every individual or traveler who came by had the right to open this door, to enter into the bedroom and to sleep there for a night. Now these bedrooms were such that the individual who went in to them never had access to the family's quarters; the visitor was absolutely the guest in transit, was not really the invited guest. (p. 26)

The last two principles appear to describe the structure and function of girls' home pages: a girl's site as a repository of images (as in the fourth principle), and the function and use factors of the guest book (related to the fifth). In terms of heterotopias being linked to slices of time that are either transitory or accumulating, we are struck by how, paradoxically, Web sites are both. The transitory nature of a child's site or any site (especially sites that have not been maintained) is immediately apparent. At the same time, girls' Web sites are often repositories of images of popular culture. These include static images of material culture that might be found in their rooms (such as dolls, stuffed animals, posters) and links to fan sites, as well as clips of popular music and musician sites. In terms of images, what is notable is that unlike material culture, the images of virtual pets or guardian angels or Powerpuff Girls and so on are from free sites. As well, the many sites devoted to girl-produced creations (art, fiction, poetry, etc.) are indeed free, although the latter two are increasingly moving to specially delegated fan sites.

In our comments about the guest book we noted how the interaction between Web site owner and visitor is limited or indirect and that it seems to form a serial community. This feature of controlled access recalls some of the features of the fifth principle of heterotopia as articulated by Foucault. We find this fascinating for many reasons. It can be seen as a virtual extension of the autograph album of girls' culture where children record their names and comments. In addition to being a useful record of a child's popularity in terms of collecting signatures, afterward it may serve as a material record or memento of a certain school grade. The idea of a guest book also evokes an imaginary leisured existence of a bygone middle-and upper-class culture in which visitors signed a guest book at the door when they came to call. This, as with adults, is a world far removed from the haste and stress of many girls' lives. The way girls personalize this standard feature can be seen as a form of "creative consumption" (Willis) by the child creator as she visits publicly available repositories of guest book options at the free home page sites and selects what she wants. Since many guest books also contain moving images, these also attract the viewer's eye.

Girls' Web sites can be considered private rooms or domains open to the public under certain conditions stipulated by the owners. The experience of

visiting a girl's site recalls Foucault's discussion of the fifth principle of heterotopia with respect to the visitors' bedrooms on South American farms.
His description of a structural situation where one can seem to gain easy
access to the private space of a bedroom seems apt. To enter a girl's home
page, as with any Web site, all one needs is the URL address. Moreover, to
continue the analogy, many of the younger girls' pages appear to be virtual
representations of their bedrooms, for they are decorated with floral and or
pastel patterns called "wallpaper"; they contain representations of objects
that resemble miniature stuffed animals or stickers from sticker albums;
images of pop stars one might find on their walls; and so on. If there is a
music file playing, it may be that of a favorite pop star, such as a girl might
listen to in the privacy of her room. At the same time, though, as Foucault
notes, the visitor never has access to the private, family quarters. This situation of separation appears to be increasingly the case with girls' Web sites.
While apparently private expressions or personal spaces, they are not often
openly confessional. Their collections of artifacts which are obtained from
public, free sites have a personal application only if one knows the owner of
the site. Otherwise they appear opaque.

Viewing a child's Web site can be a paradoxical experience. On the one
hand, an onlooker receives the impression of being invited to see private
aspects of a girl's life and also aspects closely related to the child—she may
talk about her life, her interests, her hopes. One may know her stated likes
and dislikes, maybe even see a photo of her, and read her poetry and look at
her art. As a virtual representation of a bedroom or other sort of room, the
images may even be indicators of innermost secrets and hopes (Bachelard,
in Foucault 1986). On the other hand, the images apart from personal pho-
tographs of a girl, her family, and her pets may be mainly generic or publicly accessible ones gathered from free archives. Here the creativity, as in
collections or collages of material culture artifacts, and the meaning for the
young person stem from the symbolic recycling and attribution of new
meaning (Willis 1990; Bryson and de Castell 1995). Yet despite the sometimes unsettling experience for an adult viewer on gazing at a child's site
and seeing such apparently private images, the construction of images
themselves on a site cannot be altered. The Web site creator remains apart
and untouched by the viewer. The only communication is through E-mail
or the guest book.

Conclusion

We would like to propose that girls' Web sites may also undo some opposi-
tions that Foucault considered inviolable, such as the division between
public and private spaces. If this observation is extended to include age and
gender, this "inviolable" opposition would include how girls are usually
associated with space inside the home and boys with space outside. We consider that the space of the Web and the home page may "unsettle" and,

indeed, begin to overturn this opposition. Moreover, the opposition between outer and inner psychic space may be unsettled as well, for it is on the publicly accessible, personal home page that one may find the expression of an author's innermost secrets, dreams, and passions. As we have seen, gazing at or gaining access to girls' home pages may create the impression of undergoing a contradictory experience: a viewer seems to be intruding into a private domain that resembles in some ways a virtual version of her bedroom, yet this access is an illusion. A viewer may sign the guest book, as invited to do so, but this activity of signing only heightens the status of being a transient visitor, not an invited guest.

We have become intrigued by how the common feature of the guest book in some ways extends and recapitulates the idea of a Web page. As a standard component of most Web site construction programs, the guest book is part of the "Lego" approach to building Web sites. Yet by being personalized with icons of the girl's choosing, often resembling stickers or decals, the guest book evokes (in a virtual way) girls' autograph or sticker albums, part of the material culture of girls' (bedroom) culture. The invitation to sign the guest book similarly recalls the popular practice of signing an autograph album. Indeed, the presence of a guest book evokes an imaginary leisured lifestyle far removed from any child's "real time" existence. In opposition to this fanciful aspect, the guest book, since it is combined with a counter, is the main way to record statistics about visitors to a site. A girl may interpret the numbers simply to be a record of her (virtual) "popularity." At the same time, the presence of a counter enables the Web site to become noticeable to search engines that use the number of visitors or "hits" as a criterion for inclusion in lists of sites. The presence of a guest book, then, is one way that enables the home page to be "recognized" by search engines and thereby become visible to users. In this way, the guest book records the visitors to girls' Web sites that as instances of virtual bedroom culture may be idealized spaces, but as Foucault observes about heterotopias, as opposed to utopias, they are "real" spaces. These real spaces—the guest book and the Web page itself—are constructed by the girls themselves.

A girl's home page appears to be a kind of contradictory space—a *private* space that exists openly in a *public* domain. As a private space it is like a bedroom. It can serve as a private domain where the girl can express herself creatively, whether this be to produce her own writing (analogously to the spatial requirement articulated by Virginia Woolf) or art or music, whether it be original or of a collage form. This private domain may also, as we have seen, serve as a type of private museum for virtual artifacts either created or owned by the girl. Finally, within the highly competitive and sometimes predatory "frontier" culture of the Internet and World Wide Web, girls' Web sites can also serve as a type of "safe" space, something we are certain that Virginia Woolf would have approved of in relation to issues surrounding contemporary girlhood.

References

Bryson, M., and de Castell, S. (1995). "So We've Got a Chip on Our Shoulder! Sexing the Texts of Educational Technology." In S. Gaskell and J. Willinksy (eds.), *Gender Informs Curriculum.* Toronto: OISE Press.

Buckingham, D. (2000). *After the Death of Childhood: Growing Up in the Age of Electronic Media.* Cambridge: Polity Press.

Cassell, J., and Jenkins, H. (eds.). (1998). *From Barbie to Mortal Kombat: Gender and Computer Games.* Cambridge, Mass.: MIT Press.

Christian-Smith, L. (1990). *Becoming a Woman Through Romance.* New York: Routledge.

Driscoll, C. (2002). G*irls: Feminine Adolescence in Popular Culture and Cultural Theory.* New York: Columbia University Press.

Foucault, M. (1986). "Of Other Spaces," trans. J. Miskowiec. *Diacritics* (Spring): 16 (1): 22–27.

Frith, S. (1987). *Sound Effects: Youth, Leisure, and the Politics of Rock and Roll.* New York: Pantheon.

Kline, S. (2002). "Learners, Spectators or Gamers in the Media Saturated Household? Changing Use Patterns of Canadian Adolescents." Paper presented at the Toys, Games and Media Conference, University of London, Institute of Education, August.

Luke, C. (2000). "Cyber-schooling and Technological Change: Multiliteracies for New Times." In B. Cope and M. Kalantzis (eds.), *Multiliteracies: Literacy Learning and the Design of Social Futures.* London: Routledge.

McNamee, S. (2000). "Foucault's Heterotopia and Children's Everyday Lives." *Childhood* 7 (4): 479–492.

McRobbie, A., and Garber, J. (1991). "Girls and Subcultures." In *Feminism and Youth Culture: From Jackie to Just Seventeen.* Cambridge, Mass.: Unwin. Originally printed in S. Hall and T. Jefferson (eds.), *Resistance Through Rituals: Youth Subcultures in Postwar Britain.* London: Hutchison, 1976.

Mitchell, C., and Reid-Walsh, J. (2002). *Researching Children's Popular Culture: The Cultural Spaces of Childhood.* London and New York: Routledge.

Nava, M. (1992). *Changing Cultures: Feminism, Youth and Consumerism.* London: Sage.

"Safety on the Internet." http://seahawk.scwms.mcps.k12.va.us/Curriculum/Soti/day6.htm. (Accessed March 1, 2003.)

Sefton-Green, J. and Buckingham, D. (eds.). (1998). *Digital Diversions:* Children's "Creative Uses" of Multimedia Technologies. London: UCL Press.

Takayoshi, P., Huot, E., and Huot, M. (1999). "No Boys Allowed: The World Wide Web as Clubhouse for Girls." *Computers and Composition* 16: 89–106.

Tapscott, D. (1998). *Growing Up Digital: The Rise of the Net Generation.* New York: McGraw–Hill.

Thomas, A. and Walkerdine, V. (2000). "Girls and Computer Games." Paper presented at the Bologna 4th European Feminist Research Conference. Available at http://www.women.it/cyberarchive/files/thomas.htm. (Accessed March 1, 2003.)

Tobin, J. (1998). "An American Otaku (or, a Boy's Virtual Life on the Net)." In J. Sefton-Green (ed.), *Digital Diversions: Youth Culture in the Age of Multimedia.* London: UCL Press.

Valentine, G. (1997). "'My Son's a Bit Dizzy.' 'My Wife's a Bit Soft': Gender, Children, and Cultures of Parenting." *Gender, Place and Culture* 4 (1): 37–62.

Walkderdine, V., comp. (1989). *Counting Girls Out.* London: Virago.

Walkerdine, V. (1998). "Children in Cyberspace: A New Frontier." In K. Lesnik-Oberstein (ed.), *Children in Culture: Approaches to Childhood.* Houndsmills, U.K.: Macmillan.

Willis, P. (1990). *Common Culture: Symbolic Work at Play in the Everyday Cultures of the Young.* Milton Keynes, U.K.: Open University Press.

Woolf, V. (1929). *A Room of One's Own.* New York: Harcourt, Brace.

PART **5**
Schooling

CHAPTER 16

Pleasures Within Reason: Teaching Feminism and Education

NANCY LESKO AND ANTOINETTE QUARSHIE

[P]leasure is always inevitably caught by modes of thinking and ways of being—by conventional ways of thinking. Given that conventional thinking is neither static nor all of a piece, our pleasures, though always framed, are never entirely fixed. This means, among other things, that certain ways of taking pleasure can and do offer up subversive possibilities within a lived condition of being always unfree. While fun never escapes rationality, it can and does trouble it.

(McWillliam 2000: 167)

School Memories and Pleasure

Nancy: Although I learned a lot from the Dominican nuns in grades 1–12, ideas about pleasure in teaching and learning were not among them. I came to believe that a good education involved hard work. Teaching meant cajoling, pushing, monitoring, and disciplining students to meet those expectations. Fun might be a fringe activity sneaked in by an especially humorous or compassionate sister, like a "casual Friday" reprieve from the school uniform. Pleasure was in the effort—my long Sunday afternoons at the dark mahogany dining room table with math problems—alternating between the momentary triumph of completing one and making stabs at solving the next one. Learning has been a puzzle—finding a question and then figuring out "the solution," which could be a social analysis of violence or an interdisciplinary methodology. Solving the puzzles of teaching has also been pleasurable, and new curricular puzzles are easy to think up.

185

Both my own education via the nuns and my own labors in middle school and high school classrooms made me suspicious of pedagogical pleasures and worried that good teachers and demanding professors didn't mix much with such practices. In recent years, when my classes felt fun, smoothly flowing, and starkly pleasurable, I've been haunted by worries that they must not be rigorous enough (Shank 2000). As you can see, I have been firmly in the grip of a dualist conception of teaching as work, not pleasure.

Antoinette: My early schooling experiences in Scotland include memories of nuns who broke the rules by allowing me advance entrée to school with my older brother when they learned that the precociously clever girl in their midst was an "early reader." I learned the pleasures of pleasing through academic prowess as the youngest and strongest reader in the class. Later, in a different school, on the Caribbean island of Grenada, I experienced the distinct pleasures of becoming an appropriate(d) student by acquiescing to the order of the classroom. In my complex longings and desires to belong to the body/landscape relations (Davies 2000) of my new school, I admitted to myself that being in the classroom was distinctly different from (be)longing. Belonging meant constituting my/self appropriately to become an intelligible part of the terrain as a student marked by the beliefs, routines, and rituals of the class. (Be)longing meant being recognizable to my classmates and having "a sense of being in [my] proper or usual place" (Davies 2000: 37).

As I learned that the classroom was ruled by the strictures of order and regulation, I took pleasure in silently waiting during the Friday afternoon rituals of student rankings—knowing that I would find my name at the top of the list. Each Friday, I watched the skins of my poor-performing classmates swell with welts from weekly lashings—yet I despised these peers at the bottom of the list for failing to become "good students." I was a most (un)reasonable student, full of conflicting desires, seeking secret pleasures that were subversive, (im)proper, and inappropriate(d). While I checked to make sure that my work was in order, to please my teacher, I also secretly made her dis/abled body the object of my scorn and ridicule by mocking the wooden leg that I knew was hidden under her robes. Outside of the pleasures of competing with other students for high marks, I chased (im)proper pleasures by climbing trees with boys. When I was reprimanded for crossing the invisible gendered boundaries that governed appropriate(d) behavior, I learned my primary school lesson—I had to take my "pleasures within reason" (Foucault 1985; McWilliam 2000).

Later, when I began teaching middle school students, I lived the naïve fiction of believing that if I was willing to tolerate some (dis)order, by relinquishing some decision-making power, I could create classroom spaces in which my students and I could bridge the seemingly unruly tensions between learning and pleasure. However, attempts to trouble the hierarchical relations of student/teacher, by moving beyond the boundaries of rigid conceptions of schooling embedded in the school culture, were firmly met with resistance and confusion. I had naively believed that students would readily accept student-centered pedagogical practices that invited shared decision-making, imagination, and pleasure into the classroom.

Exploring Dynamic Spaces of Teaching Together

Our disparate assumptions about learning, teaching, reason, and pleasure came into a feminist focus in the spring of 2002 when we taught an elective course, Gender, Difference, and Curriculum, and weekly exclaimed to each other as we packed up our materials, "This class is a pleasure to teach!" Our broad smiles were stoked by equal parts of surprise and delight. Those weekly exclamations of pleasurable teaching marked the beginning of this inquiry into the pleasures of teaching and the relationships between pleasure and critical inquiry. Finally, we aim to contribute a teaching-focused answer to the question of this volume: What are the futures of feminisms and education?

Are there specific pleasures to teaching with and about feminisms? Can such pleasures be counted when examining feminist futures in education? Could we trace the pleasure to the serendipity of a wonderful student population (all women graduate students in a school of education who elected the class), as many sociologists and practicing teachers do? Was the pleasure related to our working together and sharing the planning with impromptu conversations about movies, shoes, the color pink, and the identity politics of bisexuality? These questions may at first glance seem idiosyncratic and private, but the investigation of feminist teaching pleasures may offer ideas about girls and the future of feminist inquiry (depending on how one defines "girls"—we were all just a bunch of girls in our classroom).[1] We ask these questions from a position of teaching with interests in poststructural feminist approaches to pleasure (McWilliam 2000); investigations of emotions, power, and educational practices (Boler 1999); and multiple perspectives on telling life stories as instances of making selves (Morrison 1998; Lorde 1982). In addition, the course focused on discursive constructions of gender, race, class, and sexuality in popular cultural representations of schooling, through interdisciplinary readings and memoirs. We drew on ideas of writing and subjectivity (Kamler 2002), and asked students to discuss films and television programs, to write analytical papers and theorized autobiographies/biomythographies.

In the writing and telling of our lives, as we examined our individual "biomythographies" (Lorde 1982), we considered our relationships to knowledge and theory, as well as the pedagogical spaces that may be opened up and closed by the use of storytelling, literature, and textual narratives in the classroom. Since biomythographies are the constructions of life stories based on the intricate weave of personal/collective/cultural beliefs, dreams, myths, stories, memories, and histories that compose the tapestries of our lives (Lorde 1982), the telling of our stories enabled us to open up spaces for conversations across the intersections of the multiple story lines that informed our subjectivities as girls. The site of memory enabled us to begin to get outside of the text by providing the terrain for the rethinking of our present selves and the positioning of our subjectivities within temporal moments. We became aware of the ways in which memory allows us to construct the social world differently and reinvent the now through the then. In this way, we moved beyond autobiographical (re)tellings centered in constructing the self to consider how our own biomythographies fit into a collective story of experiences of women shaped by overlapping discursive practices. We chose to engage in this work because "the telling of stories, written and spoken, produces a web of experiences that are at once individual, interconnected, collective—and political" (Davies et al. 2001: 169) that enables us to see, hear, and imagine differently. We intended to critically examine the processes of our subjectification in the theorized autobiographies and to avoid essentializing our experiences by subsuming our identities under the generalized category—women.

As we describe below, the stories seemed to take on a life of their own—and we became audiences for the often intimate pleasures of the performance of personal narratives. Only months later can we now begin to unravel some of our ambivalent responses and fray the edges of the biomythographies. We are trying to implicate our own pedagogies and our pleasures in our students' biomythographies as a way to understand learning around feminism and education.

Taking Pleasure in Mapping My Geography of Self

The way we come [to take pleasure] is part of a broader set of performative practices that mark our ability to read what is proper in a particular time and place and to self-shape accordingly.

(McWilliam 2000: 164–165)

Antoinette: I selected fragments of my poetry, journals, short stories, and memoirs, with little regard for the distinction between fact and fiction (aren't both representations of truths?), to create a collage of personal truths in a biomythography that was "safe" (enough) to share with the class. In my telling of my story, I resisted the desires to share "excessive knowledges" (Orner et al.1996)—those spillages of "unofficial" or "inappropriate" knowledges—about my family histories, habits, and practices that the class could have read as (im)proper. Instead, I spoke of a nomadic geography of self, as the girlflesh of a Grenadian mother and Ghanaian father residing in the nations of Ghana, Grenada, Scotland, and the United States. In my biomythography, I explored the social and cultural terrains of my home nations within the boundaries of an impoverished cartography (of hegemonic masculinities and femininities) and discussed the scripts I received on how to be a girl and become a proper woman. In my telling of my story, I gently troubled the ways in which I tried to honor and resist the "good girl" scripts that were offered to me by parents, teachers, friends, and popular culture.

I privately considered the ways in which each telling and (re)telling of my lived experience reflected my perceptions of what is deemed proper by a particular audience—how the layers of meaning contained within the text shift as the audience explores new terrain that reflects a geography of self as social, cultural, raced, classed, and gendered bodies. I desired to interrogate my cautious decision to define myself by the contours of ambiguity. My ambiguity was in part maintained by avoiding any discussion of intimate relationships with either men or women, although I desired to trouble the heteronormative practices that were beginning to shape our collective stories.

Nancy: Yes, the class sessions in which students read and performed their biomythographies felt at particular moments like transformed classroom spaces. We portray some of those moments when personal narratives, feelings, and a special relationship between teller and audience made our class meaningful and pleasurable. But this question haunts me: How transformative were these personal narratives, that is, what kinds of gendered persons and what kinds of material practices were narrated in them? What kinds of knowledges were taken up, and what kinds resisted, in their telling? What might the transformative pedagogy and its limits tell us about the futures of feminism and education?

> [We] must become overconcerned with experience as a discourse and with competing discourses of experience that traverse and structure any narrative—[to] somehow acknowledge the differences within and among the stories of experience, how they are told, and what it is that structures the telling and the retelling. (*Britzman 2000: 32*)

In our ongoing conversations, we chose to pay attention to the small things—the day-to-day materiality of our bodies—and our lived experiences, as we located our bodies in time, space, and discourse across nations, rather than pursuing strictly theory-driven discussions of the process of our subjugation as gendered beings. As we explored the cartographies of our interior landscapes, we discovered that the uneven emotional terrain of memory was marked by our acts of remembering and our desires to forget. A few stories were interrupted as the author confronted painful knots of emotion and released streams of tears. As we acknowledged the tears, we experienced the conflicting desires to resist and embrace the painful embodied knowledges of our collective stories.

Postmodern strategies of reading/writing texts recognize that new texts are dynamically created in the discursive spaces of interaction between the reader and the written text. We took pleasure in creating spaces for "living texts" as we came to view the sharing of our biomythographies as embodied participation through performance—a delicate (inter)play between performer and audience. We could not overlook the materiality of our selves in the performance of our texts as we recognized that each printed word embodied the timbres, inflections, tones, and rhythms of our voices. We came to realize that performance may open up spaces to move beyond the boundaries/limitations of language as the dramatic power of the voice and gestures of the body shape and give meaning to the spoken text as embodied words. As embodied text, performance may call into question static notions of representation by a layering of experience that may not be apparent in the flattened texts of the page. Since "the peculiarities of where [and how] we speak are as important to the signification as the content of what we are saying" (Probyn 1997: 125), we became committed to performance as a pedagogical tool. We would have missed the nuances of meaning, interpretation, and representation contained in our women's voices if we interacted with the text only through silent reading.

The women took pleasure in braiding the threads of their lives into narratives that told their stories through a variety of unconventional narrative devices. We resisted the clichéd patterns of linear storytelling and its familiar plot structure in favor of narrative forms that moved the hearer of the tales in unexpected ways. This group of women crafted tales with cyclical narrative structures, worked their stories backward, wrote vignettes unified by a central theme, arranged narrative collages, and fashioned multigenre pastiches. We were amazed by our students' creative expressiveness. *Nancy*: For example, Maria's narrative evoked a foglike gray, watery space. I resonated with the up-and-down narrative that echoed the pool laps, the rhythms of enthusiasm, disappointment, success, and betrayal. There was also a Zenlike quality to her performance—of being "in" one's body and the joy of movement. Maria's story of repetitive, simple acts that made her strong delighted her audience. I also loved Iris's story of remaking herself—clothes, hair, music, and language—to enter her new high school as a *real* African-American young woman. Her performance as African-American for others' eyes was conscious and strategic, and it was also an exquisite portrait of the performance theory of Judith Butler.

(Re)locating the Narratives

> It is through memory and its repetitional, restorative capacity—but repetition and restoration always with a difference, in part due to the most immediate previous repetition—that the second, and beyond that, third, fourth … readings of experience are performed. It is … as if memory spreads out the text of our lives for us to read again and again … for the text is never fixed or single: it is ever rewoven, constantly renewed or reconstructed, constantly evolving, a story and a work in progress.

> (Olney 1998: 344)

Sharing stories, through performance, enabled us to bridge lives and move beyond the (im)possibilities of communicating by engaging in a collective process of remembering, recognizing, and witnessing that is so integral to our lives. Performance opened up a collective space in which we were able to take pleasure together, within reason. As we remembered, through autobiographical writing that allowed us to interrogate the site of memory, we began to call attention to biomythographies as representations of the texts of our lives as particular social constructions. In the writing of our narratives, we recognized the paradox of memory as a slippery terrain that allows us to make meaning by calling attention to details that have attained deep significance over time. What was remembered, what was forgotten, what was called forth, as we engaged in the process of narrating our lives, was as deeply individual as our conflicting desires to be recognized as intelligible subjects within reason. After all, "a narration is never a passive reflection of a reality" (Trinh 1991: 13); it is based on meaning-making through the selection of moments that have the ability to connect past, present, and future. Our narratives reflected our passion to take pleasure within reason because "narrative is both a mode of reasoning and a mode of representation" (Richardson 1997: 28) that pushes upon, yet remains within the boundaries of, recognizable cultural scripts. Each narrative and each telling pushed us to reexamine our beliefs, actions, desires, and histories—how like or unlike Anna's story was to Sandhiya's. The performance of narratives opened up transformative spaces by providing an environment for new knowledge forms to be possible as we viewed our bodies as texts in our individual tales.

Our students' writing moved our feelings, called up images, and transported us to other places and times. It also made us realize how little we know of our students. Their worlds are so multiple, densely populated with memories and desires, and our classes and assignments too narrowly academic. These biomythographies were carefully wrought, often evocative expressions that contributed to the pleasure we found in this class and made the curriculum simultaneously academic, personal, educative, emotional, aesthetic, and political.

Although Anna talked of her beloved "island" home and her ambivalence toward mainland America, she also insisted that her mother outfit her for the new part with correct blue jeans, tee shirts, and high-status shoes. Nation became a marked part of our students' narratives with Keiko's biomythography. Keiko read her narrative at the class lectern, using a microphone to amplify her "small" voice. Keiko's narrative took us to Tokyo during and after World War II and the shame of her grandmother for being a woman alone even though her husband had died fighting for Japan. Keiko's story moved circularly—away from her grandmother's shame to her mother's ultra-affluent correctness, really perfection of upperclass femininity. Keiko suggested a weakened version of female shame as she consciously performed her autobiography as an "exotic" international student side by side with her ambivalence of being without a man.

"Nation" was marked by Keiko's story. How did national boundaries, national cultures, and transnational events such as World War II construct gender and difference? Keiko's grandmother's position as female citizen was also emphasized, and even though her grandmother had land and affluence, her status as a widow made her a second-class woman-citizen. These were issues that U.S.-centered narratives muted.

Furthermore, as nation was omitted, so were most senses of the "public" sphere. Women, in our U.S. students' biomythographies, inhabited private worlds—of cooking, hair politics, finding themselves in relations with male and female friends and lovers, in harassment and rape. Family and dyadic contexts prevailed. In fact, only the three international students emphasized political contexts and gendered national politics. Their narratives could be harder for us as a class audience to respond to, for they were less individual-, emotion-, and person-centered and more analytical of women's subordinate political positions, be it in the demand for bride prices in India, the anti-abortion stance of Ireland, or the married-woman-as-normative-citizen of Japan. The international students' biomythographies emphasized national contexts as gendered and women's lives as shaped within public debates, policies, and dissent.

Our U.S. students' autobiographies resonated deeply and consistently with the understanding that the personal is political. What was missing, however, was any similar articulation of themselves as public persons, as citizens. This evacuation of the significance of nation and the elision of women as citizens in the public realm have several serious consequences for feminism and feminist education. Kaplan and Grewal (2002: 70) claim that the invisible bonds of the nation-state naturalize and reproduce "the nationalist basis of modernist scholarship." Governmental and economic aspects of women's lives are undervalued and underemphasized, while cultural and personal aspects are highlighted. Thus a U.S. cultural and analytical perspective is retained in such personal narratives. Such personalized politics may likely seem irrelevant for women and education considered transnationally. Issues of democracy and of civic life in and out of schools are also muted (Arnot and Dillabough 2000).

A second recontextualization of our students' theorized autobiographies presses on personal identities and the limits of knowing. Suzanne Luhmann recommends that queer teaching, "rather than assuming and affirming identities, takes on the problem of how identifications are made and refused in the process of learning" (1998: 153). Luhmann asks us to consider what teaching and learning emphasize, and our and our students' implications in particular kinds of knowledge. How are queer emotional reactions to a student's biomythography, for example, understood, excavated, and examined? In this course, our public reactions to the narratives (that is, our performances as an audience) tended to be scripted around appreciation, positive emotional engagement with the stories, and questions that generally asked for additional information and clarification. How could we have introduced a range of responses to peers' autobiographies—ambivalence, queer feelings, even discomfort? Apfelbaum's (2001) warning that audiences' ability to listen to counter-stories is a significant issue in the use of narrative for political change pushes us to consider how the audience norms for appreciative listening may have contributed to our class dynamics. Do classroom norms and desires for polite and civil interaction constrain the reading and writing of autobiographies that might scare, threaten, or shock? How are our pleasures as teachers who listened to our students' biomythographies constructive of recognizable stories? How might we work toward the cultivation of listening/reading selves who are willing to listen even when narratives are confusing, terrifying, or morally or politically ambiguous? How could we move beyond normative constructions of self if, as hooks suggests, the very discursive and pedagogical practices that valorize lived experience "have already been determined by a politics of race, sex and class domination" (1994: 81)? It seems that the clarity of our emotional responses—here we've emphasized and delineated our pleasurable responses—may work against a broadening of the genre of counterstories (Fine and Harris 2001).

If our pleasures remain within reason—bounded by the reasonable norms of the polite-yet-rigorous classroom and within the conventions of woman-narrated personal-yet-political lives—then what feminist futures might never be imagined, spoken, or felt? This chapter has described the feminist possibilities of personal narratives performed within education classes and their profound, pleasurable impacts on us. However, we also identified the limits of personal narratives that remain on familiar emotional terrain and elide national and public selves. In a world numbed by economic crimes against humanity, the incessant drums of war, and widespread, ongoing traumas, we middle-class feminist educators may have to cultivate more dangerous narrative pleasures. As educators, we have to cultivate the writing and hearing of more difficult, ambiguous, even dystopic stories. We wonder how feminist-inspired dangerous pleasures in teaching might play out and how to teach within strategically uncomfortable classrooms. Finally, will anyone be interested in enrolling in such a course?

Note

1. There are no unitary categories of girls or boys. However, drawing from Walkerdine (1990), we employ the term "girls" to talk about the common threads in our stories, that is, the discursive ways in which girls are produced/positioned as subjects within pedagogical practices.

References

Arnot, M., and Dillabough, J. (eds.). (2000). *Challenging Democracy: International Perspectives on Gender, Education and Citizenship*. London: Routledge Falmer.

Apfelbaum, E. (2001). "The Dread: An Essay on Communication Across Cultural Boundaries." *Critical Psychology* 4: 19–34.

Boler, M. (1999). *Feeling Power: Emotions and Education*. New York: Routledge.

Britzman, D. (2000). "The Question of Belief: Writing Post-structural Ethnography." In E.A. St. Pierre and W.S. Pillow (eds.), *Working the Ruins: Feminist Post-structural Theory and Methods in Education*, 27–40. New York: Routledge.

Butler, J. (1990/1999). *Gender Trouble: Feminism and the Subversion of Identity*. New York: Routledge.

Davies, B. (2000). *Inscribing Body/Landscape Relations*. Walnut Creek, Calif.: Alta Mira.

Davies, B., Dormer, S., Law, C., Taguchi, H., McCann, H., and Rocco, S. (2001). "Becoming Schoolgirls: The Ambivalent Project of Subjectification." *Gender and Education* 13 (2): 167–182.

Fine, M., and Harris, A. (2001). "Counterstories." *Critical Psychology* 4: 1–19.

Foucault, M. (1985). *The Uses of Pleasure: The History of Sexuality*, vol. 2, R. Hurley, trans. London: Penguin.

hooks, b. (1994). *Teaching to Transgress: Education as the Practice of Freedom*. New York: Routledge.

Kamler, B. (2002). *Relocating the Personal*. New York: Falmer Press.

Kaplan, C., and Grewal, I. (2002). "Transnational Practices and Interdisciplinary Feminist Scholarship: Refiguring Women's and Gender Studies." In R. Wiegman (ed.), *Women's Studies on Its Own*, 66–81. Durham, N.C., and London: Duke University Press.

Lorde, A. (1982). *Zami: A New Spelling of My Name*. Freedom, Calif.: The Crossing Press.

Luhmann, S. (1998). "Queering/Querying Pedagogy? Or, Pedagogy Is a Pretty Queer Thing." In W. Pinar (ed.), *Queer Theory in Education*, 141–155. Mahwah, N.J.: Lawrence Erlbaum.

McWilliam, E. (2000). "Laughing with Reason: On Pleasure, Women, and Academic Performance." In E.A. St. Pierre and W.S. Pillow (eds.), *Working the Ruins: Feminist Post-structural Theory and Methods in Education*, 164–178. New York: Routledge.

Morrison, T. (1998). "The Site of Memory." In W. Zinsser (ed.), *Inventing the Truth: The Art and Craft of Memoir*, 183–200. New York: Mariner.

Olney, J. (1998). *Memory and Narrative: The Weave of Life Writing*. Chicago and London: University of Chicago Press.

Orner, M., Miller, J., and Ellsworth, E. (1996). "Excessive Moments and Educational Discourses That Try to Contain Them." *Educational Theory* 46 (1): 71–91.

Probyn, E. (1997). "Materializing Locations, Images and Selves." In S. Kemp and J. Squires (eds.), *Feminisms*, 125–134. Oxford: Oxford University Press.

Richardson, L. (1997). *Fields of Play: Constructing an Academic Life*. New Brunswick, N.J.: Rutgers University Press.

Shank, M. (2000). "Rigor in Teacher Education." In N. Lesko (ed.), *Masculinties at School*. 213–230. Thousand Oaks, Calif.: Sage.

Trinh, T.M.H. (1991). *When the Moon Waxes Red: Representation, Gender, and Cultural Politics*. New York: Routledge.

Walkerdine, V. (1990). *Schoolgirl Fictions*. London: Verso Press.

CHAPTER 17

Girls, Schooling, and the Discourse of Self-Change: Negotiating Meanings of the High School Prom

AMY L. BEST

The high school prom is an iconic event in American culture, central not only to images of the "typical" American teen but also to our image of the American high school. To say that proms are a big deal in high school is to state the obvious. Most U.S. high schools today organize a senior prom each year and many a junior prom as well. By the time students graduate from high school, many have attended several proms. A much anticipated event for most juniors and seniors, proms tend to take on a larger-than-life importance. It is not uncommon for prom planning to begin early in the year as teachers and students (usually young women) assemble after school to make the most important prom decisions. By the time spring arrives, proms are the focal point of school life. The flurry of talk about who's taking whom, who's wearing what, and plans for after the prom often fills the halls between classes and spills over into cafeterias. It is the voices of young women that are most frequently heard as conversations among friends turn to the topic of the prom.

The high school prom figures as an important part of coming of age for many young women. Scripted by contemporary notions of romance and "the feminine," high school proms are conventionally thought to be the domain of girls. Constructed as such, the prom is a site where girls are expected to be deeply invested because they can use this space to solidify and display their feminine identities. Again and again, girls are told that going to the prom is central to their being and becoming feminine. In teen magazines, "making a statement" is the very promise of the prom; "the prom is your night to shine." "Dare To Stand Out," these magazines encourage their readers. The message is that a carefully fashioned feminine self is the key to an unforgettable prom. And why wouldn't girls want to make a dramatic statement about themselves at their high school prom? There is tremendous pleasure in the project of self-change, in becoming somebody other than who they are in school.

Drawing from interviews with and narratives written by young women across different racial-ethnic groups, and observations of four high school proms, I examine how a discourse of self-transformation gives meaning to and orders a set of prom practices that operate to secure girls' focus on constructing and reconstructing their bodies as feminine bodies.[1] I argue that the social organization of high school proms produces feminine subjects by harnessing girls' pleasure in a project of self-change and, in doing so, sustains the social/discursive organization of gender as a salient feature of girls' experiences in school. Dorothy E. Smith's (1990) understanding of "femininity as text-mediated discourse" is a useful point of entry into the complex of symbolic relations and talk through which femininity emerges around the prom. Smith seeks to locate the discursive production of social/symbolic forms like femininity within the concrete social relations that organize and coordinate the daily activities of the everyday world. She suggests that femininity as a textually organized practice emerges through ongoing relations and activities. While femininity is ordered discursively, she argues, it is constituted in and by the local and concerted activities of girls. Girls' active participation, then, is essential to its ongoing production. In what follows, I examine how girls actively negotiate the gender and sexual codes that emerge in and through the prom as they engage in the work of self-change, highlighting the varied meanings girls create as they narrate and make sense of this school event.

Given the weight of transforming the feminine self, it is not surprising that girls' talk of the prom centered on the importance of being seen. As one young African-American woman wrote:

> When I stepped out of the limo I remember thinking that I was just the princess of the night. All lights were on me and this was my night. No one and nothing was going to spoil it for me. So we walked in about an hour late. When I made my entrance everyone's eyes were on me.

The structuring of physical space at the prom ensured that the prom would be designated in this way: the entrance to the prom site was arranged so that these girls could be looked upon by others, most often by other girls. In fact, a number of girls purposely delayed their arrival at the prom so that they could "make a grand entrance."

Because of the importance of being seen in this setting, preparations are extensive and often expensive. A significant number of American girls spend what many would consider an extraordinary amount of money on their prom. According to one prom Web site, an average of $500 is spent to go to the prom (www.proms.net). A 1996 poll featured in *Your Prom*, one of the many prom magazines available for purchase each spring, reported that $188 is the average cost of a prom dress. These estimates are not surprising when one considers that many young women enlist the help of beauty professionals, even if their financial situation might prevent them from doing so on a more routine basis. One girl reported that she and her friends rented a limo to take them to the hair salon, and another girl and her friends hired a cosmetic representative to come to her home before the prom. While certainly the availability of money determines the ease with which these girls are able to engage in the extravagances of the prom, economic location does not seem to ultimately determine their willingness to do so. Girls whose economic situation might otherwise preclude their participation in such practices also manage to engage in the work of self-change for the prom.

The process of preparing for the prom for many of these girls is as important as the end product, if not more. As a young White woman wrote, "I don't remember anything eventful about the prom itself. I remember the major preparation that went into it. FINDING THE DRESS [her emphasis]." Several girls declared that getting ready for the prom was an entire day's commitment. In fact, many ditched school on the day of the prom to prepare. Hair was plucked, worked, and cajoled into shape, and faces were magically transformed. For others, preparations began months in advance; many girls attended tanning salons, some joined gyms, and others reported that they had dieted to lose weight before the prom. One young White woman wrote, "All I can remember was that the prom wore me out. From half a day at school, to a morning appointment to get my hair done, I was literally exhausted." For a number of girls, how they transformed their bodies directly related to their having a successful prom. "When the day started off I thought it would be the best day. I had the perfect dress (no one had anything else like it) and my hair was done beautifully," one young African-American woman wrote.

An important part of getting ready for the prom, of fashioning themselves to be seen, is finding the "perfect" prom dress. One local dress boutique, where a number of girls from one school bought their prom dresses, kept a detailed record of who bought which dress in an effort to prevent the unthinkable—two girls at the same prom wearing identical dresses. As one African-American young woman remarked, "You can have the same hairstyle as anyone else. It doesn't matter, but that dress." After all, an unforgettable dress secures an unforgettable night. Perhaps this also explains why one young woman never made it to her prom: her dress, which she had specially designed for the event, was not ready.

While preparations for the prom are about setting oneself apart, these preparations were a collective process. Talk began about the prom among many girls, about how they intended to prepare for the prom, months before, often transforming the culture of daily school life. Girls drew sketches of their dresses during study hall for friends to admire, and their playful chatter about who's wearing what echoed through school halls.

The process of getting ready represents, for many, a space of shared experience where a willingness to invest in feminine bodywork is collectively articulated. It is not uncommon for family and friends to assemble at one girl's house as girls dress for the prom. Even at the prom, girls talked openly about the work they undertook to achieve what many would consider an idealized feminine image. Their discussions about their bodies, dresses, and preparations were not only an obvious source of pleasure but also an integral part of the actual prom, no less important than the first dance and the crowning of the prom queen. This kind of talk represents a meaningful space where girls make sense of and articulate what it means to be young women in a culture that treats the surface of the body as central to expressing the feminine self. Many of these girls enjoyed the attention they received after such significant transformations. This, after all, is the very promise of the prom.

Transforming themselves for the prom depends on an almost endless consumption of products: makeup, dresses, hair accessories, shoes, and handbags are all products marketed as tools for feminine display at the prom. Since the expansion of a distinct teen commodity culture during the post-World War II 1940s, the prom in general has been heavily marketed as a space to consume; however, it is the particular market emphasis on feminine consumption that is most striking. Today, the prom is a multi-million-dollar industry (www.proms.net). Girls' beauty magazines, including *Seventeen* and *YM*, now dedicate entire issues to preparing for the prom, and department stores host yearly prom fashion shows. One can easily argue that the emphasis on making a statement about oneself at the prom produces disciplined bodies for consumption (Bordo 1993). But this kind of bodywork is not just about producing disciplined bodies. The meanings girls themselves attach to the work of self-transformation are significant for understanding why they engage in such practices so willingly. I was repeatedly struck by how often young women remarked how truly out of the ordinary such changes of self were.

Engaging in the work of becoming "beautiful" for the prom represents a struggle to stake a claim to one's identity. For many of these girls, participating in beauty work enables them to occupy a position within a public space, a significant fact when considering women's historical relegation to the private sphere (Brumberg 1997; Fiske 1989). Not only are these girls able to demonstrate a public commitment to feminine practices, they are also able to express their competence as beauty practitioners. While many young women are willing to endure what might be understood as the burdens of beauty for the prom in order to express their heterosexual desirability, they also do this work to experience a self-pleasure (Radner 1989). For many of these girls, the prom presents itself as an opportunity to indulge themselves in ways that many of them are unable to do in their everyday lives. Part of what made this bodywork around the prom worth doing, then, stems directly from how they experience everyday life as young women.

High school girls are often denied control over their bodies, their desire, and their self-definition. Engaging in this elaborate consumption-oriented bodywork enables them to craft a space of self-control, self-definition, and self-pleasure that is experienced immediately (even if it is ultimately illusory). Of course, the consequence is that the "discourse of self-change" conceals the ideological workings of this school event; proms structure girls' investments in upholding gender and heterosexual norms, ensure their participation in commodity culture, and focus their attention toward the all-consuming project of the body.

The activities of getting ready enabled many of these girls to demonstrate their skills at assembling a range of signs and symbols upon their bodies in a way that transformed who they were in school. "I'm going to be Miss Elegant for the night," one White girl reported. In speaking about her dress, an African-American girl commented, "I wanted to wear something that would totally surprise people." Indeed, the pleasure of the prom is to be someone different from who you are at school. "I wanted to wear something that would totally surprise people. In school, I was known to wear all black....As my huge surprise to everyone, I ended up wearing a long white dress," another young woman remarked.

By virtue of the possibility for endless consumption, the prom is a space where young women can play with a range of identities, many of which are closed off to them within what Nancy Lesko (1988) refers to as the "body curriculum" of schools, a curriculum that operates to regulate girls' sexuality and their desire. Much like the working-class girls in Angela McRobbie's (1991) study, who embraced conventional feminine practices such as applying makeup and talking about boys in the classroom to contest schools as middle-class organizations, the prom for many girls emerged as a setting to negotiate the "body curriculum" of schools.

Without romanticizing the practices of dressing up, I argue that the prom represents a meaningful space that is both safe and playful for many girls to negotiate cultural representations of adolescent girls' sexuality that organize life for them inside school. Girls repeatedly drew upon sexual codes as they discussed the dress they had selected for the prom. As one young Latina wrote:

> I'm such a tomboy. The prom was an experience. Everyone kept commenting on how beautiful I looked, "You have a great figure; you shouldn't hide behind jeans and a T-shirt." My friends barely recognized me. People who've known me all my life stared at me.

Most girls wore long, fitted dresses, many of them black, often with exposed backs and deep slits running up one leg. As one girl described her dress, what seemed most important about the dress was what it revealed. "It's got spaghetti straps and a scoop neck. It's got a slit up the mid-thigh and the back is completely open. It kind of comes in at the sides so your sides are showing."

At the prom, young women were able to display their bodies, and thus themselves, in ways that they normally are unable to at school. Arms and legs were bared, and necklines revealed. "It was cut in here and here [gesturing to her sides] and came up around my neck and it was like an open back with just the crosses and it was real tight. I loved it," one White girl offered as she described her dress.

When understood within an organization of schooling that emphasizes modesty in dress for girls and heavily sanctions violations, a sexy and often revealing prom dress symbolizes a way to negotiate the sexual terrain of school. Schools have long served as important sites to regulate and discipline girls' sexuality and desire. As a number of feminist scholars have noted, girls have few spaces where they can claim sexual agency; rarely is school one of those spaces (Fine 1993; Leahy 1994; Lesko 1988; McRobbie 1991; Tolman 1994; Walkerdine 1990). Those girls who attempt to articulate their own sexual desire must negotiate their sexuality within a discursive organization of adolescent female sexuality ordered around images of sexual victimization, teen pregnancy, and sexual promiscuity (Fine 1993). Through what they wore, many girls seemed to claim a visible sexual identity that countered a racially based, middle-class image of the adolescent girl as the bearer of sexual innocence—an image entrenched in the organization of school (Haug et al. 1987). While the activity of dressing up binds girls to an unequal order of gender, the meanings they attach to this activity reflect attempts to generate alternate meanings that enable them to exert some control over those sexual struggles that shape their everyday lives within school and beyond.

Can girls resist the high school prom as a space to solidify their feminine identities without rejecting the prom fully? The discourses of self-change that take shape around this event secure girls' investment in femininity, but girls also negotiate and at times refuse its total influence (Brown 1999; Inness 1998a, 1998b; Leadbeater et al. 1996). They move within and around the perimeters of femininity in playful ways as they forge a space for themselves in this scene through what they wear and how they assemble signs on their bodies. One young White woman from one prom I attended styled her hair into an exaggerated "beehive" bun, a symbol of middle-class femininity embodied in images of the 1950s housewife. Instead of bobby pins, which are typically used to hold the "beehive" in place, she placed little fabric bumble bees. The significance here is difficult to miss: the girl is using hair as a site to provide social commentary on women's role in society. Her modern reinterpretation of the "beehive" parodies the feminine forms that have historically confined women.

Other girls bought their dresses at second-hand consignment shops or simply wore a dress they already had, resisting the pressures to invent themselves anew. Rejecting the idea that the prom is a site to solidify their feminine identities, a few girls wore tuxedos. Wearing a tuxedo to the prom reveals nothing less than a struggle to distance themselves—if not physically, then symbolically—from the trappings of the culture of femininity paradoxically supported through the organization of high school. The tuxedo enables girls to locate themselves within an oppositional youth culture, one dominated by masculine symbols and codes, in a way that a prom dress never could, irrespective of its color or stripe. Perhaps this explains why some schools impose dress codes intended to prevent girls and boys from cross-dressing and gender-bending and, in doing so, preserve the prevailing gender and (hetero)sexual organization of this school event.

Proms, an important aspect of school life, structure particular forms of emotional investments in a range of gendered representations, meanings, and relations that take shape around the discursive codes of femininity. Proms are defining moments in the process of becoming feminine within school, inviting questions as to how particular institutional settings mediate the ways girls relate to feminine practices and feminine forms. What sorts of femininities prevail in this school space? What leads girls to invest in feminine practices, particularly those that demand dramatic altering of their bodies? The transformation of self that many of these girls desired is shaped by the ideologies organizing not only beauty culture within consumer capitalism, but also its entrenchment in a gender and heterosexual order. For most of these girls, choosing to attend the prom involved a series of negotiations that reveal a struggle to understand the perimeters of femininity in relation to their everyday experiences in school and beyond. While proms tell us something about the broader terrain in which femininity gains cultural currency, the prom also emerges as a distinct site in which context-specific forms of femininity arise.

Interestingly, many of these girls indicated that the lengths to which they were willing to go in order to transform themselves for the prom were extraordinary. A number reported that they usually do not wear makeup and only periodically visit the hair salon. If young women invest in feminine bodywork for the prom, but not necessarily daily, what, then, is the connection between gender and this cultural scene?

Proms secure girls' complicity in maintaining prevailing feminine forms. As a result, resistance seems to be possible for only a few. The limits of resistance to these gender precepts seem to be determined by the very social organization of this space—proms are the domain of the feminine, where girls' desire to make a statement about themselves is powerful. Perhaps this explains why race and class seemed to exert little influence over how girls came to invest in the prom. While one might expect meaningful race and class distinctions to be more prevalent, curiously, this is not the case in this scene. The cultural influence of gender appears to be so overwhelming that the differences across race and class lines, which are apparent elsewhere, are more or less subsumed by the force of gender.

Girls actively negotiate gender and sexual codes as they come to define this event as simultaneously an expression of school and a means to respond to school. What girls wore to their prom and the activities they participated in tied them in many ways to gender structures that concentrate their energies on their bodies. Yet, the prom also emerges as a space for girls to respond to how their schools and the larger culture in which schools reside have defined adolescent femininity, and thus them. Dressing up provided an occasion for these young women to express alternate identities to those they perform daily in school. Many girls challenged their school's emphasis on modesty and propriety in both dress and sexual expression through what they wore. However, while they may have provided a different presentation of themselves beyond being "schoolgirls" at the prom, they did so within the prevailing organization of gender and heterosexuality. Ironically, the very practices that seem to solidify their place in culture (a place feminist scholars have long found to be troubling) also become a means for them to respond to that culture. As girls make sense of their becoming women in a society where gender continues to operate as a pervasive force, they negotiate a slippery slope. These girls must find meaning in a cultural context that all too often limits the possibility for meaningful self-representation for them as girls.

Note

1. This study draws upon a range of materials for analysis, including observation, in-depth and informal interviewing, archival and contemporary documents, and narrative analysis. However, for my purposes here I rely primarily on interview and narrative data gathered between 1995 and 1998. I collected seventy-three narratives written by college students, largely first-year students, about their memories of their high school proms during 1995 and 1996. Narratives were between one-half and one-and-one-half pages long. Of these narratives, European-American women wrote forty-two. I collected nine narratives written by African-American women, five by Asian-American women, and two narratives by Latinas. I asked students to write about their prom memories, leaving it open so that they could identify those issues most relevant to their own prom experience. Additionally, I conducted twenty-two in-depth interviews with eleven male and eleven female high school students, mostly seniors, before and after their prom. I interviewed one Latina and five African-American young women, one of whom is biracial but identifies herself as African-American. Five interviews were conducted with European-American girls. In-depth interviewing allowed me not only to examine the prom and schooling from the perspective of girls, but also to analyze how particular meanings gain local currency through girls' talk about the prom. This chapter also draws from ethnographic research conducted at four public high schools located in the Northeast. In addition to attending each of these schools' proms, I was able to observe a variety of sites connected to their proms. I observed a group of girls as they prepared for their prom, attended a fund-raiser fashion show at one school, attended a post-prom party sponsored by another school, and visited three of the schools during lunch as kids signed up for the prom.

References

Best, Amy L. (2000). *Prom Night: Youth, Schools and Popular Culture*. New York: Routledge.
Bordo, Susan. (1993). *Unbearable Weight: Feminism, Western Culture and the Body*. Berkeley: University of California Press.
Brown, Mikel Lyn. (1999). *Raising Their Voices: The Politics of Girls' Anger*. Cambridge, Mass.: Harvard University Press.
Brumberg, Joan Jacobs. (1997). *The Body Project: An Intimate History of American Girls*. New York: Random House.
Fine, Michelle. (1993). "Sexuality, Schooling and Adolescent Females: The Missing Discourse of Desire." In Michelle Fine and Lois Weis (eds.), *Beyond Silenced Voices: Class, Race and Gender in United States Schools*. Albany: State University of New York Press.
Fiske, John. (1989). *Understanding Popular Culture*. Boston: Unwin Hyman.
Haug, Frigga, et al. (1987). *Feminine Sexualisation: A Collective Work of Memory*. London: Verso.
http://www.proms.net. (Accessed March 1999.)
Innes, Sherrie A. (ed.). (1998a). *Delinquents and Debutantes: Twentieth Century American Girls' Cultures*. New York: New York University Press.
Inness, Sherrie A. (ed.). (1998b). *Millennium Girls*. New York: Rowman & Littlefield.
Leadbeater, Bonnie J. Ross, and Way, Niobe (eds.). (1996). *Urban Girls: Resisting Stereotypes, Creating Identities*. New York: New York University Press.
Leahy, Terry. (1994). "Taking Up a Position: Discourse of Femininity and Adolescence in the Context of Man/Girl Relationships." *Gender and Society* 8 (1): 48–72.
Lesko, Nancy. (1988). "The Curriculum of the Body: Lessons from a Catholic High School." In Leslie G. Roman and Linda Christian-Smith (eds.), *Becoming Feminine: The Politics of Popular Culture*. London: Falmer Press.
McRobbie, Angela. (1991). *Feminism and Youth Culture: From Jackie to Just Seventeen*. Boston: Unwin Hyman.
Radner, Hillary. (1989). "'This Time's for Me': Making Up and Feminine Practice." *Cultural Studies* 3: 301–321.
Roman, Leslie G., and Linda Christian-Smith, (eds.). (1988). *Becoming Feminine: The Politics of Popular Culture*. London: Falmer Press.
Smith, Dorothy E. (1990). *Texts, Facts and Femininity: Exploring the Relations of Ruling*. New York: Routledge.
Tolman, Deborah L. (1994). "Doing Desire: Adolescent Girls' Struggle for/with Sexuality." *Gender and Society* 8 (3): 324–342.
Walkerdine, Valerie. (1990). *Schoolgirl Fictions*. London: Verso.

CHAPTER **18**

Gender and Sexuality: Continuities and Change for Girls in School

MARY JANE KEHILY

Introduction

In this chapter I want to comment upon gender and sexuality as social categories and as subject positions in the context of contemporary schooling. In particular I aim to focus upon the experiences of girls in secondary schools in order to trace some of the main changes that have taken place within this domain since the 1970s. Describing and analyzing change also brings into focus abiding features of continuity. At a point when the gendered experiences of boys and girls have become a subject of media interest and critical debate, it may be timely to ask what is new and what has remained the same in the everyday social worlds of girls in school. Proverbial themes such as failing boys and overperforming girls, the crises in masculinity, and new feminine subjectivities have become part of the lexicon of contemporary educational discourse. In commenting upon these themes, I draw upon a body of literature, in particular feminist research, that has been concerned to explore issues of gender and sexuality as a significant feature of postwar educational change in the United Kingdom and beyond. This chapter specifically draws upon ethnographic studies of sexuality and gender in schools, including my own study (Kehily 2002) based in the West Midlands area of the United Kingdom.

The fieldwork for my study took place over a total of two years, beginning in 1991 and continuing in 1995 and 1996. During this time I did the traditional ethnographic thing of hanging out in school, mainly with students, but I also built up relationships with some teachers and interviewed them as part of the study. The fieldwork took place during a period of rapid political change for schools and the education system in the United Kingdom as a whole. The National Curriculum became a statutory requirement for schools in 1988 and was implemented in subsequent years. This was followed by a wave of legislation under a Conservative government that affected the organization and management of schools. These educational reforms had two main effects: an increase in central government control and state intervention in schools and a decrease in autonomy at the level of the local education authority. While there is not scope within this chapter to detail the nature of these changes and their impact upon schools, it should be noted that many of these initiatives have parallel developments in North America, Australia, and continental European countries.

Specific features of educational change in the United Kingdom include a decrease in professional autonomy of teachers following the implementation of the National Curriculum and local management of schools (LMS), making schools responsible for their own budgets. This period also saw the introduction of appraisal schemes for teachers and the curtailment of initiatives such as anti-racist education and gender and equal opportunity issues—further changing the professional landscape in which teachers lived and worked. The overall effect of these changes made school managers and governors more responsible for what goes on within their walls, but at the same time the school was more subject to regulation and monitoring by the central government. The following section discusses the social and political changes that have taken place within the West Midlands region of the United Kingdom in the wake of deindustrialization. A section outlining my methodological approach and a further section on femininities follows this. The main body of the chapter is organized into two sections exploring issues of gender and sexuality in school, particularly cultures of femininity.

Social and Political Context

In addition to the changes referred to above that directly affected the running of schools, both schools where I carried out research were located in an area that had undergone far-reaching economic change. The Midlands region of the United Kingdom has a history of factory employment as well as an industrial heritage related to the manufacture of cars and skilled craftwork such as jewelry making. More recently the region has witnessed widespread deindustrialization, the dismantling of earlier industries, and the emergence of a competitive global economy. Furthermore, in the postwar period, the region has become synonymous with the settlement of diasporic communities from the New Commonwealth countries as well as large numbers of people who have arrived from Pakistan and Ireland.

In these "new times" of global change and development it is the convergence of time and space that has radically transformed English working-class culture. The impact of globalization can be read in different ways. Seen from one perspective, the effects of globalization can be cast as a freeing up of traditional class structures and forms of dependency around family, work, and community in ways that give subjects increased control over their own destiny (Beck 1992). Another way of looking suggests that the project of individualization and the importance of selfhood remains entrenched within class divisions that have a differential impact upon educational experiences and life trajectories (Walkerdine et al. 2001). My study recognizes the cultural specificity of the school as a local site that exists in complex interaction with wider global processes relating to migration, the economy, and culture. At the local level the very fabric of the Midlands region seems to speak of an industrial heritage that can no longer be realized, functioning as a symbol of postindustrial alienation.

Willis's (1977) classic study of working-class male counterculture (conducted in the same region) demonstrated the direct and functional relationship between school and work. For the "lads," having a "laff" at school was regarded as preparation for the workplace; the styles of trickery and subversion they engaged in became the means whereby young men "learned to labour." McRobbie's (1978) study of working-class girls argued that popular cultural forms and the practice of female friendship helped to prepare young women for their future roles as wives and mothers in the domestic sphere. In the post-Fordist era it appeared that the young people in my study were hardly "learning to labour" or preparing for domesticity; their futures in the workplace and the home were less certain and not so clearly defined. The material circumstances of young people's lives pose many big questions for schools concerning the nature and purpose of education in the present period, and the relationship between school and society in the face of global change.

The role of the school and its relationship to the local economy is seemingly less obvious as local industries and long-term manual work decline. At the same time multinational chains in the retail and service sector, together with new forms of "flexible" employment, have expanded. Observing the scope of economic change prompts more questions than answers. How has economic change impacted upon the lives of young women and men in school? What are the implications for versions of masculinity and femininity? Is there a new, emergent sex-gender order? In many respects the sex-gender identities of young men and women in the area appear to be strongly traditional and deeply embedded in older forms of social and cultural practice. It is against the backdrop of these changes and points of continuity that this study has been carried out. The following section outlines, in brief, my methodological approach to researching issues of gender and sexuality with young people in school.

Methodological Approach

My ethnographic approach aimed to explore issues of sexuality, gender, and schooling. I was interested in the ways in which school students interpret, negotiate, and relate to issues of sexuality within the context of the secondary school. In order to explore these themes, I used the concept of *student sexual cultures*. I understand student cultures to constitute informal groups of students who actively ascribe meanings to events within specific social contexts. Student sexual cultures refer specifically to the meanings ascribed to issues of sexuality by students themselves within peer groups and in social interaction more generally. My argument throughout is that this process of making meaning within the immediate realm of the local produces individual and collective identities—that is to say, ways of developing a sense of self in relation to others. This process of making sense of the world within the locale of the school can be seen as an active process that carries social and psychic investments for individuals and groups. The study documents the ways in which issues of sexuality feature in the context of student cultures, and the implications of this for sexual learning and the construction of sex-gender identities. I am particularly interested in the interrelationship between gender and sexuality, and the ways in which school students negotiate complex social relations in ways that can be both creative and constraining.

A starting point for the research is the conceptualization of schools as sites for the *production* of gendered/sexualized identities. This perspective represents a break with earlier approaches that viewed schools as *reproducers* of dominant modes of class, gender, and racial formations. The theoretical shift from reproduction to production takes into account Foucaultian insights into relations of power in which social categories are produced in the interplay of culture and power. Power, moreover, is both discursively produced as a "top-down" dynamic and created locally in sites such as school. Within this framework, school cultures can be seen as active in producing social relations that are contextually specific and productive of social identities. The next section will focus upon the ways in which the social changes discussed above have had an impact upon the lives of young women.

Femininities

Societal changes since 1945 have had a dramatic impact upon the lives and experiences of young women, particularly in relation to the labor market and the domestic sphere. Arnot et al. (1999) point out that young women in the postwar period make their own way in the world of work and no longer seek economic dependency as wives and mothers. Moreover, their analysis outlines a concomitant shift in values among young women in contemporary times marked by the desire for autonomy and self-fulfilment in work and leisure, reflecting both economic change and the cultural influence of second-wave feminism. It is a matter of some debate whether the changing value systems of young women can be seen as liberation from the confines of conventional femininity or incorporation into the project of the New Right that calls upon individuals to resolve their own economic and social subordination (Weiss 1990). Many of the positions taken up in relation to these issues hinge upon a particular conceptualization of subjectivity within the context of postmodern globalization. Walkerdine et al. (2001) cast recent features of social change in terms of the remaking of girls and women as modern neoliberal subjects. However, Walkerdine et al. challenge the idea of the demise of class and the rise of the individualized, agentic self. Rather, their analysis insists upon the salience of social class as a defining structure that differentially impacts upon the educational achievement and life trajectories of girls and women.

The wide-ranging changes in the lives of girls and women outlined above may be more difficult to discern within the school context. Indeed, Arnot et al. (1999) comment upon the 1970s and 1980s as a time when girls in school appear untouched by feminism or a feminist sensibility. Studies exploring the social experiences of young women during this period have documented the ways in which young women's lives were shaped and lived through the abiding notion of sexual reputation (e.g., McRobbie and Garber 1982; Griffin 1985; Canaan 1986; Cowie and Lees 1987). Many of these studies stress the dominant regulatory power of young men to categorize young women in terms of their sexual availability as "slags" or "drags." However, such studies also point to the role of girls themselves in regulating gender-appropriate behavior for young women. Joyce Canaan's (1986) study of U.S. middle-class girls in school considered the ways in which female friendship groups are concerned with issues of sexual reputation. Canaan cites the example of a young woman in her study who was rumored to have kinky sex with her boyfriend involving, among other things, the novel use of McDonald's french fries. Canaan documented the responses of other young women and suggested that they collectively "draw the line" (1986: 193) between acceptable sexual activity and the unacceptable.

In these moments female friendship groups incorporate spheres of practices they feel comfortable with and displace practices that do not concur with their collectively defined femininity. Young women who do not draw the line incur a reputation as "the other kinda girl" (1986: 190), the sexually promiscuous and much denigrated female figure whose lack of adherence to conventional morality serves as a "cautionary tale" reminding young women to be ever vigilant in the maintenance of their reputation. In a more recent U.K.-based study, Debbie Weekes (2002) analyzed the ways in which the notion of sexual reputation is assumed and applied in terms of ethnicity. The African-Caribbean young women in Weekes's study sexualized the identities of their White female peers in order to construct themselves *as against* prevailing stereotypes of sexual "looseness" associated with Black female sexuality and White women who go with Black men. The studies of Canaan (1986) and Weekes (2002) suggest that the notion of reputation exists as an organizing category for young women in school and, in dialogue with other social categories, becomes significant to styling particular versions of femininity. Both studies indicate that the school remains a site for the active social learning of gender and sexuality wherein young women exercise agency in the shaping and regulation of collectively defined femininities. The following section takes up the theme of social learning in relation to gender and sexuality and further explores this as a feature of student sexual cultures.

Learning Gender and Sexuality

Barrie Thorne's (1993) U.S.-based study of children and gender uses ethnographic methods to study the social worlds of boys and girls (aged nine to ten) in a public elementary school. Her study captures the energetic and highly charged nature of children's cultural worlds in which play involves multiple engagements with imaginative forms of physicality, talk, and action. To the adult researcher the rapid movements of children at play appeared haphazard and chaotic. However, after several months of observation, Thorne began to make sense of children's play from the perspective of children themselves. Thorne suggests that through patterns of friendship and rituals of play, children create meanings for themselves and others. Thorne identified an example of children creating meanings through play in playground chasing games. Here Thorne describes and comments upon the widespread invocation of "cooties" or rituals of pollution in which individuals or groups are treated as carriers of contagious "germs." Thorne documented the experiences of some unfortunate children whose undesirability was captured and pronounced by the tag "cootie queen" or "cootie king." Thorne suggests that, in general, girls are seen as a source of contamination, referred to by boys in one school as "girl stain." This involved boys treating girls, and objects associated with girls, as polluting, while the reverse did not readily occur. Thorne's analysis of these games points to the relationship between children's perceptions of gender and the broader context of power relations in which they exist:

> When pollution rituals appear, even in play, they enact larger patterns of inequality, by gender, by social class and race, and by bodily characteristics like weight and motor co-ordination....
>
> In contemporary U.S. culture even young girls are treated as symbolically contaminating in a way that boys are not. This may be because in our culture even at a young age girls are sexualised more than boys, and female sexuality, especially when "out of place" or actively associated with children, connotes danger and endangerment. (*Thorne 1993: 75–76*)

Thorne points to the further significance of gender in children's cultural worlds through her conceptualization of "borderwork," a term used to characterize the ways in which children tend to form single-sex friendship groups that serve to create and strengthen gender boundaries. Thorne suggests that children's play creates a spatial separation between boys and girls that they work to maintain through games and social interactions more generally. Drawing up boundaries, however, also creates opportunities for transgression, crossing the line to disrupt gender-appropriate behavior or "border crossing," as Thorne terms it. While most children adhered to gender-defined boundaries, Thorne did notice that border crossing appeared to be acceptable among girls or boys who had achieved a position of high status within their peer group.

In the area of secondary schooling, further research has drawn attention to sexuality and particularly the heterosexist structure of school relations (e.g., Epstein and Johnson 1998; Trudell 1993; Mac an Ghaill 1994; Nayak and Kehily 1996; Britzman 1995). This literature provides us with valuable insights and ways of understanding gendered and sexual hierarchies in schools. Within sex-gender structures in school, homosexuality may be marginalized and stigmatized through the curriculum, pedagogic practices, and pupil cultures. Moreover, these studies illustrate the ways in which schools can be seen as sites for the *production* of gendered/sexualized identities rather than agencies that passively reflect dominant power relations.

Student Sexual Cultures

I have drawn upon the insights of research discussed above to further explore the sexual cultures of young people in school. The following discussion occurred during a year 9 sex education class:

Vicky: She's [Naomi] just getting another note. What does it say, Sara?

Sara: It says, "So you want to go out with me in two weeks?" De De Derrr!

Vicky: She's told Nathan she'll go out with him in two weeks. Why d'you say you'll go out with him in two weeks?

Naomi: 'Cos Jonathan will be back then.

Vicky: You're not even going out with him, though.

Naomi: I am!

Naomi [to me]: I like Jonathan, you see, but Nathan likes me.

MJK: So what are you going to do about it? Do you feel that Jonathan isn't so interested in you as you are in him?

Naomi: Um, yeah, that's right.

Vicky: What's a matter? Why d'you tell him [Nathan] you'd go out with him in two weeks?

Naomi: I don't want to tell you. It's private.

Vicky: You tell me everything else [laughs].

Here, the interest in Naomi's affairs comes to a tentative and temporary closure. Naomi's concern to make herself available to Jonathan while holding Nathan in abeyance is a strategy which involves distancing herself from her female peer group while responding in favorable, though noncommittal, tones to Nathan's advances. Naomi's actions incur direct disapproval and censure from Vicky, who believes that Naomi has misplaced investments in Jonathan and is deliberating misleading Nathan. For Naomi, in this instance, maintaining girlfriends and having a boyfriend is a difficult balancing act, and her discomfort can be seen in terse replies and the retreat into "privacy." In courting femininity and heterosexuality, Naomi finds herself positioned by two different discourses as loyal female friend and compliant would-be girlfriend. In such moments, heterosexual relations may be consolidated through girl-boy encounters that involve a disruption of same-sex alliances. The link between heterosexuality and the management of social relations can be seen in Naomi's circumscribed and protracted negotiations with Nathan, Naomi, and Vicky, in which notes, declarations, explanations, and calls for privacy become symbolic signifiers in the paraphernalia of heterosexual practice.

At the end of the lesson Naomi told me in more detail that she feared her relationship with Jonathan may be over when he returns from his holiday, and she may then consider a relationship with Nathan because he "likes her." She, however, likes Jonathan. Naomi's attempts to exercise control in this situation illustrate the limitations of sex education practice which does not engage with the "lived" version of sexual relationships within student cultures. The emphasis on contraception and caution in these lessons does little to address the feelings of power and vulnerability experienced by young women in the negotiation of femininity and heterosexual relationships (see Kehily 2002 for a full discussion of sex education practice). Naomi wants to be recognized as sexually attractive, wants to be "liked," and wants a relationship, preferably with Jonathan. Her desire to be desired places her in the uncomfortable position of being pressured by Nathan and policed by her female peer group. As Skeggs (1997) points out, the concern of young women to validate themselves through dynamics of desirability requires the confirmation of men. Over the following weeks the dalliance between Naomi and Nathan escalated to the point where Nathan's behavior could be seen as a form of harassment. Mrs. Evans, the head of personal and social education, decided to speak to Nathan and his mother about his behavior and hoped that this intervention would resolve the situation. However, Mrs. Evans's comments to me focused upon Naomi's burgeoning sexuality:

Mrs Evans: Last year, you know, she [Naomi] wore her hair scraped back into a ponytail and this year she's got it in tresses all over her face—she's always flicking it back and playing with it—and then there's all the makeup and the ... [flutters her *eyes*].

This example illustrates the ways in which embodied femininity is read in terms of sexuality, and thus becomes the object of attention, rather than the harassment by the young males. Naomi's sexualized femininity, expressed through her physical appearance, bodily styles, and gestures, is interpreted by adults as worrying and potentially dangerous. Mrs. Evans's preoccupation with Naomi's appearance rather than Nathan's actions echoes elements of the "she-asked-for-it" argument employed in common-sense discourses to account for incidents of sexual harassment and, in some cases, assault. The suggestion here is that Naomi's demeanor displays sexuality in ways that provoke the male sex drive into action. Mrs. Evans's comments indicate an awareness of the dangers ascribed to female sexuality, particularly the power of sexuality to disrupt the rational educative process (Walkerdine and Lucey 1989). From the perspective of adults, Naomi is "playing with fire," promoting her sexuality at the risk of damaging her reputation and her chances of academic success. It is interesting to note that Naomi's behavior incurs recrimination from all of the social spheres she has contact with: Nathan's advances, her peer group's regulatory exclamations, and her teacher's disapproval. The collective reproach of Naomi during the course of this experience illustrates the many ways in which female sexuality can be seen as culpable. My field notes, written up after the discussion with Mrs. Evans, underline the gendered interpretation of the incident in which femininity is seen to bespeak a potentially dangerous form of sexuality:

> I'm sure that Catrina [Mrs. Evans] does feel that Nathan's behaviour is a form of harassment but find it strange, in retrospect, that she made hardly any comment on his behaviour and focused almost entirely on Naomi. (*field notes March 25, 1996*)

Continuities and Change

The main findings of my ethnographic study provide many points of continuity with earlier studies concerned with issues of sexuality, gender, and schooling. Obvious points of continuity in the experience of pupils in school include the persistence of gender polarities, the ways in which notions of gender difference are assumed in embodied forms of talk and action, and the constant reformulation of sex-gender hierarchies. The concern with notions of "reputation" and the naturalization of heterosexuality within the school site remain key structuring themes within student sexual cultures, and echo many of the findings of earlier work. My analysis of student sexual cultures indicates that the same-sex friendship group becomes significant in the negotiation and enactment of normative sex-gender identities. This may lead us to ask questions about the nature and scope of change that can be effected within educational arenas. In a societal context where public representations and individual practice suggest the possibility of more fluidity in sex-gender categories and identities, why is this rarely reflected in school?

In the public sphere of representations, sexual diversity becomes more visible, while shifts in the economic and the domestic spheres offer the possibility of change in gender relations and family forms. Yet young people in school remain preoccupied with the less radical and often more reactionary aspects of sexuality and gender, and utilize them to style their own forms of social learning that can be both agentic and regulatory. My work with young people in school suggests that the key to this apparent contradiction lies with the sexual cultures of young people themselves. Within the context of student sexual cultures, issues of gender and sexuality take on a logic and a momentum that make sense to the young people involved. My observations point to the abiding significance of gender and sexuality for young people as important sites for the exercise of autonomy and agency within the confined space of the school. From the perspective of young people themselves, their informal peer group cultures remain one of the few sites within school that are not shaped by the demands of teachers, parents, politicians, and policy makers. The educational experience of students in the United Kingdom is increasingly marked by policies and practices which position students as receptacles for formal learning. The National Curriculum is to be delivered *to them*, targets are set *for them*, and their "progress" is monitored and recorded in league tables and national tests.

Within this disempowering environment of educational imperative and external control, student sexual cultures become imbued with significance as adult-free and education-free zones where students collectively negotiate what is acceptable/desirable and what is "too much." The collective activity of young people exists in tension with the individualizing culture of contemporary education practice. By placing emphasis on the importance of the group over the individual, and the power of the group to negotiate and rework commonly held assumptions, young people in school work against the grain of contemporary educative processes that individualize students and prioritize personal endeavor. In the sphere of student sexual cultures, young people relate to issues of gender and sexuality by drawing upon resources available to them. My research indicates that such resources, though diverse and varied, frequently present dominant versions of sex-gender categories that can be utilized by young people to fashion their own versions of dominant sex-gender identities. Thus, the trying on of dominant forms is played out within student cultures and exists at the expense of marginal or less conventional sex-gender identities.

Concluding Comments

In this chapter I have focused upon the experiences of young women in school, and in particular the ways in which the categories and subject positions associated with gender and sexuality have had an impact upon their lives. In this respect I have attempted to provide a context by outlining some of the social changes that have taken place in the postwar period in the United Kingdom and other ways in which the experiences of young women have remained constant over successive decades. I have pointed to some of the ways in which the experiences of young women exist in tension with broad features of social change in the contemporary period. Despite changing family forms and increased participation in the workplace, young people in school continue to draw upon the notion of sexual reputation to regulate their behavior and fashion sex-gender identities that can be viewed in many ways: as normative, even reactionary, or retrogressive. My analysis of this seeming contradiction points to the significance of student sexual cultures, and particularly same-sex friendship groups, as sites for the exercise of autonomy and agency with the confined space of the school. The collective activity of young people in this domain works against the individualizing culture of contemporary education practice that seeks to control and infantilize students as receptacles for formal learning. Seen from the perspective of young people themselves, informal peer group cultures remain one of the few sites within school where they can collectively negotiate sex-gender identities on their own terms.

References

Arnot, M., David, M., and Weiner, G. (1999). *Closing the Gender Gap: Postwar Education and Social Change*. Cambridge: Polity.

Beck, U. (1992). *Risk Society: Towards a New Modernity*. London: Sage.

Britzman, D. (1995). "What Is This Thing Called Love?" *Taboo: Journal of Culture and Education* 1: 65–93.

Canaan, J. (1986). "Why a 'Slut' Is a 'Slut': Cautionary Tales of Middle-class Teenage Girls' Morality." In H. Varenne (ed.), *Symbolising America*. Lincoln: University of Nebraska Press.

Cowie, C., and Lees, S. (1987). "Slags or Drags?" In *Feminist Review* (ed.), *Sexuality: A Reader*. London: Virago.

Epstein, D., and Johnson, R. (1998). *Schooling Sexualities*. Buckingham: Open University Press.

Griffin, C. (1985). *Typical Girls? Young Women from School to the Job Market*. London: Routledge.

Kehily, M.J. (2002). *Sexuality, Gender and Schooling: Shifting Agendas in Social Learning*. London: Routledge Falmer.

Mac an Ghaill, M. (1994). *The Making of Men*. Buckingham: Open University Press.

McRobbie, A. (1978). "Working-class Girls and the Culture of Femininity." *In Women's Studies Group*, Women Take Issue, London Hutchinson Centre for Contemporary Cultural Studies, University of Birmingham.

McRobbie, A., and Garber, G. (1982). "Girls and Subcultures." In S. Hall and T. Jefferson (eds.), *Resistance Through Rituals: Youth Subcultures in Post-war Britain*. London: Hutchinson.

Nayak, A., and Kehily, M.J. (1996). "Playing It Straight: Masculinities, Homophobias and Schooling." *Journal of Gender Studies* 5 (2): 211–230.

Sears, J. (ed.). (1992). *Sexuality and the Curriculum: The Politics and Practices of Sexuality Education*. New York: Teachers' College Press.

Skeggs, B. (1997). *Formations of Class and Gender: Becoming Respectable*. London: Sage.

Thorne, B. (1993). *Gender Play: Boys and Girls in School*. New Brunswick, N.J.: Rutgers University Press.

Trudell, B. (1993). *Doing Sex Education: Gender, Politics and Schooling*. London: Routledge.

Walkerdine, V., and Lucey, H. (1989). *Democracy in the Kitchen: Regulating Mothers and Socialising Daughters*. London: Virago.

Walkerdine, V., Lucey, H., and Melody, J. (2001). *Growing Up Girl: Psychosocial Explorations of Gender and Class*. Basingstoke: Palgrave.

Weekes, D. (2002). "Get Your Freak On: How Black Girls Sexualise Identity." *Sex Education* 2 (3): 251–262.

Weiss, L. (1990). *Working Class Without Work: High School Students in a De-industrialising Economy*. New York: Routledge.

Willis, P. (1977). *Learning to Labour: How Working Class Kids Get Working Class Jobs*. Farnborough: Saxon House.

PART **6**

Research With and By Young Women

Colluding in "Compulsory Heterosexuality"? Doing Research with Young Women at School

KATHRYN MORRIS-ROBERTS

"Olivia, you're a lesbian aren't you?" ... I take a deep breath ... I start to feel uncomfortable, I am wary to look at Olivia or twist in my seat to look at the boys.

(research diary)

My contribution to this volume is fueled by the experiences and emotions I encountered when I went back to secondary school to conduct doctoral research on the construction and spatiality of young women's friendship groups (aged fourteen/fifteen) at school. The field research was conducted at a secondary school in the north of England. "Hilltop" is an oversub- scribed mixed comprehensive[1] school with 1048 pupils enrolled during the academic year 1999–2000. Unlike many schools in the United Kingdom, pupils attend "Hilltop" from all over the city. Therefore "Hilltop," and my research participants, reflect the socioeconomic and ethnic diversity of a large British city. My research used a number of in-depth qualitative research techniques: multilocational participant observation (classrooms; personal, social, and health education classroom; hang-out areas within and outside school); in-depth friendship group interviews; and self- directed photography. The thesis argues that even within a relatively progressive educational establishment such as "Hilltop," young women's discourses and practices of friendship engender normative performances of masculinity and femininity which fail to challenge the school as a site of "compulsory heterosexuality" and leave limited room for the expression of "alternative" performances of femininity.

My research raises a number of ethical dilemmas for the feminist researcher, and I have discussed this elsewhere in relation to intervening in friendship exclusion (see Morris-Roberts 2001). However, for the purpose of this chapter I concentrate on ethical dilemmas specifically related to using multilocational participant observation as a method to conduct research on heterosexuality at "Hilltop." Experiences of literally being there with girls, witnessing oppressive and exclusionary behavior first-hand, has caused me considerable ethical angst and deliberation. I attempted to deal with this through a process of "critical reflexivity" (Maxey 1999). However, "hanging out" with groups of teenage girls meant that I had to confront my "politics of intervention" head-on and deal with such issues as the policing of femininities and sexualities, and the exclusion of some girls based on style, dress, attitude, beliefs, or bodily behavior. In this chapter I use just two empirical examples to illustrate some of the ethical practicalities of being there with the young women. The examples from my research diary give a small insight into how I potentially colluded with and perpetuated the construction of the school as a site of "compulsory heterosexuality" through my research. I further consider how this potential collusion poses a problem for "feminist research praxis" and specifically a feminist "politics of intervention."

The aim of this chapter is therefore twofold. First, to provide researchers with empirical understanding of what it was like to conduct multilocational participant observation with young women in school and to discuss some of the ethical complexities that this research method raised in the field. Second, my aim is to challenge other critical feminist researchers to think through their collusionary practices, to consider how their practices of identification or (dis)identification and silencing actually perpetuate power relations in the field. I do this through the following four sections that comprise this chapter. I give a necessary background to "compulsory heterosexuality" in U.K. schools. I then follow with two empirical examples, one of which is concerned with challenging overt homophobic and heterosexist "banter" in the classroom, and the second of which considers the everyday and subtle forms of collusion in "compulsory heterosexuality." The final section of the chapter considers collusionary practices and power in the research process.

In my own empirical research I attempt to adopt a form of "feminist research practice" (WGSG 1997), through which I aim "to provide a rhetorical space where the experiences and knowledges of the marginalized can be given epistemic authority, be legitimated and taken seriously" (Skeggs 1997: 38). In so doing, "…[f]eminism implies an obligation to take moral responsibility for our politics, and so a general ethic of accountability towards the subjects of research, and the way knowledge is produced" (Holland et al. 1998: 16). Following this basic feminist ideal leads me, in principle at least, to treat young people as competent decision makers in their own right; to involve them throughout the research process, allowing them to "opt in" and "opt out," and ultimately work *with*, rather than on or for, research participants (Alderson 1995).

Furthermore, I consider it part of the moral responsibility of my critical feminist praxis to attempt to transfer these politics into practice, thus developing a critical "politics of intervention," where research participants acknowledge, and critically reflect upon, their own practices (Stanley and Wise 1993). Therefore, implicit in my desire to make visible the experiences of young women is my attempt to make explicit and to challenge injustice, exclusionary practices, and oppressive behavior (Kitchin and Hubbard 1999; Doyle 1999), specifically along the lines of age, gender, and "compulsory heterosexuality." In theory I still hold true to my "politics of intervention"; however, in practice I found my feminist politics to be aspirational. Elsewhere, I have described my research as participatory in its approach because of its feminist methodology and methods (Morris-Roberts 2001, 2002). However, it is important to note that my research is not participatory action research (PAR), which is slowly becoming popular in research with young people in the U.S. and U.K. contexts (see Reason and Bradbury 2001). Before I explore my empirical examples and discuss how my politics did or did not transfer into practice, it is important to provide a small amount of context in relation to debates concerning sexuality and education in the United Kingdom.

Schools as Sites of "Compulsory Heterosexuality" in the United Kingdom

Schools are sites and spaces for the articulation, (re)production, and contestation of young people's masculinities, femininities, and sexualities (Epstein 1994; Epstein and Johnson 1998; Haywood 1996; Holland et al. 1998; Mac an Ghaill 1996a), even though the implications of this for young people's learning and well-being in school are denied within official educational discourses and often ignored by policy makers, politicians, and the media. Critical education theorists explicate how both the formal curriculum and informal student cultures (Epstein 1994; Epstein et al. 2002; Holland et al. 1998; Mac an Ghaill 1996a, 1996b) produce and sustain the school as a site of "compulsory heterosexuality." Debbie Epstein and Richard Johnson suggest, "... like all other institutions, schools are suffused with the heterosexual presumption" (1994: 222–223). Epstein (1995: 58), following Butler (1990), goes on to argue that:

> ... the concept of genderedness becomes meaningless in the absence of heterosexuality as an institution which is compulsory and which is enforced through rewards for "appropriate" gendered and heterosexual behaviours and through punishments for deviations from the conventional "norm."

Attempts to include the experiences of lesbian, gay, and bisexual people in the formal curriculum are actively discouraged by the political climate in the United Kingdom; nowhere is this more prevalent than in the continuing debate concerning Section 28 (see Epstein 2000; Epstein et al. 2002; Sanders and Spraggs 1989; Stonewall 2000; Waites 2000; Wise 2000). Section 28 of the Local Government Act of 1988 inhibits—but, contrary to popular belief does not ban— teachers from talking openly about lesbian, gay, and bisexual relationships in school. The confusion over the law and its relevance to everyday educational practices contributes to an environment of intimidation concerning lesbian, gay, and bisexual issues in the secondary school context. The ambiguity lies in the terminology of the Act, which was brought in under the government of Margaret Thatcher; it suggests that homosexuality should not be "promoted" as a "pretend family relationship." Furthermore, since 1986 local education authorities have not been directly responsible for sex education in British schools (Epstein and Johnson 1998). In reality, therefore, the Act does not directly relate to secondary schools in the United Kigdom, but rather to local education authorities.

Sexuality is implicated in all areas of school life, through social relations with teachers and peers and also through formal curriculum provision and state education policy (Epstein and Johnson 1998). Heterosexuality is the silent term "…which is encoded in language, in institutional practices, and the encounters of everyday life" (Epstein and Johnson 1994: 198). Epstein and Johnson (1994) suggest within the book *Challenging Lesbian and Gay Inequalities in Education* (Epstein 1994) that heterosexism discriminates by failing to recognize difference. This not only excludes young lesbian, gay, and bisexual people and/or those questioning their sexuality, but also lesbian, gay, and bisexual teachers, allowing heterosexism and homophobia to continue unchallenged.

To date, therefore, researchers have had little opportunity to do ethnographic work with schools which attempt, through formal curriculum provision, to question the school as a site of "compulsory heterosexuality." Although there is an expanding body of research that looks at the ways in which educational spaces allow limited performances and discourses of masculinities, femininities, and sexualities to flourish (cf. Mac an Ghaill 1996a, 1996b). Some research has looked at sex education (Harrison 2000; Holland et al. 1998; Jackson 1999; Mac an Ghaill 1996b; Measor et al. 1996; Thomson 1994; Thorogood 2000; West 1999); however, the role of "sexuality education" (Epstein and Johnson 1998; Johnson 1996; Redman 1994) remains a utopian aspiration. However, a relatively recent edited collection (see Laskey and Beavis 1996) has looked at sexuality education and policy from the Australian perspective, and Jessica Fields (2001, 2002) has conducted an ethnography of sex education in U.S. schools.[2] Nevertheless, ethnographic research in this area is limited. However, you do not have to spend long with young people in schools to realize that both the formal and the informal curriculum are spaces for the (re)production and contestation of masculinities, femininities, and sexualities. Furthermore, even if schools are not formally talking about "it" in the classroom, sexuality, hetero and homo, is definitely a "hot topic" of conversation within student cultures. Moreover, in the past couple of years the Blair New Labour government has been struggling with an awareness that the United Kingdom has the highest teenage pregnancy rates in Europe, and that for many, sex education is failing young people (DfEE 2000).

Given the debates outlined above and the increasingly bureaucratic educational climate in the United Kingdom (Furlong and Cartmel 1997), conducting research in schools with young people, specifically when it directly concerns (hetero)sexuality, is problematic and potentially explosive. "Hilltop," however, unlike many schools in the United Kingdom, attempts to provide its students with a comprehensive personal, social, and health education (PSHE) program[3] from the ages of eleven to sixteen in which, among other age-appropriate topics, students are encouraged to explore their feelings, emotions, and opinions concerning sexuality and prejudice. There is an attempt on behalf of the PSHE teachers to move away from a biological approach to sexual health, which focuses on "bits and bodies," toward a more holistic approach to sexual health that can, and does, incorporate sexuality, self-esteem, and empowerment. However, even though the formal curriculum at "Hilltop" does raise awareness concerning gay and lesbian issues within the space of the PSHE classroom, homophobia within student and teacher culture remains prevalent through subtle and not so subtle practices of homophobia and heterosexism. I now turn to consider my first example, where I potentially did little to challenge the heterosexual presumption.

Challenging Homophobic and Heterosexist "Banter" in the Classroom

The following interaction took place during the course of a history lesson. I was sitting with Olivia, Zoë, and Jayne, who were working diligently, as usual, on their course assignment. We were sitting second row from the front, and Adam and Larry were sitting behind us:

> "Olivia, you're a lesbian aren't you?" ... I take a deep breath ... I start to feel uncomfortable, I am wary to look at Olivia or twist in my seat to look at the boys. I feel guilty but I don't want them to start on me. Olivia just replies, "Yeah." She appears calm and not embarrassed at all, certainly not how I used to feel when I was in her position at school. After a few more shouts of "lesbian," Larry says, "You all are, aren't you?" Olivia just replies, "Yeah" again.... Jayne replies "Occasionally," then Olivia and Jayne joke about being lesbians at the weekend....
> (*research diary*)

I was surprised but pleased by the way Olivia and Jayne responded to the boys' attempts to insult them; however, throughout this interaction I felt very uncomfortable. From previous interactions with Larry and Adam, I expect they wanted the girls to get upset or defensive when their presumed heterosexuality was called into question. I suspect, however, that Olivia and Jayne were able to deal productively with the previous incident because of their popularity and respectability at school. Thus far this incident remained a "humorous" interaction, one which would be explained in PSHE group discussion by young people as "harmless fun" and "banter." However:

> Adam turns to Larry and says, "You're gay…." Larry replies, "Yeah, I've got a roll of wrapping paper in my bag," Adam retorts, "Oh, and I bet you use it [for penetration purposes]." This exchange was all said in a playful manner between the two…. Steven, who is on the front row, leans over to Maggie and says, in a fairly loud and brusque manner, "Are you a lesbian?" She totally ignores him and looks down, she blushes and appears embarrassed…. Larry and Adam cease making comments to the girls and continue exchanges between themselves; these appear to be a list of insulting heterosexist comments such as "prostitutes… faggots … sucking cock." (*research diary*)

There is obviously a lot of information in this short extract that could be unpacked concerning constructions of femininity, masculinity, heterosexuality, and peer group culture. However, I want to identify just one point—my feeling of powerlessness when I was sitting in this lesson. This incident occurred during a week when there was another unsuccessful call in Parliament to abolish Section 28; media and political debates were strewn with popular homophobia. Furthermore, the above extract coincided with the start of the year 10 course on sexuality; this did little to reduce my despair at the levels of popular homophobia articulated by some young people in school. I sat there mute and very angry about my inability to intervene or question Larry and Adam on their homophobia, to challenge them on their use of inappropriate and offensive language, or to support Maggie in her embarrassment. My level of anguish also rose because within the space of the PSHE classroom it was these girls who articulated discourses of acceptance in opposition to "heterosexual laddism" (Epstein and Johnson 1998), whereas outside the classroom it was the same girls who were also confronted with heterosexism in their interactions with their male peers. Thus, I felt unable to confront the contradictory discourses described above. Interactions like these which highlight the potency of masculinity in the construction of heterosexuality (Holland et al. 1998) have become central to my thesis. However, the centrality of these contradictory and often silenced discourses of young women's friendships and sexualities has further diminished my ability to enact a feminist "politics of intervention."

Everyday and Subtle Forms of "Compulsory Heterosexuality"

The second example is subtler than the first and begins to expose the frequently undocumented ways in which "compulsory heterosexuality" works to silence deviations from the norm. Part of my research necessarily involved "hanging out" with teenage girls inside and outside lessons. As my research progressed, I was increasingly invited into my research participants' spaces of friendship. As been well documented, much "girl talk" involves the (re)enforcement of femininities through heterosexualities by talking about boyfriends, romance, and heterosex (Griffin 1985; Griffiths 1995; Hey 1997). This was fine and all very interesting when I was observing these interactions and not being asked directly for my opinion. However, the more our relationships developed, the more young women wanted reciprocation and contributions on my part, and rightly so. On this occasion I am sitting with Olivia and Abi in a Religious Education lesson; it is one of the final lessons before the end of term, and the teacher is allowing more space for chat:

> Olivia and Abi start talking about men/lads they fancy. Olivia fancies Jamie Oliver, "The Naked Chef" who appears on television [celebrity cook in the United Kingdom]; she likes the blonde, blue-eyed, messy hair "type." ... They start talking about some lad they like, but they suggest that he is a little old; he has just turned 25. "That's outrageous!" I say. Abi asks, "You're not that old are you?"... They then joke with me: "You're getting on a bit." Abi starts asking me if I fancy Jamie Oliver; I make some silly comment about his cooking abilities! They then try and think of some older men for me, Jon Bon Jovi is one of them. I try and get around having this conversation with them by talking about his music and concerts. I remark, "Jon Bon Jovi's getting better with age"—I can't believe I said that. (*research diary*)

> Following this gaffe, the conversation moves on quickly to Abi's penchant for Michael Owen, a Liverpool football (soccer) player whose picture is posted all over her RE exercise book. I am quite able and willing to engage with young women about contemporary youth culture; however, I find it very difficult to talk ethically with them about fancying "hot boys." This small incident reflects how uncomfortable I feel about potentially misrepresenting my feelings to them and consequentially (re)enforcing presumed heterosexuality. I could have lied to them directly; instead, I avoided conversations, potentially appeared standoffish, and, as in the above incident, made comments that I would more than likely attribute to someone of an older generation!

Collusionary Practices and Power in the Research Process

Reflecting back on the examples discussed above and my experiences of conducting multilocational participant observation raises one major disjuncture in doing research with young women on (hetero)sexuality in school: whether it is possible as a participant observer to challenge the school as a site of "compulsory heterosexuality" without in fact colluding in it yourself. In order to challenge young people's heterosexism, I firmly believe that the practices that (re)enforce the school as a site of "compulsory heterosexuality," thus producing prejudice and discrimination, need to be made apparent "in the field." I am sure this issue will not be new for many critical researchers. My feminist politics suggest that through my research I question the inevitability of heterosexuality; however, an overriding feeling ensues: rather than questioning and challenging "compulsory heterosexuality" in school, I actually perpetuated it. Here, I could aptly leap to my own defense and say this is strategic silencing so that I can survive "in the field" and use my networks elsewhere to challenge, and this is to some extent the case. Throughout my doctoral research and subsequently, I have attempted to interrupt the collusionary practices described in this chapter outside the space and time of participant observation. During my research I explored these issues with research participants through in-depth interviews with young women's friendship groups, and I developed alliances with PSHE staff and other local agencies to provide policy and practice development. Furthermore, I actively engage in voluntary and paid work to enhance support for young women who identify as lesbian, gay, or bisexual.

However, saying "yeah, ok, but..." does not take away the feelings of helplessness and anger that I experienced during my field research as a participant observer. Neither does it support young gay, lesbian, or bisexual pupils or straight young people (or teachers) who want to stand up and challenge, but do not have the confidence or the ability in the school context. Nor does my silence challenge the potency of heterosexism or what it means to be gay, lesbian, or, indeed, heterosexual. According to Epstein and Johnson (1994: 225), "[heterosexuality's] invisibility is part of its power"; thus my practice in the previous two examples does little to expose the ways in which heterosexuality works as a silencing mechanism within the field of education. Thus, I am still left with the question of how we as critical researchers can expose the compulsory nature of heterosexuality in an educational climate where researchers, teachers, and pupils can make space for alternative femininities, masculinities, and sexualities only through strategic silence and collusion.

From my experiences of attempting to put my politics into practice, I suggest that collusion can take on many forms that are personal to the specific research process, as well as spatially and temporally contingent. However, through a process of critical reflection I have come to understand my ethical anxieties encountered during participant observation as refracted through a process of (dis)identification (Skeggs 1997). By this I mean that in both examples, whether consciously or not, I attempted to distance myself from the power relations in the field, which theoretically I recognize as impossible. As discussed at the beginning of the chapter, my "feminist research praxis" aims to develop reciprocal research relationships with participants. Nevertheless, I am left feeling that throughout the research process I actually did the opposite, and distanced myself from the research participants because I did not feel comfortable with the dynamics. By dissociating myself, however, I feel that I have also become involved in practices of (dis)identification that are central to an understanding of young women's friendship construction at "Hilltop." Through my research I have reformulated my feminist research politics, toward a politics that is emergent and contingent upon daily ethical experiences rather than fixed and trans-situational (Stanley and Wise 1993). Nevertheless, I am still left feeling that this theoretical awareness should not allow space to excuse levels of researcher responsibility, and it certainly does not diminish ethical dilemmas and emotions encountered "in the field."

I wish I could finish this chapter with a neat conclusion that would enthuse other researchers to challenge collusionary practices and develop methods that create dialogue rather than enable collusion. On the surface, participant observation limited my ability to put my feminist "politics of intervention" into practice. However, multilocational participant observation also enabled access to young women's school experiences that I believe could not have been encountered through other qualitative methods that take the researcher out of the "here and now" context. Moreover, while my desire to put my politics into practice frequently failed, participant observation provided me with exciting, dynamic, and exhilarating experiences that magnified and made real the messiness of feminist research.

Notes

1. A U.K. comprehensive school is a system of secondary education in which children of all abilities from a particular area are educated in one school. Comprehensive schools are usually for children aged eleven to sixteen, although some take children up to the age of eighteen.

2. The "abstinence only" debate pervades discussions of sex and sexuality education in the United States. For further discussion of this and other debates in the U.S. context, see Blake and Frances (2002) and research by Fields (2001, 2002).

3. Increasingly in the United Kindom, PSHE is being taught as part of a new citizenship program in schools. Students study a range of topics including drugs, the law, sex education, and disability. In practice the topics covered and the depth to which they are discussed depend on the individual schools and teachers.

References

Alderson, P. (1995). *Listening to Children: Children, Ethics and Social Research*. Ilford, U.K.: Barnardo's.

Blake, S., and Frances, G. (2002). *Just Say No to Abstinence Education: Lessons Learnt from a Sex Education Study Tour to the United States*. London: National Children's Bureau.

Butler, J. (1990). *Gender Trouble: Feminism and Subversion of identity*. New York: Routledge.

DfEE. (2000). *Sex and Relationship Education Guidance*. Nottingham: DfEE.

Doyle, L. (1999). "The Big Issue: Empowering Homeless Women Through Academic Research?" *Area* 31 (3): 239–246.

Epstein, D. (1994). (ed.). *Challenging Lesbian and Gay Inequalities in Education*. Buckingham: Open University Press.

Epstein, D. (1995). "Girls don't do bricks." In J. Siraj-Blatchford and I. Siraj-Blatchford, *Eduacting the whole child: Cross-curricular skills, themes and dimensions,* 56–69. Buckingham: Open University Press.

Epstein, D. (2000). "Sexualities and Education: Catch 28." *Sexualities: Studies in Culture and Society* 3 (4): 387–394.

Epstein, D., and Johnson, R. (1994). "On the Straight and Narrow: The Heterosexual Presumption, Homophobias and Schools." In D. Epstein (ed.), *Challenging Lesbian and Gay Inequalities in Education,* 197–230. Buckingham: Open University Press.

Epstein, D., and Johnson, R. (eds.). (1998). *Schooling Sexualities.* Buckingham: Open University Press.

Epstein, D., O'Flynn, S., and Telford, D. (2002). *Silenced Sexualities in Schools and Universities.* London: Trentham Books.

Fields, J. (2001). "Normal Queers: Straight Parents Respond to Their Children's 'Coming Out.'" *Symbolic Interaction* 24 (2): 165–187.

Fields, J. (2002). "Risky Lessons: Sexuality and Inequality in School-based Sex Education." Ph.D. Thesis, University of North Carolina, Chapel Hill.

Furlong, A., and Cartmel, F. (1997). *Young People and Social Change: Individualization and Risk in Late Modernity.* Buckingham: Open University Press.

Griffin, C. (1985). *Typical Girls? Young Women from School to the Job Market.* London: Routledge and Kegan Paul.

Griffiths, V. (1995). *Adolescent Girls and Their Friends: A Feminist Ethnography.* Aldershot: Avebury.

Harrison, J.K. (2000). *Sex Education in Secondary Schools.* Buckingham: Open University Press.

Haywood, C. (1996). "Out of the Curriculum": Sex Talking, Talking Sex." *Curriculum Studies* 4 (2): 229–249.

Hey, V. (1997). *The Company She Keeps: An Ethnography of Girls' Friendship.* Buckingham: Open University Press.

Holland, J., Ramazanoglu, C., Sharpe, S., and Thomson, R. (1998). *The Male in the Head: Young People, Power and Heterosexuality.* London: The Tufnell Press.

Jackson, S. (1999). *Heterosexuality in ?uestion.* London: Sage.

Johnson, R. (1996). "Sexual Dissonances: Or the 'Impossibility of Sexuality Education.'" *Curriculum Studies* 4 (2): 163–189.

Kitchin, R., and Hubbard, P. (1999). "Research, Action and 'Critical' Geographies." *Area* 31(3): 195–198.

Laskey, L., and Beavis, C. (eds.). (1996). *Schooling & Sexualities: Teaching for a Positive Sexuality.* Deakin University, Deakin Centre for Education and Change, Melbourne.

Mac an Ghaill, M. (1996a). "Deconstructing Heterosexualities Within School Arenas." *Curriculum Studies* 4 (2): 191–209.

Mac an Ghaill, M. (1996b). "Towards a Reconceptualised Sex/Sexuality Education Policy: Theory and Cultural Change." *Journal of Education Policy* 11 (3): 289–302.

Maxey, I. (1999). "Beyond Boundaries? Activism, Academia, Reflexivity and Research." *Area* 31 (3): 199–208.

Measor, L., Tiffin, C., and Fry, K. (1996). "Gender and Sex Education: A Study of Adolescent Responses." *Gender and Education* 8 (3): 275–288.

Morris-Roberts, K. (2001). "Intervening in Friendship Exclusion: The Politics of Doing Feminist Research with Teenage Girls." *Ethics, Place and Environment* 4 (2): 147–152.

Morris-Roberts, K. (2002). "Individuality and (Dis)identification in Young Women's Friendships at School." Ph.D. Thesis, University of Sheffield.

Reason, P., and Bradbury, H. (eds.). (2001). *Handbook of Action Research: Participative Inquiry and Practice.* London: Sage.

Redman, P. (1994). "Shifting Ground: Rethinking Sexuality Education." In D. Epstein (ed.), *Challenging Lesbian and Gay Inequalities in Education,* 131–151. Buckingham: Open University Press.

Sanders, S., and Spraggs, G. (1989). "Section 28 and Education." In C. Jones and P. Mahony (eds.), *Learning Our Lines: Sexuality and Social Control in Education.* London: Women's Press.

Skeggs, B. (1997). *Formations of Class and Gender: Becoming Respectable.* London: Sage.

Stanley, L., and Wise, S. (1993). *Breaking Out Again: Feminist Ontology and Epistemology.* London: Routledge.

Stonewall. (2000). *Section 28 Campaign Pack*. Available from http//:www.stonewall.org.

Thomson, R. (1994). "Moral Rhetoric and Public Health Pragmatism: The Recent Politics of Sex Education." *Feminist Review* 48: 40–60.

Thorogood, N. (2000). "Sex Education as Disciplinary Technique: Policy and Practice in England and Wales." *Sexualities: Studies in Culture and Society* 3 (4): 425–438.

Waites, M. (2000). "Homosexuality and the New Right: The Legacy of the 1980's for New Delineations of Homophobia." *Sociological Research Online* 5 (1): 39–49.

West, J. (1999). "(Not) Talking About Sex: Youth Identity and Sexuality." *The Sociological Review* 47 (3): 525–547.

WGSG. (1997). *Feminist Geographies: Explorations in Diversity and Difference*. Essex: Harlam Longman.

Wise, S. (2000). "'New Right' or 'Backlash?' Section 28, Moral Panic and 'Promoting Homosexuality.'" *Sociological Research Online* 5 (1): 27–38.

CHAPTER 20

Speaking Back: Voices of Young Urban Womyn of Color Using Participatory Action Research to Challenge and Complicate Representations of Young Women

CAITLIN CAHILL AND THE "FED UP HONEYS":
ERICA ARENAS, JENNIFER CONTRERAS, JIANG NA,
INDRA RIOS-MOORE, AND TIFFANY THREATTS

THE VOICE OF A YOUNG URBAN WOMYN OF COLOR...

I am an interesting young womyn[1] who bores herself to delirium. And a comedian who can't tell a joke. I am a responsible sister and a helpful daughter. I love to be me and yet I am different around others. I am extremely emotional but want to hide my feelings. I have a hard time trusting some and put too much trust into others. This leads to hurt feelings and total vulnerability. I want to be vulnerable but it makes me feel weak. I want to feel weak but no one wants to care for me. I want to care for those I love and want them to care for me more. I never believe anyone can love me as much as I do them. I want to take care of people but don't want them to need me. I am too clingy and never see friends and family. I am a complete idiot but an intelligent person. I am lacking education. I have no communication skills and I am a good listener. I am a good listener who hates to hear people speak. I am a reader who watches way too much TV. I am a good friend and girlfriend but I have few friends and no boyfriend. I am open and bold but hold my tongue when I'm hurt. I put people in their place and yet others walk all over me. I try too hard and yet do nothing at

231

Fig. 20.1 © 2003, Fed Up Honeys, www.fed-up-honeys.org. Reprinted with permission.

all. I am a procrastinator but I am always early. I help and help and help, and get nothing in return. I am not where I would like to be, and want to be so much further. I am very opinionated and yet know nothing about the world. I know where I want to go but I am confused. I know what I want but I am confused. I know how I feel but I am confused. I know what I mean but I confuse myself. I am boring and fun, and innocent and cruel. I am trusting. I am always here. I am always there. I am always needed. I am loved and hated. I am admired. I am spiteful but not jealous. I am very jealous. I am scared of everything. My face shows bravery. I am angry. I am in love. I am confused again…. Honestly, I am too much to put into words. (Erica Arenas, www.fed-up-honeys.org, Summer 2002)

Indra: This is an example of how a young womyn describing herself manages to convey the difficulty and challenge of being a contradiction—of being many things at once. Her words exemplify our struggle to find a voice through research.

Here we reflect upon our experiences collaborating on a participatory action research project at the Graduate Center of the City University of New York (CUNY) in the summer of 2002. We represent six members of a team of seven who worked together on a qualitative research project called "Makes Me Mad: Stereotypes of Young Urban Womyn of Color," a study that considers the relationship between the lack of resources in a community (the Lower East Side neighborhood of New York City) and mischaracterizations of young women.[2] The project is for and by young urban womyn of color, and is reflective of our own concerns and the issues that personally affected us. The theme of stereotypes repeatedly came up in our group discussions. We latched onto the idea of exploring the stereotypes that we were frustrated with and challenged by. Though we are all women of color, we are a diverse collection of personalities and backgrounds; the fact that we all felt so passionately about this topic is a testament to its likely importance to all young womyn affected by stereotypes that are pervasive in popular culture and the self-image issues that stem from them. This is a snapshot of our collaborative process that we think gives a sense of where we started and the evolution of our project. Along the way we share our different perspectives on what it was like to be involved in this project, our process, the challenges we faced, and the impacts of our research.

AT THE BEGINNING

HOW WE GOT STARTED

> Caitlin: The primary focus of this research project was to study and understand young urban women's experiences and interpretations of the urban environment. The project was developed for my dissertation research on the subject of the everyday lives of young women in the city. My review of the literature found that there was little research concerning urban young women's everyday lives, and even less from a youth perspective. I wanted to create a project focusing on young urban women's perceptions of their own lives. This study took a deliberately open theoretical and methodological approach in order that the objectives of the project would be determined collaboratively by everyone involved. To this end, the project adopted a participatory research approach in order to engage young women researchers in a collective process of looking critically at their social and environmental contexts.

In order to apply to participate in this project, you had to be female, between the ages of sixteen and twenty-two, available to participate, and live on the Lower East Side. Youth researchers were recruited through neighborhood schools and community centers. Applicants had to fill out an application which included a short essay about their interest in participating. Youth researchers would be paid a stipend for their participation in the participatory action research project. The project was broadly defined because the idea was to keep it open and follow the lead of the young women involved. It was not known who would apply and what they would bring to the table.

Significantly, in the beginning the youth researchers were trained in social research skills. We spent a lot of time talking about what was research, the purposes of research, and the potential of it. I wanted the young women researchers to be involved in every aspect of developing and creating a research project. We started out in the month of July. Then we got a grant[3] which allowed us to work through August. And we have continued to meet since then to work on various aspects of the project and finish it. Collectively we have become more and more ambitious, and still we continue to meet as we reflect together and write this chapter collaboratively months later.

> Erica: On July 8, 2002, six young womyn came together as the focus of a research project, "The Lives of Young Womyn in the City." We ranged in age from sixteen to twenty-two, and different ethnic backgrounds. We are Chinese, Puerto Rican, African-American, Dominican, and Black-Latina. As diverse as we are, personalities included, we seemed to click instantly and our conversations flowed. We fed off each other's ideas and we built on them as well. We spoke of personal experiences, shared our writings, and discussed world issues we felt were impacting us.

> Indra describes us: We're almost like a boy band with members that meet pre-prescribed personality types that are different enough for any teenage girl to have a favorite. Jiang Na is quiet and shy with an undercover bravery of spirit; Shamara is loud and jovial but truly a sensitive person; Jennifer is also loud but is a storyteller who takes guff from no one and is not a big fan of school but is an excellent businesswoman; Tiffany is quiet and reserves judgments, but when she decides to talk, she lets out pearls of true wisdom; Erica is all tough on the outside but is really very sweet on the inside with a propensity for crying; Caitlin is the kind soul that keeps us all on track and at the same time makes sure that we feel free enough to let loose—she's the glue; and I'm the crazy one, I let loose with random useless facts, make weird sounds for no good reason that anyone can discern, and am the anti-establishment representative of the group.

All of us together make up "Fed-Up-Honeys,"[4] very different women with different opinions, and though it takes time to get on the same page, when we get there, we always have very interesting, fresh, new, and unique ideas to share and use.

BEFORE THE BEGINNING

> Caitlin: Some of the decisions that were made before the project started were critical. First of all, YOU decided to apply for this project. One thing that I noticed about each of you was that you were confident individuals and that you were responsible. You followed through. You came on time. You called me back. It was very important to me that you were responsible, because in order for you to participate, you had to be committed to be there—to be present. This is a prerequisite to participation.

> Jiang Na: When I joined this program, I was only in America for a year and a half. I didn't have any work experience. I tried to fill out the application form that my art teacher gave me. I really thought that I would not be accepted. Unexpectedly, I got the call from Caitlin, and she told me that I was recruited. I couldn't describe how I felt. I thought I was the most lucky person in this world.

I never thought that I could work in an office with foreign people and earn such a large wage.

Erica: One phone call, one interview, and several brief job descriptions later, and I still wasn't sure of what I'd be doing and how I would be contributing to this research project.

THE FIRST DAY

Erica: Our first day of work was also the first day I met the five other young womyn I would be working with. As each girl arrived, I couldn't help but think to myself that I was not going to get along with these girls because not one of them looked like any of my friends, as far as the way they dressed. (This was my closed-mindedness kicking in.) As we went up in the elevator, I told myself to keep an open mind and that we may turn out to be friends in the end. Still unsure.

Jiang Na: We started working at ten o'clock in the morning. I sat there and looked at others talking. They seemed to have a lot to talk about and enjoyed their time. A strange feeling came to me. I felt left out. I had a very different background from the five other women in this group. I didn't know enough English to express myself.... I still remember how I felt in the beginning: nervous, wondering, and uncertain if I have the capability to do it or not.... We began to introduce ourselves. The thing that made me surprised was that everyone is from different countries. I thought that I was the only one that was different.

Erica: We entered the room where we would be conducting our research, the room where we would be spending all our time, and I felt a sudden case of claustrophobia kick in. There was barely enough floor space for all of us to stand at the same time. I took my seat in the corner, and there it began...the silence.
The buzzing of the lights above was louder than our breathing. I found it to be funny, yet terrifying. What if my stomach growled, as it has the habit of doing for no apparent reason at all except to humiliate me? Caitlin, wanting to break the silence in the room, began with "So ... um ... hi." This was going to be something.... For the next few days our mornings began with some writing and some sharing which led into deep conversation every now and then. We spoke of what happened to us on the way to the Graduate Center.

Jiang Na: I got lost that morning on the way there.

A good beginning

The way the project started, set the tone for our work together. It is difficult to pull apart the pieces that made us identify our project as successful, but certainly our interpersonal interactions were critical to our feeling good about the project. Despite our cultural differences and our opposing views of the world and our environment, we just clicked. An unpredicted connection was made, and soon after came a natural communication. You can't plan for something like this to happen; it just has to happen, as you do not know who will be part of the project and what they will bring to it. However, critical to this was an open and comfortable atmosphere from the beginning. Early on, Caitlin, the project facilitator, made us realize that we were all equal partners and our collaborative project really would integrate all of our ideas. This atmosphere of democracy and community started us out with camaraderie and respect, and became a very important part of our research approach.

THE PROCESS

> Participatory action research starts with social concerns and lived experiences, values the knowledge produced through collaboration and in action, places emphasis upon the research process, and reconsiders the value of research as a vehicle for social change....Critical to the success of a participatory action research process is the building of a community of researchers.

> (Torre et al. 2001)

We knew a little bit about what we were getting ourselves into, even if it wasn't totally clear. The application included a brief description of the project (as follows):
A team of 6–8 youth researchers, young women who live on Lower East Side, will be trained in social research methods and will conduct research on the way they use their neighborhood, where they spend time, and if their neighborhood supports their particular needs. Youth Researchers will design and implement a research project investigating their concerns in their neighborhood.
Research questions include: Where do you spend time in your neighborhood? What places do you like? Dislike? Why? How do you think your neighborhood could be improved to meet your needs? What are your concerns and questions?

The project unfolded day by day as we made new discoveries together, as we related to each other, as we made collective decisions, and as we pushed forward in our research process that we made up as we went along. We had different experiences with research and different associations with this process.

I NEVER THOUGHT OF RESEARCH AS A TOOL TO TALK BACK ....

> Tiffany: I never thought of research as a tool to talk back to the community. I always thought of it as analyzing (sometimes overanalyzing) history. Like with researching past events, something we would get in school, or looking up a lot of information on a certain subject. I also thought of research being used like statistics, making observations about things and only using them for big companies or businesses.

Indra: Even though I've had past experience with research, it has still been hard for me to grasp the concept that research can be a tool for changing society, never mind being able to embrace it as a powerful tool for women of color in particular. For a number of reasons, namely, the fact that education alone is connoted with negative feelings and failure for communities of color, research is not understood fully and used to its full merit by communities of color. Because of this relationship, or rather lacking relationship, with education and research, I think we didn't understand the potential impact of our work at first.

Jiang Na: In the first few days, I was still not sure what we were doing. I was wondering if all we needed to do is sit there and talk and write and get paid for it. Day by day passed, and I felt we didn't do anything.

Tiffany: When we started out, we were not sure what to do the research on. We had many ideas, but not one specific idea that spoke to all of us.

Indra: When we were first starting work on creating a project of our own choice, we spent a lot of time talking and thinking about how and with whom we would like to share our research.

STRUCTURAL ISSUES

Caitlin: What was challenging about the process for me was setting up a process that you could take over, that you would feel ownership over. I knew in advance that part of working collaboratively was about being open to learning more, was about listening, and about leaving a lot of space for things to happen. So what was tricky was on the one hand creating a structure for our process, a way of working together, and on the other hand creating space for the unexpected to happen.

Indra (speaking on the lack of strict structure at inception of project): The fact that we had a very loose idea of what we were there to do gave us an opportunity to make the space our own and to express our thoughts and ideas more freely.

Tiffany: The unstructuredness of the project was great for me. I like not having barriers or a strict schedule of work to follow. It gave us time to get to know everyone and talk about what we wanted to do. Also, it made me feel like the project was actually ours.

Jiang Na: I like structure. It allows me to know what to do. I like the way no one is telling me to do this or that, but for me, in this situation—working with people from totally different backgrounds than me—I would rather have someone to set up a topic for me or tell me what I should do. Otherwise, I don't know how to satisfy them because I don't know what they want.

Indra: Because we were at CUNY, clearly an educational setting, there was potential for us to feel intimidated or feel that there were going to be specific expectations of us, but because we only knew we were going to be there to do some level of discussion and because our activities were loose enough to be group-directed, they resulted in shared thoughts and ideas that were particularly unique to us as a group.

Caitlin: I knew also that this whole process was very new to all of you and that it was my responsibility to introduce you to research. And on the other hand I didn't want to fall into the familiar role of being a teacher. I didn't want to have a student–teacher relationship with you, as I know that can be very limited and because of all the baggage that relationship brings. I also knew this might be difficult to overcome because I know from experience that many teachers you have encountered are White women, and here I was the only White woman in the room and also older than you all.

Tiffany: If it was more structured, it would have felt like school to me, and I know Caitlin was worried about coming off as a teacher, but she wasn't. She gave us the opportunity to speak our minds about every- and anything, even if it was racial. Though at times we were rushed to get work done because of little time and much conversation, we are proud of our work and of how much we have gotten done. For me the unstructuredness helped me to develop ideas on what to do and made it easier to work, knowing there were no barriers. The most important thing for me to be able to do this work was it not feeling like school.

CHALLENGES

We faced many challenges during the research process. This collaborative process challenged us to be open, and it was sometimes a difficult and painful process. We acknowledged the power of our differences in coming together, and also that sometimes these differences caused us to feel left out.

A DIFFICULT AND SOMETIMES PAINFUL PROCESS

Erica: We opened up to each other and expressed ourselves passionately. It was like I was getting paid to go to therapy.

Caitlin : Where do we go when we want to express ourselves—our feelings about the world we are living in, about social inequities, about sexism, racism, about what's happening in our neighborhoods, in our schools ... are there places for us to get angry? To get mad? To respond and do something about how we feel? I raise this question because it came up during our research process. Emotions were critical to our research. Anger/frustration/excitement/passion fueled our discussions and even made it into the title of the research project—"Makes Me Mad...."

Indra: By the end of our time together during the summer, we came to the agreement that we wanted to provoke others into rethinking the standard negative stereotypes of young urban women of color that they encountered. But before we could even realize that that was what we wanted to do, we had to (through angry eruptions, upset, and discussions) realize that we were living under the veil of those stereotypes ourselves. We had to touch upon some of those emotions that those oppressively heavy misconceptions had laid on us, and that was a difficult and sometimes painful process.

The issue of stereotypes is critical. Stereotypes set up roles for people within a society that are not self-prescribed. One must consistently question and challenge stereotypes which are entrenched not only in the minds of people outside of the stereotyped group in question, but also in the psyches of those being stereotyped, shaping their self-image and limiting their development.

In a highly patriarchal society where even White womyn still face a great deal of the same limitations and misconceptions that their grandmothers once faced, womyn of color are all the more in need of the space and the encouragement to start shaping their paths within society. Part of the journey starts with womyn of color smashing the skewed pictures of themselves that they see being constantly portrayed and reified in the world that they live in. Participatory action research is one such method of making sure that we as womyn of color could control how our voices and our thoughts would be portrayed and interpreted through the lens of research. We crafted a project that made our voices the centerpiece, and were able to develop new and innovative approaches to research that are more likely to catch the attention of our peers and urge them to rethink their own self-perceptions and those of their communities.

Differences that challenged us

One of our most significant challenges was how to manage our differences of opinion. What we realized was that not all differences of opinion need to be resolved. Not everyone has to think like you, and you don't have to think like everyone else. It's okay to disagree and express opposition, because it helps others to see things from every angle possible. This was one of our biggest accomplishments, the ability to see the world through someone else's eyes and to let others see the world through ours.

> Indra: The most difficult part of doing collaborative research was also the most rewarding. We are probably one of the most diverse groups of people I've ever spent an extended amount of time with, and when I say diverse, I'm talking about more than cultural diversity, but diversity of personality and opinion.... we never would have met due to the different ways we live, despite that fact that we're from the same small community.

> Jiang Na: I didn't know enough English to express myself. It made it more difficult for me to communicate with them, even though everybody was very understanding and tried to explain things to me. I still felt uncomfortable and guilty. I felt I was bothering them a lot. Especially after they explained the words to me, I didn't get the meaning of the words. I really thanked them for being patient, because it helps me a lot to get into their conversations. People in this project gave me a lot of encouragement.... Week after week, I felt more comfortable to work with them. I tried my best.

ON A ROLL

Proud of our accomplishments

Jiang Na: I could never have imagined how excited and proud of what we were doing I would be. When we decided to make the stickers and the Web site, I almost couldn't wait to see how they would look. For the first time in my life, my picture is on the Web site with our research team. It was a very meaningful thing to me. I can't describe how good I felt.

Tiffany: It felt great to actually follow through with our ideas, because someone like me hardly goes though with my ideas. Also, it was cool because it was like we had no barriers to what we wanted to do with our research. We created our own barriers (if needed). It was like "We're actually going to do this, it's not a dead end." It also felt like "We're actually going to do this, how are people going to take it?" It was great making the stickers, doing fieldwork, and having focus groups. I really can't explain how good it felt when we started on the stickers and Web site—it felt good thinking of something and following through with it.

Jiang Na: When the day the stickers and the Web site were finished, I thought "Wow, we've been doing a lot."

Erica: All of our "therapy sessions" eventually triggered ideas in our minds and they resulted in our sticker campaign, which received great feedback; our Web site, which we are very proud of and has been visited by many; and a study of our findings we have just recently completed and posted on our Web site. We call these our babies, and we couldn't be more proud of our accomplishments.

Recommendations for involving young people (like us) in research

Jiang Na: I think if you want a research process to engage young people, first of all the theme of the research has to be very inspiring. We need to have them feel like it is valuable to them; we need to find out what they want to know about, what they are curious about. As young people we are curious about the world. About everything in this period. We seem to know everything, but we don't. It is good to hear something from others. From other communities. We need a direction.

Indra: Honest dialogue in as safe a space as we could find was the only method that we used.

Caitlin: Too often women are dismissed as overemotional. Because of this we are especially guarded and keep our feelings to ourselves if we don't want to be stereotyped in this way ... lest we be accused of pms-ing, of being shrill, being coddled, or even be called a bitch when we get mad. Our emotional lives and responses are silenced and/or not taken seriously.... We go to school, learn about the world, about our histories, and instead of being encouraged to explore our feelings about what we learn, we are expected to memorize it and regurgitate it or write about it in a clear and concise manner that leaves out our personal feelings or the relation of knowledge to ourselves. In this way education can become alienating, and we can lose sense of what history means to us and not feel connected. This is a key issue in our research—developing our connection to our communities. Here we share our experience and offer a way of working that we think is powerful. It involves taking young people seriously, starting with their feelings, providing a structure for collaboration that is open and allows young people to take over.

Making an impact with our research

Indra: For myself, at first, I had been thinking that our main audience would be people outside of our peer group and community, because I thought that primarily these were the people that were misunderstanding us and that they were the main consumers of stereotypes of young urban womyn of color. But over time and thought, I began to feel that our main audience should be our peers. I felt that if we put our voices into the world aimed at outsiders, we were presuming that our peers and ourselves don't have the level of agency needed to make change to the predominant perceptions of us, and I strongly disagree with that.

If we were to approach our work with the level of honesty that we demand from the powers that be that aid in the production of hurtful stereotypes, we had to use our research as a method to speak our truth and get that truth out to our peers; the one group of people that hold the true power to challenge misperceptions by facing them head-on and looking to themselves for answers about who they are.

Erica: I have become more aware of the happenings in my environment and the world. Just this winter something happened to my family and I—or, should I say, it's been happening to us for a while, and it was only a matter of time.... Gentrification.... Oh! My ! God! That's what was happening to me!... These days I find myself to be angry about the situation, but I am grateful that these girls could open my eyes to something that was happening to me right under my nose. Now I can educate those who are stuck in the same predicament I was in not so long ago.

Tiffany: When we decided on researching stereotypes, then using it to educate the womyn in our community, it seemed new, like something no one has done before. Most likely there were, and are, many who do this but are not recognized, but that's where our research will be different; we have explored many options to speak to our community and have come up with very effective ways like the stickers, Web site, and paper to reach our community. Using our research to talk to our community made me realize that research is not just words of a paper for statistics, but it can be used to empower. Research can be anything the researcher wants it to be, and that is a powerful thing.

Jiang Na: Unconsciously, half a year has already passed. I discover I have grown up a lot. I am not talking about my body, it is my mind that has grown up. I think that I have had a lesson of my life. Everyone's different opinion of life gave me a lot of inspiration, it makes me know how to solve and face problems.

Erica: I finally realize the significance we played in the research. Our contributions are the result of a relationship developed by seven womyn with a mutual goal.

Notes

1. The reason we spell "womyn" with a "y" is that the "correct" spellings of "wo<u>man</u>" and "wo<u>men</u>" have the words "man" and "men" in them.
2. For more information about the "Makes Me Mad" project and stereotype sticker campaign, please visit our Web site, www.fed-up-honeys.org.
3. This research would not be possible without the generous funding from ActKnowledge, Inc. Thank you!!!
4. "Fed Up Honeys" is the name chosen by the research team for our Web site. See www.fed-up-honeys.org for more information.

References

Cahill, C. (2004, forthcoming) Defying gravity? Raising consciousness through collective research. *Children's Geographies.*

Fine, M., Torre, M.E., Boudin, K., Bowen, I., Clark, J., Hylton, D., Martinez, M., Roberts, R.A., Rivera, M., Smart, P., & Upengui, D. (2001). Participatory action research: from within and beyond prison bars. In Camie, O. Rhodes, J.E., & Yardley, L. (eds.) *Qualitative research in psychology: Expanding perspective in methodology and design.* (Washington, DC, American Psychology Association)

Torre, M.E., Fine, M., Boudin, K., Bowen, I., Clark, J., Hylton, D., Martinez, M., Roberts, R.A., Rivera, M., Smart, P., and Upegui, D. (2001). "A Space for Co-constructing Counter Stories Under Surveillance." *International Journal of Critical Psychology* 4: 149–166.

CHAPTER 21

Beneath the Surface of Voice and Silence: Researching the Home Front

ADREANNE ORMOND

This chapter discusses the voices and silences of a particular group of young indigenous Maori females from the land of Aotearoa/New Zealand.[1] The young Maori females' voices and silences contained within this chapter are based upon postgraduate research that I carried out with the "Youth First—Taking Kids' Talk Seriously" New Zealand nationwide project.[2]

This project has sought to privilege what young people ten to seventeeen years old say as a basis for evaluating the last fifteen years of economic and cultural change in New Zealand. Over the course of three years a unique methodology of focus groups and youth tribunals was used to constitute spaces where youth voice was heard (L.T. Smith et al. 2002: 169).

I discuss my postgraduate research experience by focusing upon four methodological issues, beginning with how researchers unknowingly silence young people's voices through denying their experience. What motivates these young females to cut through silence and speak out? How does an audience unintentionally silence while in the act of listening? And I conclude by offering insight into how both researcher and audience can use a methodology of listening to overcome particular aspects of silencing.

Locating the Young Maori Female Voices

This discussion begins with the premise that voice and silence are products of society, and therefore are neither pure, authentic, nor uncontaminated

(Fine 1994). On this basis it is necessary to locate the blend of social circumstances that have produced the voices and silences particular to these young Maori females. Maori are the indigenous people of New Zealand, yet we comprise a minority[3] of the population and, as such, are the only indigenous minority social group in New Zealand. Pakeha people are the non-Maori descendants of the British and North European people who settled New Zealand. Pakeha people represent the majority of New Zealand's population and are the dominant social group. This particular group of young Maori females lives on an isolated peninsula in rural New Zealand. Although their indigenous Maori culture and rural farming community surround them, their lifestyle is highly influenced by Western society. Although tourism and handmade cultural crafts are making small inroads into the area, the community's economy is largely dependent upon the two mainstay industries of beef/sheep farming and commercial fishing. Employment has been adversely affected by the removal of national economic subsidies from the farming and fishing industries. However, the community has adjusted to such economic changes, and unemployment has become an accepted feature of rural life.

The geographical landscape features Maori cultural meetinghouses, historical Maori cultural sites of significance, and ancient burial grounds. Social amenities such as supermarkets, paved sidewalks, corner dairies, shopping malls, movie theaters, and high schools are absent.[4] Instead there are blue ocean, uninhabited white sand beaches, green rolling farmland speckled with white sheep and black cattle, and one-lane narrow roads which are covered with loose metal stones. One local shop provides the community with vehicle fuel, mail, newspapers, and basic milk and bread supplies, and serves as a point of informal communal meetings and conversation. I know these roads and coastline like the back of my own hand, for this is my home community, where I grew up and take my identity from. I also know the young women who feature in this discussion personally; we descend from the same Maori genealogy, and I am ten years older than the youngest research participant.

As picturesque as my home landscape may be, there are advantages and disadvantages to carrying out research within your home community (Hill Collins 1991; Foster 1994). In the following section I name one of these disadvantages as negotiating the multiple community and academic roles involved with indigenous "inside-out/outside-in research" (L. T. Smith 1999: 7) and discuss how I unintentionally silenced the very voices I was attempting to liberate.

How a Researcher Can Unintentionally Silence

Through our kinship and shared community experiences, the young females and I share a specific knowledge which is learned through being a living piece of the community, what some people refer to as an "insider."

An insider denotes an individual who understands historic and present cultural and community traditions so that he or she is able to use that community-cultural knowledge to respond appropriately to community situations, and thereby avoid community-cultural offense and damage. Yet cultures and communities are fluid, and so are their associated roles. If an insider does not move with cultural and community changes, he or she can find the insider role changing to that of an outsider. I had this particular insight reinforced when I arrogantly assumed that within the familiar territory of my home community, my insider status guaranteed me immediate access to and understanding of the life experiences of the young Maori females. The only immediacy I was provided with was an opportunity to understand my personal researcher bias and inadequacies, and how my ignorance was silencing the young females' voices. That is, the ten-year age difference between myself and the young females meant that my insider knowledge was based upon outdated information. Therefore, instead of my insider knowledge creating a space in which the young females could speak and be understood, I was actually silencing by incorrectly anticipating what it was that they would and would not say. Therefore, the insider status that I thought would provide easy access to the young females' voices was, ironically, a passport to a methodology of silence.

I illustrate how my combined insider knowledge and researcher role silenced the voices of the young Maori females by relating a community experience. One afternoon I drove to the one and only community shop to collect the mail. As previously mentioned, this shop also serves as a communal meeting point. I collected the mail, walked out of the shop, and noticed among the parked cars and farm vehicles a group of my younger female cousins. They were listening to a Jennifer Lopez song, which was playing from a Discman. To see a group of young people hanging out around the shop and listening to music was nothing unusual. However, what did catch my attention was that they were all astride horses and, judging from the sweaty appearance of both humans and horses, their riding had been physically demanding.

Since farm four-wheeler motorbikes have nearly taken over the work that horses once performed upon farms, I had not expected to see young people riding horses to the shop. This visual impression invoked such feelings of surprise within myself that for the next few days I wrestled with, first, realizing that I had unknowingly placed a biased framework around the young Maori females' life experience and, then, questioning myself as to what, exactly, those biases were. That is, I questioned why I had unknowingly categorized certain activities as specific to the past, so that I was accepting of such a horse-riding scenario occurring twenty years ago, yet in these present times I viewed such an activity as out-of-date and therefore uninteresting to young people. I had categorized these young people as living within a new age farming community with interests centered more in Internet chat rooms, and local farming heroes being displaced by role models such as Britney Spears and Destiny's Child. Not only were my expectations stereotypical by popular culture standards, but viewing the young females upon their horses brought me face-to-face with the realization that my insider knowledge was stagnant, and as long as I continued to use it as my point of reference for understanding their life experiences, I would continue to oppress their voices into silence.

With my stereotypical assumptions framing the young females' experiences incorrectly, my community role changed from insider to outsider, and I became the young Maori females' "other." As Gentile (Ellsworth 1989: 322) writes, "[A]ny group—any position—can move into the oppressor role.... [E]veryone is someone else's 'Other.'" As a researcher I had ignored the need to continually examine how I relate to the young Maori females whom I write about and share my life with. In all of my cultural and community knowing I had become the epitome of "dull, uniform grey...laziness" (Walker 1983: 137), so that I viewed the young Maori females' lived-out experience in easy, definable myths of absoluteness. I, who was meant to be dispelling silence by encouraging voicing (Ormond 2002a), had begun speaking the language of silence.

This community experience also speaks to the relationships of social power that constitute silence and voice (Reinharz 1994; Morgan and Coombes 2001) by illustrating how social power is so insipidly entrenched within social roles that those who dominate the power dynamics are not always aware of that position or their ensuing role as potential silencers (Patai 1988; Weis and Fine 1993; Ormond 2002b). However, just as social relationships change according to the social context, so do relationships of power. One way to better understand the transposing nature of power dynamics and how this relates to voice and silence is to discuss what motivates these young Maori females to speak out and how they control the focus group space so that they are able to share their stories.

What Motivates Young People to Speak Out?

Indigenous Maori researcher Linda Smith (L. Smith et al. 2002) suggests that young people speak out to create performative spaces of encounter. In order to appreciate the necessity for such performative spaces of encounter, the young Maori female voices must be continually situated within their daily experiences of oppressive institutional and social silencing. When one's life experience is continually erased by silence, the significance of such a forum cannot be underestimated, for "Silence is like starvation. Don't be fooled. It's nothing short of that and felt most sharply when one has had a full belly most of her life" (Moraga 1983: 29).

Rysack's (1998) writings concerning immigrant women state that women speak differently in forums that they do not control. The "Youth First—Taking Kids' Talk Seriously" focus groups provided the young Maori females with performative spaces of encounter where they were the dominant social group and controlling social power. As such the focus groups were safe forums, where the young people could meet, speak, hear, test, examine, react, edit, and solidify the social messages contained within their voices. The young females exercised their social power by controlling my access to their life experiences through discerning what was public and what was private talk. They also controlled who spoke and what they spoke about according to their own defined Maori cultural and social hierarchy. Speaking out and engaging with each other's voices provided opportunities for the young females to consider how the dominant social group, community, and family members outside of the focus groups might receive their talk.

The following slices of voice are taken from the focus groups and illustrate the young females' sifting through their experiences of Maori history, ethnic identity, and experiences of colonization and racism. I reiterate that if the young females were not speaking from a forum made safe by their controlling the power dynamics and redefining social locations (Dow 1997), these particular experiences would not be voiced.

TWELVE/THIRTEEN-YEAR-OLD FEMALES FOCUS GROUP

Andy[5] (thirteen years old): I like being a Maori because you can go back and there's lots of history to the word Maori and to the land.

Lian (twelve years old): I love living here 'cause there's heaps of Maori instead of Pakeha[6] telling you what to do.

Andy: I like being a Maori because Pakeha are just, like, stuck-up. Think they can rule us Maori...we have to stand for our rights 'cause there's a lotta of history about it, and Pakehas, they think...they are just real arrogant....They always try and screw the Maori territory.

SIXTEEN-YEAR-OLD FEMALES FOCUS GROUP

Mary-ann: There's nothing bad being a Maori 'cause everyone is the same kind.

Jessica: Except for their color and skin and the size and how big they are, they can't blame Maori.

AO:[7] Who do you mean when you say "they can't blame Maori"?

Jessica: You know, Pakeha.... Like Pakeha that are not from here, but then also some of them live around here.

Mary-ann: Pakehas are all critical; they always blame Maori for something they don't do. It's like that at school, where you have Pakeha kids that don't get the blame, but if there's a Maori guy in the class, he gets the blame! It's like that all the time. They just pick on us Maori 'cause they think we're weak and we have to stay together and stick up for each other.

Jessica: Yeah, we've got to be strong for each other, 'cause that's who we've got! Each other.

The young females voices illustrate their need to express inexpressible experiences of oppression (G.H. Smith 1997; Jenkins and Pihama 2001; Cram 2001) and, by so doing, find and create communities of hope. Apfelbaum (2001) names the human need to reconstruct broken lives and maintain sanity amid personal histories of trauma as another catalyst for speaking out. When dealing with traumatic experiences, the need to examine what is and what is not real (Ormond 2001) demands courage, which can be found in those who share experiences of similar kind (Saunders 1999; Apfelbaum 2000a, 2000b). I illustrate this point by referring to a community and family tragedy involving mother and daughter suicides. The daughter was a focus group participant, and her death shattered our lives and became the center of the young females' talk. The following focus group talk captures an atmosphere fraught with questions, self-examination, and deep sorrow.

TWELVE/THIRTEEN-YEAR-OLD FEMALES FOCUS GROUP

Andy (thirteen years old): Who do we know that committed suicide?

AO:[8] In my time there was a lot that did it.

Andy: We had Ben[9] who shot himself.

Lian (twelve years old): My cousin used an exhaust pipe into the car at home.

Karen: Ruth hung herself in the shed; Auntie came out and found her.

Andy: Yeah, and she left her family behind.

Karen: Then there was Michael, who shot himself and his wife.

Andy: Plus the Smiths, who shot themselves.

Lian: Yeah, that really affected their family, too.

Andy: What's there to say about suicide?

SIXTEEN-YEAR-OLD FEMALES FOCUS GROUP

Mary-ann: I guess that you wonder why. But then you don't, 'cause you might blame yourself.

AO: What do you mean?

Jessica: Well, like I don't really know, but I just....maybe she had no one to talk to and got really down, maybe the other side was looking good.

AO: What do you mean, "the other side"?

Jessica: You know ... death, 'cause maybe she was afraid ... I don't know, just talking. I wonder if I'll do it, I just don't want to die in pain. I want to live to see my kids grow up.

Mary-ann: I guess people feel alone even out here where we're all family, they feel alone and so it all adds up and they end up hanging from a rope or putting a bullet in their head.

Speaking out is not only about testing out one's voice and negotiating social perimeters between dominant and minority social groups; it is also about reconstructing experiences of disappointment and resisting the fear and trauma that existent status quo power dynamics have incorrectly labeled as normal life experiences for the young Maori females. Understanding how speaking spaces, power relations, and social forces impact upon the young Maori female voices sets a platform for discussing the role of the audience and how they are capable of unintentionally silencing.

How Audiences Can Unintentionally Silence

As the audience reads about the experiences of attempted historical erasure, loss of land and significant cultural sites, racism, and suicide, it is easy to be drawn in by the emotional context and understandingly reciprocate with compassion. Yet it is in this humane act of emotional reciprocation that the audience silences the voices of the young Maori females by mistaking "aesthetic emotion" (Semprun 1997: 45) for comprehension. An aesthetic emotional comprehension silences by encouraging the audience to focus upon the "sentimental, the personal, and the individual" (Rysack 1998: 37), and therefore diverts attention away from the socioeconomic and cultural factors which are responsible for producing such life experiences. As Danielle, a seventeen-year-old Maori female focus group participant, voiced:

Well, they'll read what we say and they'll think they understand us ... you know, they'll think that they know what it's like for us, they will imagine that they know the solution to us, the problem, but they won't know 'cause they don't understand. They'll just think "oh, poor losties";[10] they'll feel sorry for us, but they're all talk 'cause they like us the way we are so they can keep on feeling sorry for us, gives them something to do in their offices. Nah, they won't understand, and we're poor in their eyes, poor dumb brownies....

When the audience focuses upon the emotion, the level of comprehension required in order for fundamental social change to take place is either delayed or never occurs. Unfortunately, delayed or nonoccurring comprehension only serves the dominant social group by allowing status quo, day-to-day "common sense" (Apple 1997: 122) to continue. Thus, when the audience offers sentiments of emotional politeness, it is often a case of, first, mistaking emotion for comprehension and, second, over-estimating the social value of that pseudo comprehension. The audience's emotional reciprocation is comparable to my arrogant assumption that my insider status offered a shortcut to accessing the young Maori females' voices. For example, categorizing the young Maori females' experiences from my comfortable armchair of insider community and cultural knowledge was easy because it did not require any personal risk or transformation on my part. An audience silences in a similar fashion by overestimating their knowledge about the life experiences of the "other." As Apfelbaum(2001: 31) writes, "Understanding is irrelevant (the reality always exceeds what the narrative is able to represent and convey)." If understanding is not possible and pseudo comprehension only acts to silence, then what role can the audience play in the lives of the young Maori females? Audrey Lorde (1986: 61) frames this dilemma in the following words:

> What do we want from each other,
> After we have told our stories,
> To be healed do we want
> Mossy quiet stealing over our scars,
> Do we want
> The powerful unfrightening sister,
> Who will make the pain go away
> Mother's voice in the hallway,
> You've done it right
> The first time darling.
> You will never need
> To do it again.

Indeed, what is it that research participants require from researchers? I suggest two elementary requirements and one humane invitation. First, research participants want the spaces within which they speak to be safe for themselves and those who hear their voices. Second, when they speak, they want what they say to be heard and understood for the social messages that they represent. Last, I suggest that research participants offer audiences the opportunity to reach beyond multiple barriers of isolating differences and make a human connection. In addressing these needs it is necessary to point out that as researchers, we are also an audience, and as such, our power to break the cycle of silence is magnified twofold. Therefore, the next section offers insight into how both researchers and audiences can use a methodology of listening to move away from unintentional silencing.

How an Audience Can Overcome Unintentional Silencing

Apfelbaum (2001) views the speaker–audience relationship as a transmission. I suggest that in order for any transmission to occur, the audience must be willing to participate in actively listening to the speaker. Active listening entails an awareness that in the speaker–audience relationship either participant can be the "other." Within this chapter I have mainly referred to the "other" as the insider-community member-turned-outsider. An awareness of social positions such as the "other" is essential to the speaker–audience transmission because it lays the foundation for a comprehension of depth that moves beyond the emotional to resist the social magic of the institution (Fine 1996; Bourdieu 1991) or what Greene (1995: 12) describes as the "sleepwalker's precision…the addiction to harmony and the fear of contradiction."

By resisting the dominant social group's day-to-day practices, the audience unmasks existent relationships of power between researchers and researched so that the need to "study[ing] who we are and who we are in relation to those we study" (Reinharz 1988) becomes more than a luxury of the privileged: it becomes a research necessity. For example, it was not until I examined who I was in relation to my community and the young Maori females that I realized that even though we share community experiences, I still need to build bridges of understanding so that I can listen, hear, and comprehend their personal community experiences for what they are. Therefore, I suggest that when the speaker–audience transmission is combined with an examination of the speaker–audience relationship, both parties are transformed. The audience begins to understand that to willingly participate in active listening is also to empower the speaker (Fine 1994; Reinharz 1988), which enables the speaker to redefine the speaking space so that it is safe for him or her to speak within. When such a transformation occurs, the speaker speaks from a position of verbal liberation and the audience moves beyond the words to hear the encrypted social message that is being spoken. William Carlos Williams (1951: 361) describes this transformation in the following words:

> We realize which beyond all they have been saying is what they have been trying to say.… We begin to see that the underlying meaning of all they want to tell us and have always failed to communicate is the poem, the poem which their lives are lived to realize. No one will believe it. And it is the actual words, as we hear them spoken under all circumstances, which contain it. It is actually there, in the life before us, every minute that we are listening, a rarest element—not in our imaginations but there, there in fact. It is that essence which is hidden in the very words which are going in at our ears and from which we must recover underlying meaning as realistically as we recover metal out of ore.

When this type of transformation occurs, the audience and speakers connect, as the audience comprehends that they are involved in more than just listening. That they are replacing a methodology of silence with a methodology of listening, and as such are significant participants in social change and breaking the shackles of oppressive silence.

Summary
This chapter has discussed the more obvious methodological issues involved when researching voice and silence within your home community. I have attempted to share the potential issues that arise when working within an indigenous culture and community, yet I also realize that these

issues occur across other multiple boundaries. Although this chapter has referred only to slices of voice that speak to oppressive experiences, I do not wish to represent the young females' lives as lives of despair, for that is an act of silence in itself. I reiterate that this chapter represents only one perspective, and because these young Maori females are a force unto themselves, multiple perspectives remain to be addressed. I have attempted to reinforce the young females' social identity by using their voices to inform the audience of their self-determination and courage. Finally, I have discussed their life experiences within our home community as a means of vanquishing silence and reaching out to find communities of hope, hearing, and understanding.

Notes

1. Aotearoa is the Maori name for what Pakeha people now call New Zealand.
2. This study was funded by the Marsden Fund, which is administered by the Royal Society of New Zealand.
3. The Maori population comprises approximately 15 percent of the Aotearoa/New Zealand population.
4. The community must travel one hour to the nearest rural township for shopping, doctor services, and entertainment such as movie theaters and seasonal carnivals.
5. All the names used in all of the young people's voice excerpts are aliases.
6. Pakeha people are the non-Maori descendants of British and North European settlers of New Zealand.
7. AO is an abbreviation for Adreanne Ormond.
8. AO is an abbreviation for Adreanne Ormond.
9. All the names used in all of the young people's voice excerpts are aliases.
10. "Losties" is a plural for "lost," and the young females use it in the context when an individual has lost the ability to reason.

References

Apfelbaum, E. (2000a). "The Impact of Culture in the Face of Genocide: Struggling Between a Silenced Home Culture and a Foreign Host Culture." In C. Squire (ed.), *Culture in Psychology*, 163–174. London: Routledge.

Apfelbaum, E. (2000b). "And Now What, After Such Tribulations: Memory and Dislocation in the Era of Uprooting." *American Psychologist* 55: 1008–1013.

Apfelbaum, E. (2001). "The Dread: An Essay on Communication Across Cultural Boundaries." *International Journal of Critical Psychology. Under the Covers: Theorising the Politics of Counter Stories* 4 (January): 19–34. Fine & Harris edition.

Apple, M. (1997). "Consuming the Other: Whiteness, Education, and Cheap French Fries." In M. Fine, L. Weis, C. Powell, and L.M. Wong (eds.), *Off White: Readings on Race, Power, and Society*, 121–128. New York: Routledge.

Bourdieu, P. (1991). *Language and Symbolic Power*. Cambridge, Mass.: Harvard University Press.

Cram, F. (2001). "Ma Te Wa e Whakaatu Mai: Time Will Tell." *Feminism and Psychology* 11 (3): 401–406. Special issue on feminist psychology in Aotearoa/New Zealand.

Dow, B.J. (1997). "Politicizing Voice." *Western Journal of Communication* 61 (2): 243–251.

Ellsworth. E. (1989). "Why Doesn't This Feel Empowering? Working Through the Represive Myths of Critical Pedagogy." *Harvard Educational Review* 59 (3): 297–324.

Fine, M. (1994). "Dis-stances and Other Stances: Negotiations of Power Inside Feminist Research." In A. Gitlin (ed.), *Power and Method: Political Activism and Educational Research*, 13–35. London: Routledge.

Fine, M. (1996). Foreword. In D. Kelly and J. Gaskell (eds.), *Debating Dropouts: Critical Policy and Research Perspectives on School Leaving*. New York: Teachers College Press.

Foster, M. (1994). "The Power to Know One Thing Is Never the Power to Know All Things: Methodological Notes on Two Studies of Black American Teachers." In A. Gitlin (ed.), *Power and Method: Political Activism and Educational Research*, 129–146. London: Routledge.

Greene, M. (1995). *Releasing the Imagination: Essays on Education, the Art*. San Francisco: Jossey Bass.

Hill Collins, P. (1991). "Learning from the Outsider Within: The Sociological Significance of Black Feminist Thought." In M.M. Fonow and J.A. Cook (eds.), *Beyond Methodology: Feminist Research as Lived Research*. Bloomington: Indiana University Press.

Jenkins, K., and Pihama, L. (2001). "Matauranga Wahine: Teaching Maori Women's Knowledge Alongside Feminism." *Feminism & Psychology* 11 (3): 293–303. Special issue on feminist psychology in Aotearoa/New Zealand.

Lorde, A. (1986). *Our Dead Behind Us: Poems*. New York: W.W. Norton.

Moraga, C. (1983). "La Guerra." In C. Moraga and G. Anzaldua (eds.), *This Bridge Called My Back: Writings by Radical Women of Color*, 2nd ed. New York: Kitchen Table/Women of Color Press.

Morgan, M., and Coombes, L. (2001). "Subjectivities and Silences, Mothers and Women: Theorizing an Inexperience of Silence as a Speaking Subject." *Feminism & Psychology* 11 (3): 361–375. Special issue on feminist psychology in Aotearoa/New Zealand.

Ormond, A. (2001). "What Is Real." Paper presented at A New Girl Order? Young Women and the Future of Feminist Inquiry Conference, Kings College, London University, November.

Ormond, A. (2002a). "Conspiracy of Silence." Paper presented at Crossing the Divide, Bridging Research, Building Relationships Conference, International Research Institute for Maori and Indigenous Education, University of Auckland, July.

Ormond, A. (2000b). "Voice of Maori Youth: The Other Side of Silence." *International Journal of Critical Psychology. Under the Covers: Theorising the Politics of Counter Stories* 4 (January): 49–60.

Patai, D. (1988). *Brazilian Women Speak: Contemporary Life Stories*. New Brunswick, N.J.: Rutgers University Press.

Reinharz, S. (1988). "The Concept of Voice." Paper presented at Human Diversity: Perspectives on People Context, University of Maryland-College Park, June.

Rysack, S.H. (1998). *Looking White People in the Eye*. Toronto: University of Toronto Press.

Saunders, G. (1999). "Holding and Moving: Articulating Psychology and the Visual Arts." In *Conference of the International Society for Theoretical Psychology, April 1999, Sydney*, pp. 25–28.

Semprun, J. (1997). *Life or Literature*. New York: Viking Penguin.

Smith, G.H. (1997). "The Development of Kaupapa Maori: Theory and Praxis." Ph.D. thesis, University of Auckland.

Smith, L.T. (1999). *Decolonising Methodologies*. London: Zed; Dunedin, N.Z.: Otgao University Press.

Smith, L.T. (2002). "Constituting Spaces for Countering the Stories of Encounter and Encountering the Counter Stories." *International Journal of Critical Psychology. Under the Covers: Theorising the Politics of Counter Stories* 4 (January): 167–182. Fine & Harris edition.

Smith, L.T., Boler, M., Smith, G.H., Kempton, M., Ormond, A., Chueh, H., and Waetford, R. (2002). "'Do You Guys Hate Aucklanders Too?' Youth Voicing Differences from the Rural Heartland." *Journal of Rural Studies* 18 (2): 169–178. Special issue on young rural lives.

Walker, A. (1983). *In Search of Our Mothers' Gardens*. New York: Harcourt Brace Jovanovich.

Weis, L., and Fine, M. (1993). *Beyond Silenced Voices: Class, Race and Gender in United States Schools*. Albany: State University of New York Press.

Williams, W.C. (1951). *The Autobiography of William Carlos Williams*. New York: Random House.

CHAPTER 22

Possible Selves and Pasteles: How a Group of Mothers and Daughters Took a London Conference by Storm

LORI LOBENSTINE, YASMIN PEREIRA, JENNY WHITLEY, JESSICA ROBLES, YARALIZ SOTO, JEANETTE SERGEANT, DAISY JIMENEZ, EMILY JIMENEZ, JESSENIA ORTIZ, AND SASHA CIRINO

Jessenia: Hello. My name is Jessenia, and this is Emily. First of all, we would like to thank you all for being here, and also to give special thanks to those of you who participated in our research, and those of you who helped fund our trip to London. Also, if you have any questions, feel free to ask in between or after we are done. The mothers and daughters who went to London are peer leaders, youth workers, and teen staff in our community. Emily is going to represent the three different youth organizations participating in the research project.

Emily: The three agencies are Teen Resource Project/New Visions, which is a youth theater program; Girls Inc., which is a program for girls and teens ages six to eighteen that inspires girls to be strong, smart, and bold; and Spanish American Union, which is a community health promotion agency.

These are the voices of two teenage researchers in our female-led community research project. This is an introduction piece used during our local presentation to the focus group participants, families, educators, mothers and daughters, and people who had donated money or volunteered time to our research. This presentation carried out one of our primary goals: to bring research done about our community back to our community. Other goals included:

255

- To be phenomenal, confident women willing to learn and teach
- To learn how to do our own research
- To teach academics that community groups and young women can do our research and that our research methods can be more culturally appropriate and dynamic
- Increase mother/daughter communication
- Present our findings at the "New Girl Order" International Conference in London.

Our research project was inspired by the call for papers for the New Girl Order Conference. All of us had participated in focus groups led by local students and professors. As well-meaning and useful as their research may have been, the results never found their way back to us. We decided if we could do the research ourselves, we could share our results in our community *and* in London. This chapter is our story of how we accomplished our goals and how doing so influenced our very own possible selves as researchers. Not only did we conduct research and gain skills, but valuable changes and communication occurred within the mother-and-daughter relationships of our participants.

It was through conversations about mother-and-daughter relationships of teenagers in the community that we found mothers are strong influential beings in their daughters' lives. This inspired us to take a closer look at these relationships, using a possible selves framework. Possible selves—"what we might become, hope to become, and fear becoming"—guide motivation and future behavior (Markus and Nurius 1986: 954). Teen girls spend so much time worrying, hoping, and preparing for our future, which is why we felt possible selves strongly related to teens. Literature showed that possible selves were socially constructed, relying heavily on important others in the social environment as role models, resources, and messengers about what was or was not valued in their culture (Oyserman et al. 1995: 1216). Seeing mothers as important cultural messengers, we wanted to examine the mother's role in shaping her daughter's possible selves. By looking at similarities and differences between mothers' and daughters' possible selves, we could also see what messages have remained the same or changed in terms of their identities as girls, daughters, and members of a particular (primarily Puerto Rican) culture. Our results address some important aspects of mothers' influence on the possible selves of their daughters, but also raise some critical questions about the nature of research, who does it, and who has access to it.

Research Questions

First, what are the similarities and differences between possible selves of teen girls today and those of their mothers when they were young?

Second, how would having mothers and daughters doing this research impact the research and the researchers?

METHOD

Participants

From the start, our girl researchers refused to limit the recruitment of other participants based on income, race or ethnicity, or number of parents. They felt this would be "really unfair." Despite the fact that most research on inner-city adolescent girls focuses solely on girls engaged in "high risk" behavior (Way 1990), this category did not even enter the conversation. In all probability, all of the researchers would be considered high-risk by one standard or another, but none of them identified this as a category for themselves or their friends. In the end, our participants were largely Puerto Rican and working-class, because this is the population that is most highly represented in the three youth programs doing the outreach.

A total of twenty mother–daughter pairs participated in our focus groups. Two girls counted their aunt or grandmother as their mother figure. Four pairs were also a part of our research team. All but one pair participating in the research were of Puerto Rican descent, although most were raised in the United States. Daughters ranged from thirteen to nineteen, with one ten-year-old exception. Our data set does not attempt to represent any entire age or ethnic group but, rather, is a reflection of the girls and moms with whom we regularly work and live.

Recruitment

Researcher recruitment

Staff from all three youth agencies asked their teen girls if they wanted to help design and carry out research about mothers and daughters. Three mothers of teen girls who were involved in these agencies also became researchers. All researchers had input into who our target group was, what our questions were, and what our focus group activities were. All researchers led focus groups, collected data, analyzed the data, and wrote this paper. As Sasha explained:

> Let us tell you, it is not easy at all. We are now learning how to run focus groups, how to collect data, how to run a video camera, how to speak properly so that we won't offend the audience. Even though we think we know it all, actually we really don't. So it's been very detailed.

Participant recruitment

Participants were recruited from two main pools: (1) girls who participated regularly in the three youth agencies (and their mothers), and (2) friends and family of the mothers and daughters on the research team.

Members of the research team were also participants in focus groups when they were not leading them. Recruitment was done through word of mouth, flyers, and phone calls to mothers of our participants.

Procedure

Design of the study

Our mother-and-daughter research team created the model used. As mothers and daughters themselves, they knew what kinds of activities would interest others to participate in the study. As Yara described planning our first focus group:

> For our first focus group we wanted something that would not be boring and would attract not just teens, but also their mothers. So we came up with the Pastele Night. It would be just a group of women and young ladies getting together to cook a traditional Puerto Rican dish, *pasteles*, and just have some girl talk. In the making of *pasteles*, we gave every person a specific job to do, and while everyone was doing their job to complete the dish, we chatted about how it is to be a girl in general, and how it is to be a girl in your culture. Most of the mothers and daughters participating were from Latino heritage. The focus group went well, and we were able to gather a lot of data.

Quantitative data: The maps

For the map exercise, we would split the group into two, the mothers in one group and the daughters in another. The reason for this was so that they could feel more comfortable verbalizing their feelings and opinions. We had them draw a circle, and inside the circle write or draw things about what they wanted for their future (positive possible selves), and on the outside, write or draw things that they didn't want (negative possible selves). For the moms, we had them do this thinking from the perspective of when they were their daughters' ages. Maps were intentionally open-ended to better reflect true hopes and fears, as opposed to offering set themes that may not have applied to our participants. From the maps we counted the similarities and differences between the pairs, as well as noting what possible selves came up most frequently. Personal interviews served to collect additional data in order to complete mother–daughter pairs.

Qualitative information: Group discussions

Group discussions occurred first with mothers and daughters in their separate groups, and then again as they presented their maps to each other. The discussions were powerful and emotional, and the information we gathered was important to having a better understanding of the maps. Discussions provided an in-depth look at the hopes and fears of the participants and where some of them originated. Throughout this process, participants expressed a great sense of comfort and trust because researchers were mothers and daughters.

Analysis

The entire research team worked together to compile each participant's positive and negative possible selves, first from transcribing our notes and videotapes of the discussions in which they shared what they had written and drawn, and then by adding other components directly from their artwork. We also tracked who or what they said had influenced their possible selves, and any comments they made about the influences of culture and gender.

We then coded their answers into common themes. After discarding themes with less than three percent response rate, we ended up with seven themes for positive possible selves and nine for negative ones. We compared frequencies within the themes between mother and daughter groups, and also looked at individual mother–daughter pairs for similarities and differences. Responses were clarified and enriched by the fact that we knew many of the participants, so we could easily do follow-up phone or in-person interviews.

RESULTS

Common values between mothers and daughters

We found a great many similarities between mothers and daughters in terms of their positive possible selves, that is, what they hoped for in their future. Families, education, and careers came up most frequently for both groups, and similar frequencies of response were found across all seven positive themes (see Figure 22.1). We also found the top negative possible self—drug or alcohol abuse—to be shared by both groups. Additionally, no possible selves came up as positive for a daughter and negative for a mother, or vice versa. These results demonstrate a high level of shared values and goals between mothers and daughters.

The case of Jenny and Jessica, written by Jenny, the mom, demonstrates some of these shared values and the outcome of their discussion.

CASE STUDY: Jessica and Jenny, written by Jenny (the mother)

I was born in Puerto Rico, moved to the U.S. at the age of five. I grew up with a very traditional, strict macho father. Talking about sex, drugs, and alcohol was very simple: "Never do it." Things were hidden well on the home front: (1) no arguments in front of children; (2) no drinking in front of children; and (3) no talk of sex in front of children. So I grew up very ignorant in these topics. My dad was a machista, he would say, "Women should stay home, take care of the children, clean the house, and have food ready for him." I knew I didn't want this in a marriage or in my life. Even though my dad was strict and harsh, he was very loving and caring. My dad was my inspiration; I learned a lot from him.

Jessica grew up differently; she has space and privacy, and can talk to the family or me about any issue in her life. She has a lot of knowledge on peer pressure,

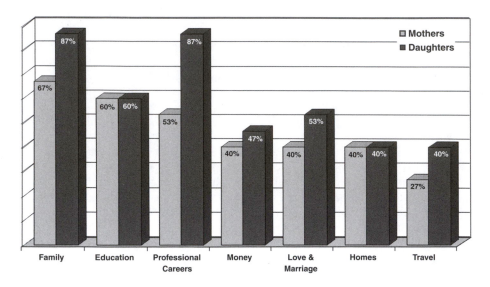

Fig. 22.1. Comparison of Positive Possible Selves.

self-esteem, drugs, alcohol, and violence. I want Jessica to learn about her culture, but she can also change a lot of it, if she wants to. I don't want her to feel that she *has* to stay home and take care of the children, only if she *chooses* it.

As a mother I thought it would be interesting to know more about my daughter (even though we have an open communication). I figure because of our age difference and our upbringing, we would pick different likes/dislikes. To my surprise, we had a lot in common. Actually, we were the team with the most in common. We both put down college, family, love, money, travel, and a home. We put down drugs, alcohol, and gang violence as things we didn't want for our futures. I was surprised when Jessica picked me as her inspiration, because she has a lot of family that helped her through a lot. Here are two women who grew up in different environments (culture) but yet want so much of the same things.

Besides writing their own case study, Jenny and Jessica presented it together each time we spoke about our work. They designed their piece as something of a research duet, going back and forth as they described their lives, and even bursting into song at one point. They were genuinely proud to have had the most in common of all the pairs, and proud of each other as well. Jessica ended each presentation by telling the audience that she was inspired to go to college because her mom had just gone back herself.

The high similarity between mothers and daughters of positive possible selves such as education, family, and careers indicates to us that (a) mothers are powerful figures in the socially constructed selves of teenage daughters and (b) daughters' identities can be both culturally affirmed and achievement oriented. Our group of mothers and daughters was primarily

Puerto Rican, but we found many similarities to the model suggested by Oyserman et al (1995: 1220) for African-American girls, which said that "by conceptualizing achievement as embedded in one's sense of self as a [Puerto Rican], youth—and especially female youths—will not experience contradiction and tension between achievement and being [Puerto Rican]." As Yasmin said, "Before this experience I felt that if I was a college graduate, I was an Americanized Puerto Rican. But now, Puerto Ricans can be successful in academics and their careers, and associate that as part of their identity."

Greater Prevalence of Negative Possible Selves for Daughters

We found many more differences between mothers and daughters when it came to negative possible selves (i.e., things they feared for their future). First of all, the daughters had over twice as many negative possible selves as their mothers (up from approximately 50 percent more on the positive possible selves). In four of the dominant themes (violence, death, poor/homeless, and lonely/heartbroken), daughters reported many more responses than mothers. Daughters mentioned each of these themes at frequencies of 50 percent–70 percent, while mothers' responses ranged from 0 percent to 30 percent (see Figure 22.2).

We talked a lot in our research group about why these particular issues came up more for daughters than for their mothers. For example, mothers and daughters in the group talked about violence, which came up the most for daughters. We felt that in some ways daughters were witnessing more violence today, both because there is a lot of violence out there nowadays

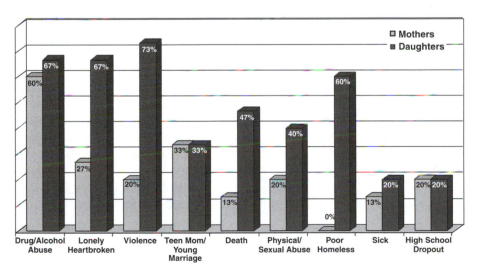

Fig. 22.2. Comparison of Negative Possible Selves.

(in their schools and communities as well as on the news and other media), but also because daughters are more likely to be outside of the home to see or feel it. "Back in the day," mothers said, their families were more protective, and they were kept at home. Nowadays, daughters are not just out at school, but in youth programs, on the streets, working, and so on.

Another reason we felt that daughters had so many more negative possible selves than their moms had was that they had fears based on both what their moms told them they had gone through, and what they watched them go through. The case study of Lisa and Sasha illustrates this trend.

CASE STUDY: *Lisa and Sasha, written by Jessica*

Here is a case about a mother, Lisa, who is 39 years old and a daughter, Sasha, who is 13 years old. Both have grown up in totally different lifestyles.

Lisa had grown up with a lot of abuse in her family. She has never had any one to inspire her. She lived with a mother that could not communicate with her, and she does not want the same for her daughter. In fact, she does not want her daughter to go through any of the negative things she has gone through herself. Before fearing these things for her daughter, Lisa feared a young and unsuccessful marriage for herself. She also feared abuse in all forms, and being like her mother.

Today, Lisa and Sasha have a good relationship, they get along and communicate well with each other. Unlike her own mother, Sasha's inspiration comes from Lisa and her older sister. She says, "I'm lucky to have such a great family and feel comfortable to talk to any one of them." However, Sasha has demonstrated she has more negative possible selves than her mother had as a teen. Sasha fears homelessness, death, violence, spousal abuse, being ugly, and [being] a teen mom. She emphasizes most her fear of any form of abuse in her life.

Oftentimes even when mothers like Lisa were proud that they had fought hard to overcome serious obstacles, their daughters feared these same situations happening to them in the future. Additionally, daughters seemed to fear going through struggles they witnessed their moms going through. As one mother and researcher commented concerning daughters worrying about being heartbroken, "Maybe girls are seeing all these single moms and worrying that they'll be like that, too." Therefore, our research suggests that the negative experiences of the mothers heavily influenced negative possible selves of the daughters.

Influence of Project on Participants and Researchers

Doing this research project and paper was a great learning experience for us. Since most of us were researchers, facilitators, *and* participants, we got to see both sides of the process. As mothers and daughters, we learned more about each other and our similarities, differences, hopes, and fears. We had some conversations we had never had before. As Daisy, Emily's mom, commented, "I couldn't believe it when we looked at our maps. We both wanted to be DJs and car mechanics!"

Most of us had never imagined ourselves as researchers. This process challenged us in many ways, even impacting our very own possible selves. Since starting this project, two of the mothers have begun college, one daughter was accepted to Barnard, and another won a national Girls Inc. Scholarship for $10,000. Meanwhile, the younger girls on the research team were busy trying to explain to friends and teachers that they were presenting at an international conference in London. As Yara retold us, "Shoot, when my friends ask me if I'm going to the prom, I tell them I have to speak at an *academic* conference, *in London*." For girls who constantly face stereotypes about dropping out of school and getting pregnant, this possible self as academic researcher is new and powerful. Sasha explained it this way in a fund-raising letter she wrote for our trip:

> So with all due respect, we come from a community that is no joke for many of us, and it's very dangerous at times. So for us to get out of Holyoke and go somewhere where they actually appreciate us and want us to do a workshop on mothers and daughters connecting, that really says something. It says that we are darn good at what we do! It says that we try our hardest even when it's hard for us teenagers. And we will never quit.

But we were not the only ones impacted by our research. Unlike many researchers, we got to see the ongoing impact of our work on the participants around us also. They're still talking about things they learned about each other, what they want for their futures, and how emotional our focus groups were. We impacted academics as well. Professors who saw our presentation in London told us later that it rearranged their expectations for their students, their own research, and their understanding of the possibilities of participant-led research. Inspired by all this feedback, we went on to become the first community-based group to be selected as research associates at the Five College Women's Study Center based at Mount Holyoke College.

Keeping with our goal of spreading what we've learned about doing our own research, we named ourselves CADRE—Compañeras Arising to Develop Researchers Everywhere. We are now working with a local boys group that wants to do father–son research, as well as with the national Girls Incorporated to look at developing a curriculum based on our work.

CONCLUSION

As a participant-led research project, we were concerned with both our product and our process. Could we produce work that was valid and added to broader knowledge of both possible selves and mother–daughter relationships? How would having mothers and daughters doing this work impact the research and the researchers? These questions wove themselves throughout our project. In fact, having mothers and daughters doing the work changed us and the work. For example, rather than formal focus groups or individual interviews, our dynamic and culturally appropriate activities led to conversations that were rich with pride and sharing. Mothers and daughters realized all that they had in common, and celebrated each other's hopes and dreams. Not only were the daughters affirmed by their own mothers, but also by the whole group, representing their culture and peer group. As Yara described it:

> While they were contributing to our research, they were having fun. Mothers were going down memory lane, and mothers found out a little bit about their daughters, and daughters found out a little bit about how their mothers used to be at their age. Every focus group managed to end on a very emotional note.

Thus our participant-designed research methods improved the data we collected while also creating a powerful experience for the participants involved.

Our presentation in London was a twofold process as well. Our group included the only girls at a conference about girls, and they were not there to just sit and listen. This demonstrated that girls truly do have something to say about the "New Girl Order," and they and their moms brought down the house. Our high-energy and interactive presentation further challenged the norms of academia, and our group was asked to present at the closing plenary session, so that everyone could hear about our work. But perhaps the biggest impact on our group was one that many academics may take for granted—the opportunity to travel, meet new people, and see new things. As we went full circle back to present our work in Holyoke, Emily had this to say: "To give you a little taste of London, it was great! It was cold, but it only rained for two days. We went sightseeing and we did our presentation at the New Girl Order Conference, and it all went well. I can't wait to go back!"

References

Markus, H., and Nurius, P. (1986). "Possible Selves." *American Psychologist* 41 (9): 954–969.

Oyserman, D., Gant, L., and Ager, J. (1995). "A Socially Contextualized Model of African-American Identity: Possible Selves and School Persistence." *Journal of Personality and Social Psychology* 69 (6): 1216–1232.

Way, N. (1995). "'Can't You See the Courage, the Strength That I Have:' Listening to Urban Adolescent Girls Speak About Their Relationships." *Psychology of Women Quarterly* 19: 107–128.

Contributor Biographies

Erica Arenas was born in Brooklyn, New York, in 1982 to young teen parents. She is currently a student at Borough of Manhattan Community College and hoping to become a literature teacher and a guidance counselor at a high needs high school in New York City.

Jennifer Baumgardner and Amy Richards are longtime collaborators. They co-authored *Manifesta: Young Women, Feminism and the Future*, and a book about activism called *Recipe Tested: An Idea Bank for Activism*.

Beth Cooper Benjamin, Ed.M., is a doctoral candidate in human development, and a research assistant with the Alliance on Gender, Culture, and School Practice, Harvard Graduate School of Education.

Amy L. Best is assistant professor of sociology at San Jose State University. Her research focuses on youth identity formation and popular culture. She is author of *Prom Night: Youth, Schools and Popular Culture* (2000), which was selected for the 2002 American Educational Studies Association Critics' Choice Award. She is currently working on a project on kids and cars.

April Burns is a doctoral student in social personality psychology at the Graduate Center of the City University of New York. Her research focuses broadly on issues of privileged consciousness and the psychology of social class.

CADRE (Compañeras Arising to Develop Researchers Everywhere) is a group of diverse women from a wide range of educational disciplines. Some of us have earned college degrees, while others are just beginning our college careers. We are diverse in many other ways as well. For instance, CADRE women are mothers, athletes, writers, and thespians. We come to stand together through our commitment to the community, especially youth, who are an integral part of our research team. We have presented our work at the "New Girl Order" Women's Studies Conference in London; a regional Girls Incorporated conference in Hampton, Virginia; and locally at Girls Incorporated of Holyoke, Massachusetts. Other than our "international" acclaim, we are known for our great cooking, spunky attitudes, and sense of humor.

Caitlin Cahill is a student at the City University of New York, where she is finishing her doctorate in environmental psychology. She thinks a better and different world is possible. She loves to teach and work collaboratively with people, and to eat good food.

Meda Chesney-Lind is professor of Women's Studies at the University of Hawaii at Manoa. She is the author of numerous books on girls' and women's crime; her most recent book, *Invisible Punishment* (edited with Marc Mauer), explores the social cost of mass imprisonment in the United States.

Sasha Cirino. See CADRE.

Jennifer Contreras is a Sagittarius living on the Lower East Side. She goes to Satellite Academy high school and plans to graduate in 2004.

Jennifer Eisenhauer is an assistant professor of art education at The Ohio State University. Her current research and teaching interests include feminist poststructural theories of pedagogy, language, and subjectivity; social and cultural issues in art and art education; and feminist zine cultures as pedagogical sites.

Michelle Fine, Distinguished Professor of Social Psychology, Women's Studies, and Urban Education at the Graduate Center, City University of New York (CUNY), has taught at CUNY since 1990. Her research focuses on how youth view distributive and procedural justice in schools, prisons, the economy, and local communities. She is also very interested in a theory of participatory methods.

Bettina Fritzsche, Ph.D., studied education at Technische Universität Berlin. While working with preadolescent girls she was inspired to write a doctoral thesis on female pop fans, which was completed in 2002. Currently she collaborates in an empirical research project on the transmission of traditions within families at Freie Universität Berlin.

Kate Gleeson and Hannah Frith are based in the Centre for Appearance Research at the University of the West of England. They are currently immersed in research projects exploring young people's visual subjectivities that draw on a range of theoretical approaches and cross disciplinary boundaries.

Christine Griffin is a reader in critical social psychology at the University of Bath in the United Kingdom. She has a long-standing interest in representations of youth, femininity, and young women's lives. Her publications include *Typical Girls?* (1985, Routledge and Kegan Paul); *Representations of Youth* (1993, Polity Press); and *Standpoints and Differences: Essays in the Practice of Feminist Psychology* (with Karen Henwood and Ann Phoenix, 1998, Sage).

Anita Harris is a lecturer in sociology at Monash University, Australia. She is the author of *Future Girl: Young Women in the Twenty-first Century* (2004, Routledge), and co-author of *Young Femininity: Girlhood, Power and Social Change* (with Sinikka Aapola and Marnina Gonick, 2004, Palgrave).

Katherine Irwin is an assistant professor of sociology at the University of Hawaii at Manoa. In addition to teaching criminology courses at the university, she has conducted research in the areas of youth violence, violence prevention, drug use, and youth culture.

Daisy Jimenez. See CADRE.

Emily Jimenez. See CADRE.

Madeleine Jowett is a lecturer in the Institute for Women's Studies at Lancaster University, United Kingdom. Her recently completed Ph.D. thesis looked at the relationship(s) between young women and feminism in contemporary Britain.

Mary Jane Kehily is a lecturer in the Faculty of Education and Language Studies at the Open University, United Kingdom. She has a background in cultural studies and education, and has research interests in gender and sexuality, narrative and identity, and popular culture. She has published widely on these themes. Recent publications include *Sexuality, Gender and Schooling: Shifting Agendas in Social Learning* (2002, Routledge Falmer) and "Sexing the Subject: Teachers, Pedagogies and Sex Education," *Sex Education* 3 (3) (2002). She is also director of a research project exploring the cultural meanings of drugs and drug use in young people's lives.

Nancy Lesko teaches gender and cultural studies in education, curriculum theory, and history, and youth studies at Teachers College, Columbia University. She has begun an exploration of curriculum in the context of terrorism/war (or other widespread social catastrophes such as HIV/AIDS, refugees, extreme poverty, etc.) and what becomes "dangerous knowledge" in such contexts.

Lori Lobenstine. See CADRE.

Angela McRobbie is professor of communications at Goldsmiths College, London. She is author of many books and articles on gender, popular culture, and, more recently, on making a living in the new cultural economies. She is currently completing a book on postfeminism.

Claudia Mitchell is a professor and chair in the School of Education, University of Natal, in Durban, South Africa. She is author of *Researching Children's Popular Culture: The Cultural Spaces of Childhood* (with Jacqueline Reid-Walsh, 2002, Routledge).

Kathryn Morris-Roberts completed her Ph.D. in 2002 at the Department of Geography, University of Sheffield, United Kingdom. She currently works as a young people's sexual health and teenage pregnancy personal adviser. She is also an Open University associate lecturer in ethnography, and continues to inform academia of her praxis through conferences and publications.

Jiang Na moved to New York from China in 2000. She is concerned about the future. She would like to be a teacher and a nurse. Her favorite things to do are to talk with friends, write poetry, draw, and knit.

Adreanne Ormond is a Ph.D. candidate in the International Research Institute for Maori and Indigenous Education at the University of Auckland, New Zealand. Her research interests include indigenous Maori youth, social injustice, voice and silence, and youth rights.

Jessenia Ortiz. See CADRE.

Yasmin Pereira. See CADRE.

Antoinette Quarshie is a doctoral student at Teachers College, Columbia University. Her dissertation maps the complex terrain of gender discourses with sixth grade students through collective biography/memory work. Ms. Quarshie is particularly interested in the contradictory emotions and desires that accompany the materiality of making and marking gendered body landscapes through body-reflexive practices.

Jacqueline Reid-Walsh teaches children's literature and popular culture at Bishop's University, Canada. She has published a number of articles and authored a book with Claudia Mitchell, *Researching Children's Popular Culture: The Cultural Spaces of Childhood* (2002, Routledge).

Indra Rios-Moore was born and raised on the Lower East Side of New York City in 1980 and has since been a devoted member of the Lower East Side community. Of Puerto Rican, African-American, and Syrian descent, she has borne the brunt of many stereotypes and has stood tall despite these resulting challenges. She has been, and continues to be, committed to contributing to communities of color and young urban youth.

Jessica Robles. See CADRE.

Jeanette Sergeant. See CADRE.

Yaraliz Soto. See CADRE.

Jessica K. Taft is a Ph.D. student in sociology at the University of California at Santa Barbara. She received her B.A. in Women's and Gender Studies from Macalester College and completed her M.A. in Sociology at University of California at Santa Barbara. Her research focuses on girls' political consciousness and activism.

Tiffany Threatts is currently attending State University of New York at Farmingdale. She loves to swim, hang out with friends (go to movies, play pool, etc.), and watch TV.

María Elena Torre is a doctoral student in social personality psychology at the Graduate Center of the City University of New York. Her research focuses on women and the criminal justice system, urban education, youth activism, and participatory action research.

Anne-Marie Tupuola is a New Zealander of Samoan descent currently affiliated with Teachers College, Columbia University. Receipt of a New Zealand Fulbright Senior Scholar Award enabled her to do postdoctoral cross-cultural research of Pacific, New Zealand, and U.S. diasporic and immigrant youth personal identity formation processes.

Janie Victoria Ward, Ed.D., is an associate professor of education and human services at Simmons College in Boston. Currently serving as the director of the Alliance on Gender, Culture and School Practice at Harvard Graduate School of Education, she is principal investigator (with Wendy Luttrell) of Project ASSERT (Assessing Strengths and Supporting Effective Resistance in Teaching), a participatory research study exploring cultural beliefs and presuppositions that underlie discourses of gender, race, and class expressed by adults working with urban youth. She is the author of four books, and many chapters and articles, and her research interests focus on the psychosocial development of African-American children and youth.

Debbie Weekes currently works as an associate lecturer in social psychology at the Open University in the United Kingdom. Her academic work has centered around the educational, ethnic, and gendered identities of young people, particularly those of African-Caribbean descent. Her research has been put to practical use in her more recent work in the charity sector, where she has developed separate programs both to support gifted Black and Asian children in schools and to enhance the leadership potential and cultural awareness of diverse groups of young people.

Jenny Whitley. See CADRE.

Index

A

Abstinence Essay Contest, 131
Abstinence-only education, 127
    anxious achievement exploitation by, 130
    Gay-Straight Alliances and, 134
Accountability
    academic, 128
    personal, 128
Achievement
    anxious, 130
    discourses of, 91
    erotics of, 130
    gap, 19, 128
Adbusting, 168
Adolescence, 16
    aggression in, 49
    American experience of, 116
    depictions of, 21
    homosexuality and, 118
    sexuality and sexual identity in, 117
Advertising, 7
Aesthetic emotional comprehension, 249
African-American girls/women. *See also*
    Black girls/women
    adolescence and, 20
    detention rates of, 52
    self-esteem of, 22
    sense of responsibility of, 129
African-Caribbean women. *See also*
    Black girls/women
    music and, 141

Age
    constitution of girls based on, 30
Age specificity
    associated with female sexuality, 118
Aggression
    relational, 19
Ahmad, Fauzia, 31
Airshop, 74
Alliance building, 19
Ally McBeal, 12
American Association of University
    Women (AAUW), 16
    campaign for equity in education, 22
American Psychological Association's
    Task Force on Adolescent Girls:
    Strengths and Stresses, 23
Anglocentrism, 29
    in teen magazines, 38
Anti-abortion policies, 127
Anti-bullying programs, 49
Anti-corporate globalization, 168
Anti-feminism, 70, 75
Anti-violence policies, 53
Anti-youth violence movement, 52
Anxious achievement, 130, 133
Arrest rates, 46, 51
Assertiveness
    common sense, 93
Attention
    attracting, 106
Awakening, 81, 87

B

Bad girls, 46
 controlling, 51
 demographics of, 50
 queen bees and, 48
Barbie, 60, 74
Beauty culture, 61, 201
Bedroom culture, 174
Bias, 18
Biomythographies, 187
Bisexuality, 189. *See also* gay women
Black girls/women. *See also* African-
 American girls/women
 contributions of feminists, 73
 music and, 141
  relationship to sexuality, 144
Body curriculum, 199
Body image
 music and, 146
Booth, Cherie, 92
Bootstrapping, 53
Borderwork, 211
Born-again virgins, 133
Boyology, 30
Boys
 arrest rates of, 46
 violence rates of, 52
Bridget Jones' Diary, 11, 60
British girls/women
 feminism and, 91
Bullying, 19, 45
 programs to combat, 49
Bust magazine, 63
BWP (Bytches with Problems), 147

C

CADRE–Compañeras Arising to
 Develop Researchers Everywhere, 263
Camp Ashema, 75
Capitalism, 62
Censure
 popular culture and, 150
Chicanas. *See* Latinas
Christian Right movement, 127

Class
 constitution of girls based on, 30
Class politics
 equality and, 72
Class-based stereotypes
 bad girls and, 46
Clique-oriented girls, 46
 behaviors of, 50
Clothing
 language of, 110
 styles and colors of, 104
 surveillance of, 106
Collaborative research, 238
Collusionary practices, 220, 226
Colonization, 247
Coming out
 challenges of, 118
Common sense assertiveness, 93
Commonalities
 significance of, 21
Communication, 76
Communism, 62
Community change girls as agents of, 76
Community of sameness, 85
Compulsory heterosexuality. *See also*
 heterosexuality
 forms of, 225
Computer gaming, 173
Conflict resolution, 76
Constructed certitude, 8
Consumer citizenship, 163
 young people and, 164
Consumer culture, 34, 62
Consumer power, 74
Consumerism
 beauty culture within, 201
 culture jamming and, 168
Consumption, 34, 163
 discursive role of, 35
Convergence, 174
Corporate globalization, 168
Creativity
 development of, 132
 sources of, 167
Criminal justice system social control
 and, 51
Crisis heterotopias, 178

Crisis literature, 21
Critique
    development of, 132
Cultural feminists, 62
Cultural production, 75
Culture
    feminism and, 3
    girl-poisoning, 17
    interplay with power, 208
Culture jamming, 167
Cyborg, 86

D

Davis, Angela, 46
Decision-making, 76
Depression
    adolescent girls, 22
Desire, 212
    costs of deferring, 134
    discourse of, 128
    life-threatening consequences of, 127
Detentions
    increase in for girls, 52
Deviancy
    popular culture and, 150
Diligence, 93
Disability
    constitution of girls based on, 30
Discourse. *See also* specific types of
    discourse
    definition of, 69
Discursive technologies, 128
Diversity
    cultural dimensions of, 29
    need for in representations of girls, 42
    sexual, 214
Dr. Dre, 151
Dropout rates
    No Child Left Behind Act and, 130
Drug dealing
    girls and, 48

E

Eating disorders, 19, 77
Economic security, 163

Education, 205
    cultural diversity and, 32
    discourses of, 143
    effect of Girl Power on, 72
    gender-equity in, 18
    peer, 134
    United States, 128
Educational Opportunity Study, 131
Elliot, Missy, 147
Emancipatory politics, 10
Emancypunx, 167
Empower Program, 50
Empowered transvestism, 155
Enforced poverty, 132
Enforcement practices, 52
Enlightenment, 87
Entrepreneurship, 93
Equal Opportunities Commission, 92
Equal opportunity
    lie of, 133
Equality, 64
    postfeminism and achievement of, 72
Equality Britain, 92
Eros, 64
Erotics of achievement, 130
Essentialist narratives, 30
Ethic of freedom, 12
Ethnic identity, 247
Eurocentric discourse
    oversexualized Black femininity
        within, 144
Excellence
    academic, 128
    desiring, 129

F

*Failing at Fairness: How America's
    Schools Cheat Girls,* 17
Familial expectations, 119
    in Samoan society, 120
Fan culture, 157
Female adolescent sexual development,
    117
Female emancipation, 98
Female individualism, 7
Female individualization, 10
Female sexuality

cultural and gender
    misinterpretations of, 118
Female spectatorship
    Hollywood cinema and, 160
Femininity, 29, 209
    as text-mediated discourse, 196
    Black girls and, 142
    feminism and, 5
    hierarchies, 143, 146
    pink and, 105
    self-change and, 200
    value of, 60
Feminism, 92, 220
    as a barrier to individuality, 65
    British girls/women and, 91
    chronology of, 7
    constructions of, 87
    consumerism and, 165, 167
    female rappers and, 148
    femininity and, 5, 61
    Girl Power and, 33
    girls and, 80
    negotiating, 96
    owning, 97
    popular culture and the undoing of, 3
    prohibitions on, 98
    racial homogeneity and Western bias
     in theories of, 82
    taken into account, 5
    teaching about, 187
    waves of, 59
Feminist identity, 91
Feminist mystique, 66
Feminist pedagogy, 86
Feminist research praxis, 220, 226
Feminist theory
    definitive self-critique, 4
Feminists
    cultural, 62
    educational futures of, 187
    legacy of, 85
    young, 82
First World
    representations of girlhood contexts
     in, 31
Foster teens, 77
Foucalt, 10, 178

Friedan, Betty, 66
Friendship exclusion, 220

G

Gangs
    girls in, 47
Gay women
    challenges of coming out, 118
    contributions of, 73
Gay-Straight Alliances, 133
    activities of, 135
Gender
    analysis, 75
    bias and stereotyping, 75
    inequality, 95
    interaction with race, 72
    learning, 210
    polarities, 213
    schooling and, 205
    treachery, 134
Gender awareness, 9
Gender equity, 19
    educators, 18
Gender relations
    dynamics of social change in, 5
Gender studies
    declining enrollment in, 6
General TK, 149
Generational repudiation of feminism, 4
Gentrification, 241
Ghetto culture
    sexual depravity in, 143
Gilbert, Jeremy, 93
Gilligan, Carol, 64
Girl magazines, 36
Girl Power, 33, 69, 92, 155, 170
    consumerism and, 166
    interpretations and applications of,
     159
    sexuality of, 40
Girl's studies, 86
    American, 16
Girl's studies, 30
    polarity in, 22, 25
Girlhood
    consumption and, 34

popular culture and, 150
Girlie, 60, 105
   applicability of, 64
Girls
   accountability of, 133
   arrest rates of, 46, 51
   cliques and, 46
   consumer citizenship of, 165
   definition of, 60
      contradiction in, 82
   feminism and, 80
   impact of societal changes on, 208
   music and, 141
   objectification of, 35
   political agency of, 77
   subcultures of, 175
   subversive relationship of with music, 149
   use of term in feminist context, 63
   violent offending, 51
Girls Inc., 255, 263
   study of violence, 51
Glenbrook High School
   hazing incident at, 49, 54
Global AIDS Bill, 128
Globalization. *See also* corporate globalization effects of, 207
Group decision-making, 75
Group dynamics, 214
Growing up, 81
Guest books, 177, 181
Guilds, 176

H

Hacktivists, 168
Haraway, Donna, 86
Harvard Project on Women's Psychology and Girl's Development, 16
Hearst, Patti, 46
Heterosexuality, 118, 159
   compulsory, 220
   dominance of, 148
   fan culture and, 160
   naturalization of, 213
   norms of
      high school proms and, 199

schools and, 211
   silencing mechanism of, 226
Heterotopia, 178
High heels, 105
High school prom. *See* proms
Hip-hop
   b-girls, 143
   imagery in, 142
Hollywood cinema
   female spectatorship of, 160
Home pages, 173
   as idealized space, 178
Homophobia, 223
Homosexuality, 118. *See also* gay women
   Samoan culture and, 122
   schools and, 211, 222
How Schools Shortchange Girls, 16
Human rights, 64
Hyperresponsibility, 130, 133

I

In a Different Voice, 65
Incarceration
   trends, 52
Individual initiative, 93
Individual power, 73, 75
Individual rehabilitation, 133
Individualism, 7
Individuality
   barriers to, 65
Individualization, 163, 207
Inequality, 73, 92
   voicing, 94
Intellectual engagement in education, 128
Internet
   girls and, 173
   guest books, 177
   virtual community of, 170
Interpersonal skills, 22
Intersectionality, 21, 73

J

Jamming girl culture, 167
Johnson, Lesley, 30
Juvenile justice system
   girls in, 19

K

Krabbe, Friederike, 46

L

Labor market
    feminization of, 165
Lady Saw, 147
Ladybomb, 169
Language
    as a barrier, 79
Latinas
    contributions of, 73
    detention rates of, 52
Life politics, 10
Lil' Kim, 147
Listen Up: Voices from the Next Feminist Generation, 82
Living texts, 189
Local Government Act of 1988, 222
Local management of schools, 206

M

Mad About Boys, 36
Madonna, 155
Madonna/whore discourse, 146
Magazines
    Bust, 63
    power of, 36
Makeovers, 38
Male adolescent sexual development, 117
Maori females
    voice and silence of, 243
Marginalization
    in teen magazines, 38
Marketing
    consumer citizenship and, 165
    Girl Power and, 74
Masculinity
    Black popular culture and, 143
McRobbie, Angela, 33, 93, 167, 199, 207
Mean girls, 45
Media
    Girl Power portrayal in, 69
    literacy, 17

moral panic due to, 52
    sexual codes of conduct definitions by, 7
Mental health, 77
Meritocracy, 170
    lie of, 133
Mimetic acts, 157
Modern girlhood, 31
Monetarization, 163
Moral panic, 52
    youth violence and, 53
Moral standards
    discourses of, 128
Multilocational participant observation, 220, 225
Music, 141
    body image and, 146
    effect of on young Black women, 148
Muslim women, 31

N

Narratives, 190
    essentialist, 30
    personal, 193
National Curriculum, 206
National Women's Association, 81
National Women's Party
    Student Action Committee, 84
New gender regime, 4, 11
New Girl Order Conference, 256
New Labour government, 93, 223
New media, 170
New sexualities, 33
Nihilism
    in rap music, 144
No Child Left Behind Act, 130
Nonverbal aggression, 19
Normative perceptions of adolescent sexuality, 119
Nylon, 168

O

Objectification
    popular culture and, 150
Odd Girl Out, 19
Oppression, 76, 98

Optimism
   discourses of, 91
Ostracism, 45
Othering, 151

P

Parenting
   of girls, 19
Participant-led research, 263
Patra, 147
Patriarchy, 65, 84, 134
   gangsta rap and, 150
   Spice Girls and, 70
Pedagogy
   feminist, 86
   transformative, 189
Peer education, 134
Performance theory, 190
Performative spaces of encounter, 246
Personal accountability, 128
Personal narratives, 193
Phantom, 66
Pink, 60
   rejecting, 104
   significance of, 103
Pleasure
   poststructural feminist approaches to,
      187
Political agency, 77
Politics
   emancipatory, 10
   engagement in, 75
   equality and, 72
   life, 10
   repudiation of feminism in, 4
Politics of intervention, 220
Polynesian females
   sexuality and, 115
Pop feminist phenomena, 156
Popular culture, 157
   computers and, 174
   developing identities of young Black
      women and, 143
   feminism and, 3
Pornography
   normalization of, 8

Possible selves, 256
Postfeminism, 3, 6, 33, 72
Poverty
   enforced, 132
Power
   interplay with culture, 208
   social, 246
   sources of, 167
Power dynamics, 246
   gendered, 72
   issues of in research, 111
Power relationships
   Girl Power and, 73
Pregnancy, 77, 150
   escape mechanism of, 122
Privatization, 165
Problem-solving, 76
Progress, 87
   discourses of, 91
Proms, 118, 195
Prostitution, 30
Proto-communities, 177
Psychic space, 181
Psychological development
   theories of, 22
Psychologizing, 19
Public spheres
   creating new, 169
Purchasing power, 74

Q

Queen bees, 45
   bad girls and, 48
Queen Bees and Wannabes, 45, 50
Queer women. *See* gay women
Quiz genre, 38
Quizzes
   disciplinary nature of, 38

R

R&B music
   imagery in, 142
Race
   constitution of girls based on, 30
Race-based stereotypes
   bad girls and, 46

Racialization
  Girl Power, 33
Racism, 34, 50, 72, 247
Ragga
  Black female sexuality and, 144
  gyals, 143
  imagery embedded in, 141
  reconstruction of sexuality by female
    performers, 147
  references to Black females in, 146
Rap
  reconstruction of sexuality by female
    performers, 147
Rape, 48
Red diaper babies, 62
Reflective celebration, 91
Reflexive modernization, 10
Regulation of clothing, 106
Relabeling, 53
Relational aggression, 19, 45, 49
Relational awareness, 22
Relational discourse, 143
Reproductive health, 76
Reputation, 213
  respectability and, 143
Research
  complexity of dynamics, 111
  insider, 245
  participant-led, 263
Respectability
  reputation and, 143
Responsibility
  discourse of, 130
*Reviving Ophelia: Saving the Selves of
  Adolescent Girls,* 17
Riot grrrl, 66, 155
Risk-taking behavior, 118, 132
Rock music
  sexism in, 151
Rumor spreading, 19

S

Sabrina the Teenage Witch, 72
Safety, 64
Samoan females
  sexuality of, 115, 121

Saroyan, Strawberry, 61
Sartorial identities, 104
Scare tactics
  abstinence-only programs and, 131, 133
Schlafly, Phyllis, 61
School. *See also* education
  compulsory heterosexuality in, 221
  local management, 206
  memories and pleasure, 185
  violence, 49
*Schoolgirls: Young Women, Self-Esteem
  and the Confidence Gap,* 17
Second World
  girlhood in, 31
Second-wave feminism, 4, 59, 82, 209
The Secret Lives of Girls, Odd Girl Out, 45
Secret telling, 19
Self-advocacy skills, 76
Self-assessment, 76
Self-blame, 133
Self-change
  discourse of, 199
Self-confidence
  fan culture and, 160
Self-esteem
  bullying and, 49
  declining, 22
  sexism and, 67
Self-image
  relationship between star ideals and,
    160
Self-invention, 170
Self-monitoring, 11
Self-organization, 10
Self-representation
  fan culture and, 160
Self-transformation
  high school proms and, 196
Serial community, 177
Sex in the City, 12, 60
Sex education programs, 212, 222
  abstinence-only, 127
Sexism, 64
  self-esteem and, 67
Sexual agency, 200
Sexual codes of conduct
  media definition of, 7

Sexual cultures, 208
Sexual development, 19
Sexual politics, 4
    equality and, 72
Sexual violence
    femininity and, 64
Sexuality, 30, 209
    adolescent, 115
        definition of, 123
    body curriculum and, 199
    clothing and, 103
    commercial, 9
    contexts of, 117
    girl's, 19
    learning, 210
    life-threatening consequences of, 127
    music and, 142
    new, 33
    popular culture and, 150
    rationalizing images of in music, 144
    risk-taking nature of, 118
    Samoan contexts of, 119
    schooling and, 205, 222
Sexualized clothing, 105
Sexually transmitted disease, 150
Short skirts, 105
Signifying, 144
Silence
    audience and, 249
    insider research and, 245
Snoop Doggy Dogg, 151
Social activism
    defusing, 133
Social changes
    dynamics of gender relations and, 5
    postfeminism and, 72
Social class
    stratification of, 20
Social control, 46, 51, 54
Social engagement, 75
Social marginalization, 50
Social mobility, 93
Social order
    exposure of the body and, 106
Social power, 246
Social research, 233
Social rights, 164

Social transformation, 10
Socialism, 62
Socialization
    constitution of girls', 29
Societal changes
    impact of, 208
Sociocultural expectations, 119
Sociopolitical power, 75
South Asian women, 31
South Pacific
    stereotypes of female sexuality in, 115
Spanish American Union, 255
Speaker-audience relationship, 251
Spears, Britney, 64, 151
Spice Girls, 35, 61, 70, 92, 155
    as a source of empowerment, 159
Standardized testing, 130
Standards
    academic, 128
Stereotypes, 233
    bad girls and, 46
    difficulties of developing sexuality
        due to, 145
    female sexuality in the South Pacific,
        115
    researching, 241
Stoller, Debbie, 63
Stress, 76
Student sexual cultures, 208
Style
    semiotics of, 110
Subpolitics, 10
Suicide
    Maori females and, 248
    Samoan females and, 122
Sunni Muslim women, 32
Superpredators, 55
Surveillance of clothing, 106

T

Take Back the Night Marches, 66
Teaching. See also education
    pleasures of, 187
Teen magazines, 36
    racial dimensions of, 40
Teen pregnancy, 19
Teen Resource Project/New Visions, 255

Teen Women's Action Program, 76
Teenage consumers, 34
Test-driven educational policies, 132
Thatcher, Margaret, 92
The Third Wave: Feminist Perspectives on Racism, 81
Third Wave Agenda: Being Feminist, Doing Feminism, 82
Third World
    girlhood in, 31
Third-wave feminism, 59, 62
    contradictions in definition of, 81
    goals of, 63
Thorne, Barrie, 210
To Be Real: Telling the Truth and Changing the Face of Feminism, 82
Tokenism, 34
Traditional cultures, 31
Transformative pedagogy, 189
Trauma, 248
Tweenies, 35
    web sites by, 176

U

U.S. Women's Soccer Team (1999), 71
United States Department of Health and Human Services
    Girl Power Initiative, 22
Up-criming, 53
Utopia, 178

V

The Vagina Monologues, 64
Violence, 76
    against women
        legitimization of in rap music, 144
    race and, 54
    sexual
        femininity and, 64
Violent girls, 46
Virtual communities, 170

Voice
    insider research and, 245

W

Walkerdine, Valerie, 29
Web forums, 177
Web sites, 134
    generic construction of, 176
    textual approaches to, 175
Welfare
    rollback of, 164
White girls
    detention rates of, 52
Women of color. *See* Black girls/women
Women's magazines
    power of, 36
Women's studies
    declining enrollment in, 6
Work
    as a mechanism of identity formation, 165
World Wide Web. *See* Internet

Y

Young British women. *See* British girls/ women
Young Maori female voices, 243
Young women. *See* adolescence; girls
Youth leisure
    commercialization of, 165
Youth studies, 30

Z

Zero tolerance policies, 53
Zines, 134, 169